CZECH

VOCABULARY

FOR ENGLISH SPEAKERS

ENGLISH-CZECH

The most useful words
To expand your lexicon and sharpen
your language skills

9000 words

Czech vocabulary for English speakers - 9000 words

By Andrey Taranov

T&P Books vocabularies are intended for helping you learn, memorize and review foreign words. The dictionary is divided into themes, covering all major spheres of everyday activities, business, science, culture, etc.

The process of learning words using T&P Books' theme-based dictionaries gives you the following advantages:

- Correctly grouped source information predetermines success at subsequent stages of word memorization
- Availability of words derived from the same root allowing memorization of word units (rather than separate words)
- Small units of words facilitate the process of establishing associative links needed for consolidation of vocabulary
- Level of language knowledge can be estimated by the number of learned words

T&P Books Publishing
www.tpbooks.com

ISBN: 978-1-78071-817-0

This book is also available in E-book formats.
Please visit www.tpbooks.com or the major online bookstores.

CZECH VOCABULARY
for English speakers

T&P Books vocabularies are intended to help you learn, memorize, and review foreign words. The vocabulary contains over 9000 commonly used words arranged thematically.

- Vocabulary contains the most commonly used words
- Recommended as an addition to any language course
- Meets the needs of beginners and advanced learners of foreign languages
- Convenient for daily use, revision sessions, and self-testing activities
- Allows you to assess your vocabulary

Special features of the vocabulary

- Words are organized according to their meaning, not alphabetically
- Words are presented in three columns to facilitate the reviewing and self-testing processes
- Words in groups are divided into small blocks to facilitate the learning process
- The vocabulary offers a convenient and simple transcription of each foreign word

The vocabulary has 256 topics including:

Basic Concepts, Numbers, Colors, Months, Seasons, Units of Measurement, Clothing & Accessories, Food & Nutrition, Restaurant, Family Members, Relatives, Character, Feelings, Emotions, Diseases, City, Town, Sightseeing, Shopping, Money, House, Home, Office, Working in the Office, Import & Export, Marketing, Job Search, Sports, Education, Computer, Internet, Tools, Nature, Countries, Nationalities and more ...

T&P BOOKS' THEME-BASED DICTIONARIES

The Correct System for Memorizing Foreign Words

Acquiring vocabulary is one of the most important elements of learning a foreign language, because words allow us to express our thoughts, ask questions, and provide answers. An inadequate vocabulary can impede communication with a foreigner and make it difficult to understand a book or movie well.

The pace of activity in all spheres of modern life, including the learning of modern languages, has increased. Today, we need to memorize large amounts of information (grammar rules, foreign words, etc.) within a short period. However, this does not need to be difficult. All you need to do is to choose the right training materials, learn a few special techniques, and develop your individual training system.

Having a system is critical to the process of language learning. Many people fail to succeed in this regard; they cannot master a foreign language because they fail to follow a system comprised of selecting materials, organizing lessons, arranging new words to be learned, and so on. The lack of a system causes confusion and eventually, lowers self-confidence.

T&P Books' theme-based dictionaries can be included in the list of elements needed for creating an effective system for learning foreign words. These dictionaries were specially developed for learning purposes and are meant to help students effectively memorize words and expand their vocabulary.

Generally speaking, the process of learning words consists of three main elements:

- Reception (creation or acquisition) of a training material, such as a word list
- Work aimed at memorizing new words
- Work aimed at reviewing the learned words, such as self-testing

All three elements are equally important since they determine the quality of work and the final result. All three processes require certain skills and a well-thought-out approach.

New words are often encountered quite randomly when learning a foreign language and it may be difficult to include them all in a unified list. As a result, these words remain written on scraps of paper, in book margins, textbooks, and so on. In order to systematize such words, we have to create and continually update a "book of new words." A paper notebook, a netbook, or a tablet PC can be used for these purposes.

This "book of new words" will be your personal, unique list of words. However, it will only contain the words that you came across during the learning process. For example, you might have written down the words "Sunday," "Tuesday," and "Friday." However, there are additional words for days of the week, for example, "Saturday," that are missing, and your list of words would be incomplete. Using a theme dictionary, in addition to the "book of new words," is a reasonable solution to this problem.

The theme-based dictionary may serve as the basis for expanding your vocabulary.

It will be your big "book of new words" containing the most frequently used words of a foreign language already included. There are quite a few theme-based dictionaries available, and you should ensure that you make the right choice in order to get the maximum benefit from your purchase.

Therefore, we suggest using theme-based dictionaries from T&P Books Publishing as an aid to learning foreign words. Our books are specially developed for effective use in the sphere of vocabulary systematization, expansion and review.

Theme-based dictionaries are not a magical solution to learning new words. However, they can serve as your main database to aid foreign-language acquisition. Apart from theme dictionaries, you can have copybooks for writing down new words, flash cards, glossaries for various texts, as well as other resources; however, a good theme dictionary will always remain your primary collection of words.

T&P Books' theme-based dictionaries are specialty books that contain the most frequently used words in a language.

The main characteristic of such dictionaries is the division of words into themes. For example, the *City* theme contains the words "street," "crossroads," "square," "fountain," and so on. The *Talking* theme might contain words like "to talk," "to ask," "question," and "answer".

All the words in a theme are divided into smaller units, each comprising 3–5 words. Such an arrangement improves the perception of words and makes the learning process less tiresome. Each unit contains a selection of words with similar meanings or identical roots. This allows you to learn words in small groups and establish other associative links that have a positive effect on memorization.

The words on each page are placed in three columns: a word in your native language, its translation, and its transcription. Such positioning allows for the use of techniques for effective memorization. After closing the translation column, you can flip through and review foreign words, and vice versa. "This is an easy and convenient method of review – one that we recommend you do often."

Our theme-based dictionaries contain transcriptions for all the foreign words. Unfortunately, none of the existing transcriptions are able to convey the exact nuances of foreign pronunciation. That is why we recommend using the transcriptions only as a supplementary learning aid. Correct pronunciation can only be acquired with the help of sound. Therefore our collection includes audio theme-based dictionaries.

The process of learning words using T&P Books' theme-based dictionaries gives you the following advantages:

- You have correctly grouped source information, which predetermines your success at subsequent stages of word memorization
- Availability of words derived from the same root (lazy, lazily, lazybones), allowing you to memorize word units instead of separate words
- Small units of words facilitate the process of establishing associative links needed for consolidation of vocabulary
- You can estimate the number of learned words and hence your level of language knowledge
- The dictionary allows for the creation of an effective and high-quality revision process
- You can revise certain themes several times, modifying the revision methods and techniques
- Audio versions of the dictionaries help you to work out the pronunciation of words and develop your skills of auditory word perception

The T&P Books' theme-based dictionaries are offered in several variants differing in the number of words: 1.500, 3.000, 5.000, 7.000, and 9.000 words. There are also dictionaries containing 15,000 words for some language combinations. Your choice of dictionary will depend on your knowledge level and goals.

We sincerely believe that our dictionaries will become your trusty assistant in learning foreign languages and will allow you to easily acquire the necessary vocabulary.

TABLE OF CONTENTS

T&P Books' Theme-Based Dictionaries 4
Pronunciation guide 15
Abbreviations 16

BASIC CONCEPTS 18
Basic concepts. Part 1 18

1. Pronouns 18
2. Greetings. Salutations. Farewells 18
3. How to address 19
4. Cardinal numbers. Part 1 19
5. Cardinal numbers. Part 2 20
6. Ordinal numbers 21
7. Numbers. Fractions 21
8. Numbers. Basic operations 21
9. Numbers. Miscellaneous 22
10. The most important verbs. Part 1 22
11. The most important verbs. Part 2 23
12. The most important verbs. Part 3 24
13. The most important verbs. Part 4 25
14. Colors 26
15. Questions 27
16. Prepositions 28
17. Function words. Adverbs. Part 1 28
18. Function words. Adverbs. Part 2 30

Basic concepts. Part 2 32

19. Weekdays 32
20. Hours. Day and night 32
21. Months. Seasons 33
22. Time. Miscellaneous 35
23. Opposites 36
24. Lines and shapes 38
25. Units of measurement 39
26. Containers 40
27. Materials 41
28. Metals 41

HUMAN BEING 43
Human being. The body 43

29. Humans. Basic concepts 43
30. Human anatomy 43
31. Head 44
32. Human body 45

Clothing & Accessories 46

33. Outerwear. Coats 46
34. Men's & women's clothing 46
35. Clothing. Underwear 47
36. Headwear 47
37. Footwear 47
38. Textile. Fabrics 48
39. Personal accessories 48
40. Clothing. Miscellaneous 49
41. Personal care. Cosmetics 50
42. Jewelry 51
43. Watches. Clocks 51

Food. Nutricion 53

44. Food 53
45. Drinks 55
46. Vegetables 56
47. Fruits. Nuts 56
48. Bread. Candy 57
49. Cooked dishes 58
50. Spices 59
51. Meals 59
52. Table setting 60
53. Restaurant 60

Family, relatives and friends 62

54. Personal information. Forms 62
55. Family members. Relatives 62
56. Friends. Coworkers 64
57. Man. Woman 64
58. Age 65
59. Children 65
60. Married couples. Family life 66

Character. Feelings. Emotions 68

61. Feelings. Emotions 68

62. Character. Personality 69
63. Sleep. Dreams 70
64. Humour. Laughter. Gladness 71
65. Discussion, conversation. Part 1 72
66. Discussion, conversation. Part 2 73
67. Discussion, conversation. Part 3 74
68. Agreement. Refusal 75
69. Success. Good luck. Failure 76
70. Quarrels. Negative emotions 76

Medicine 79

71. Diseases 79
72. Symptoms. Treatments. Part 1 80
73. Symptoms. Treatments. Part 2 81
74. Symptoms. Treatments. Part 3 82
75. Doctors 83
76. Medicine. Drugs. Accessories 83
77. Smoking. Tobacco products 84

HUMAN HABITAT 85
City 85

78. City. Life in the city 85
79. Urban institutions 86
80. Signs 88
81. Urban transportation 89
82. Sightseeing 90
83. Shopping 90
84. Money 91
85. Post. Postal service 92

Dwelling. House. Home 94

86. House. Dwelling 94
87. House. Entrance. Lift 95
88. House. Electricity 95
89. House. Doors. Locks 95
90. Country house 96
91. Villa. Mansion 97
92. Castle. Palace 97
93. Apartment 98
94. Apartment. Cleaning 98
95. Furniture. Interior 98
96. Bedding 99
97. Kitchen 99
98. Bathroom 101
99. Household appliances 101
100. Repairs. Renovation 102

101. Plumbing 102
102. Fire. Conflagration 103

HUMAN ACTIVITIES 105
Job. Business. Part 1 105

103. Office. Working in the office 105
104. Business processes. Part 1 106
105. Business processes. Part 2 107
106. Production. Works 108
107. Contract. Agreement 110
108. Import & Export 110
109. Finances 111
110. Marketing 112
111. Advertising 112
112. Banking 113
113. Telephone. Phone conversation 114
114. Cell phone 114
115. Stationery 115
116. Various kinds of documents 115
117. Kinds of business 116

Job. Business. Part 2 119

118. Show. Exhibition 119
119. Mass Media 120
120. Agriculture 121
121. Building. Building process 122
122. Science. Research. Scientists 123

Professions and occupations 125

123. Job search. Dismissal 125
124. Business people 125
125. Service professions 127
126. Military professions and ranks 127
127. Officials. Priests 128
128. Agricultural professions 129
129. Art professions 129
130. Various professions 130
131. Occupations. Social status 131

Sports 133

132. Kinds of sports. Sportspersons 133
133. Kinds of sports. Miscellaneous 134
134. Gym 135

135. Hockey 135
136. Soccer 135
137. Alpine skiing 137
138. Tennis. Golf 138
139. Chess 138
140. Boxing 139
141. Sports. Miscellaneous 139

Education 141

142. School 141
143. College. University 142
144. Sciences. Disciplines 143
145. Writing system. Orthography 143
146. Foreign languages 145
147. Fairy tale characters 146
148. Zodiac Signs 146

Arts 148

149. Theater 148
150. Cinema 149
151. Painting 150
152. Literature & Poetry 151
153. Circus 152
154. Music. Pop music 153

Rest. Entertainment. Travel 155

155. Trip. Travel 155
156. Hotel 156
157. Books. Reading 156
158. Hunting. Fishing 158
159. Games. Billiards 159
160. Games. Playing cards 159
161. Casino. Roulette 160
162. Rest. Games. Miscellaneous 160
163. Photography 161
164. Beach. Swimming 162

TECHNICAL EQUIPMENT. TRANSPORTATION 164
Technical equipment 164

165. Computer 164
166. Internet. E-mail 165
167. Electricity 166
168. Tools 167

Transportation 170

169. Airplane 170
170. Train 171
171. Ship 172
172. Airport 174
173. Bicycle. Motorcycle 175

Cars 176

174. Types of cars 176
175. Cars. Bodywork 176
176. Cars. Passenger compartment 178
177. Cars. Engine 178
178. Cars. Crash. Repair 179
179. Cars. Road 180
180. Traffic signs 181

PEOPLE. LIFE EVENTS 183
Life events 183

181. Holidays. Event 183
182. Funerals. Burial 184
183. War. Soldiers 185
184. War. Military actions. Part 1 186
185. War. Military actions. Part 2 187
186. Weapons 189
187. Ancient people 190
188. Middle Ages 191
189. Leader. Chief. Authorities 193
190. Road. Way. Directions 193
191. Breaking the law. Criminals. Part 1 195
192. Breaking the law. Criminals. Part 2 196
193. Police. Law. Part 1 197
194. Police. Law. Part 2 198

NATURE 201
The Earth. Part 1 201

195. Outer space 201
196. The Earth 202
197. Cardinal directions 203
198. Sea. Ocean 203
199. Seas' and Oceans' names 204
200. Mountains 205
201. Mountains names 206
202. Rivers 206
203. Rivers' names 207

204. Forest 208
205. Natural resources 209

The Earth. Part 2 211

206. Weather 211
207. Severe weather. Natural disasters 212
208. Noises. Sounds 212
209. Winter 213

Fauna 215

210. Mammals. Predators 215
211. Wild animals 215
212. Domestic animals 217
213. Dogs. Dog breeds 218
214. Sounds made by animals 218
215. Young animals 219
216. Birds 219
217. Birds. Singing and sounds 221
218. Fish. Marine animals 221
219. Amphibians. Reptiles 222
220. Insects 222
221. Animals. Body parts 223
222. Actions of animals 224
223. Animals. Habitats 224
224. Animal care 225
225. Animals. Miscellaneous 225
226. Horses 226

Flora 228

227. Trees 228
228. Shrubs 229
229. Mushrooms 229
230. Fruits. Berries 229
231. Flowers. Plants 230
232. Cereals, grains 231
233. Vegetables. Greens 232

REGIONAL GEOGRAPHY 234
Countries. Nationalities 234

234. Western Europe 234
235. Central and Eastern Europe 236
236. Former USSR countries 237
237. Asia 238

238. North America 240
239. Central and South America 241
240. Africa 242
241. Australia. Oceania 242
242. Cities 243
243. Politics. Government. Part 1 244
244. Politics. Government. Part 2 246
245. Countries. Miscellaneous 247
246. Major religious groups. Confessions 248
247. Religions. Priests 249
248. Faith. Christianity. Islam 249

MISCELLANEOUS 252

249. Various useful words 252
250. Modifiers. Adjectives. Part 1 253
251. Modifiers. Adjectives. Part 2 256

MAIN 500 VERBS 259

252. Verbs A-C 259
253. Verbs D-G 261
254. Verbs H-M 264
255. Verbs N-R 266
256. Verbs S-W 268

PRONUNCIATION GUIDE

T&P phonetic alphabet	Czech example	English example
[a]	**lavina** [lavɪna]	shorter than in ask
[a:]	**banán** [bana:n]	calf, palm
[e]	**beseda** [bɛsɛda]	elm, medal
[ɛ:]	**chléb** [xlɛ:p]	longer than bed, fell
[ɪ]	**Bible** [bɪblɛ]	big, America
[i:]	**chudý** [xudi:]	feet, meter
[o]	**epocha** [ɛpoxa]	pod, John
[o:]	**diagnóza** [dɪagno:za]	fall, bomb
[u]	**dokument** [dokumɛnt]	book
[u:]	**chůva** [xu:va]	pool, room
[b]	**babička** [babɪʧka]	baby, book
[ʦ]	**celnice** [ʦɛlnɪʦɛ]	cats, tsetse fly
[ʧ]	**vlčák** [vlʧa:k]	church, French
[x]	**archeologie** [arxɛologɪe]	as in Scots 'loch'
[d]	**delfín** [dɛlfi:n]	day, doctor
[dʲ]	**Holanďan** [holandʲan]	median, radio
[f]	**atmosféra** [atmosfɛ:ra]	face, food
[g]	**galaxie** [galaksɪe]	game, gold
[h]	**knihovna** [knɪhovna]	huge, hat
[j]	**jídlo** [ji:dlo]	yes, New York
[k]	**zaplakat** [zaplakat]	clock, kiss
[l]	**chlapec** [xlapɛʦ]	lace, people
[m]	**modelář** [modɛla:rʃ]	magic, milk
[n]	**imunita** [ɪmunɪta]	name, normal
[nʲ]	**báseň** [ba:sɛnʲ]	canyon, new
[ŋk]	**vstupenka** [vstupɛŋka]	bank, trunk
[p]	**poločas** [poloʧas]	pencil, private
[r]	**senátor** [sɛna:tor]	rice, radio
[rʒ], [rʃ]	**bouřka** [bourʃka]	urgent, flash
[s]	**svoboda** [svoboda]	city, boss
[ʃ]	**šiška** [ʃɪʃka]	machine, shark
[t]	**turista** [turɪsta]	tourist, trip
[tʲ]	**poušť** [pouʃtʲ]	tune, student
[v]	**veverka** [vɛvɛrka]	very, river
[z]	**zapomínat** [zapomi:nat]	zebra, please
[ʒ]	**ložisko** [loʒɪsko]	forge, pleasure

ABBREVIATIONS used in the vocabulary

English abbreviations

ab.	-	about
adj	-	adjective
adv	-	adverb
anim.	-	animate
as adj	-	attributive noun used as adjective
e.g.	-	for example
etc.	-	et cetera
fam.	-	familiar
fem.	-	feminine
form.	-	formal
inanim.	-	inanimate
masc.	-	masculine
math	-	mathematics
mil.	-	military
n	-	noun
pl	-	plural
pron.	-	pronoun
sb	-	somebody
sing.	-	singular
sth	-	something
v aux	-	auxiliary verb
vi	-	intransitive verb
vi, vt	-	intransitive, transitive verb
vt	-	transitive verb

Czech abbreviations

ž	-	feminine noun
ž mn	-	feminine plural
m	-	masculine noun
m mn	-	masculine plural
m, ž	-	masculine, feminine

mn	-	plural
s	-	neuter
s mn	-	neuter plural

BASIC CONCEPTS

Basic concepts. Part 1

1. Pronouns

I, me	**já**	[ja:]
you	**ty**	[tɪ]
he	**on**	[on]
she	**ona**	[ona]
we	**my**	[mɪ]
you (to a group)	**vy**	[vɪ]
they (inanim.)	**ony**	[onɪ]
they (anim.)	**oni**	[onɪ]

2. Greetings. Salutations. Farewells

Hello! (fam.)	**Dobrý den!**	[dobri: dɛn]
Hello! (form.)	**Dobrý den!**	[dobri: dɛn]
Good morning!	**Dobré jitro!**	[dobrɛ: jɪtro]
Good afternoon!	**Dobrý den!**	[dobri: dɛn]
Good evening!	**Dobrý večer!**	[dobri: vɛʧɛr]
to say hello	**zdravit**	[zdravɪt]
Hi! (hello)	**Ahoj!**	[ahoj]
greeting (n)	**pozdrav** (m)	[pozdraf]
to greet (vt)	**zdravit**	[zdravɪt]
How are you?	**Jak se máte?**	[jak sɛ ma:tɛ]
What's new?	**Co je nového?**	[ʦo jɛ novɛ:ho]
Bye-Bye! Goodbye!	**Na shledanou!**	[na sxlɛdanou]
See you soon!	**Brzy na shledanou!**	[brzɪ na sxlɛdanou]
Farewell!	**Sbohem!**	[zbohɛm]
to say goodbye	**loučit se**	[louʧɪt sɛ]
So long!	**Ahoj!**	[ahoj]
Thank you!	**Děkuji!**	[dekujɪ]
Thank you very much!	**Děkuji mnohokrát!**	[dekujɪ mnohokra:t]
You're welcome	**Prosím**	[prosi:m]
Don't mention it!	**Nemoci se dočkat**	[nɛmoʦɪ sɛ doʧkat]
It was nothing	**Není zač**	[nɛni: zaʧ]

Excuse me! (fam.)	**Promiň!**	[promɪnʲ]
Excuse me! (form.)	**Promiňte!**	[promɪnʲtɛ]
to excuse (forgive)	**omlouvat**	[omlouvat]
to apologize (vi)	**omlouvat se**	[omlouvat sɛ]
My apologies	**Má soustrast**	[ma: soustrast]
I'm sorry!	**Promiňte!**	[promɪnʲtɛ]
to forgive (vt)	**omlouvat**	[omlouvat]
please (adv)	**prosím**	[prosi:m]
Don't forget!	**Nezapomeňte!**	[nɛzapomɛnʲtɛ]
Certainly!	**Jistě!**	[jɪste]
Of course not!	**Rozhodně ne!**	[rozhodne nɛ]
Okay! (I agree)	**Souhlasím!**	[souhlasi:m]
That's enough!	**Dost!**	[dost]

3. How to address

Excuse me, ...	**Promiňte, ...**	promɪnʲtɛ, ...
mister, sir	**Pane**	[panɛ]
ma'am	**Paní**	[pani:]
miss	**Slečno**	[slɛʧno]
young man	**Mladý muži**	[mladi: muʒɪ]
young man (little boy, kid)	**Chlapče**	[xlapʧɛ]
miss (little girl)	**Děvče**	[devʧɛ]

4. Cardinal numbers. Part 1

0 zero	**nula** (ž)	[nula]
1 one	**jeden**	[jɛdɛn]
2 two	**dva**	[dva]
3 three	**tři**	[trʃɪ]
4 four	**čtyři**	[ʧtɪrʒɪ]
5 five	**pět**	[pet]
6 six	**šest**	[ʃɛst]
7 seven	**sedm**	[sɛdm]
8 eight	**osm**	[oʒm]
9 nine	**devět**	[dɛvet]
10 ten	**deset**	[dɛsɛt]
11 eleven	**jedenáct**	[jɛdɛna:ʦt]
12 twelve	**dvanáct**	[dvana:ʦt]
13 thirteen	**třináct**	[trʃɪna:ʦt]
14 fourteen	**čtrnáct**	[ʧtrna:ʦt]
15 fifteen	**patnáct**	[patna:ʦt]
16 sixteen	**šestnáct**	[ʃɛstna:ʦt]

17 seventeen	**sedmnáct**	[sɛdmna:ʦt]
18 eighteen	**osmnáct**	[osmna:ʦt]
19 nineteen	**devatenáct**	[dɛvatɛna:ʦt]
20 twenty	**dvacet**	[dvaʦɛt]
21 twenty-one	**dvacet jeden**	[dvaʦɛt jɛdɛn]
22 twenty-two	**dvacet dva**	[dvaʦɛt dva]
23 twenty-three	**dvacet tři**	[dvaʦɛt trʃɪ]
30 thirty	**třicet**	[trʃɪʦɛt]
31 thirty-one	**třicet jeden**	[trʃɪʦɛt jɛdɛn]
32 thirty-two	**třicet dva**	[trʃɪʦɛt dva]
33 thirty-three	**třicet tři**	[trʃɪʦɛt trʃɪ]
40 forty	**čtyřicet**	[ʧtɪrʒɪʦɛt]
41 forty-one	**čtyřicet jeden**	[ʧtɪrʒɪʦɛt jɛdɛn]
42 forty-two	**čtyřicet dva**	[ʧtɪrʒɪʦɛt dva]
43 forty-three	**čtyřicet tři**	[ʧtɪrʒɪʦɛt trʃɪ]
50 fifty	**padesát**	[padesa:t
51 fifty-one	**padesát jeden**	[padesa:t jɛdɛn]
52 fifty-two	**padesát dva**	[padesa:t dva]
53 fifty-three	**padesát tři**	[padesa:t trʃɪ]
60 sixty	**šedesát**	[ʃɛdɛsa:t
61 sixty-one	**šedesát jeden**	[ʃɛdɛsa:t jɛdɛn]
62 sixty-two	**šedesát dva**	[ʃɛdɛsa:t dva]
63 sixty-three	**šedesát tři**	[ʃɛdɛsa:t trʃɪ]
70 seventy	**sedmdesát**	[sɛdmdɛsa:t
71 seventy-one	**sedmdesát jeden**	[sɛdmdɛsa:t jɛdɛn]
72 seventy-two	**sedmdesát dva**	[sɛdmdɛsa:t dva]
73 seventy-three	**sedmdesát tři**	[sɛdmdɛsa:t trʃɪ]
80 eighty	**osmdesát**	[osmdɛsa:t
81 eighty-one	**osmdesát jeden**	[osmdɛsa:t jɛdɛn]
82 eighty-two	**osmdesát dva**	[osmdɛsa:t dva]
83 eighty-three	**osmdesát tři**	[osmdɛsa:t trʃɪ]
90 ninety	**devadesát**	[dɛvadɛsa:t
91 ninety-one	**devadesát jeden**	[dɛvadɛsa:t jɛdɛn]
92 ninety-two	**devadesát dva**	[dɛvadɛsa:t dva]
93 ninety-three	**devadesát tři**	[dɛvadɛsa:t trʃɪ]

5. Cardinal numbers. Part 2

100 one hundred	**sto**	[sto]
200 two hundred	**dvě stě**	[dve ste]
300 three hundred	**tři sta**	[trʃɪ sta]
400 four hundred	**čtyři sta**	[ʧtɪrʒɪ sta]

500 five hundred	**pět set**	[pet sɛt]
600 six hundred	**šest set**	[ʃɛst sɛt]
700 seven hundred	**sedm set**	[sɛdm sɛt]
800 eight hundred	**osm set**	[osm sɛt]
900 nine hundred	**devět set**	[dɛvet sɛt]
1000 one thousand	**tisíc** (m)	[tɪsi:ʦ]
2000 two thousand	**dva tisíce**	[dva tɪsi:ʦɛ]
3000 three thousand	**tři tisíce**	[trʃɪ tɪsi:ʦɛ]
10000 ten thousand	**deset tisíc**	[dɛsɛt tɪsi:ʦ]
one hundred thousand	**sto tisíc**	[sto tɪsi:ʦ]
million	**milión** (m)	[mɪlɪo:n]
billion	**miliarda** (ž)	[mɪlɪarda]

6. Ordinal numbers

first (adj)	**první**	[prvni:]
second (adj)	**druhý**	[druhi:]
third (adj)	**třetí**	[trʃɛti:]
fourth (adj)	**čtvrtý**	[ʧtvrti:]
fifth (adj)	**pátý**	[pa:ti:]
sixth (adj)	**šestý**	[ʃɛsti:]
seventh (adj)	**sedmý**	[sɛdmi:]
eighth (adj)	**osmý**	[osmi:]
ninth (adj)	**devátý**	[dɛva:ti:]
tenth (adj)	**desátý**	[dɛsa:ti:]

7. Numbers. Fractions

fraction	**zlomek** (m)	[zlomɛk]
one half	**polovina** (ž)	[polovɪna]
one third	**třetina** (ž)	[trʃɛtɪna]
one quarter	**čtvrtina** (ž)	[ʧtvrtɪna]
one eighth	**osmina** (ž)	[osmɪna]
one tenth	**desetina** (ž)	[dɛsɛtɪna]
two thirds	**dvě třetiny** (ž)	[dve trʃɛtɪnɪ]
three quarters	**tři čtvrtiny** (ž)	[trʃɪ ʧtvrtɪnɪ]

8. Numbers. Basic operations

subtraction	**odčítání** (s)	[odʧi:ta:ni:]
to subtract (vi, vt)	**odčítat**	[odʧi:tat]
division	**dělení** (s)	[delɛni:]
to divide (vt)	**dělit**	[delɪt]

addition	**sčítání** (s)	[stʃi:ta:ni:]
to add up (vt)	**sečíst**	[sɛtʃi:st]
to add (vi, vt)	**přidávat**	[prʃɪda:vat]
multiplication	**násobení** (s)	[na:sobɛni:]
to multiply (vt)	**násobit**	[na:sobɪt]

9. Numbers. Miscellaneous

digit, figure	**číslice** (ž)	[tʃi:slɪtsɛ]
number	**číslo** (s)	[tʃi:slo]
numeral	**číslovka** (ž)	[tʃi:slofka]
minus sign	**minus** (m)	[mi:nus]
plus sign	**plus** (m)	[plus]
formula	**vzorec** (m)	[vzorɛts]
calculation	**vypočítávání** (s)	[vɪpotʃi:ta:va:ni:]
to count (vi, vt)	**počítat**	[potʃi:tat]
to count up	**vypočítávat**	[vɪpotʃi:ta:vat]
to compare (vt)	**srovnávat**	[srovna:vat]
How much?	**Kolik?**	[kolɪk]
sum, total	**součet** (m)	[soutʃɛt]
result	**výsledek** (m)	[vi:slɛdɛk]
remainder	**zůstatek** (m)	[zu:statɛk]
a few (e.g., ~ years ago)	**několik**	[nekolɪk]
little (I had ~ time)	**málo**	[ma:lo]
few (I have ~ friends)	**nemnoho**	nɛmnoho]
a little (~ water)	**trochu**	[troxu]
the rest	**zbytek** (m)	[zbɪtɛk]
one and a half	**půl druhého**	[pu:l druhɛ:ho]
dozen	**tucet** (m)	[tutsɛt]
in half (adv)	**napolovic**	[napolovɪts]
equally (evenly)	**stejně**	[stɛjne]
half	**polovina** (ž)	[polovɪna]
time (three ~s)	**krát**	[kra:t]

10. The most important verbs. Part 1

to advise (vt)	**radit**	[radɪt]
to agree (say yes)	**souhlasit**	[souhlasɪt]
to answer (vi, vt)	**odpovídat**	[otpovi:dat]
to apologize (vi)	**omlouvat se**	[omlouvat sɛ]
to arrive (vi)	**přijíždět**	[prʃɪji:ʒdet]
to ask (~ oneself)	**ptát se**	[pta:t sɛ]
to ask (~ sb to do sth)	**prosit**	[prosɪt]

to be (vi)	**být**	[bi:t]
to be afraid	**bát se**	[ba:t sɛ]
to be hungry	**mít hlad**	[mi:t hlat]
to be interested in ...	**zajímat se**	[zaji:mat sɛ]
to be needed	**být potřebný**	[bi:t potrʃɛbni:]
to be surprised	**divit se**	[dɪvɪt sɛ]
to be thirsty	**mít žízeň**	[mi:t ʒi:zɛnʲ]
to begin (vt)	**začínat**	[zaʧi:nat]
to belong to ...	**patřit**	[patrʃɪt]
to boast (vi)	**vychloubat se**	[vɪxloubat sɛ]
to break (split into pieces)	**lámat**	[la:mat]
to call (~ for help)	**volat**	[volat]
can (v aux)	**moci**	[moʦɪ]
to catch (vt)	**chytat**	[xɪtat]
to change (vt)	**změnit**	[zmnenɪt]
to choose (select)	**vybírat**	[vɪbi:rat]
to come down (the stairs)	**jít dolů**	[ji:t dolu:]
to compare (vt)	**porovnávat**	[porovna:vat]
to complain (vi, vt)	**stěžovat si**	[steʒovat sɪ]
to confuse (mix up)	**plést**	[plɛ:st]
to continue (vt)	**pokračovat**	[pokraʧovat]
to control (vt)	**kontrolovat**	[kontrolovat]
to cook (dinner)	**vařit**	[varʒɪt]
to cost (vt)	**stát**	[sta:t]
to count (add up)	**počítat**	[poʧi:tat]
to count on ...	**spoléhat na ...**	[spolɛ:hat na]
to create (vt)	**vytvořit**	[vɪtvorʒɪt]
to cry (weep)	**plakat**	[plakat]

11. The most important verbs. Part 2

to deceive (vi, vt)	**podvádět**	[podva:det]
to decorate (tree, street)	**zdobit**	[zdobɪt]
to defend (a country, etc.)	**bránit**	[bra:nɪt]
to demand (request firmly)	**žádat**	[ʒa:dat]
to dig (vt)	**rýt**	[ri:t]
to discuss (vt)	**projednávat**	[projɛdna:vat]
to do (vt)	**dělat**	[delat]
to doubt (have doubts)	**pochybovat**	[poxɪbovat]
to drop (let fall)	**pouštět**	[pouʃtet]
to enter (room, house, etc.)	**vcházet**	[vxa:zet]
to excuse (forgive)	**omlouvat**	[omlouvat]
to exist (vi)	**existovat**	[ɛgzɪstovat]

to expect (foresee)	**předvídat**	[prʃɛdvi:dat]
to explain (vt)	**vysvětlovat**	[vɪsvetlovat]
to fall (vi)	**padat**	[padat]
to find (vt)	**nacházet**	[naxa:zɛt]
to finish (vt)	**končit**	[kontʃɪt]
to fly (vi)	**letět**	[lɛtet]
to follow ... (come after)	**následovat**	[na:slɛdovat]
to forget (vi, vt)	**zapomínat**	[zapomi:nat]
to forgive (vt)	**odpouštět**	[otpouʃtet]
to give (vt)	**dávat**	[da:vat]
to give a hint	**narážet**	[nara:ʒet]
to go (on foot)	**jít**	[ji:t]
to go for a swim	**koupat se**	[koupat sɛ]
to go out (for dinner, etc.)	**vycházet**	[vɪxa:zɛt]
to guess (the answer)	**rozluštit**	[rozluʃtɪt]
to have (vt)	**mít**	[mi:t]
to have breakfast	**snídat**	[sni:dat]
to have dinner	**večeřet**	[vɛtʃɛrʒɛt]
to have lunch	**obědvat**	[obedvat]
to hear (vt)	**slyšet**	[slɪʃɛt]
to help (vt)	**pomáhat**	[poma:hat]
to hide (vt)	**schovávat**	[sxova:vat]
to hope (vi, vt)	**doufat**	[doufat]
to hunt (vi, vt)	**lovit**	[lovɪt]
to hurry (vi)	**spěchat**	[spexat]

12. The most important verbs. Part 3

to inform (vt)	**informovat**	[ɪnformovat]
to insist (vi, vt)	**trvat**	[trvat]
to insult (vt)	**urážet**	[ura:ʒet]
to invite (vt)	**zvát**	[zva:t]
to joke (vi)	**žertovat**	[ʒertovat]
to keep (vt)	**zachovávat**	[zaxova:vat]
to keep silent, to hush	**mlčet**	[mltʃɛt]
to kill (vt)	**zabíjet**	[zabi:jɛt]
to know (sb)	**znát**	[zna:t]
to know (sth)	**vědět**	[vedet]
to laugh (vi)	**smát se**	[sma:t sɛ]
to liberate (city, etc.)	**osvobozovat**	[osvobozovat]
to like (I like ...)	**líbit se**	[li:bɪt sɛ]
to look for ... (search)	**hledat**	[hlɛdat]
to love (sb)	**milovat**	[mɪlovat]

to make a mistake	**mýlit se**	[mi:lɪt sɛ]
to manage, to run	**řídit**	[rʒi:dɪt]
to mean (signify)	**znamenat**	[znamɛnat]
to mention (talk about)	**zmiňovat se**	[zmɪnʲovat sɛ]
to miss (school, etc.)	**zameškávat**	[zameʃka:vat]
to notice (see)	**všímat si**	[vʃi:mat sɪ]
to object (vi, vt)	**namítat**	[nami:tat]
to observe (see)	**pozorovat**	[pozorovat]
to open (vt)	**otvírat**	[otvi:rat]
to order (meal, etc.)	**objednávat**	[objɛdna:vat]
to order (mil.)	**rozkazovat**	[roskazovat]
to own (possess)	**vlastnit**	[vlastnɪt]
to participate (vi)	**zúčastnit se**	[zu:ʧastnɪt sɛ]
to pay (vi, vt)	**platit**	[platɪt]
to permit (vt)	**dovolovat**	[dovolovat]
to plan (vt)	**plánovat**	[pla:novat]
to play (children)	**hrát**	[hra:t]
to pray (vi, vt)	**modlit se**	[modlɪt sɛ]
to prefer (vt)	**dávat přednost**	[da:vat prʃɛdnost]
to promise (vt)	**slibovat**	[slɪbovat]
to pronounce (vt)	**vyslovovat**	[vɪslovovat]
to propose (vt)	**nabízet**	[nabi:zɛt]
to punish (vt)	**trestat**	[trɛstat]

13. The most important verbs. Part 4

to read (vi, vt)	**číst**	[ʧi:st]
to recommend (vt)	**doporučovat**	[doporuʧovat]
to refuse (vi, vt)	**odmítat**	[odmi:tat]
to regret (be sorry)	**litovat**	[lɪtovat]
to rent (sth from sb)	**pronajímat si**	[pronaji:mat sɪ]
to repeat (say again)	**opakovat**	[opakovat]
to reserve, to book	**rezervovat**	[rɛzɛrvovat]
to run (vi)	**běžet**	[beʒet]
to save (rescue)	**zachraňovat**	[zaxranʲovat]
to say (~ thank you)	**říci**	[rʒi:tsɪ]
to scold (vt)	**nadávat**	[nada:vat]
to see (vt)	**vidět**	[vɪdet]
to sell (vt)	**prodávat**	[proda:vat]
to send (vt)	**odesílat**	[odɛsi:lat]
to shoot (vi)	**střílet**	[strʃi:lɛt]
to shout (vi)	**křičet**	[krʃɪʧɛt]
to show (vt)	**ukazovat**	[ukazovat]
to sign (document)	**podepisovat**	[podɛpɪsovat]

to sit down (vi)	**sednout si**	[sɛdnout sɪ]
to smile (vi)	**usmívat se**	[usmi:vat sɛ]
to speak (vi, vt)	**mluvit**	[mluvɪt]
to steal (money, etc.)	**krást**	[kra:st]
to stop (for pause, etc.)	**zastavovat se**	[zastavovat sɛ]
to stop (please ~ calling me)	**zastavovat**	[zastavovat]
to study (vt)	**studovat**	[studovat]
to swim (vi)	**plavat**	[plavat]
to take (vt)	**brát**	[bra:t]
to think (vi, vt)	**myslit**	[mɪslɪt]
to threaten (vt)	**vyhrožovat**	[vɪhroʒovat]
to touch (with hands)	**dotýkat se**	[doti:kat sɛ]
to translate (vt)	**překládat**	[prʃɛkla:dat]
to trust (vt)	**důvěřovat**	[du:verʒovat]
to try (attempt)	**zkoušet**	[skouʃɛt]
to turn (e.g., ~ left)	**zatáčet**	[zata:ʧɛt]
to underestimate (vt)	**podceňovat**	[podʦɛnʲovat]
to understand (vt)	**rozumět**	[rozumnet]
to unite (vt)	**sjednocovat**	[sjɛdnoʦovat]
to wait (vt)	**čekat**	[ʧɛkat]
to want (wish, desire)	**chtít**	[xti:t]
to warn (vt)	**upozorňovat**	[upozornʲovat]
to work (vi)	**pracovat**	[praʦovat]
to write (vt)	**psát**	[psa:t]
to write down	**zapisovat si**	[zapɪsovat sɪ]

14. Colors

color	**barva** (ž)	[barva]
shade (tint)	**odstín** (m)	[otsti:n]
hue	**tón** (m)	[to:n]
rainbow	**duha** (ž)	[duha]
white (adj)	**bílý**	[bi:li:]
black (adj)	**černý**	[ʧɛrni:]
gray (adj)	**šedý**	[ʃɛdi:]
green (adj)	**zelený**	[zɛlɛni:]
yellow (adj)	**žlutý**	[ʒluti:]
red (adj)	**červený**	[ʧɛrvɛni:]
blue (adj)	**modrý**	[modri:]
light blue (adj)	**bledě modrý**	[blɛde modri:]
pink (adj)	**růžový**	[ru:ʒovi:]
orange (adj)	**oranžový**	[oranʒovi:]

violet (adj)	**fialový**	[fɪalovi:]
brown (adj)	**hnědý**	[hnedi:]
golden (adj)	**zlatý**	[zlati:]
silvery (adj)	**stříbřitý**	[strʃi:brʒɪti:]
beige (adj)	**béžový**	[bɛ:ʒovi:]
cream (adj)	**krémový**	[krɛ:movi:]
turquoise (adj)	**tyrkysový**	[tɪrkɪsovi:]
cherry red (adj)	**višňový**	[vɪʃnʲovi:]
lilac (adj)	**lila**	[lɪla]
crimson (adj)	**malinový**	[malɪnovi:]
light (adj)	**světlý**	[svetli:]
dark (adj)	**tmavý**	[tmavi:]
bright, vivid (adj)	**jasný**	[jasni:]
colored (pencils)	**barevný**	[barɛvni:]
color (e.g., ~ film)	**barevný**	[barɛvni:]
black-and-white (adj)	**černobílý**	[ʧɛrnobi:li:]
plain (one-colored)	**jednobarevný**	[jɛdnobarɛvni:]
multicolored (adj)	**různobarevný**	[ru:znobarɛvni:]

15. Questions

Who?	**Kdo?**	[gdo]
What?	**Co?**	[ʦo]
Where? (at, in)	**Kde?**	[gdɛ]
Where (to)?	**Kam?**	[kam]
From where?	**Odkud?**	[otkut]
When?	**Kdy?**	[gdɪ]
Why? (What for?)	**Proč?**	[proʧ]
Why? (~ are you crying?)	**Proč?**	[proʧ]
What for?	**Na co?**	[na ʦo]
How? (in what way)	**Jak?**	[jak]
What? (What kind of ...?)	**Jaký?**	[jaki:]
Which?	**Který?**	[ktɛri:]
To whom?	**Komu?**	[komu]
About whom?	**O kom?**	[o kom]
About what?	**O čem?**	[o ʧɛm]
With whom?	**S kým?**	[s ki:m]
How many? How much?	**Kolik?**	[kolɪk]
Whose?	**Čí?**	[ʧi:]

16. Prepositions

with (accompanied by)	**s, se**	[s], [sɛ]
without	**bez**	[bɛz]
to (indicating direction)	**do**	[do]
about (talking ~ ...)	**o**	[o]
before (in time)	**před**	[prʃɛt]
in front of ...	**před**	[prʃɛt]
under (beneath, below)	**pod**	[pot]
above (over)	**nad**	[nat]
on (atop)	**na**	[na]
from (off, out of)	**z**	[z]
of (made from)	**z**	[z]
in (e.g., ~ ten minutes)	**za**	[za]
over (across the top of)	**přes**	[prʃɛs]

17. Function words. Adverbs. Part 1

Where? (at, in)	**Kde?**	[gdɛ]
here (adv)	**zde**	[zdɛ]
there (adv)	**tam**	[tam]
somewhere (to be)	**někde**	[negdɛ]
nowhere (not in any place)	**nikde**	[nɪgdɛ]
by (near, beside)	**u ...**	[u]
by the window	**u okna**	[u okna]
Where (to)?	**Kam?**	[kam]
here (e.g., come ~!)	**sem**	[sɛm]
there (e.g., to go ~)	**tam**	[tam]
from here (adv)	**odsud**	[otsut]
from there (adv)	**odtamtud**	[odtamtut]
close (adv)	**blízko**	[bli:sko]
far (adv)	**daleko**	[dalɛko]
near (e.g., ~ Paris)	**kolem**	[kolɛm]
nearby (adv)	**poblíž**	[pobli:ʒ]
not far (adv)	**nedaleko**	[nɛdalɛko]
left (adj)	**levý**	[lɛvi:]
on the left	**zleva**	[zlɛva]
to the left	**vlevo**	[vlɛvo]
right (adj)	**pravý**	[pravi:]
on the right	**zprava**	[sprava]

to the right	**vpravo**	[vpravo]
in front (adv)	**zpředu**	[sprʃɛdu]
front (as adj)	**přední**	[prʃɛdni:]
ahead (the kids ran ~)	**vpřed**	[vprʃɛt]
behind (adv)	**za**	[za]
from behind	**zezadu**	[zɛzadu]
back (towards the rear)	**zpět**	[spet]
middle	**střed** (m)	[strʃɛt]
in the middle	**uprostřed**	[uprostrʃɛt]
at the side	**z boku**	[z boku]
everywhere (adv)	**všude**	[vʃudɛ]
around (in all directions)	**kolem**	[kolɛm]
from inside	**zevnitř**	[zɛvnɪtrʃ]
somewhere (to go)	**někam**	[nekam]
straight (directly)	**přímo**	[prʃi:mo]
back (e.g., come ~)	**zpět**	[spet]
from anywhere	**odněkud**	[odnekut]
from somewhere	**odněkud**	[odnekut]
firstly (adv)	**za prvé**	[za prvɛ:]
secondly (adv)	**za druhé**	[za druhɛ:]
thirdly (adv)	**za třetí**	[za trʃɛti:]
suddenly (adv)	**najednou**	[najɛdnou]
at first (in the beginning)	**zpočátku**	[spoʧa:tku]
for the first time	**poprvé**	[poprvɛ:]
long before ...	**dávno před ...**	[da:vno prʃɛt]
anew (over again)	**znovu**	[znovu]
for good (adv)	**navždy**	[navʒdɪ]
never (adv)	**nikdy**	[nɪgdɪ]
again (adv)	**opět**	[opet]
now (at present)	**nyní**	[nɪni:]
often (adv)	**často**	[ʧasto]
then (adv)	**tehdy**	[tɛhdɪ]
urgently (quickly)	**neodkladně**	[nɛotkladne]
usually (adv)	**obyčejně**	[obɪʧɛjne]
by the way, ...	**mimochodem**	[mɪmoxodɛm]
possibly	**možná**	[moʒna:]
probably (adv)	**asi**	[asɪ]
maybe (adv)	**možná**	[moʒna:]
besides ...	**kromě toho ...**	[kromne toho]
that's why ...	**proto ...**	[proto]
in spite of ...	**nehledě na ...**	[nɛhlɛde na]
thanks to ...	**díky ...**	[di:kɪ]
what (pron.)	**co**	[ʦo]

that (conj.)	**že**	[ʒe]
something	**něco**	[netso]
anything (something)	**něco**	[netso]
nothing	**nic**	[nɪts]
who (pron.)	**kdo**	[gdo]
someone	**někdo**	[negdo]
somebody	**někdo**	[negdo]
nobody	**nikdo**	[nɪgdo]
nowhere (a voyage to ~)	**nikam**	[nɪkam]
nobody's	**ničí**	[nɪtʃi:]
somebody's	**něčí**	[netʃi:]
so (I'm ~ glad)	**tak**	[tak]
also (as well)	**také**	[takɛ:]
too (as well)	**také**	[takɛ:]

18. Function words. Adverbs. Part 2

Why?	**Proč?**	[protʃ]
for some reason	**z nějakých důvodů**	[z nejaki:x du:vodu:]
because ...	**protože ...**	[protoʒe]
for some purpose	**z nějakých důvodů**	[z nejaki:x du:vodu:]
and	**a**	[a]
or	**nebo**	[nɛbo]
but	**ale**	[alɛ]
for (e.g., ~ me)	**pro**	[pro]
too (~ many people)	**příliš**	[prʃi:lɪʃ]
only (exclusively)	**jenom**	[jɛnom]
exactly (adv)	**přesně**	[prʃɛsne]
about (more or less)	**kolem**	[kolɛm]
approximately (adv)	**přibližně**	[prʃɪblɪʒne]
approximate (adj)	**přibližný**	[prʃɪblɪʒni:]
almost (adv)	**skoro**	[skoro]
the rest	**zbytek** (m)	[zbɪtɛk]
the other (second)	**druhý**	[druhi:]
other (different)	**jiný**	[jɪni:]
each (adj)	**každý**	[kaʒdi:]
any (no matter which)	**každý**	[kaʒdi:]
many, much (a lot of)	**mnoho**	[mnoho]
many people	**mnozí**	[mnozi:]
all (everyone)	**všichni**	[vʃɪxnɪ]
in return for ...	**výměnou za ...**	[vi:mnenou za]
in exchange (adv)	**místo**	[mi:sto]

by hand (made)	**ručně**	[rutʃne]
hardly (negative opinion)	**sotva**	[sotva]
probably (adv)	**asi**	[asɪ]
on purpose (intentionally)	**schválně**	[sxva:lne]
by accident (adv)	**náhodou**	[na:hodou]
very (adv)	**velmi**	[vɛlmɪ]
for example (adv)	**například**	[naprʃi:klat]
between	**mezi**	[mɛzɪ]
among	**mezi**	[mɛzɪ]
so much (such a lot)	**tolik**	[tolɪk]
especially (adv)	**zejména**	[zɛjmɛ:na]

Basic concepts. Part 2

19. Weekdays

Monday	**pondělí** (s)	[pondeli:]
Tuesday	**úterý** (s)	[u:tɛri:]
Wednesday	**středa** (ž)	[strʃɛda]
Thursday	**čtvrtek** (m)	[ʧtvrtɛk]
Friday	**pátek** (m)	[pa:tɛk]
Saturday	**sobota** (ž)	[sobota]
Sunday	**neděle** (ž)	[nɛdelɛ]
today (adv)	**dnes**	[dnɛs]
tomorrow (adv)	**zítra**	[zi:tra]
the day after tomorrow	**pozítří**	[pozi:trʃi:]
yesterday (adv)	**včera**	[vʧɛra]
the day before yesterday	**předevčírem**	[prʃɛdɛvʧi:rɛm]
day	**den** (m)	[dɛn]
working day	**pracovní den** (m)	[praʦovni: dɛn]
public holiday	**sváteční den** (m)	[sva:tɛʧni: dɛn]
day off	**volno** (s)	[volno]
weekend	**víkend** (m)	[vi:kɛnt]
all day long	**celý den**	[ʦɛli: dɛn]
the next day (adv)	**příští den**	[prʃi:ʃti: dɛn]
two days ago	**před dvěma dny**	[prʃɛd dvema dnɪ]
the day before	**den předtím**	[dɛn prʃɛdti:m]
daily (adj)	**denní**	[dɛnni:]
every day (adv)	**denně**	[dɛnne]
week	**týden** (m)	[ti:dɛn]
last week (adv)	**minulý týden**	[mɪnuli: ti:dɛn]
next week (adv)	**příští týden**	[prʃi:ʃti: ti:dɛn]
weekly (adj)	**týdenní**	[ti:dɛnni:]
every week (adv)	**týdně**	[ti:dne]
twice a week	**dvakrát týdně**	[dvakra:t ti:dne]
every Tuesday	**každé úterý**	[kaʒdɛ: u:tɛri:]

20. Hours. Day and night

morning	**ráno** (s)	[ra:no]
in the morning	**ráno**	[ra:no]
noon, midday	**poledne** (s)	[polɛdnɛ]

in the afternoon	**odpoledne**	[otpolɛdnɛ]
evening	**večer** (m)	[vɛʧɛr]
in the evening	**večer**	[vɛʧɛr]
night	**noc** (ž)	[noʦ]
at night	**v noci**	[v noʦɪ]
midnight	**půlnoc** (ž)	[pu:lnoʦ]

second	**sekunda** (ž)	[sɛkunda]
minute	**minuta** (ž)	[mɪnuta]
hour	**hodina** (ž)	[hodɪna]
half an hour	**půlhodina** (ž)	[pu:lhodɪna]
a quarter-hour	**čtvrthodina** (ž)	[ʧtvrthodɪna]
fifteen minutes	**patnáct minut**	[patna:ʦt mɪnut]
24 hours	**den a noc**	[dɛn a noʦ]

sunrise	**východ** (m) **slunce**	[vi:xod sluntsɛ]
dawn	**úsvit** (m)	[u:svɪt]
early morning	**časné ráno** (s)	[ʧasnɛ: ra:no]
sunset	**západ** (m) **slunce**	[za:pat sluntsɛ]

early in the morning	**brzy ráno**	[brzɪ ra:no]
this morning	**dnes ráno**	[dnɛs ra:no]
tomorrow morning	**zítra ráno**	[zi:tra ra:no]

this afternoon	**dnes odpoledne**	[dnɛs otpolɛdnɛ]
in the afternoon	**odpoledne**	[otpolɛdnɛ]
tomorrow afternoon	**zítra odpoledne**	[zi:tra otpolɛdnɛ]

tonight (this evening)	**dnes večer**	[dnɛs vɛʧɛr]
tomorrow night	**zítra večer**	[zi:tra vɛʧɛr]

at 3 o'clock sharp	**přesně ve tři hodiny**	[prʃɛsne vɛ trʃɪ hodɪnɪ]
about 4 o'clock	**kolem čtyř hodin**	[kolɛm ʧtɪrʒ hodɪn]
by 12 o'clock	**do dvanácti hodin**	[do dvana:ʦtɪ hodɪn]

in 20 minutes	**za dvacet minut**	[za dvaʦɛt mɪnut]
in an hour	**za hodinu**	[za hodɪnu]
on time (adv)	**včas**	[vʧas]

a quarter to ...	**tři čtvrtě**	[trʃɪ ʧtvrte]
within an hour	**během hodiny**	[behɛm hodɪnɪ]
every 15 minutes	**každých patnáct minut**	[kaʒdi:x patna:ʦt mɪnut]
round the clock	**celodenně**	[ʦɛlodɛnne]

21. Months. Seasons

January	**leden** (m)	[lɛdɛn]
February	**únor** (m)	[u:nor]
March	**březen** (m)	[brʒɛzɛn]
April	**duben** (m)	[dubɛn]

May	**květen** (m)	[kvetɛn]
June	**červen** (m)	[ʧɛrvɛn]
July	**červenec** (m)	[ʧɛrvɛnɛʦ]
August	**srpen** (m)	[srpɛn]
September	**září** (s)	[za:rʒi:]
October	**říjen** (m)	[rʒi:jɛn]
November	**listopad** (m)	[lɪstopat]
December	**prosinec** (m)	[prosɪnɛʦ]
spring	**jaro** (s)	[jaro]
in spring	**na jaře**	[na jarʒɛ]
spring (as adj)	**jarní**	[jarni:]
summer	**léto** (s)	[lɛ:to]
in summer	**v létě**	[v lɛ:te]
summer (as adj)	**letní**	[lɛtni:]
fall	**podzim** (m)	[podzɪm]
in fall	**na podzim**	[na podzɪm]
fall (as adj)	**podzimní**	[podzɪmni:]
winter	**zima** (ž)	[zɪma]
in winter	**v zimě**	[v zɪmne]
winter (as adj)	**zimní**	[zɪmni:]
month	**měsíc** (m)	[mnesi:ʦ]
this month	**tento měsíc**	[tɛnto mnesi:ʦ]
next month	**příští měsíc**	[prʃi:ʃti: mnesi:ʦ]
last month	**minulý měsíc**	[mɪnuli: mnesi:ʦ]
a month ago	**před měsícem**	[prʃɛd mnesi:ʦɛm]
in a month (a month later)	**za měsíc**	[za mnesi:ʦ]
in 2 months (2 months later)	**za dva měsíce**	[za dva mnesi:ʦɛ]
the whole month	**celý měsíc**	[ʦɛli: mnesi:ʦ]
all month long	**celý měsíc**	[ʦɛli: mnesi:ʦ]
monthly (~ magazine)	**měsíční**	[mnesi:ʧni:]
monthly (adv)	**každý měsíc**	[kaʒdi: mnesi:ʦ]
every month	**měsíčně**	[mnesi:ʧne]
twice a month	**dvakrát měsíčně**	[dvakra:t mnesi:ʧne]
year	**rok** (m)	[rok]
this year	**letos**	[lɛtos]
next year	**příští rok**	[prʃi:ʃti: rok]
last year	**vloni**	[vlonɪ]
a year ago	**před rokem**	[prʃɛd rokɛm]
in a year	**za rok**	[za rok]
in two years	**za dva roky**	[za dva rokɪ]
the whole year	**celý rok**	[ʦɛli: rok]

all year long	**celý rok**	[tsɛli: rok]
every year	**každý rok**	[kaʒdi: rok]
annual (adj)	**každoroční**	[kaʒdorotʃni:]
annually (adv)	**každoročně**	[kaʒdorotʃne]
4 times a year	**čtyřikrát za rok**	[tʃtɪrʒɪkra:t za rok]
date (e.g., today's ~)	**datum** (s)	[datum]
date (e.g., ~ of birth)	**datum** (s)	[datum]
calendar	**kalendář** (m)	[kalɛnda:rʃ]
half a year	**půl roku**	[pu:l roku]
six months	**půlrok** (m)	[pu:lrok]
season (summer, etc.)	**období** (s)	[obdobi:]
century	**století** (s)	[stolɛti:]

22. Time. Miscellaneous

time	**čas** (m)	[tʃas]
moment	**okamžik** (m)	[okamʒɪk]
instant (n)	**okamžik** (m)	[okamʒɪk]
instant (adj)	**okamžitý**	[okamʒɪti:]
lapse (of time)	**časový úsek** (m)	[tʃasovi: u:sɛk]
life	**život** (m)	[ʒɪvot]
eternity	**věčnost** (ž)	[vetʃnost]
epoch	**epocha** (ž)	[ɛpoxa]
era	**éra** (ž)	[ɛ:ra]
cycle	**cyklus** (m)	[tsɪklus]
period	**období** (s)	[obdobi:]
term (short-~)	**doba** (ž)	[doba]
the future	**budoucnost** (ž)	[budoutsnost]
future (as adj)	**příští**	[prʃi:ʃti:]
next time	**příště**	[prʃi:ʃte]
the past	**minulost** (ž)	[mɪnulost]
past (recent)	**minulý**	[mɪnuli:]
last time	**minule**	[mɪnulɛ]
later (adv)	**později**	[pozdejɪ]
after (prep.)	**po**	[po]
nowadays (adv)	**nyní**	[nɪni:]
now (at this moment)	**teď**	[tɛtʲ]
immediately (adv)	**okamžitě**	[okamʒɪte]
soon (adv)	**brzo**	[brzo]
in advance (beforehand)	**předem**	[prʃɛdɛm]
a long time ago	**dávno**	[da:vno]
recently (adv)	**nedávno**	[nɛda:vno]
destiny	**osud** (m)	[osut]
memories (childhood ~)	**paměť** (ž)	[pamnetʲ]

archives	**archív** (m)	[arxi:f]
during ...	**během ...**	[behɛm]
long, a long time (adv)	**dlouho**	[dlouho]
not long (adv)	**nedlouho**	[nɛdlouho]
early (in the morning)	**brzy**	[brzɪ]
late (not early)	**pozdě**	[pozde]
forever (for good)	**navždy**	[navʒdɪ]
to start (begin)	**začínat**	[zatʃi:nat]
to postpone (vt)	**posunout**	[posunout]
at the same time	**současně**	[soutʃasne]
permanently (adv)	**stále**	[sta:lɛ]
constant (noise, pain)	**neustálý**	[nɛusta:li:]
temporary (adj)	**dočasný**	[dotʃasni:]
sometimes (adv)	**někdy**	[negdɪ]
rarely (adv)	**málokdy**	[ma:logdɪ]
often (adv)	**často**	[tʃasto]

23. Opposites

rich (adj)	**bohatý**	[bohati:]
poor (adj)	**chudý**	[xudi:]
ill, sick (adj)	**nemocný**	[nɛmotsni:]
well (not sick)	**zdravý**	[zdravi:]
big (adj)	**velký**	[vɛlki:]
small (adj)	**malý**	[mali:]
quickly (adv)	**rychle**	[rɪxlɛ]
slowly (adv)	**pomalu**	[pomalu]
fast (adj)	**rychlý**	[rɪxli:]
slow (adj)	**pomalý**	[pomali:]
glad (adj)	**veselý**	[vɛsɛli:]
sad (adj)	**smutný**	[smutni:]
together (adv)	**spolu**	[spolu]
separately (adv)	**zvlášť**	[zvla:ʃtʲ]
aloud (to read)	**nahlas**	[nahlas]
silently (to oneself)	**pro sebe**	[pro sɛbɛ]
tall (adj)	**vysoký**	[vɪsoki:]
low (adj)	**nízký**	[ni:ski:]
deep (adj)	**hluboký**	[hluboki:]
shallow (adj)	**mělký**	[mnelki:]

yes	**ano**	[ano]
no	**ne**	[nɛ]
distant (in space)	**daleký**	[dalɛki:]
nearby (adj)	**blízký**	[bli:ski:]
far (adv)	**daleko**	[dalɛko]
nearby (adv)	**vedle**	[vɛdlɛ]
long (adj)	**dlouhý**	[dlouhi:]
short (adj)	**krátký**	[kra:tki:]
good (kindhearted)	**dobrý**	[dobri:]
evil (adj)	**zlý**	[zli:]
married (adj)	**ženatý**	[ʒenati:]
single (adj)	**svobodný**	[svobodni:]
to forbid (vt)	**zakázat**	[zaka:zat]
to permit (vt)	**dovolit**	[dovolɪt]
end	**konec** (m)	[konɛʦ]
beginning	**začátek** (m)	[zaʧa:tɛk]
left (adj)	**levý**	[lɛvi:]
right (adj)	**pravý**	[pravi:]
first (adj)	**první**	[prvni:]
last (adj)	**poslední**	[poslɛdni:]
crime	**zločin** (m)	[zloʧɪn]
punishment	**trest** (m)	[trɛst]
to order (vt)	**rozkázat**	[roska:zat]
to obey (vi, vt)	**podřídit se**	[podrʒi:dɪt sɛ]
straight (adj)	**přímý**	[prʃi:mi:]
curved (adj)	**křivý**	[krʃɪvi:]
paradise	**ráj** (m)	[ra:j]
hell	**peklo** (s)	[pɛklo]
to be born	**narodit se**	[narodɪt sɛ]
to die (vi)	**umřít**	[umrʒi:t]
strong (adj)	**silný**	[sɪlni:]
weak (adj)	**slabý**	[slabi:]
old (adj)	**starý**	[stari:]
young (adj)	**mladý**	[mladi:]
old (adj)	**starý**	[stari:]
new (adj)	**nový**	[novi:]

hard (adj)	**tvrdý**	[tvrdi:]
soft (adj)	**měkký**	[mneki:]
warm (tepid)	**teplý**	[tɛpli:]
cold (adj)	**studený**	[studɛni:]
fat (adj)	**tlustý**	[tlusti:]
thin (adj)	**hubený**	[hubɛni:]
narrow (adj)	**úzký**	[u:ski:]
wide (adj)	**široký**	[ʃɪroki:]
good (adj)	**dobrý**	[dobri:]
bad (adj)	**špatný**	[ʃpatni:]
brave (adj)	**chrabrý**	[xrabri:]
cowardly (adj)	**bázlivý**	[ba:zlɪvi:]

24. Lines and shapes

square	**čtverec** (m)	[ʧtvɛrɛʦ]
square (as adj)	**čtvercový**	[ʧtvɛrʦovi:]
circle	**kruh** (m)	[krux]
round (adj)	**kulatý**	[kulati:]
triangle	**trojúhelník** (m)	[troju:hɛlni:k]
triangular (adj)	**trojúhelníkový**	[troju:hɛlni:kovi:]
oval	**ovál** (m)	[ova:l]
oval (as adj)	**oválný**	[ova:lni:]
rectangle	**obdélník** (m)	[obdɛ:lni:k]
rectangular (adj)	**obdélníkový**	[obdɛ:lni:kovi:]
pyramid	**jehlan** (m)	[jɛhlan]
rhombus	**kosočtverec** (m)	[kosoʧtvɛrɛʦ]
trapezoid	**lichoběžník** (m)	[lɪxobeʒni:k]
cube	**krychle** (ž)	[krɪxlɛ]
prism	**hranol** (m)	[hranol]
circumference	**kružnice** (ž)	[kruʒnɪʦɛ]
sphere	**sféra** (ž)	[sfɛ:ra]
ball (solid sphere)	**koule** (ž)	[koulɛ]
diameter	**průměr** (m)	[pru:mner]
radius	**poloměr** (m)	[polomner]
perimeter (circle's ~)	**obvod** (m)	[obvot]
center	**střed** (m)	[strʃɛt]
horizontal (adj)	**vodorovný**	[vodorovni:]
vertical (adj)	**svislý**	[svɪsli:]
parallel (n)	**rovnoběžka** (ž)	[rovnobeʃka]
parallel (as adj)	**paralelní**	[paralɛlni:]

line	**linie** (ž)	[lɪnɪe]
stroke	**čára** (ž)	[ʧa:ra]
straight line	**přímka** (ž)	[prʃi:mka]
curve (curved line)	**křivka** (ž)	[krʃɪfka]
thin (line, etc.)	**tenký**	[tɛŋki:]
contour (outline)	**obrys** (m)	[obrɪs]
intersection	**průsečík** (m)	[pru:sɛʧi:k]
right angle	**pravý úhel** (m)	[pravi: u:hɛl]
segment	**segment** (m)	[sɛgmɛnt]
sector (circular ~)	**sektor** (m)	[sɛktor]
side (of triangle)	**strana** (ž)	[strana]
angle	**úhel** (m)	[u:hɛl]

25. Units of measurement

weight	**váha** (ž)	[va:ha]
length	**délka** (ž)	[dɛ:lka]
width	**šířka** (ž)	[ʃi:rʃka]
height	**výška** (ž)	[vi:ʃka]
depth	**hloubka** (ž)	[hloupka]
volume	**objem** (m)	[objɛm]
area	**plocha** (ž)	[ploxa]
gram	**gram** (m)	[gram]
milligram	**miligram** (m)	[mɪlɪgram]
kilogram	**kilogram** (m)	[kɪlogram]
ton	**tuna** (ž)	[tuna]
pound	**libra** (ž)	[lɪbra]
ounce	**unce** (ž)	[unʦɛ]
meter	**metr** (m)	[mɛtr]
millimeter	**milimetr** (m)	[mɪlɪmɛtr]
centimeter	**centimetr** (m)	[ʦɛntɪmɛtr]
kilometer	**kilometr** (m)	[kɪlomɛtr]
mile	**míle** (ž)	[mi:lɛ]
inch	**coul** (m)	[ʦoul]
foot	**stopa** (ž)	[stopa]
yard	**yard** (m)	[jart]
square meter	**čtvereční metr** (m)	[ʧtvɛrɛʧni: mɛtr]
hectare	**hektar** (m)	[hɛktar]
liter	**litr** (m)	[lɪtr]
degree	**stupeň** (m)	[stupɛnʲ]
volt	**volt** (m)	[volt]
ampere	**ampér** (m)	[ampɛ:r]
horsepower	**koňská síla** (ž)	[konʲska: si:la]
quantity	**množství** (s)	[mnoʒstvi:]

a little bit of ...	**trochu ...**	[troxu]
half	**polovina** (ž)	[polovɪna]
dozen	**tucet** (m)	[tuʦɛt]
piece (item)	**kus** (m)	[kus]
size	**rozměr** (m)	[rozmnɛr]
scale (map ~)	**měřítko** (s)	[mnerʒi:tko]
minimal (adj)	**minimální**	[mɪnɪma:lni:]
the smallest (adj)	**nejmenší**	[nɛjmɛnʃi:]
medium (adj)	**střední**	[strʃɛdni:]
maximal (adj)	**maximální**	[maksɪma:lni:]
the largest (adj)	**největší**	[nɛjvetʃi:]

26. Containers

canning jar (glass ~)	**sklenice** (ž)	[sklɛnɪʦɛ]
can	**plechovka** (ž)	[plɛxofka]
bucket	**vědro** (s)	[vedro]
barrel	**sud** (m)	[sut]
wash basin (e.g., plastic ~)	**mísa** (ž)	[mi:sa]
tank (100L water ~)	**nádrž** (ž)	[na:drʃ]
hip flask	**plochá láhev** (ž)	[ploxa: la:gɛf]
jerrycan	**kanystr** (m)	[kanɪstr]
tank (e.g., tank car)	**cisterna** (ž)	[ʦɪstɛrna]
mug	**hrníček** (m)	[hrni:ʧɛk]
cup (of coffee, etc.)	**šálek** (m)	[ʃa:lɛk]
saucer	**talířek** (m)	[tali:rʒɛk]
glass (tumbler)	**sklenice** (ž)	[sklɛnɪʦɛ]
wine glass	**sklenka** (ž)	[sklɛŋka]
stock pot (soup pot)	**hrnec** (m)	[hrnɛʦ]
bottle (~ of wine)	**láhev** (ž)	[la:hɛf]
neck (of the bottle, etc.)	**hrdlo** (s)	[hrdlo]
carafe (decanter)	**karafa** (ž)	[karafa]
pitcher	**džbán** (m)	[ʤba:n]
vessel (container)	**nádoba** (ž)	[na:doba]
pot (crock, stoneware ~)	**hrnec** (m)	[hrnɛʦ]
vase	**váza** (ž)	[va:za]
flacon, bottle (perfume ~)	**flakón** (m)	[flako:n]
vial, small bottle	**lahvička** (ž)	[lahvɪʧka]
tube (of toothpaste)	**tuba** (ž)	[tuba]
sack (bag)	**pytel** (m)	[pɪtɛl]
bag (paper ~, plastic ~)	**sáček** (m)	[sa:ʧɛk]
pack (of cigarettes, etc.)	**balíček** (m)	[bali:ʧɛk]

box (e.g., shoebox)	**krabice** (ž)	[krabɪʦɛ]
crate	**schránka** (ž)	[sxra:ŋka]
basket	**koš** (m)	[koʃ]

27. Materials

material	**materiál** (m)	[matɛrɪa:l]
wood (n)	**dřevo** (s)	[drʒɛvo]
wood-, wooden (adj)	**dřevěný**	[drʒɛveni:]
glass (n)	**sklo** (s)	[sklo]
glass (as adj)	**skleněný**	[sklɛneni:]
stone (n)	**kámen** (m)	[ka:mɛn]
stone (as adj)	**kamenný**	[kamɛnni:]
plastic (n)	**plast** (m)	[plast]
plastic (as adj)	**plastový**	[plastovi:]
rubber (n)	**guma** (ž)	[guma]
rubber (as adj)	**gumový**	[gumovi:]
cloth, fabric (n)	**látka** (ž)	[la:tka]
fabric (as adj)	**z látky**	[z la:tkɪ]
paper (n)	**papír** (m)	[papi:r]
paper (as adj)	**papírový**	[papi:rovi:]
cardboard (n)	**kartón** (m)	[karto:n]
cardboard (as adj)	**kartónový**	[karto:novi:]
polyethylene	**polyetylén** (m)	[poliɛtɪlɛ:n]
cellophane	**celofán** (m)	[ʦɛlofa:n]
linoleum	**linoleum** (s)	[lɪnolɛum]
plywood	**dýha** (ž)	[di:ha]
porcelain (n)	**porcelán** (m)	[porʦɛla:n]
porcelain (as adj)	**porcelánový**	[porʦɛla:novi:]
clay (n)	**hlína** (ž)	[hli:na]
clay (as adj)	**hliněný**	[hlɪneni:]
ceramic (n)	**keramika** (ž)	[kɛramɪka]
ceramic (as adj)	**keramický**	[kɛramɪʦki:]

28. Metals

metal (n)	**kov** (m)	[kof]
metal (as adj)	**kovový**	[kovovi:]
alloy (n)	**slitina** (ž)	[slɪtɪna]

gold (n)	**zlato** (s)	[zlato]
gold, golden (adj)	**zlatý**	[zlati:]
silver (n)	**stříbro** (s)	[strʃi:bro]
silver (as adj)	**stříbrný**	[strʃi:brni:]
iron (n)	**železo** (s)	[ʒelɛzo]
iron-, made of iron (adj)	**železný**	[ʒelɛzni:]
steel (n)	**ocel** (ž)	[ot͡sɛl]
steel (as adj)	**ocelový**	[ot͡sɛlovi:]
copper (n)	**měď** (ž)	[mnetʲ]
copper (as adj)	**měděný**	[mnedeni:]
aluminum (n)	**hliník** (m)	[hlɪni:k]
aluminum (as adj)	**hliníkový**	[hlɪni:kovi:]
bronze (n)	**bronz** (m)	[bronz]
bronze (as adj)	**bronzový**	[bronzovi:]
brass	**mosaz** (ž)	[mosaz]
nickel	**nikl** (m)	[nɪkl]
platinum	**platina** (ž)	[platɪna]
mercury	**rtuť** (ž)	[rtutʲ]
tin	**cín** (m)	[t͡si:n]
lead	**olovo** (s)	[olovo]
zinc	**zinek** (m)	[zɪnɛk]

HUMAN BEING

Human being. The body

29. Humans. Basic concepts

human being	**člověk** (m)	[ʧlovek]
man (adult male)	**muž** (m)	[muʃ]
woman	**žena** (ž)	[ʒena]
child	**dítě** (s)	[di:te]
girl	**děvče** (s)	[devʧɛ]
boy	**chlapec** (m)	[xlapɛʦ]
teenager	**výrostek** (m)	[vi:rostɛk]
old man	**stařec** (m)	[starʒɛʦ]
old woman	**stařena** (ž)	[starʒɛna]

30. Human anatomy

organism (body)	**organismus** (m)	[organɪzmus]
heart	**srdce** (s)	[srdʦɛ]
blood	**krev** (ž)	[krɛf]
artery	**tepna** (ž)	[tɛpna]
vein	**žíla** (ž)	[ʒi:la]
brain	**mozek** (m)	[mozɛk]
nerve	**nerv** (m)	[nɛrf]
nerves	**nervy** (m mn)	[nɛrvɪ]
vertebra	**obratel** (m)	[obratɛl]
spine (backbone)	**páteř** (ž)	[pa:tɛrʃ]
stomach (organ)	**žaludek** (m)	[ʒaludɛk]
intestines, bowels	**střeva** (s mn)	[strʃɛva]
intestine (e.g., large ~)	**střevo** (s)	[strʃɛvo]
liver	**játra** (s mn)	[ja:tra]
kidney	**ledvina** (ž)	[lɛdvɪna]
bone	**kost** (ž)	[kost]
skeleton	**kostra** (ž)	[kostra]
rib	**žebro** (s)	[ʒebro]
skull	**lebka** (ž)	[lɛpka]
muscle	**sval** (m)	[sval]
biceps	**biceps** (m)	[bɪʦɛps]

triceps	**triceps** (m)	[trɪtsɛps]
tendon	**šlacha** (ž)	[ʃlaxa]
joint	**kloub** (m)	[kloup]
lungs	**plíce** (ž mn)	[pli:tsɛ]
genitals	**pohlavní orgány** (m mn)	[pohlavni: orga:nɪ]
skin	**pleť** (ž)	[plɛtʲ]

31. Head

head	**hlava** (ž)	[hlava]
face	**obličej** (ž)	[oblɪtʃɛj]
nose	**nos** (m)	[nos]
mouth	**ústa** (s mn)	[u:sta]
eye	**oko** (s)	[oko]
eyes	**oči** (s mn)	[otʃɪ]
pupil	**zornice** (ž)	[zornɪtsɛ]
eyebrow	**obočí** (s)	[obotʃi:]
eyelash	**řasa** (ž)	[rʒasa]
eyelid	**víčko** (s)	[vi:tʃko]
tongue	**jazyk** (m)	[jazɪk]
tooth	**zub** (m)	[zup]
lips	**rty** (m mn)	[rtɪ]
cheekbones	**lícní kosti** (ž mn)	[li:tsni: kostɪ]
gum	**dáseň** (ž)	[da:sɛnʲ]
palate	**patro** (s)	[patro]
nostrils	**chřípí** (s)	[xrʃi:pi:]
chin	**brada** (ž)	[brada]
jaw	**čelist** (ž)	[tʃɛlɪst]
cheek	**tvář** (ž)	[tva:rʃ]
forehead	**čelo** (s)	[tʃɛlo]
temple	**spánek** (s)	[spa:nɛk]
ear	**ucho** (s)	[uxo]
back of the head	**týl** (m)	[ti:l]
neck	**krk** (m)	[krk]
throat	**hrdlo** (s)	[hrdlo]
hair	**vlasy** (m mn)	[vlasɪ]
hairstyle	**účes** (m)	[u:tʃɛs]
haircut	**střih** (m)	[strʃɪx]
wig	**paruka** (ž)	[paruka]
mustache	**vousy** (m mn)	[vousɪ]
beard	**plnovous** (m)	[plnovous]
to have (a beard, etc.)	**nosit**	[nosɪt]
braid	**cop** (m)	[tsop]
sideburns	**licousy** (m mn)	[lɪtsousɪ]

red-haired (adj)	**zrzavý**	[zrzavi:]
gray (hair)	**šedivý**	[ʃɛdɪvi:]
bald (adj)	**lysý**	[lɪsi:]
bald patch	**lysina** (ž)	[lɪsɪna]
ponytail	**ocas** (m)	[otsas]
bangs	**ofina** (ž)	[ofɪna]

32. Human body

hand	**ruka** (ž)	[ruka]
arm	**ruka** (ž)	[ruka]
finger	**prst** (m)	[prst]
toe	**prst** (m) **na noze**	[prst na nozɛ]
thumb	**palec** (m)	[palɛts]
little finger	**malíček** (m)	[mali:tʃɛk]
nail	**nehet** (m)	[nɛhɛt]
fist	**pěst** (ž)	[pest]
palm	**dlaň** (ž)	[dlanʲ]
wrist	**zápěstí** (s)	[za:pɛsti:]
forearm	**předloktí** (s)	[prʃɛdlokti:]
elbow	**loket** (m)	[lokɛt]
shoulder	**rameno** (s)	[ramɛno]
leg	**noha** (ž)	[noha]
foot	**chodidlo** (s)	[xodɪdlo]
knee	**koleno** (s)	[kolɛno]
calf (part of leg)	**lýtko** (s)	[li:tko]
hip	**stehno** (s)	[stɛhno]
heel	**pata** (ž)	[pata]
body	**tělo** (s)	[telo]
stomach	**břicho** (s)	[brʒɪxo]
chest	**prsa** (s mn)	[prsa]
breast	**prs** (m)	[prs]
flank	**bok** (m)	[bok]
back	**záda** (s mn)	[za:da]
lower back	**kříž** (m)	[krʃi:ʃ]
waist	**pás** (m)	[pa:s]
navel (belly button)	**pupek** (m)	[pupɛk]
buttocks	**hýždě** (ž mn)	[hi:ʒde]
bottom	**zadek** (m)	[zadɛk]
beauty mark	**mateřské znaménko** (s)	[matɛrʃskɛ: znamɛ:ŋko]
tattoo	**tetování** (s)	[tɛtova:ni:]
scar	**jizva** (ž)	[jɪzva]

Clothing & Accessories

33. Outerwear. Coats

clothes	**oblečení** (s)	[oblɛʧɛni:]
outerwear	**svrchní oděv** (m)	[svrxni: odeʃ]
winter clothing	**zimní oděv** (m)	[zɪmni: odeʃ]
coat (overcoat)	**kabát** (m)	[kaba:t]
fur coat	**kožich** (m)	[koʒɪx]
fur jacket	**krátký kožich** (m)	[kra:tki: koʒɪx]
down coat	**peřová bunda** (ž)	[pɛrʒova: bunda]
jacket (e.g., leather ~)	**bunda** (ž)	[bunda]
raincoat (trenchcoat, etc.)	**plášť** (m)	[pla:ʃtʲ]
waterproof (adj)	**nepromokavý**	[nɛpromokavi:]

34. Men's & women's clothing

shirt (button shirt)	**košile** (ž)	[koʃɪlɛ]
pants	**kalhoty** (ž mn)	[kalhotɪ]
jeans	**džínsy** (m mn)	[ʤi:nsɪ]
suit jacket	**sako** (s)	[sako]
suit	**pánský oblek** (m)	[pa:nski: oblɛk]
dress (frock)	**šaty** (m mn)	[ʃatɪ]
skirt	**sukně** (ž)	[sukne]
blouse	**blůzka** (ž)	[blu:ska]
knitted jacket (cardigan, etc.)	**svetr** (m)	[svɛtr]
jacket (of woman's suit)	**žaket** (m)	[ʒakɛt]
T-shirt	**tričko** (s)	[trɪʧko]
shorts (short trousers)	**šortky** (ž mn)	[ʃortkɪ]
tracksuit	**tepláková souprava** (ž)	[tɛpla:kova: souprava]
bathrobe	**župan** (m)	[ʒupan]
pajamas	**pyžamo** (s)	[piʒamo]
sweater	**svetr** (m)	[svɛtr]
pullover	**pulovr** (m)	[pulovr]
vest	**vesta** (ž)	[vɛsta]
tailcoat	**frak** (m)	[frak]
tuxedo	**smoking** (m)	[smokɪŋk]

uniform	**uniforma** (ž)	[unɪforma]
workwear	**pracovní oděv** (m)	[praʦovni: odef]
overalls	**kombinéza** (ž)	[kombɪnɛ:za]
coat (e.g., doctor's smock)	**plášť** (m)	[illegible]

35. Clothing. Underwear

underwear	**spodní prádlo** (s)	[spodni: pra:dlo]
boxers, briefs	**boxerky** (mn)	[boksɛrkɪ]
panties	**kalhotky** (mn)	[kalhotkɪ]
undershirt (A-shirt)	**tílko** (s)	[tilko]
socks	**ponožky** (ž mn)	[ponoʃkɪ]
nightdress	**noční košile** (ž)	[noʧni: koʃɪlɛ]
bra	**podprsenka** (ž)	[potprsɛŋka]
knee highs (knee-high socks)	**podkolenky** (ž mn)	[potkolɛŋkɪ]
pantyhose	**punčochové kalhoty** (ž mn)	[punʧoxovɛ: kalgotɪ]
stockings (thigh highs)	**punčochy** (ž mn)	[punʧoxɪ]
bathing suit	**plavky** (ž mn)	[plafkɪ]

36. Headwear

hat	**čepice** (ž)	[ʧɛpɪʦɛ]
fedora	**klobouk** (m)	[klobouk]
baseball cap	**kšiltovka** (ž)	[kʃɪltofka]
flatcap	**čepice** (ž)	[ʧɛpɪʦɛ]
beret	**baret** (m)	[barɛt]
hood	**kapuce** (ž)	[kapuʦɛ]
panama hat	**panamský klobouk** (m)	[panamski: klobouk]
knit cap (knitted hat)	**pletená čepice** (ž)	[plɛtɛna: ʧɛpɪʦɛ]
headscarf	**šátek** (m)	[ʃa:tɛk]
women's hat	**klobouček** (m)	[kloboutʃɛk]
hard hat	**přilba** (ž)	[prʃɪlba]
garrison cap	**lodička** (ž)	[lodɪʧka]
helmet	**helma** (ž)	[hɛlma]
derby	**tvrďák** (m)	[tvrdʲa:k]
top hat	**válec** (m)	[va:lɛʦ]

37. Footwear

footwear	**obuv** (ž)	[obuf]
shoes (men's shoes)	**boty** (ž mn)	[botɪ]

shoes (women's shoes)	**střevíce** (m mn)	[strʃɛvi:ʦɛ]
boots (e.g., cowboy ~)	**holínky** (ž mn)	[holi:ŋkɪ]
slippers	**bačkory** (ž mn)	[batʃkorɪ]
tennis shoes (e.g., Nike ~)	**tenisky** (ž mn)	[tɛnɪskɪ]
sneakers (e.g., Converse ~)	**kecky** (ž mn)	[kɛʦkɪ]
sandals	**sandály** (m mn)	[sanda:lɪ]
cobbler (shoe repairer)	**obuvník** (m)	[obuvni:k]
heel	**podpatek** (m)	[potpatɛk]
pair (of shoes)	**pár** (m)	[pa:r]
shoestring	**tkanička** (ž)	[tkanɪtʃka]
to lace (vt)	**šněrovat**	[ʃnerovat]
shoehorn	**lžíce** (ž) **na boty**	[lʒi:ʦɛ na botɪ]
shoe polish	**krém** (m) **na boty**	[krɛ:m na botɪ]

38. Textile. Fabrics

cotton (n)	**bavlna** (ž)	[bavlna]
cotton (as adj)	**bavlněný**	[bavlneni:]
flax (n)	**len** (m)	[lɛn]
flax (as adj)	**lněný**	[lneni:]
silk (n)	**hedvábí** (s)	[hɛdva:bi:]
silk (as adj)	**hedvábný**	[hɛdva:bni:]
wool (n)	**vlna** (ž)	[vlna]
wool (as adj)	**vlněný**	[vlneni:]
velvet	**samet** (m)	[samɛt]
suede	**semiš** (m)	[sɛmɪʃ]
corduroy	**manšestr** (m)	[manʃɛstr]
nylon (n)	**nylon** (m)	[nɪlon]
nylon (as adj)	**nylonový**	[nɪlonovi:]
polyester (n)	**polyester** (m)	[poliɛstɛr]
polyester (as adj)	**polyesterový**	[poliɛstɛrovi:]
leather (n)	**kůže** (ž)	[ku:ʒe]
leather (as adj)	**z kůže, kožený**	[z ku:ʒe], [koʒeni:]
fur (n)	**kožešina** (ž)	[koʒeʃɪna]
fur (e.g., ~ coat)	**kožešinový**	[koʒeʃɪnovi:]

39. Personal accessories

gloves	**rukavice** (ž mn)	[rukavɪʦɛ]
mittens	**palčáky** (m mn)	[paltʃa:kɪ]

scarf (muffler)	**šála** (ž)	[ʃa:la]
glasses (eyeglasses)	**brýle** (ž mn)	[bri:lɛ]
frame (eyeglass ~)	**obroučky** (m mn)	[obroutʃkɪ]
umbrella	**deštník** (m)	[dɛʃtni:k]
walking stick	**hůl** (ž)	[hu:l]
hairbrush	**kartáč** (m) **na vlasy**	[karta:tʃ na vlasɪ]
fan	**vějíř** (m)	[veji:rʃ]
tie (necktie)	**kravata** (ž)	[kravata]
bow tie	**motýlek** (m)	[moti:lɛk]
suspenders	**šle** (ž mn)	[ʃlɛ]
handkerchief	**kapesník** (m)	[kapesni:k]
comb	**hřeben** (m)	[hrʒɛbɛn]
barrette	**sponka** (ž)	[spoŋka]
hairpin	**vlásnička** (ž)	[vla:snɪtʃka]
buckle	**spona** (ž)	[spona]
belt	**pás** (m)	[pa:s]
shoulder strap	**řemen** (m)	[rʒɛmɛn]
bag (handbag)	**taška** (ž)	[taʃka]
purse	**kabelka** (ž)	[kabɛlka]
backpack	**batoh** (m)	[batox]

40. Clothing. Miscellaneous

fashion	**móda** (ž)	[mo:da]
in vogue (adj)	**módní**	[mo:dni:]
fashion designer	**modelář** (m)	[modɛla:rʃ]
collar	**límec** (m)	[li:mɛʦ]
pocket	**kapsa** (ž)	[kapsa]
pocket (as adj)	**kapesní**	[kapɛsni:]
sleeve	**rukáv** (m)	[ruka:f]
hanging loop	**poutko** (s)	[poutko]
fly (on trousers)	**poklopec** (m)	[poklopɛʦ]
zipper (fastener)	**zip** (m)	[zɪp]
fastener	**spona** (ž)	[spona]
button	**knoflík** (m)	[knofli:k]
buttonhole	**knoflíková dírka** (ž)	[knofli:kova: di:rka]
to come off (ab. button)	**utrhnout se**	[utrhnout sɛ]
to sew (vi, vt)	**šít**	[ʃi:t]
to embroider (vi, vt)	**vyšívat**	[vɪʃi:vat]
embroidery	**výšivka** (ž)	[vi:ʃɪfka]
sewing needle	**jehla** (ž)	[jɛhla]
thread	**nit** (ž)	[nɪt]
seam	**šev** (m)	[ʃɛf]

to get dirty (vi)	**ušpinit se**	[uʃpɪnɪt sɛ]
stain (mark, spot)	**skvrna** (ž)	[skvrna]
to crease, crumple (vi)	**pomačkat se**	[pomatʃkat sɛ]
to tear, to rip (vt)	**roztrhat**	[roztrhat]
clothes moth	**mol** (m)	[mol]

41. Personal care. Cosmetics

toothpaste	**zubní pasta** (ž)	[zubni: pasta]
toothbrush	**kartáček** (m) **na zuby**	[karta:tʃɛk na zubɪ]
to brush one's teeth	**čistit si zuby**	[tʃɪstɪt sɪ zubɪ]
razor	**holicí strojek** (m)	[holɪtsi: strojɛk]
shaving cream	**krém** (m) **na holení**	[krɛ:m na holɛni:]
to shave (vi)	**holit se**	[holɪt sɛ]
soap	**mýdlo** (s)	[mi:dlo]
shampoo	**šampon** (m)	[ʃampon]
scissors	**nůžky** (ž mn)	[nu:ʃkɪ]
nail file	**pilník** (m) **na nehty**	[pɪlni:k na nɛxtɪ]
nail clippers	**kleštičky** (ž mn) **na nehty**	[klɛʃtɪtʃkɪ na nɛxtɪ]
tweezers	**pinzeta** (ž)	[pɪnzeta]
cosmetics	**kosmetika** (ž)	[kosmɛtɪka]
face mask	**kosmetická maska** (ž)	[kosmɛtɪtska: maska]
manicure	**manikúra** (ž)	[manɪku:ra]
to have a manicure	**dělat manikúru**	[delat manɪku:ru]
pedicure	**pedikúra** (ž)	[pɛdɪku:ra]
make-up bag	**kosmetická kabelka** (ž)	[kosmɛtɪtska: kabɛlka]
face powder	**pudr** (m)	[pudr]
powder compact	**pudřenka** (ž)	[pudrʒɛŋka]
blusher	**červené líčidlo** (s)	[tʃɛrvɛnɛ: li:tʃɪdlo]
perfume (bottled)	**voňavka** (ž)	[vonʲafka]
toilet water (lotion)	**toaletní voda** (ž)	[toalɛtni: voda]
lotion	**pleťová voda** (ž)	[plɛtʲova: voda]
cologne	**kolínská voda** (ž)	[koli:nska: voda]
eyeshadow	**oční stíny** (m mn)	[otʃni: sti:nɪ]
eyeliner	**tužka** (ž) **na oči**	[tuʃka na otʃɪ]
mascara	**řasenka** (ž)	[rʒasɛŋka]
lipstick	**rtěnka** (ž)	[rteŋka]
nail polish, enamel	**lak** (m) **na nehty**	[lak na nɛxtɪ]
hair spray	**lak** (m) **na vlasy**	[lak na vlasɪ]
deodorant	**deodorant** (m)	[dɛodorant]
cream	**krém** (m)	[krɛ:m]
face cream	**pleťový krém** (m)	[plɛtʲovi: krɛ:m]

hand cream	**krém** (m) **na ruce**	[krɛ:m na rutsɛ]
anti-wrinkle cream	**krém** (m) **proti vráskám**	[krɛ:m protɪ vra:ska:m]
day cream	**denní krém** (m)	[dɛnni:]krɛ:m]
night cream	**noční krém** (m)	[notʃni: krɛ:m]
day (as adj)	**denní**	[dɛnni:]
night (as adj)	**noční**	[notʃni:]
tampon	**tampón** (m)	[tampo:n]
toilet paper (toilet roll)	**toaletní papír** (m)	[toalɛtni: papi:r]
hair dryer	**fén** (m)	[fɛ:n]

42. Jewelry

jewelry, jewels	**šperk** (m)	[ʃpɛrk]
precious (e.g., ~ stone)	**drahý**	[drahi:]
hallmark stamp	**punc** (m)	[punts]
ring	**prsten** (m)	[prstɛn]
wedding ring	**snubní prsten** (m)	[snubni: prstɛn]
bracelet	**náramek** (m)	[na:ramɛk]
earrings	**náušnice** (ž mn)	[na:uʃnɪtsɛ]
necklace (~ of pearls)	**náhrdelník** (m)	[na:hrdɛlni:k]
crown	**koruna** (ž)	[koruna]
bead necklace	**korály** (m mn)	[kora:lɪ]
diamond	**diamant** (m)	[dɪamant]
emerald	**smaragd** (m)	[smarakt]
ruby	**rubín** (m)	[rubi:n]
sapphire	**safír** (m)	[safi:r]
pearl	**perly** (ž mn)	[pɛrlɪ]
amber	**jantar** (m)	[jantar]

43. Watches. Clocks

watch (wristwatch)	**hodinky** (ž mn)	[hodɪŋkɪ]
dial	**ciferník** (m)	[tsɪfɛrni:k]
hand (of clock, watch)	**ručička** (ž)	[rutʃɪtʃka]
metal watch band	**náramek** (m)	[na:ramɛk]
watch strap	**pásek** (m)	[pa:sɛk]
battery	**baterka** (ž)	[batɛrka]
to be dead (battery)	**vybít se**	[vɪbi:t sɛ]
to change a battery	**vyměnit baterku**	[vɪmnenɪt batɛrku]
to run fast	**jít napřed**	[ji:t naprʃɛt]
to run slow	**opožďovat se**	[opoʒdʲovat sɛ]
wall clock	**nástěnné hodiny** (ž mn)	[na:stennɛ: hodɪnɪ]
hourglass	**přesýpací hodiny** (ž mn)	[prʃɛsi:patsi: hodɪnɪ]

sundial	**sluneční hodiny** (ž mn)	[slunɛʧni: hodɪnɪ]
alarm clock	**budík** (m)	[budi:k]
watchmaker	**hodinář** (m)	[hodɪna:rʃ]
to repair (vt)	**opravovat**	[opravovat]

Food. Nutricion

44. Food

meat	**maso** (s)	[maso]
chicken	**slepice** (ž)	[slɛpɪʦɛ]
Rock Cornish hen (poussin)	**kuře** (s)	[kurʒɛ]
duck	**kachna** (ž)	[kaxna]
goose	**husa** (ž)	[husa]
game	**zvěřina** (ž)	[zverʒɪna]
turkey	**krůta** (ž)	[kru:ta]
pork	**vepřové** (s)	[vɛprʃovɛ:]
veal	**telecí** (s)	[tɛlɛʦi:]
lamb	**skopové** (s)	[skopovɛ:]
beef	**hovězí** (s)	[hovezi:]
rabbit	**králík** (m)	[kra:li:k]
sausage (bologna, etc.)	**salám** (m)	[sala:m]
vienna sausage (frankfurter)	**párek** (m)	[pa:rɛk]
bacon	**slanina** (ž)	[slanɪna]
ham	**šunka** (ž)	[ʃuŋka]
gammon	**kýta** (ž)	[ki:ta]
pâté	**paštika** (ž)	[paʃtɪka]
liver	**játra** (s mn)	[ja:tra]
hamburger (ground beef)	**mleté maso** (s)	[mlɛtɛ: maso]
tongue	**jazyk** (m)	[jazɪk]
egg	**vejce** (s)	[vɛjʦɛ]
eggs	**vejce** (s mn)	[vɛjʦɛ]
egg white	**bílek** (m)	[bi:lɛk]
egg yolk	**žloutek** (m)	[ʒloutɛk]
fish	**ryby** (ž mn)	[rɪbɪ]
seafood	**mořské plody** (m mn)	[morʃskɛ: plodɪ]
crustaceans	**korýši** (m mn)	[kori:ʃɪ]
caviar	**kaviár** (m)	[kavɪa:r]
crab	**krab** (m)	[krap]
shrimp	**kreveta** (ž)	[krɛvɛta]
oyster	**ústřice** (ž)	[u:strʃɪʦɛ]
spiny lobster	**langusta** (ž)	[langusta]
octopus	**chobotnice** (ž)	[xobotnɪʦɛ]

squid	**sépie** (ž)	[sɛ:pɪe]
sturgeon	**jeseter** (m)	[jɛsɛtɛr]
salmon	**losos** (m)	[losos]
halibut	**platýs** (m)	[plati:s]
cod	**treska** (ž)	[trɛska]
mackerel	**makrela** (ž)	[makrɛla]
tuna	**tuňák** (m)	[tunʲa:k]
eel	**úhoř** (m)	[u:horʃ]
trout	**pstruh** (m)	[pstrux]
sardine	**sardinka** (ž)	[sardɪŋka]
pike	**štika** (ž)	[ʃtɪka]
herring	**sleď** (ž)	[slɛtʲ]
bread	**chléb** (m)	[xlɛ:p]
cheese	**sýr** (m)	[si:r]
sugar	**cukr** (m)	[ʦukr]
salt	**sůl** (ž)	[su:l]
rice	**rýže** (ž)	[ri:ʒe]
pasta (macaroni)	**makaróny** (m mn)	[makaro:nɪ]
noodles	**nudle** (ž mn)	[nudlɛ]
butter	**máslo** (s)	[ma:slo]
vegetable oil	**olej** (m)	[olɛj]
sunflower oil	**slunečnicový olej** (m)	[slunɛʧnɪʦovi: olɛj]
margarine	**margarín** (m)	[margari:n]
olives	**olivy** (ž)	[olɪvɪ]
olive oil	**olivový olej** (m)	[olɪvovi: olɛj]
milk	**mléko** (s)	[mlɛ:ko]
condensed milk	**kondenzované mléko** (s)	[kondɛnzovanɛ: mlɛ:ko]
yogurt	**jogurt** (m)	[jogurt]
sour cream	**kyselá smetana** (ž)	[kɪsɛla: smɛtana]
cream (of milk)	**sladká smetana** (ž)	[slatka: smɛtana]
mayonnaise	**majonéza** (ž)	[majonɛ:za]
buttercream	**krém** (m)	[krɛ:m]
groats (barley ~, etc.)	**kroupy** (ž mn)	[kroupɪ]
flour	**mouka** (ž)	[mouka]
canned food	**konzerva** (ž)	[konzɛrva]
cornflakes	**kukuřičné vločky** (ž mn)	[kukurʒɪʧnɛ: vloʧkɪ]
honey	**med** (m)	[mɛt]
jam	**džem** (m)	[ʤem]
chewing gum	**žvýkačka** (ž)	[ʒvi:kaʧka]

45. Drinks

water	**voda** (ž)	[voda]
drinking water	**pitná voda** (ž)	[pɪtna: voda]
mineral water	**minerální voda** (ž)	[mɪnɛra:lni: voda]
still (adj)	**neperlivý**	[nɛpɛrlɪvi:]
carbonated (adj)	**perlivý**	[pɛrlɪvi:]
sparkling (adj)	**perlivý**	[pɛrlɪvi:]
ice	**led** (m)	[lɛt]
with ice	**s ledem**	[s lɛdɛm]
non-alcoholic (adj)	**nealkoholický**	[nɛalkoholɪʦki:]
soft drink	**nealkoholický nápoj** (m)	[nɛalkoholɪʦki: na:poj]
refreshing drink	**osvěžující nápoj** (m)	[osveʒuji:ʦi: na:poj]
lemonade	**limonáda** (ž)	[lɪmona:da]
liquors	**alkoholické nápoje** (m mn)	[alkoholɪʦkɛ: na:pojɛ]
wine	**víno** (s)	[vi:no]
white wine	**bílé víno** (s)	[bi:lɛ: vi:no]
red wine	**červené víno** (s)	[ʧɛrvɛnɛ: vi:no]
liqueur	**likér** (m)	[lɪkɛ:r]
champagne	**šampaňské** (s)	[ʃampanʲskɛ:]
vermouth	**vermut** (m)	[vɛrmut]
whiskey	**whisky** (ž)	[vɪskɪ]
vodka	**vodka** (ž)	[votka]
gin	**džin** (m)	[ʤɪn]
cognac	**koňak** (m)	[konʲak]
rum	**rum** (m)	[rum]
coffee	**káva** (ž)	[ka:va]
black coffee	**černá káva** (ž)	[ʧɛrna: ka:va]
coffee with milk	**bílá káva** (ž)	[bi:la: ka:va]
cappuccino	**kapučíno** (s)	[kapuʧi:no]
instant coffee	**rozpustná káva** (ž)	[rozpustna: ka:va]
milk	**mléko** (s)	[mlɛ:ko]
cocktail	**koktail** (m)	[koktajl]
milkshake	**mléčný koktail** (m)	[mlɛʧni: koktajl]
juice	**šťáva** (ž), **džus** (m)	[ʃtʲa:va], [ʤus]
tomato juice	**rajčatová šťáva** (ž)	[rajʧatova: ʃtʲa:va]
orange juice	**pomerančový džus** (m)	[pomɛranʧovi: ʤus]
freshly squeezed juice	**vymačkaná šťáva** (ž)	[vɪmaʧkana: ʃtʲa:va]
beer	**pivo** (s)	[pɪvo]
light beer	**světlé pivo** (s)	[svetlɛ: pɪvo]
dark beer	**tmavé pivo** (s)	[tmavɛ: pɪvo]
tea	**čaj** (m)	[ʧaj]

black tea	**černý čaj** (m)	[ʧɛrni: ʧaj]
green tea	**zelený čaj** (m)	[zɛlɛni: ʧaj]

46. Vegetables

vegetables	**zelenina** (ž)	[zɛlɛnɪna]
greens	**zelenina** (ž)	[zɛlɛnɪna]
tomato	**rajské jablíčko** (s)	[rajskɛ: jabli:ʧko]
cucumber	**okurka** (ž)	[okurka]
carrot	**mrkev** (ž)	[mrkɛf]
potato	**brambory** (ž mn)	[bramborɪ]
onion	**cibule** (ž)	[ʦɪbulɛ]
garlic	**česnek** (m)	[ʧɛsnɛk]
cabbage	**zelí** (s)	[zɛli:]
cauliflower	**květák** (m)	[kvɛta:k]
Brussels sprouts	**růžičková kapusta** (ž)	[ru:ʒɪʧkova: kapusta]
broccoli	**brokolice** (ž)	[brokolɪʦɛ]
beet	**červená řepa** (ž)	[ʧɛrvena: rʒɛpa]
eggplant	**lilek** (m)	[lɪlɛk]
zucchini	**cukina, cuketa** (ž)	[ʦukɪna], [ʦuketa]
pumpkin	**tykev** (ž)	[tɪkɛf]
turnip	**vodní řepa** (ž)	[vodni: rʒɛpa]
parsley	**petržel** (ž)	[pɛtrʒel]
dill	**kopr** (m)	[kopr]
lettuce	**salát** (m)	[sala:t]
celery	**celer** (m)	[ʦɛlɛr]
asparagus	**chřest** (m)	[xrʃɛst]
spinach	**špenát** (m)	[ʃpɛna:t]
pea	**hrách** (m)	[hra:x]
beans	**boby** (m mn)	[bobɪ]
corn (maize)	**kukuřice** (ž)	[kukurʒɪʦɛ]
kidney bean	**fazole** (ž)	[fazolɛ]
bell pepper	**pepř** (m)	[pɛprʃ]
radish	**ředkvička** (ž)	[rʒɛtkvɪʧka]
artichoke	**artyčok** (m)	[artɪʧok]

47. Fruits. Nuts

fruit	**ovoce** (s)	[ovoʦɛ]
apple	**jablko** (s)	[jablko]
pear	**hruška** (ž)	[hruʃka]
lemon	**citrón** (m)	[ʦɪtro:n]

orange	**pomeranč** (m)	[pomɛrantʃ]
strawberry (garden ~)	**zahradní jahody** (ž mn)	[zahradni: jahodɪ]
mandarin	**mandarinka** (ž)	[mandarɪŋka]
plum	**švestka** (ž)	[ʃvɛstka]
peach	**broskev** (ž)	[broskɛf]
apricot	**meruňka** (ž)	[mɛrunʲka]
raspberry	**maliny** (ž mn)	[malɪnɪ]
pineapple	**ananas** (m)	[ananas]
banana	**banán** (m)	[bana:n]
watermelon	**vodní meloun** (m)	[vodni: mɛloun]
grape	**hroznové víno** (s)	[hroznovɛ: vi:no]
sour cherry	**višně** (ž)	[vɪʃne]
sweet cherry	**třešně** (ž)	[trʃɛʃne]
melon	**cukrový meloun** (m)	[tsukrovi: mɛloun]
grapefruit	**grapefruit** (m)	[grɛjpfru:t]
avocado	**avokádo** (s)	[avoka:do]
papaya	**papája** (ž)	[papa:ja]
mango	**mango** (s)	[mango]
pomegranate	**granátové jablko** (s)	[grana:tovɛ: jablko]
redcurrant	**červený rybíz** (m)	[tʃɛrvɛni: rɪbi:z]
blackcurrant	**černý rybíz** (m)	[tʃɛrni: rɪbi:z]
gooseberry	**angrešt** (m)	[angrɛʃt]
bilberry	**borůvky** (ž mn)	[boru:fkɪ]
blackberry	**ostružiny** (ž mn)	[ostruʒɪnɪ]
raisin	**hrozinky** (ž mn)	[hrozɪŋkɪ]
fig	**fík** (m)	[fi:k]
date	**datle** (ž)	[datlɛ]
peanut	**burský oříšek** (m)	[burski: orʒi:ʃɛk]
almond	**mandle** (ž)	[mandlɛ]
walnut	**vlašský ořech** (m)	[vlaʃski: orʒɛx]
hazelnut	**lískový ořech** (m)	[li:skovi: orʒɛx]
coconut	**kokos** (m)	[kokos]
pistachios	**pistácie** (ž)	[pɪsta:tsɪe]

48. Bread. Candy

bakers' confectionery (pastry)	**cukroví** (s)	[tsukrovi:]
bread	**chléb** (m)	[xlɛ:p]
cookies	**sušenky** (ž mn)	[suʃɛŋkɪ]
chocolate (n)	**čokoláda** (ž)	[tʃokola:da]
chocolate (as adj)	**čokoládový**	[tʃokola:dovi:]
candy (wrapped)	**bonbón** (m)	[bonbo:n]

cake (e.g., cupcake)	**zákusek** (m)	[za:kusɛk]
cake (e.g., birthday ~)	**dort** (m)	[dort]
pie (e.g., apple ~)	**koláč** (m)	[kola:ʧ]
filling (for cake, pie)	**nádivka** (ž)	[na:dɪfka]
jam (whole fruit jam)	**zavařenina** (ž)	[zavarʒɛnɪna]
marmalade	**marmeláda** (ž)	[marmɛla:da]
wafers	**oplatky** (mn)	[oplatkɪ]
ice-cream	**zmrzlina** (ž)	[zmrzlɪna]
pudding	**pudink** (m)	[pudɪŋk]

49. Cooked dishes

course, dish	**jídlo** (s)	[ji:dlo]
cuisine	**kuchyně** (ž)	[kuxɪne]
recipe	**recept** (m)	[rɛʦɛpt]
portion	**porce** (ž)	[porʦɛ]
salad	**salát** (m)	[sala:t]
soup	**polévka** (ž)	[polɛ:fka]
clear soup (broth)	**vývar** (m)	[vi:var]
sandwich (bread)	**obložený chlebíček** (m)	[oblozeni: xlɛbi:ʧɛk]
fried eggs	**míchaná vejce** (s mn)	[mi:xana: vɛjʦɛ]
hamburger (beefburger)	**hamburger** (m)	[hamburgɛr]
beefsteak	**biftek** (m)	[bɪftɛk]
side dish	**příloha** (ž)	[prʃi:loha]
spaghetti	**spagety** (m mn)	[spagɛtɪ]
mashed potatoes	**bramborová kaše** (ž)	[bramborova: kaʃɛ]
pizza	**pizza** (ž)	[pɪʦa]
porridge (oatmeal, etc.)	**kaše** (ž)	[kaʃɛ]
omelet	**omeleta** (ž)	[omɛlɛta]
boiled (e.g., ~ beef)	**vařený**	[varʒɛni:]
smoked (adj)	**uzený**	[uzɛni:]
fried (adj)	**smažený**	[smaʒeni:]
dried (adj)	**sušený**	[suʃɛni:]
frozen (adj)	**zmražený**	[zmraʒeni:]
pickled (adj)	**marinovaný**	[marɪnovani:]
sweet (sugary)	**sladký**	[slatki:]
salty (adj)	**slaný**	[slani:]
cold (adj)	**studený**	[studɛni:]
hot (adj)	**teplý**	[tɛpli:]
bitter (adj)	**hořký**	[horʃki:]
tasty (adj)	**chutný**	[xutni:]
to cook in boiling water	**vařit**	[varʒɪt]

to cook (dinner)	**vařit**	[varʒɪt]
to fry (vt)	**smažit**	[smaʒɪt]
to heat up (food)	**ohřívat**	[ohrʒi:vat]
to salt (vt)	**solit**	[solɪt]
to pepper (vt)	**pepřit**	[pɛprʃɪt]
to grate (vt)	**strouhat**	[strouhat]
peel (n)	**slupka** (ž)	[slupka]
to peel (vt)	**loupat**	[loupat]

50. Spices

salt	**sůl** (ž)	[su:l]
salty (adj)	**slaný**	[slani:]
to salt (vt)	**solit**	[solɪt]
black pepper	**černý pepř** (m)	[ʧɛrni: pɛprʃ]
red pepper (milled ~)	**červená paprika** (ž)	[ʧɛrvɛna: paprɪka]
mustard	**hořčice** (ž)	[horʃʧɪʦɛ]
horseradish	**křen** (m)	[krʃɛn]
condiment	**ochucovadlo** (s)	[oxutsovadlo]
spice	**koření** (s)	[korʒɛni:]
sauce	**omáčka** (ž)	[oma:ʧka]
vinegar	**ocet** (m)	[oʦɛt]
anise	**anýz** (m)	[ani:z]
basil	**bazalka** (ž)	[bazalka]
cloves	**hřebíček** (m)	[hrʒɛbi:ʧɛk]
ginger	**zázvor** (m)	[za:zvor]
coriander	**koriandr** (m)	[korɪandr]
cinnamon	**skořice** (ž)	[skorʒɪʦɛ]
sesame	**sezam** (m)	[sɛzam]
bay leaf	**bobkový list** (m)	[bopkovi: lɪst]
paprika	**paprika** (ž)	[paprɪka]
caraway	**kmín** (m)	[kmi:n]
saffron	**šafrán** (m)	[ʃafra:n]

51. Meals

food	**jídlo** (s)	[ji:dlo]
to eat (vi, vt)	**jíst**	[ji:st]
breakfast	**snídaně** (ž)	[sni:dane]
to have breakfast	**snídat**	[sni:dat]
lunch	**oběd** (m)	[obet]
to have lunch	**obědvat**	[obedvat]

dinner	**večeře** (ž)	[vɛʧɛrʒɛ]
to have dinner	**večeřet**	[vɛʧɛrʒɛt]
appetite	**chuť** (ž) **k jídlu**	[xutʲ k ji:dlu]
Enjoy your meal!	**Dobrou chuť!**	[dobrou xutʲ]
to open (~ a bottle)	**otvírat**	[otvi:rat]
to spill (liquid)	**rozlít**	[rozli:t]
to spill out (vi)	**rozlít se**	[rozli:t sɛ]
to boil (vi)	**vřít**	[vrʒi:t]
to boil (vt)	**vařit**	[varʒɪt]
boiled (~ water)	**svařený**	[svarʒɛni:]
to chill, cool down (vt)	**ochladit**	[oxladɪt]
to chill (vi)	**ochlazovat se**	[oxlazovat sɛ]
taste, flavor	**chuť** (ž)	[xutʲ]
aftertaste	**příchuť** (ž)	[prʃi:xutʲ]
to slim down (lose weight)	**držet dietu**	[drʒet dɪetu]
diet	**dieta** (ž)	[dɪeta]
vitamin	**vitamín** (m)	[vɪtami:n]
calorie	**kalorie** (ž)	[kalorɪe]
vegetarian (n)	**vegetarián** (m)	[vɛgɛtarɪa:n]
vegetarian (adj)	**vegetariánský**	[vɛgɛtarɪa:nski:]
fats (nutrient)	**tuky** (m)	[tukɪ]
proteins	**bílkoviny** (ž)	[bi:lkovɪnɪ]
carbohydrates	**karbohydráty** (mn)	[karbohɪdrati:]
slice (of lemon, ham)	**plátek** (m)	[pla:tɛk]
piece (of cake, pie)	**kousek** (m)	[kousɛk]
crumb (of bread, cake, etc.)	**drobek** (m)	[drobɛk]

52. Table setting

spoon	**lžíce** (ž)	[lʒi:ʦɛ]
knife	**nůž** (m)	[nu:ʃ]
fork	**vidlička** (ž)	[vɪdlɪʧka]
cup (e.g., coffee ~)	**šálek** (m)	[ʃa:lɛk]
plate (dinner ~)	**talíř** (m)	[tali:rʃ]
saucer	**talířek** (m)	[tali:rʒɛk]
napkin (on table)	**ubrousek** (m)	[ubrousɛk]
toothpick	**párátko** (s)	[pa:ra:tko]

53. Restaurant

restaurant	**restaurace** (ž)	[rɛstauraʦɛ]
coffee house	**kavárna** (ž)	[kava:rna]

pub, bar	**bar** (m)	[bar]
tearoom	**čajovna** (ž)	[ʧajovna]
waiter	**číšník** (m)	[ʧi:ʃni:k]
waitress	**číšnice** (ž)	[ʧi:ʃnɪʦɛ]
bartender	**barman** (m)	[barman]
menu	**jídelní lístek** (m)	[ji:dɛlni: li:stɛk]
wine list	**nápojový lístek** (m)	[na:pojovi: li:stɛk]
to book a table	**rezervovat stůl**	[rɛzɛrvovat stu:l]
course, dish	**jídlo** (s)	[ji:dlo]
to order (meal)	**objednat si**	[objɛdnat sɪ]
to make an order	**objednat si**	[objɛdnat sɪ]
aperitif	**aperitiv** (m)	[apɛrɪtɪf]
appetizer	**předkrm** (m)	[prʃɛtkrm]
dessert	**desert** (m)	[dɛsɛrt]
check	**účet** (m)	[u:ʧɛt]
to pay the check	**zaplatit účet**	[zaplatɪt u:ʧɛt]
to give change	**dát nazpátek**	[da:t naspa:tɛk]
tip	**spropitné** (s)	[spropɪtnɛ:]

Family, relatives and friends

54. Personal information. Forms

name (first name)	**jméno** (s)	[jmɛ:no]
surname (last name)	**příjmení** (s)	[prʃi:jmɛni:]
date of birth	**datum** (s) **narození**	[datum narozɛni:]
place of birth	**místo** (s) **narození**	[mi:sto narozɛni:]
nationality	**národnost** (ž)	[na:rodnost]
place of residence	**bydliště** (s)	[bɪdlɪʃte]
country	**země** (ž)	[zɛmnɛ]
profession (occupation)	**povolání** (s)	[povola:ni:]
gender, sex	**pohlaví** (s)	[pohlavi:]
height	**postava** (ž)	[postava]
weight	**váha** (ž)	[va:ha]

55. Family members. Relatives

mother	**matka** (ž)	[matka]
father	**otec** (m)	[otɛʦ]
son	**syn** (m)	[sɪn]
daughter	**dcera** (ž)	[dʦɛra]
younger daughter	**nejmladší dcera** (ž)	[nɛjmladʃi: dʦɛra]
younger son	**nejmladší syn** (m)	[nɛjmladʃi: sɪn]
eldest daughter	**nejstarší dcera** (ž)	[nɛjstarʃi: dʦɛra]
eldest son	**nejstarší syn** (m)	[nɛjstarʃi: sɪn]
brother	**bratr** (m)	[bratr]
elder brother	**starší bratr** (m)	[starʃi: bratr]
younger brother	**mladší bratr** (m)	[mladʃi: bratr]
sister	**sestra** (ž)	[sɛstra]
elder sister	**starší sestra** (ž)	[starʃi: sɛstra]
younger sister	**mladší sestra** (ž)	[mladʃi: sɛstra]
cousin (masc.)	**bratranec** (m)	[bratranɛʦ]
cousin (fem.)	**sestřenice** (ž)	[sɛstrʃɛnɪʦɛ]
mom, mommy	**maminka** (ž)	[mamɪŋka]
dad, daddy	**táta** (m)	[ta:ta]
parents	**rodiče** (m mn)	[rodɪʧɛ]
child	**dítě** (s)	[di:te]
children	**děti** (ž mn)	[detɪ]

grandmother	**babička** (ž)	[babɪʧka]
grandfather	**dědeček** (m)	[dedɛʧɛk]
grandson	**vnuk** (m)	[vnuk]
granddaughter	**vnučka** (ž)	[vnuʧka]
grandchildren	**vnuci** (m mn)	[vnuʦɪ]
uncle	**strýc** (m)	[stri:ʦ]
aunt	**teta** (ž)	[tɛta]
nephew	**synovec** (m)	[sɪnovɛʦ]
niece	**neteř** (ž)	[nɛtɛrʃ]
mother-in-law (wife's mother)	**tchyně** (ž)	[txɪne]
father-in-law (husband's father)	**tchán** (m)	[txa:n]
son-in-law (daughter's husband)	**zeť** (m)	[zɛtʲ]
stepmother	**nevlastní matka** (ž)	[nɛvlastni: matka]
stepfather	**nevlastní otec** (m)	[nɛvlastni: otɛʦ]
infant	**kojenec** (m)	[kojɛnɛʦ]
baby (infant)	**nemluvně** (s)	[nɛmluvne]
little boy, kid	**děcko** (s)	[deʦko]
wife	**žena** (ž)	[ʒena]
husband	**muž** (m)	[muʃ]
spouse (husband)	**manžel** (m)	[manʒel]
spouse (wife)	**manželka** (ž)	[manʒelka]
married (masc.)	**ženatý**	[ʒenati:]
married (fem.)	**vdaná**	[vdana:]
single (unmarried)	**svobodný**	[svobodni:]
bachelor	**mládenec** (m)	[mla:dɛnɛʦ]
divorced (masc.)	**rozvedený**	[rozvɛdɛni:]
widow	**vdova** (ž)	[vdova]
widower	**vdovec** (m)	[vdovɛʦ]
relative	**příbuzný** (m)	[prʃi:buzni:]
close relative	**blízký příbuzný** (m)	[bli:skɪ: prʃi:buzni:]
distant relative	**vzdálený příbuzný** (m)	[vzda:lɛni: prʃi:buzni:]
relatives	**příbuzenstvo** (s)	[prʃi:buzɛnstvo]
orphan (boy or girl)	**sirotek** (m, ž)	[sɪrotɛk]
orphan (boy)	**sirotek** (m)	[sɪrotɛk]
orphan (girl)	**sirotek** (ž)	[sɪrotɛk]
guardian (of a minor)	**poručník** (m)	[poruʧni:k]
to adopt (a boy)	**adoptovat**	[adoptovat]
to adopt (a girl)	**adoptovat dívku**	[adoptovat difku]

56. Friends. Coworkers

friend (masc.)	**přítel** (m)	[prʃi:tɛl]
friend (fem.)	**přítelkyně** (ž)	[prʃi:tɛlkɪne]
friendship	**přátelství** (s)	[prʃa:tɛlstvi:]
to be friends	**kamarádit**	[kamara:dɪt]
buddy (masc.)	**kamarád** (m)	[kamara:t]
buddy (fem.)	**kamarádka** (ž)	[kamara:tka]
partner	**partner** (m)	[partnɛr]
chief (boss)	**šéf** (m)	[ʃɛ:f]
superior (n)	**vedoucí** (m)	[vɛdouʦi:]
owner, proprietor	**vlastník** (m)	[vlastni:k]
subordinate (n)	**podřízený** (m)	[podrʒi:zɛni:]
colleague	**kolega** (m)	[kolɛga]
acquaintance (person)	**známý** (m)	[zna:mi:]
fellow traveler	**spolucestující** (m)	[spoluʦɛstuji:ʦi:]
classmate	**spolužák** (m)	[spoluʒa:k]
neighbor (masc.)	**soused** (m)	[sousɛt]
neighbor (fem.)	**sousedka** (ž)	[sousɛtka]
neighbors	**sousedé** (m mn)	[sousɛdɛ:]

57. Man. Woman

woman	**žena** (ž)	[ʒena]
girl (young woman)	**slečna** (ž)	[slɛʧna]
bride	**nevěsta** (ž)	[nɛvesta]
beautiful (adj)	**pěkná**	[pekna:]
tall (adj)	**vysoká**	[vɪsoka:]
slender (adj)	**štíhlá**	[ʃti:hla:]
short (adj)	**menší**	[mɛnʃi:]
blonde (n)	**blondýna** (ž)	[blondi:na]
brunette (n)	**bruneta** (ž)	[brunɛta]
ladies' (adj)	**dámský**	[da:mski:]
virgin (girl)	**panna** (ž)	[panna]
pregnant (adj)	**těhotná**	[tehotna:]
man (adult male)	**muž** (m)	[muʃ]
blond (n)	**blondýn** (m)	[blondi:n]
brunet (n)	**brunet** (m)	[brunɛt]
tall (adj)	**vysoký**	[vɪsoki:]
short (adj)	**menší**	[mɛnʃi:]
rude (rough)	**hrubý**	[hrubi:]

stocky (adj)	**zavalitý**	[zavalɪti:]
robust (adj)	**statný, zdatný**	[statni:], [zdatni:]
strong (adj)	**silný**	[sɪlni:]
strength	**síla** (ž)	[si:la]
stout, fat (adj)	**tělnatý**	[telnati:]
swarthy (adj)	**snědý**	[snedi:]
slender (well-built)	**štíhlý**	[ʃti:hli:]
elegant (adj)	**elegantní**	[ɛlɛgantni:]

58. Age

age	**věk** (m)	[vek]
youth (young age)	**mladost** (ž)	[mladost]
young (adj)	**mladý**	[mladi:]
younger (adj)	**mladší**	[mladʃi:]
older (adj)	**starší**	[starʃi:]
young man	**jinoch** (m)	[jɪnox]
teenager	**výrostek** (m)	[vi:rostɛk]
guy, fellow	**kluk** (m)	[kluk]
old man	**stařec** (m)	[starʒɛʦ]
old woman	**stařena** (ž)	[starʒɛna]
adult (adj)	**dospělý**	[dospeli:]
middle-aged (adj)	**středního věku**	[strʃɛdni:ho veku]
elderly (adj)	**starší**	[starʃi:]
old (adj)	**starý**	[stari:]
retirement	**důchod** (m)	[du:xot]
to retire (from job)	**odejít do důchodu**	[odɛji:t do du:xodu]
retiree	**důchodce** (m)	[du:xodʦɛ]

59. Children

child	**dítě** (s)	[di:te]
children	**děti** (ž mn)	[detɪ]
twins	**blíženci** (m mn)	[bli:ʒenʦɪ]
cradle	**kolébka** (ž)	[kolɛ:pka]
rattle	**chrastítko** (s)	[xrasti:tko]
diaper	**plenka** (ž)	[plɛŋka]
pacifier	**dudlík** (m)	[dudli:k]
baby carriage	**kočárek** (m)	[koʧa:rɛk]
kindergarten	**mateřská škola** (ž)	[matɛrʃska: ʃkola]

babysitter	**chůva** (ž)	[xu:va]
childhood	**dětství** (s)	[detstvi:]
doll	**panenka** (ž)	[panɛŋka]
toy	**hračka** (ž)	[hraʧka]
construction set (toy)	**dětská stavebnice** (ž)	[detska: stavɛbnɪʦɛ]
well-bred (adj)	**vychovaný**	[vɪxovani:]
ill-bred (adj)	**nevychovaný**	[nɛvɪxovani:]
spoiled (adj)	**rozmazlený**	[rozmazlɛni:]
to be naughty	**dovádět**	[dova:det]
mischievous (adj)	**nezbedný**	[nɛzbɛdni:]
mischievousness	**nezbednost** (ž)	[nɛzbɛdnost]
mischievous child	**nezbedník** (m)	[nɛzbɛdni:k]
obedient (adj)	**poslušný**	[posluʃni:]
disobedient (adj)	**neposlušný**	[nɛposluʃni:]
docile (adj)	**poslušný**	[posluʃni:]
clever (smart)	**rozumný**	[rozumni:]
child prodigy	**zázračné dítě** (s)	[za:zraʧnɛ: di:te]

60. Married couples. Family life

to kiss (vt)	**líbat**	[li:bat]
to kiss (vi)	**líbat se**	[li:bat sɛ]
family (n)	**rodina** (ž)	[rodɪna]
family (as adj)	**rodinný**	[rodɪnni:]
couple	**pár** (m)	[pa:r]
marriage (state)	**manželství** (s)	[manʒelstvi:]
hearth (home)	**rodinný krb** (m)	[rodɪnni: krp]
dynasty	**dynastie** (ž)	[dɪnastɪe]
date	**rande** (s)	[randɛ]
kiss	**pusa** (ž)	[pusa]
love (for sb)	**láska** (ž)	[la:ska]
to love (sb)	**milovat**	[mɪlovat]
beloved	**milovaný**	[mɪlovani:]
tenderness	**něžnost** (ž)	[neʒnost]
tender (affectionate)	**něžný**	[neʒni:]
faithfulness	**věrnost** (ž)	[vernost]
faithful (adj)	**věrný**	[verni:]
care (attention)	**péče** (ž)	[pɛ:ʧɛ]
caring (~ father)	**starostlivý**	[starostlɪvi:]
newlyweds	**novomanželé** (m mn)	[novomanʒelɛ:]
honeymoon	**líbánky** (ž mn)	[li:ba:ŋkɪ]
to get married (ab. woman)	**vdát se**	[vda:t sɛ]

to get married (ab. man)	**ženit se**	[ʒenɪt sɛ]
wedding	**svatba** (ž)	[svatba]
golden wedding	**zlatá svatba** (ž)	[zlata: svatba]
anniversary	**výročí** (s)	[vi:rotʃi:]
lover (masc.)	**milenec** (m)	[mɪlɛnɛts]
mistress (lover)	**milenka** (ž)	[mɪlɛŋka]
adultery	**nevěra** (ž)	[nɛvera]
to cheat on ... (commit adultery)	**podvést**	[podvɛ:st]
jealous (adj)	**žárlivý**	[ʒa:rlɪvi:]
to be jealous	**žárlit**	[ʒa:rlɪt]
divorce	**rozvod** (m)	[rozvot]
to divorce (vi)	**rozvést se**	[rozvɛ:st sɛ]
to quarrel (vi)	**hádat se**	[ha:dat sɛ]
to be reconciled (after an argument)	**smiřovat se**	[smɪrʒovat sɛ]
together (adv)	**spolu**	[spolu]
sex	**sex** (m)	[sɛks]
happiness	**štěstí** (s)	[ʃtesti:]
happy (adj)	**šťastný**	[ʃtʲastni:]
misfortune (accident)	**neštěstí** (s)	[nɛʃtesti:]
unhappy (adj)	**nešťastný**	[nɛʃtʲastni:]

Character. Feelings. Emotions

61. Feelings. Emotions

feeling (emotion)	**pocit** (m)	[potsɪt]
feelings	**pocity** (m mn)	[potsɪtɪ]
to feel (vt)	**cítit**	[tsi:tɪt]
hunger	**hlad** (m)	[hlat]
to be hungry	**mít hlad**	[mi:t hlat]
thirst	**žízeň** (ž)	[ʒi:zɛnʲ]
to be thirsty	**mít žízeň**	[mi:t ʒi:zɛnʲ]
sleepiness	**ospalost** (ž)	[ospalost]
to feel sleepy	**chtít spát**	[xti:t spa:t]
tiredness	**únava** (ž)	[u:nava]
tired (adj)	**unavený**	[unavɛni:]
to get tired	**unavit se**	[unavɪt sɛ]
mood (humor)	**nálada** (ž)	[na:lada]
boredom	**nuda** (ž)	[nuda]
to be bored	**nudit se**	[nudɪt sɛ]
seclusion	**samota** (ž)	[samota]
to seclude oneself	**odloučit se**	[odloutʃɪt sɛ]
to worry (make anxious)	**znepokojovat**	[znɛpokojovat]
to be worried	**znepokojovat se**	[znɛpokojovat sɛ]
worrying (n)	**úzkost** (ž)	[u:skost]
anxiety	**nepokoj** (m)	[nɛpokoj]
preoccupied (adj)	**ustaraný**	[ustarani:]
to be nervous	**být nervózní**	[bi:t nɛrvo:zni:]
to panic (vi)	**panikařit**	[panɪkarʒɪt]
hope	**naděje** (ž)	[nadejɛ]
to hope (vi, vt)	**doufat**	[doufat]
certainty	**jistota** (ž)	[jɪstota]
certain, sure (adj)	**jistý**	[jɪsti:]
uncertainty	**nejistota** (ž)	[nɛjɪstota]
uncertain (adj)	**nejistý**	[nɛjɪsti:]
drunk (adj)	**opilý**	[opɪli:]
sober (adj)	**střízlivý**	[strʒi:zlɪvi:]
weak (adj)	**slabý**	[slabi:]
happy (adj)	**šťastný**	[ʃtʲastni:]
to scare (vt)	**polekat**	[polɛkat]

fury (madness)	**zuřivost** (ž)	[zurʒɪvost]
rage (fury)	**vztek** (m)	[vstɛk]
depression	**deprese** (ž)	[dɛprɛsɛ]
discomfort (unease)	**neklid** (m)	[nɛklɪt]
comfort	**klid** (m)	[klɪt]
to regret (be sorry)	**litovat**	[lɪtovat]
regret	**lítost** (ž)	[li:tost]
bad luck	**smůla** (ž)	[smu:la]
sadness	**rozladění** (s)	[rozladeni:]
shame (remorse)	**stud** (m)	[stut]
gladness	**radost** (ž)	[radost]
enthusiasm, zeal	**nadšení** (s)	[nadʃɛni:]
enthusiast	**nadšenec** (m)	[nadʃɛnɛʦ]
to show enthusiasm	**projevit nadšení**	[projɛvɪt nadʃɛni:]

62. Character. Personality

character	**povaha** (ž)	[povaha]
character flaw	**vada** (ž)	[vada]
mind, reason	**rozum** (m)	[rozum]
conscience	**svědomí** (s)	[svedomi:]
habit (custom)	**zvyk** (m)	[zvɪk]
ability (talent)	**schopnost** (ž)	[sxopnost]
can (e.g., ~ swim)	**umět**	[umnet]
patient (adj)	**trpělivý**	[trpelɪvi:]
impatient (adj)	**opilý**	[opɪli:]
curious (inquisitive)	**zvědavý**	[zvedavi:]
curiosity	**zvědavost** (ž)	[zvedavost]
modesty	**skromnost** (ž)	[skromnost]
modest (adj)	**skromný**	[skromni:]
immodest (adj)	**neskromný**	[nɛskromni:]
laziness	**lenost** (ž)	[lɛnost]
lazy (adj)	**líný**	[li:ni:]
lazy person (masc.)	**lenoch** (m)	[lɛnox]
cunning (n)	**vychytralost** (ž)	[vɪxɪtralost]
cunning (as adj)	**vychytralý**	[vɪxɪtrali:]
distrust	**nedůvěra** (ž)	[nɛdu:vera]
distrustful (adj)	**nedůvěřivý**	[nɛdu:verʒɪvi:]
generosity	**štědrost** (ž)	[ʃtedrost]
generous (adj)	**štědrý**	[ʃtedri:]
talented (adj)	**nadaný**	[nadani:]
talent	**nadání** (s)	[nada:ni:]

courageous (adj)	**smělý**	[smneli:]
courage	**smělost** (ž)	[smnelost]
honest (adj)	**poctivý**	[potstɪvi:]
honesty	**poctivost** (ž)	[potstɪvost]
careful (cautious)	**opatrný**	[opatrni:]
brave (courageous)	**odvážný**	[odva:ʒni:]
serious (adj)	**vážný**	[va:ʒni:]
strict (severe, stern)	**přísný**	[prʃi:sni:]
decisive (adj)	**rozhodný**	[rozhodni:]
indecisive (adj)	**nerozhodný**	[nɛrozhodni:]
shy, timid (adj)	**nesmělý**	[nɛsmneli:]
shyness, timidity	**nesmělost** (ž)	[nɛsmnelost]
confidence (trust)	**důvěra** (ž)	[du:vera]
to believe (trust)	**věřit**	[verʒɪt]
trusting (credulous)	**důvěřivý**	[du:verʒɪvi:]
sincerely (adv)	**upřímně**	[uprʃi:mne]
sincere (adj)	**upřímný**	[uprʃi:mni:]
sincerity	**upřímnost** (ž)	[uprʃi:mnost]
open (person)	**otevřený**	[otɛvrʒɛni:]
calm (adj)	**tichý**	[tɪxi:]
frank (sincere)	**upřímný**	[uprʃi:mni:]
naïve (adj)	**naivní**	[naɪvni:]
absent-minded (adj)	**roztržitý**	[roztrʒɪti:]
funny (odd)	**směšný**	[smneʃni:]
greed, stinginess	**lakomost** (ž)	[lakomost]
greedy, stingy (adj)	**lakomý**	[lakomi:]
stingy (adj)	**skoupý**	[skoupi:]
evil (adj)	**zlý**	[zli:]
stubborn (adj)	**tvrdohlavý**	[tvrdohlavi:]
unpleasant (adj)	**nepříjemný**	[nɛprʃi:jɛmni:]
selfish person (masc.)	**sobec** (m)	[sobɛts]
selfish (adj)	**sobecký**	[sobɛtski:]
coward	**zbabělec** (m)	[zbabelɛts]
cowardly (adj)	**bázlivý**	[ba:zlɪvi:]

63. Sleep. Dreams

to sleep (vi)	**spát**	[spa:t]
sleep, sleeping	**spaní** (s)	[spani:]
dream	**sen** (m)	[sɛn]
to dream (in sleep)	**snít**	[sni:t]
sleepy (adj)	**ospalý**	[ospali:]
bed	**lůžko** (s)	[lu:ʃko]

mattress	**matrace** (ž)	[matratsɛ]
blanket (comforter)	**deka** (ž)	[dɛka]
pillow	**polštář** (m)	[polʃta:rʃ]
sheet	**prostěradlo** (s)	[prosteradlo]
insomnia	**nespavost** (ž)	[nɛspavost]
sleepless (adj)	**bezesný**	[bɛzɛsni:]
sleeping pill	**prášek** (m) **pro spaní**	[pra:ʃɛk pro spani:]
to take a sleeping pill	**vzít prášek pro spaní**	[vzi:t pra:ʃɛk pro spani:]
to feel sleepy	**chtít spát**	[xti:t spa:t]
to yawn (vi)	**zívnout**	[zi:vnout]
to go to bed	**jít spát**	[ji:t spa:t]
to make up the bed	**stlát postel**	[stla:t postɛl]
to fall asleep	**usnout**	[usnout]
nightmare	**noční můra** (ž)	[notʃni: mu:ra]
snore, snoring	**chrápání** (s)	[xra:pa:ni:]
to snore (vi)	**chrápat**	[xra:pat]
alarm clock	**budík** (m)	[budi:k]
to wake (vt)	**vzbudit**	[vzbudɪt]
to wake up	**probouzet se**	[probouzɛt sɛ]
to get up (vi)	**vstávat**	[vsta:vat]
to wash up (wash face)	**umýt se**	[umi:t sɛ]

64. Humour. Laughter. Gladness

humor (wit, fun)	**humor** (m)	[humor]
sense of humor	**smysl** (m)	[smɪsl]
to enjoy oneself	**bavit se**	[bavɪt sɛ]
cheerful (merry)	**veselý**	[vɛsɛli:]
merriment (gaiety)	**zábava** (ž)	[za:bava]
smile	**úsměv** (m)	[u:smnef]
to smile (vi)	**usmívat se**	[usmi:vat sɛ]
to start laughing	**zasmát se**	[zasma:t sɛ]
to laugh (vi)	**smát se**	[sma:t sɛ]
laugh, laughter	**smích** (m)	[smi:x]
anecdote	**anekdota** (ž)	[anɛgdota]
funny (anecdote, etc.)	**směšný**	[smneʃni:]
funny (odd)	**směšný**	[smneʃni:]
to joke (vi)	**žertovat**	[ʒertovat]
joke (verbal)	**žert** (m)	[ʒert]
joy (emotion)	**radost** (ž)	[radost]
to rejoice (vi)	**radovat se**	[radovat sɛ]
joyful (adj)	**radostný**	[radostni:]

65. Discussion, conversation. Part 1

communication	**styk** (m)	[stɪk]
to communicate	**komunikovat**	[komunɪkovat]
conversation	**rozhovor** (m)	[rozhovor]
dialog	**dialog** (m)	[dɪalok]
discussion (discourse)	**diskuse** (ž)	[dɪskusɛ]
dispute (debate)	**debata** (ž)	[dɛbata]
to dispute	**diskutovat**	[dɪskutovat]
interlocutor	**účastník** (m) **rozhovoru**	[u:ʧastni:k rozhovoru]
topic (theme)	**téma** (s)	[tɛ:ma]
point of view	**stanovisko** (s)	[stanovɪsko]
opinion (point of view)	**názor** (m)	[na:zor]
speech (talk)	**projev** (m)	[projɛf]
discussion (of report, etc.)	**diskuse** (ž)	[dɪskusɛ]
to discuss (vt)	**projednávat**	[projɛdna:vat]
talk (conversation)	**beseda** (ž)	[bɛsɛda]
to talk (to chat)	**besedovat**	[bɛsɛdovat]
meeting (encounter)	**setkání** (s)	[sɛtka:ni:]
to meet (vi, vt)	**utkávat se**	[utka:vat sɛ]
proverb	**přísloví** (s)	[prʃi:slovi:]
saying	**pořekadlo** (s)	[porʒɛkadlo]
riddle (poser)	**hádanka** (ž)	[ha:daŋka]
to pose a riddle	**dávat hádat**	[da:vat ha:dat]
password	**heslo** (s)	[hɛslo]
secret	**tajemství** (s)	[tajɛmstvi:]
oath (vow)	**přísaha** (ž)	[prʃi:saha]
to swear (an oath)	**přísahat**	[prʃi:sahat]
promise	**slib** (m)	[slɪp]
to promise (vt)	**slibovat**	[slɪbovat]
advice (counsel)	**rada** (ž)	[rada]
to advise (vt)	**radit**	[radɪt]
to follow one's advice	**řídit se čí radou**	[rʒi:dɪt sɛ ʧi: radou]
to listen to ... (obey)	**poslouchat**	[poslouxat]
news	**novina** (ž)	[novɪna]
sensation (news)	**senzace** (ž)	[sɛnzaʦɛ]
information (report)	**údaje** (m mn)	[u:dajɛ]
conclusion (decision)	**závěr** (m)	[za:ver]
voice	**hlas** (m)	[hlas]
compliment	**lichotka** (ž)	[lɪxotka]
kind (nice)	**laskavý**	[laskavi:]
word	**slovo** (s)	[slovo]
phrase	**věta** (ž)	[veta]

answer	**odpověď** (ž)	[otpovetʲ]
truth	**pravda** (ž)	[pravda]
lie	**lež** (ž)	[lɛʃ]
thought	**myšlenka** (ž)	[mɪʃlɛŋka]
idea (inspiration)	**idea** (ž)	[ɪdɛa]
fantasy	**fantazie** (ž)	[fantazɪe]

66. Discussion, conversation. Part 2

respected (adj)	**vážený**	[va:ʒeni:]
to respect (vt)	**vážit si**	[va:ʒɪt sɪ]
respect	**respekt** (m)	[rɛspɛkt]
Dear ... (letter)	**vážený**	[va:ʒeni:]
to introduce (sb to sb)	**seznámit**	[sɛzna:mɪt]
to make acquaintance	**navázat známost**	[nava:zat zna:most]
intention	**úmysl** (m)	[u:mɪsl]
to intend (have in mind)	**mít v úmyslu**	[mi:t v u:mɪslu]
wish	**přání** (s)	[prʃa:ni:]
to wish (~ good luck)	**popřát**	[poprʃa:t]
surprise (astonishment)	**překvapení** (s)	[prʃɛkvapɛnɪ]
to surprise (amaze)	**udivovat**	[udɪvovat]
to be surprised	**divit se**	[dɪvɪt sɛ]
to give (vt)	**dát**	[da:t]
to take (get hold of)	**vzít**	[vzi:t]
to give back	**vrátit**	[vra:tɪt]
to return (give back)	**odevzdat**	[odɛvzdat]
to apologize (vi)	**omlouvat se**	[omlouvat sɛ]
apology	**omluva** (ž)	[omluva]
to forgive (vt)	**odpouštět**	[otpouʃtet]
to talk (speak)	**mluvit**	[mluvɪt]
to listen (vi)	**poslouchat**	[poslouxat]
to hear out	**vyslechnout**	[vɪslɛxnout]
to understand (vt)	**pochopit**	[poxopɪt]
to show (to display)	**ukázat**	[uka:zat]
to look at ...	**dívat se**	[di:vat sɛ]
to call (yell for sb)	**zavolat**	[zavolat]
to distract (disturb)	**rušit**	[ruʃɪt]
to disturb (vt)	**rušit**	[ruʃɪt]
to pass (to hand sth)	**předat**	[prʃɛdat]
demand (request)	**prosba** (ž)	[prozba]
to request (ask)	**prosit**	[prosɪt]
demand (firm request)	**požadavek** (m)	[poʒadavɛk]

to demand (request firmly)	**žádat**	[ʒa:dat]
to tease (call names)	**škádlit**	[ʃka:dlɪt]
to mock (make fun of)	**vysmívat se**	[vɪsmi:vat sɛ]
mockery, derision	**výsměch** (m)	[vi:smnex]
nickname	**přezdívka** (ž)	[prʃɛzdi:fka]
insinuation	**narážka** (ž)	[nara:ʃka]
to insinuate (imply)	**narážet**	[nara:ʒet]
to mean (vt)	**mínit**	[mi:nɪt]
description	**popis** (m)	[popɪs]
to describe (vt)	**popsat**	[popsat]
praise (compliments)	**pochvala** (ž)	[poxvala]
to praise (vt)	**pochválit**	[poxva:lɪt]
disappointment	**zklamání** (s)	[sklama:ni:]
to disappoint (vt)	**zklamat**	[sklamat]
to be disappointed	**zklamat se**	[sklamat sɛ]
supposition	**předpoklad** (m)	[prʃɛtpoklat]
to suppose (assume)	**předpokládat**	[prʃɛtpokla:dat]
warning (caution)	**varování** (s)	[varova:ni:]
to warn (vt)	**varovat**	[varovat]

67. Discussion, conversation. Part 3

to talk into (convince)	**přemluvit**	[prʃɛmluvɪt]
to calm down (vt)	**uklidňovat**	[uklɪdnʲovat]
silence (~ is golden)	**mlčení** (s)	[mltʃɛni:]
to be silent (not speaking)	**mlčet**	[mltʃɛt]
to whisper (vi, vt)	**šeptnout**	[ʃɛptnout]
whisper	**šepot** (m)	[ʃɛpot]
frankly, sincerely (adv)	**otevřeně**	[otɛvrʒɛne]
in my opinion ...	**podle mého názoru ...**	[podlɛ mɛ:ho na:zoru]
detail (of the story)	**podrobnost** (ž)	[podrobnost]
detailed (adj)	**podrobný**	[podrobni:]
in detail (adv)	**podrobně**	[podrobne]
hint, clue	**nápověda** (ž)	[na:poveda]
to give a hint	**napovídat**	[napovi:dat]
look (glance)	**pohled** (m)	[pohlɛt]
to have a look	**pohlédnout**	[pohlɛ:dnout]
fixed (look)	**ustrnulý**	[ustrnuli:]
to blink (vi)	**mrkat**	[mrkat]
to wink (vi)	**mrknout**	[mrknout]
to nod (in assent)	**kývnout**	[ki:vnout]

sigh	**vzdech** (m)	[vzdɛx]
to sigh (vi)	**vzdechnout**	[vzdɛxnout]
to shudder (vi)	**zachvívat se**	[zaxvi:vat sɛ]
gesture	**gesto** (s)	[gɛsto]
to touch (one's arm, etc.)	**dotknout se**	[dotknout sɛ]
to seize (e.g., ~ by the arm)	**chytat**	[xɪtat]
to tap (on the shoulder)	**plácat**	[pla:ʦat]
Look out!	**Pozor!**	[pozor]
Really?	**Opravdu?**	[opravdu]
Are you sure?	**Jsi si tím jist?**	[jsɪ sɪ ti:m jɪst]
Good luck!	**Hodně zdaru!**	[hodne zdaru]
I see!	**Jasně!**	[jasne]
What a pity!	**Škoda!**	[ʃkoda]

68. Agreement. Refusal

consent	**souhlas** (m)	[souhlas]
to consent (vi)	**souhlasit**	[souhlasɪt]
approval	**schválení** (s)	[sxva:lɛni:]
to approve (vt)	**schválit**	[sxva:lɪt]
refusal	**odmítnutí** (s)	[odmi:tnuti:]
to refuse (vi, vt)	**odmítat**	[odmi:tat]
Great!	**Výborně!**	[vi:borne]
All right!	**Dobře!**	[dobrʒɛ]
Okay! (I agree)	**Platí!**	[plati:]
forbidden (adj)	**zakázaný**	[zaka:zani:]
it's forbidden	**nesmí se**	[nɛsmi: sɛ]
it's impossible	**není možno**	[nɛni: moʒno]
incorrect (adj)	**nesprávný**	[nɛspra:vni:]
to reject (~ a demand)	**zamítnout**	[zami:tnout]
to support (cause, idea)	**podpořit**	[potporʒɪt]
to accept (~ an apology)	**akceptovat**	[akʦɛptovat]
to confirm (vt)	**potvrdit**	[potvrdɪt]
confirmation	**potvrzení** (s)	[potvrzɛni:]
permission	**povolení** (s)	[povolɛni:]
to permit (vt)	**dovolit**	[dovolɪt]
decision	**rozhodnutí** (s)	[rozhodnuti:]
to say nothing (hold one's tongue)	**nepromluvit**	[nɛpromluvɪt]
condition (term)	**podmínka** (ž)	[podmi:ŋka]
excuse (pretext)	**výmluva** (ž)	[vi:mluva]
praise (compliments)	**pochvala** (ž)	[poxvala]
to praise (vt)	**chválit**	[xva:lɪt]

69. Success. Good luck. Failure

success	**úspěch** (m)	[u:spex]
successfully (adv)	**úspěšně**	[u:speʃne]
successful (adj)	**úspěšný**	[u:spɛʃni:]
luck (good luck)	**zdar** (m)	[zdar]
Good luck!	**Hodně zdaru!**	[hodne zdaru]
lucky (e.g., ~ day)	**zdařilý**	[zdarʒɪli:]
lucky (fortunate)	**mít štěstí**	[mi:t ʃtɛsti:]
failure	**nezdar** (m)	[nɛzdar]
misfortune	**neštěstí** (s)	[nɛʃtesti:]
bad luck	**smůla** (ž)	[smu:la]
unsuccessful (adj)	**nepodařený**	[nɛpodarʒɛni:]
catastrophe	**katastrofa** (ž)	[katastrofa]
pride	**hrdost** (ž)	[hrdost]
proud (adj)	**hrdý**	[hrdi:]
to be proud	**být hrdý**	[bi:t hrdi:]
winner	**vítěz** (m)	[vi:tez]
to win (vi)	**zvítězit**	[zvi:tezɪt]
to lose (not win)	**prohrát**	[prohra:t]
try	**pokus** (m)	[pokus]
to try (vi)	**pokoušet se**	[pokouʃɛt sɛ]
chance (opportunity)	**šance** (ž)	[ʃantsɛ]

70. Quarrels. Negative emotions

shout (scream)	**křik** (m)	[krʃɪk]
to shout (vi)	**křičet**	[krʃɪʧɛt]
to start to cry out	**zakřičet**	[zakrʃɪʧɛt]
quarrel	**hádka** (ž)	[ha:tka]
to quarrel (vi)	**hádat se**	[ha:dat sɛ]
fight (squabble)	**skandál** (m)	[skanda:l]
to make a scene	**dělat skandál**	[delat skanda:l]
conflict	**konflikt** (m)	[konflɪkt]
misunderstanding	**nedorozumění** (s)	[nɛdorozumneni:]
insult	**urážka** (ž)	[ura:ʃka]
to insult (vt)	**urážet**	[ura:ʒet]
insulted (adj)	**uražený**	[uraʒeni:]
resentment	**urážka** (ž)	[ura:ʃka]
to offend (vt)	**urazit**	[urazɪt]
to take offense	**urazit se**	[urazɪt sɛ]
indignation	**rozhořčení** (s)	[rozhorʃʧɛni:]
to be indignant	**rozhořčovat se**	[rozhorʃʧovat sɛ]

complaint	**stížnost** (ž)	[sti:ʒnost]
to complain (vi, vt)	**stěžovat si**	[steʒovat sɪ]
apology	**omluva** (ž)	[omluva]
to apologize (vi)	**omlouvat se**	[omlouvat sɛ]
to beg pardon	**prosit o prominutí**	[prosɪt o promɪnuti:]
criticism	**kritika** (ž)	[krɪtɪka]
to criticize (vt)	**kritizovat**	[krɪtɪzovat]
accusation (charge)	**obvinění** (s)	[obvɪneni:]
to accuse (vt)	**obviňovat**	[obvɪnʲovat]
revenge	**pomsta** (ž)	[pomsta]
to avenge (get revenge)	**mstít se**	[msti:t sɛ]
to pay back	**odplatit**	[otplatɪt]
disdain	**opovržení** (s)	[opovrʒeni:]
to despise (vt)	**pohrdat**	[pohrdat]
hatred, hate	**nenávist** (ž)	[nɛna:vɪst]
to hate (vt)	**nenávidět**	[nɛna:vɪdet]
nervous (adj)	**nervózní**	[nɛrvo:zni:]
to be nervous	**být nervózní**	[bi:t nɛrvo:zni:]
angry (mad)	**rozčilený**	[roztʃɪleni:]
to make angry	**rozčilit**	[roztʃɪlɪt]
humiliation	**ponížení** (s)	[poni:ʒeni:]
to humiliate (vt)	**ponižovat**	[ponɪʒovat]
to humiliate oneself	**ponižovat se**	[ponɪʒovat sɛ]
shock	**šok** (m)	[ʃok]
to shock (vt)	**šokovat**	[ʃokovat]
trouble (e.g., serious ~)	**nepříjemnost** (ž)	[nɛprʃi:jɛmnost]
unpleasant (adj)	**nepříjemný**	[nɛprʃi:jɛmni:]
fear (dread)	**strach** (m)	[strax]
terrible (storm, heat)	**strašný**	[straʃni:]
scary (e.g., ~ story)	**strašný**	[straʃni:]
horror	**hrůza** (ž)	[hru:za]
awful (crime, news)	**hrůzyplný**	[hru:zɪplni:]
to begin to tremble	**zatřást se**	[zatrʃa:st sɛ]
to cry (weep)	**plakat**	[plakat]
to start crying	**zaplakat**	[zaplakat]
tear	**slza** (ž)	[slza]
fault	**provinění** (s)	[provɪneni:]
guilt (feeling)	**vina** (ž)	[vɪna]
dishonor (disgrace)	**hanba** (ž)	[hanba]
protest	**protest** (m)	[protɛst]
stress	**stres** (m)	[strɛs]

to disturb (vt)	**rušit**	[ruʃɪt]
to be furious	**zlobit se**	[zlobɪt sɛ]
mad, angry (adj)	**naštvaný**	[naʃtvani:]
to end (~ a relationship)	**přerušovat**	[prʃɛruʃovat]
to swear (at sb)	**hádat se**	[ha:dat sɛ]
to scare (become afraid)	**lekat se**	[lɛkat sɛ]
to hit (strike with hand)	**udeřit**	[udɛrʒɪt]
to fight (street fight, etc.)	**prát se**	[pra:t sɛ]
to settle (a conflict)	**urovnat**	[urovnat]
discontented (adj)	**nespokojený**	[nɛspokojɛni:]
furious (adj)	**vzteklý**	[vstɛkli:]
It's not good!	**To není dobře!**	[to nɛni: dobrʒɛ]
It's bad!	**To je špatné!**	[to jɛ ʃpatnɛ:]

Medicine

71. Diseases

sickness	**nemoc** (ž)	[nɛmots]
to be sick	**být nemocný**	[bi:t nɛmotsni:]
health	**zdraví** (s)	[zdravi:]
runny nose (coryza)	**rýma** (ž)	[ri:ma]
tonsillitis	**angína** (ž)	[angi:na]
cold (illness)	**nachlazení** (s)	[naxlazɛni:]
to catch a cold	**nachladit se**	[naxladɪt sɛ]
bronchitis	**bronchitida** (ž)	[bronxɪti:da]
pneumonia	**zápal** (m) **plic**	[za:pal plɪts]
flu, influenza	**chřipka** (ž)	[xrʃɪpka]
nearsighted (adj)	**krátkozraký**	[kra:tkozraki:]
farsighted (adj)	**dalekozraký**	[dalɛkozraki:]
strabismus (crossed eyes)	**šilhavost** (ž)	[ʃɪlhavost]
cross-eyed (adj)	**šilhavý**	[ʃɪlhavi:]
cataract	**šedý zákal** (m)	[ʃɛdi: za:kal]
glaucoma	**zelený zákal** (m)	[zɛlɛni: za:kal]
stroke	**mozková mrtvice** (ž)	[moskova: mrtvɪtsɛ]
heart attack	**infarkt** (m)	[ɪnfarkt]
myocardial infarction	**infarkt** (m) **myokardu**	[ɪnfarkt mɪokardu]
paralysis	**obrna** (ž)	[obrna]
to paralyze (vt)	**paralyzovat**	[paralɪzovat]
allergy	**alergie** (ž)	[alɛrgɪe]
asthma	**astma** (s)	[astma]
diabetes	**cukrovka** (ž)	[tsukrofka]
toothache	**bolení** (s) **zubů**	[bolɛni: zubu:]
caries	**zubní kaz** (m)	[zubni: kaz]
diarrhea	**průjem** (m)	[pru:jɛm]
constipation	**zácpa** (ž)	[za:tspa]
stomach upset	**žaludeční potíže** (ž mn)	[ʒaludɛtʃni: poti:ʒe]
food poisoning	**otrava** (ž)	[otrava]
to get food poisoning	**otrávit se**	[otra:vɪt sɛ]
arthritis	**artritida** (ž)	[artrɪtɪda]
rickets	**rachitida** (ž)	[raxɪtɪda]
rheumatism	**revmatismus** (m)	[rɛvmatɪzmus]

atherosclerosis	**ateroskleróza** (ž)	[atɛrosklɛro:za]
gastritis	**gastritida** (ž)	[gastrɪtɪda]
appendicitis	**apendicitida** (ž)	[apɛndɪtsɪtɪda]
cholecystitis	**zánět** (m) **žlučníku**	[za:net ʒluʧni:ku]
ulcer	**vřed** (m)	[vrʒɛt]
measles	**spalničky** (ž mn)	[spalnɪʧki:]
rubella (German measles)	**zarděnky** (ž mn)	[zardeŋkɪ]
jaundice	**žloutenka** (ž)	[ʒloutɛŋka]
hepatitis	**hepatitida** (ž)	[hɛpatɪtɪda]
schizophrenia	**schizofrenie** (ž)	[sxɪzofrɛnɪe]
rabies (hydrophobia)	**vzteklina** (ž)	[vstɛklɪna]
neurosis	**neuróza** (ž)	[nɛuro:za]
concussion	**otřes** (m) **mozku**	[otrʃɛs mosku]
cancer	**rakovina** (ž)	[rakovɪna]
sclerosis	**skleróza** (ž)	[sklɛro:za]
multiple sclerosis	**roztroušená skleróza** (ž)	[roztrouʃɛna: sklɛro:za]
alcoholism	**alkoholismus** (m)	[alkoholɪzmus]
alcoholic (n)	**alkoholik** (m)	[alkoholɪk]
syphilis	**syfilida** (ž)	[sɪfɪlɪda]
AIDS	**AIDS** (m)	[ajts]
tumor	**nádor** (m)	[na:dor]
malignant (adj)	**zhoubný**	[zhoubni:]
benign (adj)	**nezhoubný**	[nɛzhoubni:]
fever	**zimnice** (ž)	[zɪmnɪtsɛ]
malaria	**malárie** (ž)	[mala:rɪe]
gangrene	**gangréna** (ž)	[gangrɛ:na]
seasickness	**mořská nemoc** (ž)	[morʃska: nɛmots]
epilepsy	**padoucnice** (ž)	[padoutsnɪtsɛ]
epidemic	**epidemie** (ž)	[ɛpɪdɛmɪe]
typhus	**tyf** (m)	[tɪf]
tuberculosis	**tuberkulóza** (ž)	[tubɛrkulo:za]
cholera	**cholera** (ž)	[xolɛra]
plague (bubonic ~)	**mor** (m)	[mor]

72. Symptoms. Treatments. Part 1

symptom	**příznak** (m)	[prʃi:znak]
temperature	**teplota** (ž)	[tɛplota]
high temperature (fever)	**vysoká teplota** (ž)	[vɪsoka: tɛplota]
pulse (heartbeat)	**tep** (m)	[tɛp]
dizziness (vertigo)	**závrať** (ž)	[za:vratʲ]
hot (adj)	**horký**	[horki:]

shivering	**mrazení** (s)	[mrazɛni:]
pale (e.g., ~ face)	**bledý**	[blɛdi:]
cough	**kašel** (m)	[kaʃɛl]
to cough (vi)	**kašlat**	[kaʃlat]
to sneeze (vi)	**kýchat**	[ki:xat]
faint	**mdloby** (ž mn)	[mdlobɪ]
to faint (vi)	**upadnout do mdlob**	[upadnout do mdlop]
bruise (hématome)	**modřina** (ž)	[modrʒɪna]
bump (lump)	**boule** (ž)	[boulɛ]
to bang (bump)	**uhodit se**	[uhodɪt sɛ]
contusion (bruise)	**pohmožděnina** (ž)	[pohmoʒdenɪna]
to get a bruise	**uhodit se**	[uhodɪt sɛ]
to limp (vi)	**kulhat**	[kulhat]
dislocation	**vykloubení** (s)	[vɪkloubɛni:]
to dislocate (vt)	**vykloubit**	[vɪkloubɪt]
fracture	**zlomenina** (ž)	[zlomɛnɪna]
to have a fracture	**dostat zlomeninu**	[dostat zlomɛnɪnu]
cut (e.g., paper ~)	**říznutí** (s)	[rʒi:znuti:]
to cut oneself	**říznout se**	[rʒi:znout sɛ]
bleeding	**krvácení** (s)	[krva:ʦɛni:]
burn (injury)	**popálenina** (ž)	[popa:lɛnɪna]
to get burned	**spálit se**	[spa:lɪt sɛ]
to prick (vt)	**píchnout**	[pi:xnout]
to prick oneself	**píchnout se**	[pi:xnout sɛ]
to injure (vt)	**pohmoždit**	[pohmoʒdɪt]
injury	**pohmoždění** (s)	[pohmoʒdeni:]
wound	**rána** (ž)	[ra:na]
trauma	**úraz** (m)	[u:raz]
to be delirious	**blouznit**	[blouznɪt]
to stutter (vi)	**zajíkat se**	[zaji:kat sɛ]
sunstroke	**úpal** (m)	[u:pal]

73. Symptoms. Treatments. Part 2

pain, ache	**bolest** (ž)	[bolɛst]
splinter (in foot, etc.)	**tříska** (ž)	[trʃi:ska]
sweat (perspiration)	**pot** (m)	[pot]
to sweat (perspire)	**potit se**	[potɪt sɛ]
vomiting	**zvracení** (s)	[zvraʦɛni:]
convulsions	**křeče** (ž mn)	[krʃɛʧɛ]
pregnant (adj)	**těhotná**	[tehotna:]
to be born	**narodit se**	[narodɪt sɛ]

delivery, labor	**porod** (m)	[porot]
to deliver (~ a baby)	**rodit**	[rodɪt]
abortion	**umělý potrat** (m)	[umneli: potrat]
breathing, respiration	**dýchání** (s)	[di:xa:ni:]
in-breath (inhalation)	**vdech** (m)	[vdɛx]
out-breath (exhalation)	**výdech** (m)	[vi:dɛx]
to exhale (breathe out)	**vydechnout**	[vɪdɛxnout]
to inhale (vi)	**nadechnout se**	[nadɛxnout sɛ]
disabled person	**invalida** (m)	[ɪnvalɪda]
cripple	**mrzák** (m)	[mrza:k]
drug addict	**narkoman** (m)	[narkoman]
deaf (adj)	**hluchý**	[hluxi:]
mute (adj)	**němý**	[nemi:]
deaf mute (adj)	**hluchoněmý**	[hluxonemi:]
mad, insane (adj)	**šílený**	[ʃi:lɛni:]
madman (demented person)	**šílenec** (m)	[ʃi:lɛnɛʦ]
madwoman	**šílenec** (ž)	[ʃi:lɛnɛʦ]
to go insane	**zešílet**	[zɛʃi:lɛt]
gene	**gen** (m)	[gɛn]
immunity	**imunita** (ž)	[ɪmunɪta]
hereditary (adj)	**dědičný**	[dedɪʧni:]
congenital (adj)	**vrozený**	[vrozɛni:]
virus	**virus** (m)	[vɪrus]
microbe	**mikrob** (m)	[mɪkrop]
bacterium	**baktérie** (ž)	[baktɛ:rɪe]
infection	**infekce** (ž)	[ɪnfɛkʦɛ]

74. Symptoms. Treatments. Part 3

hospital	**nemocnice** (ž)	[nɛmoʦnɪʦɛ]
patient	**pacient** (m)	[paʦɪent]
diagnosis	**diagnóza** (ž)	[dɪagno:za]
cure	**léčení** (s)	[lɛ:ʧɛni:]
medical treatment	**léčba** (ž)	[lɛ:ʧba]
to get treatment	**léčit se**	[lɛ:ʧɪt sɛ]
to treat (~ a patient)	**léčit**	[lɛ:ʧɪt]
to nurse (look after)	**ošetřovat**	[oʃɛtrʃovat]
care (nursing ~)	**ošetřování** (s)	[oʃɛtrʃova:ni:]
operation, surgery	**operace** (ž)	[opɛraʦɛ]
to bandage (head, limb)	**obvázat**	[obva:zat]
bandaging	**obvazování** (s)	[obvazova:ni:]

vaccination	**očkování** (s)	[otʃkova:ni:]
to vaccinate (vt)	**dělat očkování**	[delat otʃkova:ni:]
injection, shot	**injekce** (ž)	[ɪnjɛktsɛ]
to give an injection	**dávat injekci**	[da:vat ɪnjɛktsɪ]
attack	**záchvat** (m)	[za:xvat]
amputation	**amputace** (ž)	[amputatsɛ]
to amputate (vt)	**amputovat**	[amputovat]
coma	**kóma** (s)	[ko:ma]
to be in a coma	**být v kómatu**	[bi:t v ko:matu]
intensive care	**reanimace** (ž)	[rɛanɪmatsɛ]
to recover (~ from flu)	**uzdravovat se**	[uzdravovat sɛ]
condition (patient's ~)	**stav** (m)	[staf]
consciousness	**vědomí** (s)	[vedomi:]
memory (faculty)	**paměť** (ž)	[pamnetʲ]
to pull out (tooth)	**trhat**	[trhat]
filling	**plomba** (ž)	[plomba]
to fill (a tooth)	**plombovat**	[plombovat]
hypnosis	**hypnóza** (ž)	[hɪpno:za]
to hypnotize (vt)	**hypnotizovat**	[hɪpnotɪzovat]

75. Doctors

doctor	**lékař** (m)	[lɛ:karʃ]
nurse	**zdravotní sestra** (ž)	[zdravotni: sɛstra]
personal doctor	**osobní lékař** (m)	[osobni: lɛ:karʃ]
dentist	**zubař** (m)	[zubarʃ]
eye doctor	**oční lékař** (m)	[otʃni: lɛ:karʃ]
internist	**internista** (m)	[ɪntɛrnɪsta]
surgeon	**chirurg** (m)	[xɪrurg]
psychiatrist	**psychiatr** (m)	[psɪxɪatr]
pediatrician	**pediatr** (m)	[pɛdɪatr]
psychologist	**psycholog** (m)	[psɪxolog]
gynocologist	**gynekolog** (m)	[gɪnɛkolog]
cardiologist	**kardiolog** (m)	[kardɪolog]

76. Medicine. Drugs. Accessories

medicine, drug	**lék** (m)	[lɛ:k]
remedy	**prostředek** (m)	[prostrʃɛdɛk]
to prescribe (vt)	**předepsat**	[prʒɛdɛpsat]
prescription	**recept** (m)	[rɛtsɛpt]
tablet, pill	**tableta** (ž)	[tablɛta]

ointment	**mast** (ž)	[mast]
ampule	**ampule** (ž)	[ampulɛ]
mixture, solution	**mixtura** (ž)	[mɪkstura]
syrup	**sirup** (m)	[sɪrup]
capsule	**pilulka** (ž)	[pɪlulka]
powder	**prášek** (m)	[pra:ʃɛk]
gauze bandage	**obvaz** (m)	[obvaz]
cotton wool	**vata** (ž)	[vata]
iodine	**jód** (m)	[jo:t]
Band-Aid	**leukoplast** (m)	[lɛukoplast]
eyedropper	**pipeta** (ž)	[pɪpɛta]
thermometer	**teploměr** (m)	[tɛplomner]
syringe	**injekční stříkačka** (ž)	[ɪnjɛkʧni: strʃi:kaʧka]
wheelchair	**vozík** (m)	[vozi:k]
crutches	**berle** (ž mn)	[bɛrlɛ]
painkiller	**anestetikum** (s)	[anɛstɛtɪkum]
laxative	**projímadlo** (s)	[proji:madlo]
spirits (ethanol)	**líh** (m)	[li:x]
medicinal herbs	**bylina** (ž)	[bɪlɪna]
herbal (~ tea)	**bylinný**	[bɪlɪnni:]

77. Smoking. Tobacco products

tobacco	**tabák** (m)	[taba:k]
cigarette	**cigareta** (ž)	[ʦɪgarɛta]
cigar	**doutník** (m)	[doutni:k]
pipe	**dýmka** (ž)	[di:mka]
pack (of cigarettes)	**krabička** (ž)	[krabɪʧka]
matches	**zápalky** (ž mn)	[za:palkɪ]
matchbox	**krabička** (ž) **zápalek**	[krabɪʧka za:palek]
lighter	**zapalovač** (m)	[zapalovaʧ]
ashtray	**popelník** (m)	[popɛlni:k]
cigarette case	**pouzdro** (s) **na cigarety**	[pouzdro na ʦɪgarɛtɪ]
cigarette holder	**špička** (ž) **na cigarety**	[ʃpɪʧka na ʦɪgarɛtɪ]
filter (cigarette tip)	**filtr** (m)	[fɪltr]
to smoke (vi, vt)	**kouřit**	[kourʒɪt]
to light a cigarette	**zapálit si**	[zapa:lɪt sɪ]
smoking	**kouření** (s)	[kourʒɛni:]
smoker	**kuřák** (m)	[kurʒa:k]
stub, butt (of cigarette)	**nedopalek** (m)	[nɛdopalɛk]
smoke, fumes	**kouř** (m)	[kourʃ]
ash	**popel** (m)	[popɛl]

HUMAN HABITAT

City

78. City. Life in the city

city, town	**město** (s)	[mnesto]
capital city	**hlavní město** (s)	[hlavni: mnesto]
village	**venkov** (m)	[vɛŋkof]
city map	**plán** (m) **města**	[pla:n mnesta]
downtown	**střed** (m) **města**	[strʃɛd mnesta]
suburb	**předměstí** (s)	[prʃɛdmnesti:]
suburban (adj)	**předměstský**	[prʃɛdmnestski:]
outskirts	**okraj** (m)	[okraj]
environs (suburbs)	**okolí** (s)	[okoli:]
city block	**čtvrť** (ž)	[ʧtvrtʲ]
residential block (area)	**obytná čtvrť** (ž)	[obɪtna: ʧtvrtʲ]
traffic	**provoz** (m)	[provoz]
traffic lights	**semafor** (m)	[sɛmafor]
public transportation	**městská doprava** (ž)	[mnestska: doprava]
intersection	**křižovatka** (ž)	[krʃɪʒovatka]
crosswalk	**přechod** (m)	[prʃɛxot]
pedestrian underpass	**podchod** (m)	[podxot]
to cross (~ the street)	**přecházet**	[prʃɛxa:zɛt]
pedestrian	**chodec** (m)	[xodɛʦ]
sidewalk	**chodník** (m)	[xodni:k]
bridge	**most** (m)	[most]
embankment (river walk)	**nábřeží** (s)	[na:brʒɛʒi:]
fountain	**fontána** (ž)	[fonta:na]
allée (garden walkway)	**alej** (ž)	[alɛj]
park	**park** (m)	[park]
boulevard	**bulvár** (m)	[bulva:r]
square	**náměstí** (s)	[na:mnesti:]
avenue (wide street)	**třída** (ž)	[trʃi:da]
street	**ulice** (ž)	[ulɪʦɛ]
side street	**boční ulice** (ž)	[boʧni: ulɪʦɛ]
dead end	**slepá ulice** (ž)	[slɛpa: ulɪʦɛ]
house	**dům** (m)	[du:m]
building	**budova** (ž)	[budova]

skyscraper	**mrakodrap** (m)	[mrakodrap]
facade	**fasáda** (ž)	[fasa:da]
roof	**střecha** (ž)	[strʃɛxa]
window	**okno** (s)	[okno]
arch	**oblouk** (m)	[oblouk]
column	**sloup** (m)	[sloup]
corner	**roh** (m)	[rox]
store window	**výloha** (ž)	[vi:loha]
signboard (store sign, etc.)	**vývěsní tabule** (ž)	[vi:vesni: tabulɛ]
poster (e.g., playbill)	**plakát** (m)	[plaka:t]
advertising poster	**reklamní plakát** (m)	[rɛklamni: plaka:t]
billboard	**billboard** (m)	[bɪlbo:rt]
garbage, trash	**odpadky** (m mn)	[otpatki:]
trash can (public ~)	**popelnice** (ž)	[popɛlnɪʦɛ]
to litter (vi)	**dělat smetí**	[delat smɛti:]
garbage dump	**smetiště** (s)	[smɛtɪʃte]
phone booth	**telefonní budka** (ž)	[tɛlɛfonni: butka]
lamppost	**pouliční svítilna** (ž)	[poulɪʧni: svi:tɪlna]
bench (park ~)	**lavička** (ž)	[lavɪʧka]
police officer	**policista** (m)	[polɪʦɪsta]
police	**policie** (ž)	[polɪʦɪe]
beggar	**žebrák** (m)	[ʒebra:k]
homeless (n)	**bezdomovec** (m)	[bɛzdomovɛʦ]

79. Urban institutions

store	**obchod** (m)	[obxot]
drugstore, pharmacy	**lékárna** (ž)	[lɛ:ka:rna]
eyeglass store	**oční optika** (ž)	[oʧni: optɪka]
shopping mall	**obchodní středisko** (s)	[obxodni: strʃɛdɪsko]
supermarket	**supermarket** (m)	[supɛrmarket]
bakery	**pekařství** (s)	[pɛkarʃstvi:]
baker	**pekař** (m)	[pɛkarʃ]
pastry shop	**cukrárna** (ž)	[ʦukra:rna]
grocery store	**smíšené zboží** (s)	[smiʃɛnɛ: zboʒi:]
butcher shop	**řeznictví** (s)	[rʒɛznɪʦtvi:]
produce store	**zelinářství** (s)	[zɛlɪna:rʃstvi:]
market	**tržnice** (ž)	[trʒnɪʦɛ]
coffee house	**kavárna** (ž)	[kava:rna]
restaurant	**restaurace** (ž)	[rɛstauraʦɛ]
pub, bar	**pivnice** (ž)	[pɪvnɪʦɛ]
pizzeria	**pizzerie** (ž)	[pɪʦɛrɪe]
hair salon	**holičství** (s) **a kadeřnictví**	[holɪʧstvi: a kadɛrʒnɪʦtvi:]

post office	**pošta** (ž)	[poʃta]
dry cleaners	**čistírna** (ž)	[ʧɪsti:rna]
photo studio	**fotografický ateliér** (m)	[fotografɪʦki: atɛlɪe:r]
shoe store	**obchod** (m) **s obuví**	[obxot s obuvi:]
bookstore	**knihkupectví** (s)	[knɪxkupɛʦtvi:]
sporting goods store	**sportovní potřeby** (ž mn)	[sportovni: potrʃɛbɪ]
clothes repair shop	**opravna** (ž) **oděvů**	[opravna odevu:]
formal wear rental	**půjčovna** (ž) **oděvů**	[pu:jʧovna odevu:]
video rental store	**půjčovna** (ž) **filmů**	[pu:jʧovna fɪlmu:]
circus	**cirkus** (m)	[ʦɪrkus]
zoo	**zoologická zahrada** (ž)	[zoologɪʦka: zahrada]
movie theater	**biograf** (m)	[bɪograf]
museum	**muzeum** (s)	[muzɛum]
library	**knihovna** (ž)	[knɪhovna]
theater	**divadlo** (s)	[dɪvadlo]
opera (opera house)	**opera** (ž)	[opɛra]
nightclub	**noční klub** (m)	[noʧni: klup]
casino	**kasino** (s)	[kasi:no]
mosque	**mešita** (ž)	[mɛʃɪta]
synagogue	**synagóga** (ž)	[sinago:ga]
cathedral	**katedrála** (ž)	[katɛdra:la]
temple	**chrám** (m)	[xra:m]
church	**kostel** (m)	[kostɛl]
college	**vysoká škola** (ž)	[vɪsoka: ʃkola]
university	**univerzita** (ž)	[unɪvɛrzɪta]
school	**škola** (ž)	[ʃkola]
prefecture	**prefektura** (ž)	[prɛfɛktura]
city hall	**magistrát** (m)	[magɪstra:t]
hotel	**hotel** (m)	[hotɛl]
bank	**banka** (ž)	[baŋka]
embassy	**velvyslanectví** (s)	[vɛlvɪslanɛʦtvi:]
travel agency	**cestovní kancelář** (ž)	[ʦɛstovni: kanʦɛla:rʃ]
information office	**informační kancelář** (ž)	[ɪnformaʧni: kanʦɛla:rʃ]
currency exchange	**směnárna** (ž)	[smnena:rna]
subway	**metro** (s)	[mɛtro]
hospital	**nemocnice** (ž)	[nɛmoʦnɪʦɛ]
gas station	**benzínová stanice** (ž)	[bɛnzi:nova: stanɪʦɛ]
parking lot	**parkoviště** (s)	[parkovɪʃte]

80. Signs

signboard (store sign, etc.)	**ukazatel** (m) **směru**	[ukazatɛl smneru]
notice (door sign, etc.)	**nápis** (m)	[na:pɪs]
poster	**plakát** (m)	[plaka:t]
direction sign	**ukazatel** (m)	[ukazatɛl]
arrow (sign)	**šípka** (ž)	[ʃi:pka]
caution	**varování** (s)	[varova:ni:]
warning sign	**výstraha** (ž)	[vi:straha]
to warn (vt)	**upozorňovat**	[upozornʲovat]
rest day (weekly ~)	**volný den** (m)	[volni: dɛn]
timetable (schedule)	**jízdní řád** (m)	[ji:zdni: rʒa:t]
opening hours	**pracovní doba** (ž)	[praʦovni: doba]
WELCOME!	**VÍTEJTE!**	[vi:tɛjtɛ]
ENTRANCE	**VCHOD**	[vxot]
EXIT	**VÝCHOD**	[vi:xot]
PUSH	**TAM**	[tam]
PULL	**SEM**	[sɛm]
OPEN	**OTEVŘENO**	[otɛvrʒɛno]
CLOSED	**ZAVŘENO**	[zavrʒɛno]
WOMEN	**ŽENY**	[ʒenɪ]
MEN	**MUŽI**	[muʒɪ]
DISCOUNTS	**SLEVY**	[slɛvɪ]
SALE	**VÝPRODEJ**	[vi:prodɛj]
NEW!	**NOVINKA!**	[novɪŋka]
FREE	**ZDARMA**	[zdarma]
ATTENTION!	**POZOR!**	[pozor]
NO VACANCIES	**VOLNÁ MÍSTA NEJSOU**	[volna: mi:sta nɛjsou]
RESERVED	**ZADÁNO**	[zada:no]
ADMINISTRATION	**KANCELÁŘ**	[kanʦɛla:rʒ]
STAFF ONLY	**POUZE PRO PERSONÁL**	[pouzɛ pro pɛrsona:l]
BEWARE OF THE DOG!	**POZOR! ZLÝ PES**	[pozor zli: pɛs]
NO SMOKING	**ZÁKAZ KOUŘENÍ**	[za:kaz kourʒɛni:]
DO NOT TOUCH!	**NEDOTÝKEJTE SE!**	[nɛdoti:kɛjtɛ sɛ]
DANGEROUS	**NEBEZPEČNÉ**	[nɛbɛzpɛʧnɛ:]
DANGER	**NEBEZPEČÍ**	[nɛbɛzpɛʧi:]
HIGH VOLTAGE	**VYSOKÉ NAPĚTÍ**	[vɪsokɛ: napeti:]
NO SWIMMING!	**KOUPÁNÍ ZAKÁZÁNO**	[koupa:ni: zaka:za:no]
OUT OF ORDER	**MIMO PROVOZ**	[mɪmo provoz]
FLAMMABLE	**VYSOCE HOŘLAVÝ**	[vɪsoʦɛ horʒlavi:]
FORBIDDEN	**ZÁKAZ**	[za:kaz]

NO TRESPASSING!	**PRŮCHOD ZAKÁZÁN**	[pru:xot zaka:za:n]
WET PAINT	**ČERSTVĚ NATŘENO**	[ʧɛrstve natrʃɛno]

81. Urban transportation

bus	**autobus** (m)	[autobus]
streetcar	**tramvaj** (ž)	[tramvaj]
trolley bus	**trolejbus** (m)	[trolɛjbus]
route (of bus, etc.)	**trasa** (ž)	[trasa]
number (e.g., bus ~)	**číslo** (s)	[ʧi:slo]
to go by ...	**jet**	[jɛt]
to get on (~ the bus)	**nastoupit do ...**	[nastoupɪt do]
to get off ...	**vystoupit z ...**	[vɪstoupɪt z]
stop (e.g., bus ~)	**zastávka** (ž)	[zasta:fka]
next stop	**příští zastávka** (ž)	[prʃi:ʃti: zasta:fka]
terminus	**konečná stanice** (ž)	[konɛʧna: stanɪʦɛ]
schedule	**jízdní řád** (m)	[ji:zdni: rʒa:t]
to wait (vt)	**čekat**	[ʧɛkat]
ticket	**jízdenka** (ž)	[ji:zdɛŋka]
fare	**jízdné** (s)	[ji:zdnɛ:]
cashier (ticket seller)	**pokladník** (m)	[pokladni:k]
ticket inspection	**kontrola** (ž)	[kontrola]
ticket inspector	**revizor** (m)	[rɛvɪzor]
to be late (for ...)	**mít zpoždění**	[mi:t spoʒdɛni:]
to miss (~ the train, etc.)	**opozdit se**	[opozdɪt sɛ]
to be in a hurry	**pospíchat**	[pospi:xat]
taxi, cab	**taxík** (m)	[taksi:k]
taxi driver	**taxikář** (m)	[taksɪka:rʃ]
by taxi	**taxíkem**	[taksi:kɛm]
taxi stand	**stanoviště** (s) **taxíků**	[stanovɪʃte taksi:ku:]
to call a taxi	**zavolat taxíka**	[zavolat taksi:ka]
to take a taxi	**vzít taxíka**	[vzi:t taksi:ka]
traffic	**uliční provoz** (m)	[ulɪʧni: provoz]
traffic jam	**zácpa** (ž)	[za:ʦpa]
rush hour	**špička** (ž)	[ʃpɪʧka]
to park (vi)	**parkovat se**	[parkovat sɛ]
to park (vt)	**parkovat**	[parkovat]
parking lot	**parkoviště** (s)	[parkovɪʃte]
subway	**metro** (s)	[mɛtro]
station	**stanice** (ž)	[stanɪʦɛ]
to take the subway	**jet metrem**	[jɛt mɛtrɛm]
train	**vlak** (m)	[vlak]
train station	**nádraží** (s)	[na:draʒi:]

82. Sightseeing

monument	**památka** (ž)	[pama:tka]
fortress	**pevnost** (ž)	[pɛvnost]
palace	**palác** (m)	[pala:ʦ]
castle	**zámek** (m)	[za:mɛk]
tower	**věž** (ž)	[veʃ]
mausoleum	**mauzoleum** (s)	[mauzolɛum]
architecture	**architektura** (ž)	[arxɪtɛktura]
medieval (adj)	**středověký**	[strʃɛdoveki:]
ancient (adj)	**starobylý**	[starobɪli:]
national (adj)	**národní**	[na:rodni:]
famous (monument, etc.)	**známý**	[zna:mi:]
tourist	**turista** (m)	[turɪsta]
guide (person)	**průvodce** (m)	[pru:vodʦɛ]
excursion, sightseeing tour	**výlet** (m)	[vi:lɛt]
to show (vt)	**ukazovat**	[ukazovat]
to tell (vt)	**povídat**	[povi:dat]
to find (vt)	**najít**	[naji:t]
to get lost (lose one's way)	**ztratit se**	[stratɪʦɛ]
map (e.g., subway ~)	**plán** (m)	[pla:n]
map (e.g., city ~)	**plán** (m)	[pla:n]
souvenir, gift	**suvenýr** (m)	[suvɛni:r]
gift shop	**prodejna** (ž) **suvenýrů**	[prodɛjna suvɛni:ru:]
to take pictures	**fotografovat**	[fotografovat]
to have one's picture taken	**fotografovat se**	[fotografovat sɛ]

83. Shopping

to buy (purchase)	**kupovat**	[kupovat]
purchase	**nákup** (m)	[na:kup]
to go shopping	**dělat nákupy**	[delat na:kupɪ]
shopping	**nakupování** (s)	[nakupova:ni:]
to be open (ab. store)	**být otevřen**	[bi:t otɛvrʒɛn]
to be closed	**být zavřen**	[bi:t zavrʒɛn]
footwear, shoes	**obuv** (ž)	[obuf]
clothes, clothing	**oblečení** (s)	[oblɛʧɛni:]
cosmetics	**kosmetika** (ž)	[kosmɛtɪka]
food products	**potraviny** (ž mn)	[potravɪnɪ]
gift, present	**dárek** (m)	[da:rɛk]
salesman	**prodavač** (m)	[prodavaʧ]
saleswoman	**prodavačka** (ž)	[prodavaʧka]

check out, cash desk	**pokladna** (ž)	[pokladna]
mirror	**zrcadlo** (s)	[zrtsadlo]
counter (store ~)	**pult** (m)	[pult]
fitting room	**zkušební kabinka** (ž)	[skuʃɛbni: kabɪŋka]
to try on	**zkusit**	[skusɪt]
to fit (ab. dress, etc.)	**hodit se**	[hodɪt sɛ]
to like (I like ...)	**líbit se**	[li:bɪt sɛ]
price	**cena** (ž)	[tsɛna]
price tag	**cenovka** (ž)	[tsɛnofka]
to cost (vt)	**stát**	[sta:t]
How much?	**Kolik?**	[kolɪk]
discount	**sleva** (ž)	[slɛva]
inexpensive (adj)	**levný**	[lɛvni:]
cheap (adj)	**levný**	[lɛvni:]
expensive (adj)	**drahý**	[drahi:]
It's expensive	**To je drahé**	[to jɛ drahɛ:]
rental (n)	**půjčování** (s)	[pu:jtʃova:ni:]
to rent (~ a tuxedo)	**vypůjčit si**	[vɪpu:jtʃɪt sɪ]
credit (trade credit)	**úvěr** (m)	[u:ver]
on credit (adv)	**na splátky**	[na spla:tkɪ]

84. Money

money	**peníze** (m mn)	[pɛni:zɛ]
currency exchange	**výměna** (ž)	[vi:mnena]
exchange rate	**kurz** (m)	[kurs]
ATM	**bankomat** (m)	[baŋkomat]
coin	**mince** (ž)	[mɪntsɛ]
dollar	**dolar** (m)	[dolar]
euro	**euro** (s)	[ɛuro]
lira	**lira** (ž)	[lɪra]
Deutschmark	**marka** (ž)	[marka]
franc	**frank** (m)	[fraŋk]
pound sterling	**libra** (ž) **šterlinků**	[lɪbra ʃtɛrlɪŋku:]
yen	**jen** (m)	[jɛn]
debt	**dluh** (m)	[dlux]
debtor	**dlužník** (m)	[dluʒni:k]
to lend (money)	**půjčit**	[pu:jtʃɪt]
to borrow (vi, vt)	**půjčit si**	[pu:jtʃɪt sɪ]
bank	**banka** (ž)	[baŋka]
account	**účet** (m)	[u:tʃɛt]
to deposit (vt)	**uložit**	[uloʒɪt]

to deposit into the account	**uložit na účet**	[uloʒɪt na u:ʧɛt]
to withdraw (vt)	**vybrat z účtu**	[vɪbrat s u:ʧtu]
credit card	**kreditní karta** (ž)	[krɛdɪtni: karta]
cash	**hotové peníze** (m mn)	[hotovɛ: pɛni:zɛ]
check	**šek** (m)	[ʃɛk]
to write a check	**vystavit šek**	[vɪstavɪt ʃɛk]
checkbook	**šeková knížka** (ž)	[ʃɛkova: kni:ʃka]
wallet	**náprsní taška** (ž)	[na:prsni: taʃka]
change purse	**peněženka** (ž)	[pɛneʒeŋka]
safe	**trezor** (m)	[trɛzor]
heir	**dědic** (m)	[dedɪʦ]
inheritance	**dědictví** (s)	[dedɪʦtvi:]
fortune (wealth)	**majetek** (m)	[majɛtɛk]
lease	**nájem** (m)	[na:jɛm]
rent (money)	**činže** (ž)	[ʧɪnʒe]
to rent (sth from sb)	**pronajímat si**	[pronaji:mat sɪ]
price	**cena** (ž)	[ʦɛna]
cost	**cena** (ž)	[ʦɛna]
sum	**částka** (ž)	[ʧa:stka]
to spend (vt)	**utrácet**	[utra:ʦɛt]
expenses	**náklady** (m mn)	[na:kladɪ]
to economize (vi, vt)	**šetřit**	[ʃɛtrʃɪt]
economical	**úsporný**	[u:sporni:]
to pay (vi, vt)	**platit**	[platɪt]
payment	**platba** (ž)	[platba]
change (give the ~)	**peníze** (m mn) **nazpět**	[pɛni:zɛ naspet]
tax	**daň** (ž)	[danʲ]
fine	**pokuta** (ž)	[pokuta]
to fine (vt)	**pokutovat**	[pokutovat]

85. Post. Postal service

post office	**pošta** (ž)	[poʃta]
mail (letters, etc.)	**pošta** (ž)	[poʃta]
mailman	**listonoš** (m)	[lɪstonoʃ]
opening hours	**pracovní doba** (ž)	[praʦovni: doba]
letter	**dopis** (m)	[dopɪs]
registered letter	**doporučený dopis** (m)	[doporuʧɛni: dopɪs]
postcard	**pohlednice** (ž)	[pohlɛdnɪʦɛ]
telegram	**telegram** (m)	[tɛlɛgram]
package (parcel)	**balík** (m)	[bali:k]

money transfer	**peněžní poukázka** (ž)	[pɛneʒni: pouka:ska]
to receive (vt)	**dostat**	[dostat]
to send (vt)	**odeslat**	[odɛslat]
sending	**odeslání** (s)	[odɛsla:ni:]
address	**adresa** (ž)	[adrɛsa]
ZIP code	**poštovní směrovací číslo** (s)	[poʃtovni: smnerovaʦi: ʧi:slo]
sender	**odesílatel** (m)	[odɛsi:latɛl]
receiver	**příjemce** (m)	[prʃi:jɛmʦɛ]
name (first name)	**jméno** (s)	[jmɛ:no]
surname (last name)	**příjmení** (s)	[prʃi:jmɛni:]
postage rate	**tarif** (m)	[tarɪf]
standard (adj)	**obyčejný**	[obɪʧɛjni:]
economical (adj)	**zlevněný**	[zlɛvneni:]
weight	**váha** (ž)	[va:ha]
to weigh (~ letters)	**vážit**	[va:ʒɪt]
envelope	**obálka** (ž)	[oba:lka]
postage stamp	**známka** (ž)	[zna:mka]
to stamp an envelope	**nalepovat známku**	[nalɛpovat zna:mku]

Dwelling. House. Home

86. House. Dwelling

house	**dům** (m)	[du:m]
at home (adv)	**doma**	[doma]
yard	**dvůr** (m)	[dvu:r]
fence (iron ~)	**ohrada** (ž)	[ohrada]
brick (n)	**cihla** (ž)	[ʦɪhla]
brick (as adj)	**cihlový**	[ʦɪhlovi:]
stone (n)	**kámen** (m)	[ka:mɛn]
stone (as adj)	**kamenný**	[kamɛnni:]
concrete (n)	**beton** (m)	[bɛton]
concrete (as adj)	**betonový**	[bɛtonovi:]
new (new-built)	**nový**	[novi:]
old (adj)	**starý**	[stari:]
decrepit (house)	**sešlý**	[sɛʃli:]
modern (adj)	**moderní**	[modɛrni:]
multistory (adj)	**vícepatrový**	[vi:ʦɛpatrovi:]
tall (~ building)	**vysoký**	[vɪsoki:]
floor, story	**poschodí** (s)	[posxodi:]
single-story (adj)	**přizemní**	[prʃɪzɛmni:]
1st floor	**dolní podlaží** (s)	[dolni: podlaʒi:]
top floor	**horní podlaží** (s)	[horni: podlaʒi:]
roof	**střecha** (ž)	[strʃɛxa]
chimney	**komín** (m)	[komi:n]
roof tiles	**taška** (ž)	[taʃka]
tiled (adj)	**taškový**	[taʃkovi:]
attic (storage place)	**půda** (ž)	[pu:da]
window	**okno** (s)	[okno]
glass	**sklo** (s)	[sklo]
window ledge	**parapet** (m)	[parapɛt]
shutters	**okenice** (ž mn)	[okɛnɪʦɛ]
wall	**stěna** (ž)	[stena]
balcony	**balkón** (m)	[balko:n]
downspout	**okapová roura** (ž)	[okapova: roura]
upstairs (to be ~)	**nahoře**	[nahorʒɛ]
to go upstairs	**vystupovat**	[vɪstupovat]

to come down (the stairs)	**jít dolů**	[ji:t dolu:]
to move (to new premises)	**stěhovat se**	[stehovat sɛ]

87. House. Entrance. Lift

entrance	**vchod** (m)	[vxot]
stairs (stairway)	**schodiště** (s)	[sxodɪʃte]
steps	**schody** (m mn)	[sxodɪ]
banister	**zábradlí** (s)	[za:bradli:]
lobby (hotel ~)	**hala** (ž)	[hala]
mailbox	**poštovní schránka** (ž)	[poʃtovni: sxra:ŋka]
garbage can	**popelnice** (ž)	[popɛlnɪʦɛ]
trash chute	**šachta** (ž) **na odpadky**	[ʃaxta na otpatkɪ]
elevator	**výtah** (m)	[vi:tax]
freight elevator	**nákladní výtah** (m)	[na:kladni: vi:tax]
elevator cage	**kabina** (ž)	[kabɪna]
to take the elevator	**jet výtahem**	[jɛt vi:tahɛm]
apartment	**byt** (m)	[bɪt]
residents (~ of a building)	**nájemníci** (m)	[na:jɛmni:ʦɪ]
neighbor (masc.)	**soused** (m)	[sousɛt]
neighbor (fem.)	**sousedka** (ž)	[sousɛtka]
neighbors	**sousedé** (m mn)	[sousɛdɛ:]

88. House. Electricity

electricity	**elektřina** (ž)	[ɛlɛktrʃɪna]
light bulb	**žárovka** (ž)	[ʒa:rofka]
switch	**vypínač** (m)	[vɪpi:natʃ]
fuse (plug fuse)	**pojistka** (ž)	[pojɪstka]
cable, wire (electric ~)	**vodič** (m)	[vodɪtʃ]
wiring	**vedení** (s)	[vɛdɛni:]
electricity meter	**elektroměr** (m)	[ɛlɛktromnɛr]
readings	**údaj** (m)	[u:daj]

89. House. Doors. Locks

door	**dveře** (ž mn)	[dvɛrʒɛ]
gate (vehicle ~)	**vrata** (s mn)	[vrata]
handle, doorknob	**klika** (ž)	[klɪka]
to unlock (unbolt)	**odemknout**	[odɛmknout]
to open (vt)	**otvírat**	[otvi:rat]
to close (vt)	**zavírat**	[zavi:rat]

key	**klíč** (m)	[kli:tʃ]
bunch (of keys)	**svazek** (m)	[svazɛk]
to creak (door, etc.)	**vrzat**	[vrzat]
creak	**vrzání** (s)	[vrza:ni:]
hinge (door ~)	**závěs** (m)	[za:ves]
doormat	**kobereček** (m)	[kobɛrɛtʃɛk]
door lock	**zámek** (m)	[za:mɛk]
keyhole	**klíčová dírka** (ž)	[kli:tʃova: di:rka]
crossbar (sliding bar)	**závora** (ž)	[za:vora]
door latch	**zástrčka** (ž)	[za:strtʃka]
padlock	**visací zámek** (m)	[vɪsaʦi: za:mɛk]
to ring (~ the door bell)	**zvonit**	[zvonɪt]
ringing (sound)	**zvonění** (s)	[zvoneni:]
doorbell	**zvonek** (m)	[zvonɛk]
doorbell button	**knoflík** (m)	[knofli:k]
knock (at the door)	**klepání** (s)	[klɛpa:ni:]
to knock (vi)	**klepat**	[klɛpat]
code	**kód** (m)	[ko:t]
combination lock	**kódový zámek** (m)	[ko:dovi: za:mɛk]
intercom	**domácí telefon** (m)	[doma:ʦi: tɛlɛfon]
number (on the door)	**číslo** (s)	[tʃi:slo]
doorplate	**štítek** (m)	[ʃtitɛk]
peephole	**kukátko** (s)	[kuka:tko]

90. Country house

village	**venkov** (m)	[vɛŋkof]
vegetable garden	**zelinářská zahrada** (ž)	[zɛlɪna:rʃska: zahrada]
fence	**plot** (m)	[plot]
picket fence	**pletený plot** (m)	[plɛtɛni: plot]
wicket gate	**vrátka** (s mn)	[vra:tka]
granary	**sýpka** (ž)	[si:pka]
root cellar	**sklep** (m)	[sklɛp]
shed (garden ~)	**kůlna** (ž)	[ku:lna]
water well	**studna** (ž)	[studna]
stove (wood-fired ~)	**kamna** (s mn)	[kamna]
to stoke the stove	**topit**	[topɪt]
firewood	**dříví** (s)	[drʒi:vi:]
log (firewood)	**poleno** (s)	[polɛno]
veranda	**veranda** (ž)	[vɛranda]
deck (terrace)	**terasa** (ž)	[tɛrasa]
stoop (front steps)	**schody** (m mn) **před vchodem**	[sxodɪ prʃɛd vxodɛm]
swing (hanging seat)	**houpačky** (ž mn)	[houpatʃkɪ]

91. Villa. Mansion

country house	**venkovský dům** (m)	[vɛŋkovski: du:m]
villa (seaside ~)	**vila** (ž)	[vɪla]
wing (~ of a building)	**křídlo** (s)	[krʃi:dlo]
garden	**zahrada** (ž)	[zahrada]
park	**park** (m)	[park]
conservatory (greenhouse)	**oranžérie** (ž)	[oranʒe:rɪe]
to look after (garden, etc.)	**zahradničit**	[zahradnɪʧɪt]
swimming pool	**bazén** (m)	[bazɛ:n]
gym (home gym)	**tělocvična** (ž)	[telotsvɪʧna]
tennis court	**tenisový kurt** (m)	[tɛnɪsovi: kurt]
home theater (room)	**biograf** (m)	[bɪograf]
garage	**garáž** (ž)	[gara:ʃ]
private property	**soukromé vlastnictví** (s)	[soukromɛ: vlastnɪtstvi:]
private land	**soukromý pozemek** (m)	[soukromi: pozɛmɛk]
warning (caution)	**výstraha** (ž)	[vi:straha]
warning sign	**výstražný nápis** (m)	[vi:straʒni: na:pɪs]
security	**stráž** (ž)	[stra:ʃ]
security guard	**strážce** (m)	[stra:ʒtsɛ]
burglar alarm	**signalizace** (ž)	[sɪgnalɪzatsɛ]

92. Castle. Palace

castle	**zámek** (m)	[za:mɛk]
palace	**palác** (m)	[pala:ts]
fortress	**pevnost** (ž)	[pɛvnost]
wall (round castle)	**zeď** (ž)	[zɛtʲ]
tower	**věž** (ž)	[veʃ]
keep, donjon	**hlavní věž** (ž)	[hlavni: veʃ]
portcullis	**zvedací vrata** (s mn)	[zvɛdatsi: vrata]
underground passage	**podzemní chodba** (ž)	[podzɛmni: xodba]
moat	**příkop** (m)	[prʃi:kop]
chain	**řetěz** (m)	[rʒɛtez]
arrow loop	**střílna** (ž)	[strʃi:lna]
magnificent (adj)	**velkolepý**	[vɛlkolɛpi:]
majestic (adj)	**majestátní**	[majɛsta:tni:]
impregnable (adj)	**nedobytný**	[nɛdobɪtni:]
medieval (adj)	**středověký**	[strʃɛdoveki:]

93. Apartment

apartment	**byt** (m)	[bɪt]
room	**pokoj** (m)	[pokoj]
bedroom	**ložnice** (ž)	[loʒnɪʦɛ]
dining room	**jídelna** (ž)	[ji:dɛlna]
living room	**přijímací pokoj** (m)	[prʃɪji:maʦi: pokoj]
study (home office)	**pracovna** (ž)	[praʦovna]
entry room	**předsíň** (ž)	[prʃɛtsi:nʲ]
bathroom (room with a bath or shower)	**koupelna** (ž)	[koupɛlna]
half bath	**záchod** (m)	[za:xot]
ceiling	**strop** (m)	[strop]
floor	**podlaha** (ž)	[podlaha]
corner	**kout** (m)	[kout]

94. Apartment. Cleaning

to clean (vi, vt)	**uklízet**	[ukli:zɛt]
to put away (to stow)	**odklízet**	[otkli:zɛt]
dust	**prach** (m)	[prax]
dusty (adj)	**zaprášený**	[zapra:ʃɛni:]
to dust (vt)	**utírat prach**	[uti:rat prax]
vacuum cleaner	**vysavač** (m)	[vɪsavaʧ]
to vacuum (vt)	**vysávat**	[vɪsa:vat]
to sweep (vi, vt)	**zametat**	[zamɛtat]
sweepings	**smetí** (s)	[smɛti:]
order	**pořádek** (m)	[porʒa:dɛk]
disorder, mess	**nepořádek** (m)	[nɛporʒa:dɛk]
mop	**mop** (m)	[mop]
dust cloth	**hadr** (m)	[hadr]
short broom	**koště** (s)	[koʃte]
dustpan	**lopatka** (ž) **na smetí**	[lopatka na smɛti:]

95. Furniture. Interior

furniture	**nábytek** (m)	[na:bɪtɛk]
table	**stůl** (m)	[stu:l]
chair	**židle** (ž)	[ʒɪdlɛ]
bed	**lůžko** (s)	[lu:ʃko]
couch, sofa	**pohovka** (ž)	[pohofka]
armchair	**křeslo** (s)	[krʃɛslo]
bookcase	**knihovna** (ž)	[knɪhovna]

shelf	**police** (ž)	[polɪʦɛ]
wardrobe	**skříň** (ž)	[skrʃi:nʲ]
coat rack (wall-mounted ~)	**předsíňový věšák** (m)	[prʃɛdsi:novi: veʃa:k]
coat stand	**stojanový věšák** (m)	[stojanovi: veʃa:k]
bureau, dresser	**prádelník** (m)	[pra:dɛlni:k]
coffee table	**konferenční stolek** (m)	[konfɛrɛnʧni: stolɛk]
mirror	**zrcadlo** (s)	[zrʦadlo]
carpet	**koberec** (m)	[kobɛrɛʦ]
rug, small carpet	**kobereček** (m)	[kobɛrɛʧɛk]
fireplace	**krb** (m)	[krp]
candle	**svíce** (ž)	[svi:ʦɛ]
candlestick	**svícen** (m)	[svi:ʦɛn]
drapes	**záclony** (ž mn)	[za:ʦlonɪ]
wallpaper	**tapety** (ž mn)	[tapɛtɪ]
blinds (jalousie)	**žaluzie** (ž)	[ʒaluzɪe]
table lamp	**stolní lampa** (ž)	[stolni: lampa]
wall lamp (sconce)	**svítidlo** (s)	[svi:tɪdlo]
floor lamp	**stojací lampa** (ž)	[stojaʦi: lampa]
chandelier	**lustr** (m)	[lustr]
leg (of chair, table)	**noha** (ž)	[noha]
armrest	**područka** (ž)	[podruʧka]
back (backrest)	**opěradlo** (s)	[operadlo]
drawer	**zásuvka** (ž)	[za:sufka]

96. Bedding

bedclothes	**ložní prádlo** (s)	[loʒni: pra:dlo]
pillow	**polštář** (m)	[polʃta:rʃ]
pillowcase	**povlak** (m) **na polštář**	[povlak na polʃta:rʒ]
duvet, comforter	**deka** (ž)	[dɛka]
sheet	**prostěradlo** (s)	[prosteradlo]
bedspread	**přikrývka** (ž)	[prʃɪkri:fka]

97. Kitchen

kitchen	**kuchyně** (ž)	[kuxɪne]
gas	**plyn** (m)	[plɪn]
gas stove (range)	**plynový sporák** (m)	[plɪnovi: spora:k]
electric stove	**elektrický sporák** (m)	[ɛlɛktrɪʦki: spora:k]
oven	**trouba** (ž)	[trouba]
microwave oven	**mikrovlnná pec** (ž)	[mɪkrovlnna: pɛʦ]
refrigerator	**lednička** (ž)	[lɛdnɪʧka]

freezer	**mrazicí komora** (ž)	[mrazɪʦi: komora]
dishwasher	**myčka** (ž) **nádobí**	[mɪʧka na:dobi:]
meat grinder	**mlýnek** (m) **na maso**	[mli:nɛk na maso]
juicer	**odšťavňovač** (m)	[otʃtʲavnʲovaʧ]
toaster	**opékač** (m) **topinek**	[opɛ:kaʧ topɪnɛk]
mixer	**mixér** (m)	[mɪksɛ:r]
coffee machine	**kávovar** (m)	[ka:vovar]
coffee pot	**konvice** (ž) **na kávu**	[konvɪʦɛ na ka:vu]
coffee grinder	**mlýnek** (m) **na kávu**	[mli:nɛk na ka:vu]
kettle	**čajník** (m)	[ʧajni:k]
teapot	**čajová konvice** (ž)	[ʧajova: konvɪʦɛ]
lid	**poklička** (ž)	[poklɪʧka]
tea strainer	**cedítko** (s)	[ʦɛdi:tko]
spoon	**lžíce** (ž)	[lʒi:ʦɛ]
teaspoon	**kávová lžička** (ž)	[ka:vova: lʒɪʧka]
soup spoon	**polévková lžíce** (ž)	[polɛ:fkova: lʒi:ʦɛ]
fork	**vidlička** (ž)	[vɪdlɪʧka]
knife	**nůž** (m)	[nu:ʃ]
tableware (dishes)	**nádobí** (s)	[na:dobi:]
plate (dinner ~)	**talíř** (m)	[tali:rʃ]
saucer	**talířek** (m)	[tali:rʒɛk]
shot glass	**sklenička** (ž)	[sklɛnɪʧka]
glass (tumbler)	**sklenice** (ž)	[sklɛnɪʦɛ]
cup	**šálek** (m)	[ʃa:lɛk]
sugar bowl	**cukřenka** (ž)	[ʦukrʃɛŋka]
salt shaker	**solnička** (ž)	[solnɪʧka]
pepper shaker	**pepřenka** (ž)	[pɛprʃɛŋka]
butter dish	**nádobka** (ž) **na máslo**	[na:dopka na ma:slo]
stock pot (soup pot)	**hrnec** (m)	[hrnɛʦ]
frying pan (skillet)	**pánev** (ž)	[pa:nɛf]
ladle	**naběračka** (ž)	[naberaʧka]
colander	**cedník** (m)	[ʦɛdni:k]
tray (serving ~)	**podnos** (m)	[podnos]
bottle	**láhev** (ž)	[la:hɛf]
jar (glass)	**sklenice** (ž)	[sklɛnɪʦɛ]
can	**plechovka** (ž)	[plɛxofka]
bottle opener	**otvírač** (m) **lahví**	[otvi:raʧ lahvi:]
can opener	**otvírač** (m) **konzerv**	[otvi:raʧ konzɛrf]
corkscrew	**vývrtka** (ž)	[vi:vrtka]
filter	**filtr** (m)	[fɪltr]
to filter (vt)	**filtrovat**	[fɪltrovat]
trash, garbage (food waste, etc.)	**odpadky** (m mn)	[otpatki:]
trash can (kitchen ~)	**kbelík** (m) **na odpadky**	[gbɛli:k na otpatkɪ]

98. Bathroom

bathroom	**koupelna** (ž)	[koupɛlna]
water	**voda** (ž)	[voda]
faucet	**kohout** (m)	[kohout]
hot water	**teplá voda** (ž)	[tɛpla: voda]
cold water	**studená voda** (ž)	[studɛna: voda]
toothpaste	**zubní pasta** (ž)	[zubni: pasta]
to brush one's teeth	**čistit si zuby**	[ʧɪstɪt sɪ zubɪ]
toothbrush	**kartáček** (m) **na zuby**	[karta:ʧɛk na zubɪ]
to shave (vi)	**holit se**	[holɪt sɛ]
shaving foam	**pěna** (ž) **na holení**	[pena na holɛni:]
razor	**holicí strojek** (m)	[holɪʦi: strojɛk]
to wash (one's hands, etc.)	**mýt**	[mi:t]
to take a bath	**mýt se**	[mi:t sɛ]
shower	**sprcha** (ž)	[sprxa]
to take a shower	**sprchovat se**	[sprxovat sɛ]
bathtub	**vana** (ž)	[vana]
toilet (toilet bowl)	**záchodová mísa** (ž)	[za:xodova: mi:sa]
sink (washbasin)	**umývadlo** (s)	[umi:vadlo]
soap	**mýdlo** (m)	[mi:dlo]
soap dish	**miska** (ž) **na mýdlo**	[mɪska na mi:dlo]
sponge	**mycí houba** (ž)	[mɪʦi: houba]
shampoo	**šampon** (m)	[ʃampon]
towel	**ručník** (m)	[ruʧni:k]
bathrobe	**župan** (m)	[ʒupan]
laundry (laundering)	**praní** (s)	[prani:]
washing machine	**pračka** (ž)	[praʧka]
to do the laundry	**prát**	[pra:t]
laundry detergent	**prací prášek** (m)	[praʦi: pra:ʃɛk]

99. Household appliances

TV set	**televizor** (m)	[tɛlɛvɪzor]
tape recorder	**magnetofon** (m)	[magnɛtofon]
VCR (video recorder)	**videomagnetofon** (m)	[vɪdɛomagnɛtofon]
radio	**přijímač** (m)	[prʃɪji:maʧ]
player (CD, MP3, etc.)	**přehrávač** (m)	[prʃɛhra:vaʧ]
video projector	**projektor** (m)	[projɛktor]
home movie theater	**domácí biograf** (m)	[doma:ʦi: bɪograf]
DVD player	**DVD přehrávač** (m)	[dɛvɛdɛ prʃɛhra:vaʧ]

amplifier	**zesilovač** (m)	[zɛsɪlovaʧ]
video game console	**hrací přístroj** (m)	[hraʦi: prʃi:stroj]
video camera	**videokamera** (ž)	[vɪdɛokamɛra]
camera (photo)	**fotoaparát** (m)	[fotoapara:t]
digital camera	**digitální fotoaparát** (m)	[dɪgɪta:lni: fotoapara:t]
vacuum cleaner	**vysavač** (m)	[vɪsavaʧ]
iron (e.g., steam ~)	**žehlička** (ž)	[ʒehlɪʧka]
ironing board	**žehlicí prkno** (s)	[ʒehlɪʦi: prkno]
telephone	**telefon** (m)	[tɛlɛfon]
cell phone	**mobilní telefon** (m)	[mobɪlni: tɛlɛfon]
typewriter	**psací stroj** (m)	[psaʦi: stroj]
sewing machine	**šicí stroj** (m)	[ʃɪʦi: stroj]
microphone	**mikrofon** (m)	[mɪkrofon]
headphones	**sluchátka** (s mn)	[sluxa:tka]
remote control (TV)	**ovládač** (m)	[ovla:daʧ]
CD, compact disc	**CD disk** (m)	[ʦɛ:dɛ: dɪsk]
cassette, tape	**kazeta** (ž)	[kazɛta]
vinyl record	**deska** (ž)	[dɛska]

100. Repairs. Renovation

renovations	**oprava** (ž)	[oprava]
to renovate (vt)	**dělat opravu**	[delat opravu]
to repair, to fix (vt)	**opravovat**	[opravovat]
to put in order	**dávat do pořádku**	[da:vat do porʒa:tku]
to redo (do again)	**předělávat**	[prʃɛdela:vat]
paint	**barva** (ž)	[barva]
to paint (~ a wall)	**natírat**	[nati:rat]
house painter	**malíř** (m) **pokojů**	[mali:rʃ pokoju:]
paintbrush	**štětec** (m)	[ʃtetɛʦ]
whitewash	**omítka** (ž)	[omi:tka]
to whitewash (vt)	**bílit**	[bi:lɪt]
wallpaper	**tapety** (ž mn)	[tapɛtɪ]
to wallpaper (vt)	**vytapetovat**	[vɪtapɛtovat]
varnish	**lak** (m)	[lak]
to varnish (vt)	**lakovat**	[lakovat]

101. Plumbing

water	**voda** (ž)	[voda]
hot water	**teplá voda** (ž)	[tɛpla: voda]

cold water	**studená voda** (ž)	[studɛna: voda]
faucet	**kohout** (m)	[kohout]
drop (of water)	**kapka** (ž)	[kapka]
to drip (vi)	**kapat**	[kapat]
to leak (ab. pipe)	**téci**	[tɛ:ʦɪ]
leak (pipe ~)	**tečení** (s)	[tɛʧɛni:]
puddle	**louže** (ž)	[louʒe]
pipe	**trubka** (ž)	[trupka]
valve (e.g., ball ~)	**ventil** (m)	[vɛntɪl]
to be clogged up	**zacpat se**	[zaʦpat sɛ]
tools	**nástroje** (m mn)	[nastrojɛ]
adjustable wrench	**stavitelný klíč** (m)	[stavɪtɛlni: kli:ʧ]
to unscrew (lid, filter, etc.)	**ukroutit**	[ukroutɪt]
to screw (tighten)	**zakroutit**	[zakroutɪt]
to unclog (vt)	**pročišťovat**	[proʧɪʃtʲovat]
plumber	**instalatér** (m)	[ɪnstalatɛ:r]
basement	**sklep** (m)	[sklɛp]
sewerage (system)	**kanalizace** (ž)	[kanalɪzaʦɛ]

102. Fire. Conflagration

fire (accident)	**oheň** (m)	[ohɛnʲ]
flame	**plamen** (m)	[plamɛn]
spark	**jiskra** (ž)	[jɪskra]
smoke (from fire)	**kouř** (m)	[kourʃ]
torch (flaming stick)	**pochodeň** (ž)	[poxodɛnʲ]
campfire	**oheň** (m)	[ohɛnʲ]
gas, gasoline	**benzín** (m)	[bɛnzi:n]
kerosene (type of fuel)	**petrolej** (m)	[pɛtrolɛj]
flammable (adj)	**hořlavý**	[horʒlavi:]
explosive (adj)	**výbušný**	[vi:buʃni:]
NO SMOKING	**ZÁKAZ KOUŘENÍ**	[za:kaz kourʒɛni:]
safety	**bezpečnost** (ž)	[bɛzpɛʧnost]
danger	**nebezpečí** (s)	[nɛbɛzpɛʧi:]
dangerous (adj)	**nebezpečný**	[nɛbɛzpɛʧni:]
to catch fire	**začít hořet**	[zaʧi:t horʒɛt]
explosion	**výbuch** (m)	[vi:bux]
to set fire	**zapálit**	[zapa:lɪt]
arsonist	**žhář** (m)	[ʒha:rʃ]
arson	**žhářství** (s)	[ʒha:rʃstvi:]
to blaze (vi)	**planout**	[planout]
to burn (be on fire)	**hořet**	[horʒɛt]

to burn down	**shořet**	[sxorʒɛt]
to call the fire department	**zavolat hasiče**	[zavolat hasiʧɛ]
firefighter, fireman	**hasič** (m)	[hasɪʧ]
fire truck	**hasičské auto** (m)	[hasɪʧske: auto]
fire department	**hasičský sbor** (m)	[hasɪʧski: zbor]
fire truck ladder	**požární žebřík** (m)	[poʒa:rni: ʒebrʒi:k]
fire hose	**hadice** (ž)	[hadɪʦɛ]
fire extinguisher	**hasicí přístroj** (m)	[hasɪʦi: prʃi:stroj]
helmet	**přilba** (ž)	[prʃɪlba]
siren	**houkačka** (ž)	[houkaʧka]
to cry (for help)	**křičet**	[krʃɪʧɛt]
to call for help	**volat o pomoc**	[volat o pomoʦ]
rescuer	**záchranář** (m)	[za:xrana:rʃ]
to rescue (vt)	**zachraňovat**	[zaxranʲovat]
to arrive (vi)	**přijet**	[prʃɪjɛt]
to extinguish (vt)	**hasit**	[hasɪt]
water	**voda** (ž)	[voda]
sand	**písek** (m)	[pi:sɛk]
ruins (destruction)	**zřícenina** (ž)	[zrʒi:ʦɛnɪna]
to collapse (building, etc.)	**zřítit se**	[zrʒi:tɪt sɛ]
to fall down (vi)	**zhroutit se**	[zhroutɪt sɛ]
to cave in (ceiling, floor)	**zřítit se**	[zrʒi:tɪt sɛ]
piece of debris	**úlomek** (m)	[u:lomɛk]
ash	**popel** (m)	[popɛl]
to suffocate (die)	**udusit se**	[udusɪt sɛ]
to be killed (perish)	**zahynout**	[zahɪnout]

HUMAN ACTIVITIES

Job. Business. Part 1

103. Office. Working in the office

office (company ~)	**kancelář** (ž)	[kantsɛla:rʃ]
office (of director, etc.)	**pracovna** (ž)	[pratsovna]
reception desk	**recepce** (ž)	[rɛtsɛptsɛ]
secretary	**sekretář** (m)	[sɛkrɛta:rʃ]
secretary (fem.)	**sekretářka** (ž)	[sɛkrɛta:rʃka]
director	**ředitel** (m)	[rʒɛdɪtɛl]
manager	**manažer** (m)	[manaʒer]
accountant	**účetní** (m, ž)	[u:ʧɛtni:]
employee	**zaměstnanec** (m)	[zamnestnanɛts]
furniture	**nábytek** (m)	[na:bɪtɛk]
desk	**stůl** (m)	[stu:l]
desk chair	**křeslo** (s)	[krʃɛslo]
drawer unit	**zásuvkový díl** (ž)	[za:sufkovi: di:l]
coat stand	**věšák** (m)	[veʃa:k]
computer	**počítač** (m)	[poʧi:taʧ]
printer	**tiskárna** (ž)	[tɪska:rna]
fax machine	**fax** (m)	[faks]
photocopier	**kopírovací přístroj** (m)	[kopi:rovatsi: prʃi:stroj]
paper	**papír** (m)	[papi:r]
office supplies	**kancelářské potřeby** (ž mn)	[kantsɛlarʃskɛ: potrʃɛbɪ]
mouse pad	**podložka** (ž) **pro myš**	[podloʃka pro mɪʃ]
sheet (of paper)	**list** (m)	[lɪst]
binder	**fascikl** (m)	[fastsɪkl]
catalog	**katalog** (m)	[katalok]
phone directory	**příručka** (ž)	[prʃi:ruʧka]
documentation	**dokumentace** (ž)	[dokumɛntatsɛ]
brochure (e.g., 12 pages ~)	**brožura** (ž)	[broʒura]
leaflet (promotional ~)	**leták** (m)	[lɛta:k]
sample	**vzor** (m)	[vzor]
training meeting	**trénink** (m)	[trɛ:nɪŋk]
meeting (of managers)	**porada** (ž)	[porada]
lunch time	**polední přestávka** (ž)	[polɛdni: prʃɛsta:fka]

to make a copy	**dělat kopii**	[delat kopɪjɪ]
to make multiple copies	**rozmnožit**	[rozmnoʒɪt]
to receive a fax	**přijímat fax**	[prʃɪji:mat faks]
to send a fax	**odesílat fax**	[odɛsi:lat faks]
to call (by phone)	**zavolat**	[zavolat]
to answer (vt)	**odpovědět**	[otpovedet]
to put through	**spojit**	[spojɪt]
to arrange, to set up	**stanovovat**	[stanovovat]
to demonstrate (vt)	**demonstrovat**	[dɛmonstrovat]
to be absent	**být nepřítomen**	[bi:t nɛprʃi:tomɛn]
absence	**absence** (ž)	[apsɛntsɛ]

104. Business processes. Part 1

business	**podnik** (m)	[podnɪk]
occupation	**práce** (ž)	[pra:tsɛ]
firm	**firma** (ž)	[fɪrma]
company	**společnost** (ž)	[spolɛtʃnost]
corporation	**korporace** (ž)	[korporatsɛ]
enterprise	**podnik** (m)	[podnɪk]
agency	**agentura** (ž)	[agɛntura]
agreement (contract)	**smlouva** (ž)	[smlouva]
contract	**kontrakt** (m)	[kontrakt]
deal	**obchod** (m)	[obxot]
order (to place an ~)	**objednávka** (ž)	[objɛdna:fka]
terms (of the contract)	**podmínka** (ž)	[podmi:ŋka]
wholesale (adv)	**ve velkém**	[vɛ vɛlkɛ:m]
wholesale (adj)	**velkoobchodní**	[vɛlkoobxodni:]
wholesale (n)	**prodej** (m) **ve velkém**	[prodɛj vɛ vɛlkɛ:m]
retail (adj)	**maloobchodní**	[maloobxodni:]
retail (n)	**prodej** (m) **v drobném**	[prodɛj v drobnɛ:m]
competitor	**konkurent** (m)	[koŋkurɛnt]
competition	**konkurence** (ž)	[koŋkurɛntsɛ]
to compete (vi)	**konkurovat**	[koŋkurovat]
partner (associate)	**partner** (m)	[partnɛr]
partnership	**partnerství** (s)	[partnɛrstvi:]
crisis	**krize** (ž)	[krɪzɛ]
bankruptcy	**bankrot** (m)	[baŋkrot]
to go bankrupt	**zbankrotovat**	[zbaŋkrotovat]
difficulty	**potíž** (ž)	[poti:ʃ]
problem	**problém** (m)	[problɛ:m]
catastrophe	**katastrofa** (ž)	[katastrofa]
economy	**ekonomika** (ž)	[ɛkonomɪka]

economic (~ growth)	**ekonomický**	[ɛkonomɪʦki:]
economic recession	**hospodářský pokles** (m)	[hospoda:rʃski: poklɛs]
goal (aim)	**cíl** (m)	[ʦi:l]
task	**úkol** (m)	[u:kol]
to trade (vi)	**obchodovat**	[obxodovat]
network (distribution ~)	**síť** (ž)	[si:tʲ]
inventory (stock)	**sklad** (m)	[sklat]
range (assortment)	**sortiment** (m)	[sortɪmɛnt]
leader (leading company)	**předák** (m)	[prʃɛda:k]
large (~ company)	**velký**	[vɛlki:]
monopoly	**monopol** (m)	[monopol]
theory	**teorie** (ž)	[tɛorɪe]
practice	**praxe** (ž)	[praksɛ]
experience (in my ~)	**zkušenost** (ž)	[skuʃɛnost]
trend (tendency)	**tendence** (ž)	[tɛndɛnʦɛ]
development	**rozvoj** (m)	[rozvoj]

105. Business processes. Part 2

profit (foregone ~)	**výhoda** (ž)	[vi:hoda]
profitable (~ deal)	**výhodný**	[vi:hodni:]
delegation (group)	**delegace** (ž)	[dɛlɛgaʦɛ]
salary	**mzda** (ž)	[mzda]
to correct (an error)	**opravovat**	[opravovat]
business trip	**služební cesta** (ž)	[sluʒebni: ʦɛsta]
commission	**komise** (ž)	[komɪsɛ]
to control (vt)	**kontrolovat**	[kontrolovat]
conference	**konference** (ž)	[konfɛrɛnʦɛ]
license	**licence** (ž)	[lɪʦɛnʦɛ]
reliable (~ partner)	**spolehlivý**	[spolɛhlɪvi:]
initiative (undertaking)	**iniciativa** (ž)	[ɪnɪʦɪatɪva]
norm (standard)	**norma** (ž)	[norma]
circumstance	**okolnost** (ž)	[okolnost]
duty (of employee)	**povinnost** (ž)	[povɪnnost]
organization (company)	**organizace** (ž)	[organɪzaʦɛ]
organization (process)	**organizace** (ž)	[organɪzaʦɛ]
organized (adj)	**organizovaný**	[organɪzovani:]
cancellation	**zrušení** (s)	[zruʃɛni:]
to cancel (call off)	**zrušit**	[zruʃɪt]
report (official ~)	**zpráva** (ž)	[spra:va]
patent	**patent** (m)	[patɛnt]
to patent (obtain patent)	**patentovat**	[patɛntovat]

to plan (vt)	**plánovat**	[pla:novat]
bonus (money)	**prémie** (ž)	[prɛ:mɪe]
professional (adj)	**profesionální**	[profɛsɪona:lni:]
procedure	**procedura** (ž)	[proʦɛdura]
to examine (contract, etc.)	**projednat**	[projɛdnat]
calculation	**výpočet** (m)	[vi:poʧɛt]
reputation	**reputace** (ž)	[rɛputaʦɛ]
risk	**riziko** (s)	[rɪzɪko]
to manage, to run	**řídit**	[rʒi:dɪt]
information (report)	**údaje** (m mn)	[u:dajɛ]
property	**vlastnictví** (s)	[vlastnɪʦtvi:]
union	**unie** (ž)	[unɪe]
life insurance	**pojištění** (s) **života**	[pojɪʃteni: ʒɪvota]
to insure (vt)	**pojišťovat**	[pojɪʃtʲovat]
insurance	**pojistka** (ž)	[pojɪstka]
auction (~ sale)	**dražba** (ž)	[draʒba]
to notify (inform)	**uvědomit**	[uvedomɪt]
management (process)	**řízení** (s)	[rʒi:zɛni:]
service (~ industry)	**služba** (ž)	[sluʒba]
forum	**fórum** (s)	[fo:rum]
to function (vi)	**fungovat**	[fungovat]
stage (phase)	**etapa** (ž)	[ɛtapa]
legal (~ services)	**právnický**	[pra:vnɪʦki:]
lawyer (legal advisor)	**právník** (m)	[pra:vni:k]

106. Production. Works

plant	**závod** (m)	[za:vot]
factory	**továrna** (ž)	[tova:rna]
workshop	**dílna** (ž)	[di:lna]
works, production site	**podnik** (m)	[podnɪk]
industry (manufacturing)	**průmysl** (m)	[pru:mɪsl]
industrial (adj)	**průmyslový**	[pru:mɪslovi:]
heavy industry	**těžký průmysl** (m)	[teʃki: pru:mɪsl]
light industry	**lehký průmysl** (m)	[lɛhki: pru:mɪsl]
products	**výroba** (ž)	[vi:roba]
to produce (vt)	**vyrábět**	[vɪra:bet]
raw materials	**surovina** (ž)	[surovɪna]
foreman (construction ~)	**četař** (m)	[ʧɛtarʃ]
workers team (crew)	**brigáda** (ž)	[brɪga:da]
worker	**dělník** (m)	[delni:k]
working day	**pracovní den** (m)	[praʦovni: dɛn]

pause (rest break)	**přestávka** (ž)	[prʃɛsta:fka]
meeting	**schůze** (ž)	[sxu:zɛ]
to discuss (vt)	**projednávat**	[projɛdna:vat]
plan	**plán** (m)	[pla:n]
to fulfill the plan	**plnit plán**	[plnɪt pla:n]
rate of output	**norma** (ž)	[norma]
quality	**kvalita** (ž)	[kvalɪta]
control (checking)	**kontrola** (ž)	[kontrola]
quality control	**kontrola** (ž) **kvality**	[kontrola kvalɪtɪ]
workplace safety	**bezpečnost** (ž) **práce**	[bɛzpɛʧnost pra:ʦɛ]
discipline	**kázeň** (ž)	[ka:zɛnʲ]
violation (of safety rules, etc.)	**přestupek** (m)	[prʃɛstupɛk]
to violate (rules)	**nedodržovat**	[nɛdodrʒovat]
strike	**stávka** (ž)	[sta:fka]
striker	**stávkující** (m)	[sta:fkuji:ʦi:]
to be on strike	**stávkovat**	[sta:fkovat]
labor union	**odbory** (m)	[odborɪ]
to invent (machine, etc.)	**vynalézat**	[vɪnalɛ:zat]
invention	**vynález** (m)	[vɪnalɛ:z]
research	**výzkum** (m)	[vi:skum]
to improve (make better)	**zlepšovat**	[zlɛpʃovat]
technology	**technologie** (ž)	[tɛxnologɪe]
technical drawing	**výkres** (m)	[vi:krɛs]
load, cargo	**náklad** (m)	[na:klat]
loader (person)	**nakládač** (m)	[nakla:daʧ]
to load (vehicle, etc.)	**nakládat**	[nakla:dat]
loading (process)	**nakládání** (s)	[nakla:da:ni:]
to unload (vi, vt)	**vykládat**	[vɪkla:dat]
unloading	**vykládání** (s)	[vɪkla:da:ni:]
transportation	**doprava** (ž)	[doprava]
transportation company	**dopravní společnost** (ž)	[dopravni: spolɛʧnost]
to transport (vt)	**dopravovat**	[dopravovat]
freight car	**nákladní vůz** (m)	[na:kladni: vu:z]
tank (e.g., oil ~)	**cisterna** (ž)	[ʦɪstɛrna]
truck	**nákladní auto** (s)	[na:kladni: auto]
machine tool	**stroj** (m)	[stroj]
mechanism	**mechanismus** (m)	[mɛxanɪzmus]
industrial waste	**odpad** (m)	[otpat]
packing (process)	**balení** (s)	[balɛni:]
to pack (vt)	**zabalit**	[zabalɪt]

107. Contract. Agreement

contract	**kontrakt** (m)	[kontrakt]
agreement	**dohoda** (ž)	[dohoda]
addendum	**příloha** (ž)	[prʃi:loha]
to sign a contract	**uzavřít kontrakt**	[uzavrʒi:t kontrakt]
signature	**podpis** (m)	[potpɪs]
to sign (vt)	**podepsat**	[podɛpsat]
seal (stamp)	**razítko** (s)	[razi:tko]
subject of the contract	**předmět** (m) **smlouvy**	[prʃɛdmnet smlouvɪ]
clause	**bod** (m)	[bot]
parties (in contract)	**strany** (ž mn)	[stranɪ]
legal address	**sídlo** (s)	[si:dlo]
to violate the contract	**porušit kontrakt**	[poruʃɪt kontrakt]
commitment (obligation)	**závazek** (m)	[za:vazɛk]
responsibility	**odpovědnost** (ž)	[otpovednost]
force majeure	**vyšší moc** (ž)	[vɪʃi: mots]
dispute	**spor** (m)	[spor]
penalties	**sankční pokuta** (ž)	[saŋktʃni: pokuta]

108. Import & Export

import	**dovoz, import** (m)	[dovoz], [ɪmport]
importer	**dovozce** (m)	[dovoztsɛ]
to import (vt)	**dovážet**	[dova:ʒet]
import (as adj.)	**dovozový**	[dovozovi:]
export (exportation)	**vývoz, export** (m)	[vi:vos], [ɛksport]
exporter	**vývozce** (m)	[vi:voztsɛ]
to export (vi, vt)	**vyvážet**	[vɪva:ʒet]
export (as adj.)	**vývozní**	[vi:vozni:]
goods (merchandise)	**zboží** (s)	[zboʒi:]
consignment, lot	**partie** (ž)	[partɪe]
weight	**váha** (ž)	[va:ha]
volume	**objem** (m)	[objɛm]
cubic meter	**krychlový metr** (m)	[krɪxlovi: mɛtr]
manufacturer	**výrobce** (m)	[vi:robtsɛ]
transportation company	**dopravní společnost** (ž)	[dopravni: spolɛtʃnost]
container	**kontejner** (m)	[kontɛjnɛr]
border	**hranice** (ž)	[hranɪtsɛ]
customs	**celnice** (ž)	[tsɛlnɪtsɛ]
customs duty	**clo** (s)	[tslo]

customs officer	**celník** (m)	[ʦɛlni:k]
smuggling	**pašování** (s)	[paʃova:ni:]
contraband (smuggled goods)	**pašované zboží** (s mn)	[paʃovanɛ: zboʒi:]

109. Finances

stock (share)	**akcie** (ž)	[akʦɪe]
bond (certificate)	**dluhopis** (m)	[dluhopɪs]
promissory note	**směnka** (ž)	[smneŋka]
stock exchange	**burza** (ž)	[burza]
stock price	**kurz** (m) **akcií**	[kurs akʦɪji:]
to go down (become cheaper)	**zlevnět**	[zlɛvnet]
to go up (become more expensive)	**zdražit**	[zdraʒɪt]
share	**podíl** (m)	[podi:l]
controlling interest	**kontrolní balík** (m)	[kontrolni: bali:k]
investment	**investice** (ž mn)	[ɪnvɛstɪʦɛ]
to invest (vt)	**investovat**	[ɪnvɛstovat]
percent	**procento** (s)	[proʦɛnto]
interest (on investment)	**úroky** (m mn)	[u:rokɪ]
profit	**zisk** (m)	[zɪsk]
profitable (adj)	**ziskový**	[zɪskovi:]
tax	**daň** (ž)	[danʲ]
currency (foreign ~)	**měna** (ž)	[mnena]
national (adj)	**národní**	[na:rodni:]
exchange (currency ~)	**výměna** (ž)	[vi:mnena]
accountant	**účetní** (m, ž)	[u:ʧɛtni:]
accounting	**účtárna** (ž)	[u:ʧta:rna]
bankruptcy	**bankrot** (m)	[baŋkrot]
collapse, crash	**krach** (m)	[krax]
ruin	**bankrot** (m)	[baŋkrot]
to be ruined (financially)	**zkrachovat**	[skraxovat]
inflation	**inflace** (ž)	[ɪnflaʦɛ]
devaluation	**devalvace** (ž)	[dɛvalvaʦɛ]
capital	**kapitál** (m)	[kapɪta:l]
income	**příjem** (m)	[prʃi:jɛm]
turnover	**obrat** (m)	[obrat]
resources	**zdroje** (m mn)	[zdrojɛ]
monetary resources	**peněžní prostředky** (m mn)	[pɛneʒni: prostrʃɛtkɪ]

overhead	**režijní náklady** (m mn)	[rɛʒɪjni: na:kladɪ]
to reduce (expenses)	**snížit**	[sni:ʒɪt]

110. Marketing

marketing	**marketing** (m)	[markɛtɪŋk]
market	**trh** (m)	[trx]
market segment	**segment** (m) **trhu**	[sɛgmɛnt trhu]
product	**produkt** (m)	[produkt]
goods (merchandise)	**zboží** (s)	[zboʒi:]
brand	**obchodní značka** (ž)	[obxodni: znaʧka]
logotype	**firemní značka** (ž)	[fɪrɛmni: znaʧka]
logo	**logo** (s)	[logo]
demand	**poptávka** (ž)	[popta:fka]
supply	**nabídka** (ž)	[nabi:tka]
need	**potřeba** (ž)	[potrʃɛba]
consumer	**spotřebitel** (m)	[spotrʃɛbɪtɛl]
analysis	**analýza** (ž)	[anali:za]
to analyze (vt)	**analyzovat**	[analɪzovat]
positioning	**určování** (s) **pozice**	[urʧova:ni: pozɪʦɛ]
to position (vt)	**určovat pozici**	[urʧovat pozɪʦɪ]
price	**cena** (ž)	[ʦɛna]
pricing policy	**cenová politika** (ž)	[ʦɛnova: polɪtɪka]
price formation	**tvorba** (ž) **cen**	[tvorba ʦɛn]

111. Advertising

advertising	**reklama** (ž)	[rɛklama]
to advertise (vt)	**dělat reklamu**	[delat rɛklamu]
budget	**rozpočet** (m)	[rozpoʧɛt]
ad, advertisement	**reklama** (ž)	[rɛklama]
TV advertising	**televizní reklama** (ž)	[tɛlɛvɪzni: rɛklama]
radio advertising	**rozhlasová reklama** (ž)	[rozhlasova: rɛklama]
outdoor advertising	**venkovní reklama** (ž)	[vɛŋkovni: rɛklama]
mass media	**média** (s mn)	[mɛ:dɪa]
periodical (n)	**periodikum** (s)	[pɛrɪodɪkum]
image (public appearance)	**image** (ž)	[ɪmɪʤ]
slogan	**heslo** (s)	[hɛslo]
motto (maxim)	**heslo** (s)	[hɛslo]
campaign	**kampaň** (ž)	[kampanʲ]
advertising campaign	**reklamní kampaň** (ž)	[rɛklamni: kampanʲ]

target group	**cílové posluchačstvo** (s)	[ʦi:lovɛ: posluxaʧstvo]
business card	**vizitka** (ž)	[vɪzɪtka]
leaflet (promotional ~)	**leták** (m)	[lɛta:k]
brochure (e.g., 12 pages ~)	**brožura** (ž)	[broʒura]
pamphlet	**skládanka** (ž)	[skla:daŋka]
newsletter	**bulletin** (m)	[bɪltɛ:n]
signboard (store sign, etc.)	**reklamní tabule** (ž)	[rɛklamni: tabulɛ]
poster	**plakát** (m)	[plaka:t]
billboard	**billboard** (m)	[bɪlbo:rt]

112. Banking

bank	**banka** (ž)	[baŋka]
branch (of bank, etc.)	**pobočka** (ž)	[pobotʃka]
bank clerk, consultant	**konzultant** (m)	[konzultant]
manager (director)	**správce** (m)	[spra:vʦɛ]
bank account	**účet** (m)	[u:ʧɛt]
account number	**číslo** (s) **účtu**	[ʧi:slo u:ʧtu]
checking account	**běžný účet** (m)	[beʒni: u:ʧɛt]
savings account	**spořitelní účet** (m)	[sporʒɪtɛlni: u:ʧɛt]
to open an account	**založit účet**	[zaloʒɪt u:ʧɛt]
to close the account	**uzavřít účet**	[uzavrʒi:t u:ʧɛt]
to deposit into the account	**uložit na účet**	[uloʒɪt na u:ʧɛt]
to withdraw (vt)	**vybrat z účtu**	[vɪbrat s u:ʧtu]
deposit	**vklad** (m)	[fklat]
to make a deposit	**uložit vklad**	[uloʒɪt fklat]
wire transfer	**převod** (m)	[prʃɛvot]
to wire, to transfer	**převést**	[prʃɛvɛ:st]
sum	**částka** (ž)	[ʧa:stka]
How much?	**Kolik?**	[kolɪk]
signature	**podpis** (m)	[potpɪs]
to sign (vt)	**podepsat**	[podɛpsat]
credit card	**kreditní karta** (ž)	[krɛdɪtni: karta]
code (PIN code)	**kód** (m)	[ko:t]
credit card number	**číslo** (s) **kreditní karty**	[ʧi:slo krɛdɪtni: kartɪ]
ATM	**bankomat** (m)	[baŋkomat]
check	**šek** (m)	[ʃɛk]
to write a check	**vystavit šek**	[vɪstavɪt ʃɛk]
checkbook	**šeková knížka** (ž)	[ʃɛkova: kni:ʃka]
loan (bank ~)	**úvěr** (m)	[u:ver]

to apply for a loan	**žádat o úvěr**	[ʒa:dat o u:ver]
to get a loan	**brát na úvěr**	[bra:t na u:ver]
to give a loan	**poskytovat úvěr**	[poskɪtovat u:ver]
guarantee	**kauce** (ž)	[kautsɛ]

113. Telephone. Phone conversation

telephone	**telefon** (m)	[tɛlɛfon]
cell phone	**mobilní telefon** (m)	[mobɪlni: tɛlɛfon]
answering machine	**záznamník** (m)	[za:znamni:k]
to call (by phone)	**volat**	[volat]
phone call	**hovor** (m), **volání** (s)	[hovor], [vola:ni:]
to dial a number	**vytočit číslo**	[vɪtotʃɪt tʃi:slo]
Hello!	**Prosím!**	[prosi:m]
to ask (vt)	**zeptat se**	[zɛptat sɛ]
to answer (vi, vt)	**odpovědět**	[otpovedet]
to hear (vt)	**slyšet**	[slɪʃɛt]
well (adv)	**dobře**	[dobrʒɛ]
not well (adv)	**špatně**	[ʃpatne]
noises (interference)	**poruchy** (ž mn)	[poruxɪ]
receiver	**sluchátko** (s)	[sluxa:tko]
to pick up (~ the phone)	**vzít sluchátko**	[vzi:t sluxa:tko]
to hang up (~ the phone)	**zavěsit sluchátko**	[zavesɪt sluxa:tko]
busy (engaged)	**obsazeno**	[opsazɛno]
to ring (ab. phone)	**zvonit**	[zvonɪt]
telephone book	**telefonní seznam** (m)	[tɛlɛfonni: sɛznam]
local (adj)	**místní**	[mi:stni:]
local call	**místní hovor** (m)	[mi:stni: hovor]
long distance (~ call)	**dálkový**	[da:lkovi:]
long-distance call	**dálkový hovor** (m)	[da:lkovi: hovor]
international (adj)	**mezinárodní**	[mɛzɪna:rodni:]
international call	**mezinárodní hovor** (m)	[mɛzɪna:rodni: hovor]

114. Cell phone

cell phone	**mobilní telefon** (m)	[mobɪlni: tɛlɛfon]
display	**displej** (m)	[dɪsplɛj]
button	**tlačítko** (s)	[tlatʃi:tko]
SIM card	**SIM karta** (ž)	[sɪm karta]
battery	**baterie** (ž)	[batɛrɪe]
to be dead (battery)	**vybít se**	[vɪbi:t sɛ]

charger	**nabíječka** (ž)	[nabi:jɛʧka]
menu	**nabídka** (ž)	[nabi:tka]
settings	**nastavení** (s)	[nastavɛni:]
tune (melody)	**melodie** (ž)	[mɛlodɪe]
to select (vt)	**vybrat**	[vɪbrat]
calculator	**kalkulačka** (ž)	[kalkulaʧka]
voice mail	**hlasová schránka** (ž)	[hlasova: sxra:ŋka]
alarm clock	**budík** (m)	[budi:k]
contacts	**telefonní seznam** (m)	[tɛlɛfonni: sɛznam]
SMS (text message)	**SMS zpráva** (ž)	[ɛsɛmɛs spra:va]
subscriber	**účastník** (m)	[u:ʧastni:k]

115. Stationery

ballpoint pen	**pero** (s)	[pɛro]
fountain pen	**plnicí pero** (s)	[plnɪʦi: pɛro]
pencil	**tužka** (ž)	[tuʃka]
highlighter	**značkovač** (m)	[znaʧkovaʧ]
felt-tip pen	**fix** (m)	[fɪks]
notepad	**notes** (m)	[notɛs]
agenda (diary)	**diář** (m)	[dɪa:rʃ]
ruler	**pravítko** (s)	[pravi:tko]
calculator	**kalkulačka** (ž)	[kalkulaʧka]
eraser	**guma** (ž)	[guma]
thumbtack	**napínáček** (m)	[napi:na:ʧɛk]
paper clip	**svorka** (ž)	[svorka]
glue	**lepidlo** (s)	[lɛpɪdlo]
stapler	**sešívačka** (ž)	[sɛʃi:vaʧka]
hole punch	**dírkovačka** (ž)	[di:rkovaʧka]
pencil sharpener	**ořezávátko** (s)	[orʒɛza:va:tko]

116. Various kinds of documents

account (report)	**zpráva** (ž)	[spra:va]
agreement	**dohoda** (ž)	[dohoda]
application form	**přihláška** (ž)	[prʃɪhla:ʃka]
authentic (adj)	**původní**	[pu:vodni:]
badge (identity tag)	**jmenovka** (ž)	[jmɛnofka]
business card	**vizitka** (ž)	[vɪzɪtka]
certificate (~ of quality)	**certifikát** (m)	[ʦɛrtɪfɪka:t]
check (e.g., draw a ~)	**šek** (m)	[ʃɛk]

check (in restaurant)	**účet** (m)	[u:ʧɛt]
constitution	**ústava** (ž)	[u:stava]
contract (agreement)	**smlouva** (ž)	[smlouva]
copy	**kopie** (ž)	[kopɪe]
copy (of contract, etc.)	**výtisk** (m)	[vi:tɪsk]
customs declaration	**prohlášení** (s)	[prohla:ʃɛni:]
document	**dokument** (m)	[dokumɛnt]
driver's license	**řidičský průkaz** (m)	[rʒɪdɪʧski: pru:kaz]
addendum	**příloha** (ž)	[prʃi:loha]
form	**anketa** (ž)	[aŋkɛta]
ID card (e.g., FBI ~)	**průkaz** (m)	[pru:kaz]
inquiry (request)	**dotaz** (m)	[dotaz]
invitation card	**pozvánka** (ž)	[pozva:ŋka]
invoice	**účet** (m)	[u:ʧɛt]
law	**zákon** (m)	[za:kon]
letter (mail)	**dopis** (m)	[dopɪs]
letterhead	**blanket** (m)	[blaŋkɛt]
list (of names, etc.)	**seznam** (m)	[sɛznam]
manuscript	**rukopis** (m)	[rukopɪs]
newsletter	**bulletin** (m)	[bɪltɛ:n]
note (short letter)	**zpráva** (ž)	[spra:va]
pass (for worker, visitor)	**propustka** (ž)	[propustka]
passport	**pas** (m)	[pas]
permit	**povolení** (s)	[povolɛni:]
résumé	**resumé** (s)	[rɛzimɛ:]
debt note, IOU	**dlužní úpis** (m)	[dluʒnɪ u:pɪs]
receipt (for purchase)	**stvrzenka** (ž)	[stvrzɛŋka]
sales slip, receipt	**stvrzenka** (ž)	[stvrzɛŋka]
report (mil.)	**hlášení** (s)	[hla:ʃɛni:]
to show (ID, etc.)	**předkládat**	[prʃɛtkla:dat]
to sign (vt)	**podepsat**	[podɛpsat]
signature	**podpis** (m)	[potpɪs]
seal (stamp)	**razítko** (s)	[razi:tko]
text	**text** (m)	[tɛkst]
ticket (for entry)	**průkaz** (m)	[pru:kaz]
to cross out	**škrtnout**	[ʃkrtnout]
to fill out (~ a form)	**vyplnit**	[vɪplnɪt]
waybill (shipping invoice)	**dodací list** (m)	[dodaʦi: li:st]
will (testament)	**testament** (m)	[tɛstamɛnt]

117. Kinds of business

accounting services	**účetnické služby** (ž mn)	[u:ʧɛtnɪʦkɛ: sluʒbɪ]
advertising	**reklama** (ž)	[rɛklama]

advertising agency	**reklamní agentura** (ž)	[rɛklamni: agɛntura]
air-conditioners	**klimatizátory** (m mn)	[klɪmatɪza:torɪ]
airline	**letecká společnost** (ž)	[lɛtɛtska: spolɛtʃnost]
alcoholic beverages	**alkoholické nápoje** (m mn)	[alkoholɪtskɛ: na:pojɛ]
antiques (antique dealers)	**starožitnictví** (s)	[staroʒɪtnɪtstvi:]
art gallery (contemporary ~)	**galerie** (ž)	[galɛrɪe]
audit services	**auditorské služby** (ž mn)	[audɪtorskɛ: sluʒbɪ]
banking industry	**bankovnictví** (s)	[baŋkovnɪtstvi:]
bar	**bar** (m)	[bar]
beauty parlor	**kosmetický salón** (m)	[kosmɛtɪtski: salo:n]
bookstore	**knihkupectví** (s)	[knɪxkupɛtstvi:]
brewery	**pivovar** (m)	[pɪvovar]
business center	**obchodní centrum** (s)	[obxodni: tsɛntrum]
business school	**obchodní škola** (ž)	[obxodni: ʃkola]
casino	**kasino** (s)	[kasi:no]
construction	**stavebnictví** (s)	[stavɛbnɪtstvi:]
consulting	**poradenství** (s)	[poradɛnstvi:]
dental clinic	**stomatologie** (ž)	[stomatologɪe]
design	**design** (m)	[dɪzajn]
drugstore, pharmacy	**lékárna** (ž)	[lɛ:ka:rna]
dry cleaners	**čistírna** (ž)	[tʃɪsti:rna]
employment agency	**kádrová kancelář** (ž)	[ka:drova: kantsɛla:rʃ]
financial services	**finanční služby** (ž mn)	[fɪnantʃni: sluʒbɪ]
food products	**potraviny** (ž mn)	[potravɪnɪ]
funeral home	**pohřební ústav** (m)	[pohrʒɛbni: u:staf]
furniture (e.g., house ~)	**nábytek** (m)	[na:bɪtɛk]
clothing, garment	**oblečení** (s)	[oblɛtʃɛni:]
hotel	**hotel** (m)	[hotɛl]
ice-cream	**zmrzlina** (ž)	[zmrzlɪna]
industry (manufacturing)	**průmysl** (m)	[pru:mɪsl]
insurance	**pojištění** (s)	[pojɪʃtɛni:]
Internet	**internet** (m)	[ɪntɛrnɛt]
investments (finance)	**investice** (ž mn)	[ɪnvɛstɪtsɛ]
jeweler	**klenotník** (m)	[klɛnotni:k]
jewelry	**klenotnické výrobky** (m mn)	[klɛnotnɪtskɛ: vi:ropkɪ]
laundry (shop)	**prádelna** (ž)	[pra:dɛlna]
legal advisor	**právnické služby** (ž mn)	[pra:vnɪtskɛ: sluʒbɪ]
light industry	**lehký průmysl** (m)	[lɛhki: pru:mɪsl]
magazine	**časopis** (m)	[tʃasopɪs]
mail order selling	**prodej** (m) **podle katalogu**	[prodɛj podlɛ katalogu]
medicine	**lékařství** (s)	[lɛ:karʃstvi:]
movie theater	**biograf** (m)	[bɪograf]

museum	**muzeum** (s)	[muzɛum]
news agency	**zpravodajská agentura** (ž)	[spravodajska: agɛntura]
newspaper	**noviny** (ž mn)	[novɪnɪ]
nightclub	**noční klub** (m)	[notʃni: klup]
oil (petroleum)	**ropa** (ž)	[ropa]
courier services	**kurýrská služba** (ž)	[kuri:rska: sluʒba]
pharmaceutics	**farmacie** (ž)	[farmatsɪe]
printing (industry)	**polygrafie** (ž)	[polɪgrafɪe]
publishing house	**nakladatelství** (s)	[nakladatɛlstvi:]
radio (~ station)	**rozhlas** (m)	[rozhlas]
real estate	**nemovitost** (ž)	[nɛmovɪtost]
restaurant	**restaurace** (ž)	[rɛstauratsɛ]
security company	**bezpečnostní agentura** (ž)	[bɛzpɛtʃnostni: agɛntura]
sports	**sport** (m)	[sport]
stock exchange	**burza** (ž)	[burza]
store	**obchod** (m)	[obxot]
supermarket	**supermarket** (m)	[supɛrmarket]
swimming pool (public ~)	**bazén** (m)	[bazɛ:n]
tailor shop	**módní salón** (m)	[mo:dni: salo:n]
television	**televize** (ž)	[tɛlɛvɪzɛ]
theater	**divadlo** (s)	[dɪvadlo]
trade (commerce)	**obchod** (m)	[obxot]
transportation	**přeprava** (ž)	[prʃɛprava]
travel	**cestovní ruch** (m)	[tsɛstovni: rux]
veterinarian	**zvěrolékař** (m)	[zverolɛ:karʃ]
warehouse	**sklad** (m)	[sklat]
waste collection	**vyvážení** (s) **odpadků**	[vɪva:ʒeni: otpatku:]

Job. Business. Part 2

118. Show. Exhibition

exhibition, show	**výstava** (ž)	[vi:stava]
trade show	**obchodní výstava** (ž)	[obxodni: vi:stava]
participation	**účast** (ž)	[u:ʧast]
to participate (vi)	**zúčastnit se**	[zu:ʧastnɪt sɛ]
participant (exhibitor)	**účastník** (m)	[u:ʧastni:k]
director	**ředitel** (m)	[rʒɛdɪtɛl]
organizers' office	**organizační výbor** (m)	[organɪzaʧni: vi:bor]
organizer	**organizátor** (m)	[organɪza:tor]
to organize (vt)	**organizovat**	[organɪzovat]
participation form	**přihláška** (ž) **k účasti**	[prʃɪhla:ʃka k u:ʧastɪ]
to fill out (vt)	**vyplnit**	[vɪplnɪt]
details	**podrobnosti** (ž mn)	[podrobnostɪ]
information	**informace** (ž)	[ɪnformaʦɛ]
price (cost, rate)	**cena** (ž)	[ʦɛna]
including	**včetně**	[vʧɛtne]
to include (vt)	**zahrnovat**	[zahrnovat]
to pay (vi, vt)	**platit**	[platɪt]
registration fee	**registrační poplatek** (m)	[rɛgɪstraʧni: poplatɛk]
entrance	**vchod** (m)	[vxot]
pavilion, hall	**pavilón** (m)	[pavɪlo:n]
to register (vt)	**registrovat**	[rɛgɪstrovat]
badge (identity tag)	**jmenovka** (ž)	[jmɛnofka]
booth, stand	**stánek** (m)	[sta:nɛk]
to reserve, to book	**rezervovat**	[rɛzɛrvovat]
display case	**vitrina** (ž)	[vɪtrɪna]
spotlight	**svítidlo** (s)	[svi:tɪdlo]
design	**design** (m)	[dɪzajn]
to place (put, set)	**rozmisťovat**	[rozmɪsťovat]
distributor	**distributor** (m)	[dɪstrɪbutor]
supplier	**dodavatel** (m)	[dodavatɛl]
to supply (vt)	**dodávat**	[doda:vat]
country	**země** (ž)	[zɛmnɛ]
foreign (adj)	**zahraniční**	[zahranɪʧni:]

product	**produkt** (m)	[produkt]
association	**asociace** (ž)	[asotsɪatsɛ]
conference hall	**konferenční sál** (m)	[konfɛrɛntʃni: sa:l]
congress	**kongres** (m)	[kongrɛs]
contest (competition)	**soutěž** (ž)	[souteʃ]
visitor (attendee)	**návštěvník** (m)	[na:vʃtevni:k]
to visit (attend)	**navštěvovat**	[navʃtevovat]
customer	**zákazník** (m)	[za:kazni:k]

119. Mass Media

newspaper	**noviny** (ž mn)	[novɪnɪ]
magazine	**časopis** (m)	[tʃasopɪs]
press (printed media)	**tisk** (m)	[tɪsk]
radio	**rozhlas** (m)	[rozhlas]
radio station	**rozhlasová stanice** (ž)	[rozhlasova: stanɪtsɛ]
television	**televize** (ž)	[tɛlɛvɪzɛ]
presenter, host	**moderátor** (m)	[modɛra:tor]
newscaster	**hlasatel** (m)	[hlasatɛl]
commentator	**komentátor** (m)	[komɛnta:tor]
journalist	**novinář** (m)	[novɪna:rʃ]
correspondent (reporter)	**zpravodaj** (m)	[spravodaj]
press photographer	**fotožurnalista** (m)	[fotoʒurnalɪsta]
reporter	**reportér** (m)	[rɛportɛ:r]
editor	**redaktor** (m)	[rɛdaktor]
editor-in-chief	**šéfredaktor** (m)	[ʃɛ:frɛdaktor]
to subscribe (to ...)	**předplatit si**	[prʃɛtplatɪt sɪ]
subscription	**předplacení** (s)	[prʃɛtplatsɛni:]
subscriber	**předplatitel** (m)	[prʃɛtplatɪtɛl]
to read (vi, vt)	**číst**	[tʃi:st]
reader	**čtenář** (m)	[tʃtɛna:rʃ]
circulation (of newspaper)	**náklad** (m)	[na:klat]
monthly (adj)	**měsíční**	[mnesi:tʃni:]
weekly (adj)	**týdenní**	[ti:dɛnni:]
issue (edition)	**číslo** (s)	[tʃi:slo]
new (~ issue)	**čerstvý**	[tʃɛrstvi:]
headline	**titulek** (m)	[tɪtulɛk]
short article	**noticka** (ž)	[notɪtska]
column (regular article)	**rubrika** (ž)	[rubrɪka]
article	**článek** (m)	[tʃla:nɛk]
page	**stránka** (ž)	[stra:ŋka]
reportage, report	**reportáž** (ž)	[rɛporta:ʃ]
event (happening)	**událost** (ž)	[uda:lost]

sensation (news)	**senzace** (ž)	[sɛnzat͡sɛ]
scandal	**skandál** (m)	[skanda:l]
scandalous (adj)	**skandální**	[skanda:lni:]
great (~ scandal)	**halasný**	[halasni:]
show (e.g., cooking ~)	**pořad** (m)	[porʒat]
interview	**rozhovor** (m)	[rozhovor]
live broadcast	**přímý přenos** (m)	[prʃi:mi: prʃɛnos]
channel	**kanál** (m)	[kana:l]

120. Agriculture

agriculture	**zemědělství** (s)	[zɛmnedelstvi:]
peasant (masc.)	**rolník** (m)	[rolni:k]
peasant (fem.)	**rolnice** (ž)	[rolnɪt͡sɛ]
farmer	**farmář** (m)	[farma:rʃ]
tractor (farm ~)	**traktor** (m)	[traktor]
combine, harvester	**kombajn** (m)	[kombajn]
plow	**pluh** (m)	[plux]
to plow (vi, vt)	**orat**	[orat]
plowland	**ornice** (ž)	[ornɪt͡sɛ]
furrow (in field)	**brázda** (ž)	[bra:zda]
to sow (vi, vt)	**sít**	[si:t]
seeder	**sečka** (ž)	[sɛt͡ʃka]
sowing (process)	**setí** (s)	[sɛti:]
scythe	**kosa** (ž)	[kosa]
to mow, to scythe	**kosit**	[kosɪt]
spade (tool)	**lopata** (ž)	[lopata]
to till (vt)	**rýt**	[ri:t]
hoe	**motyka** (ž)	[motɪka]
to hoe, to weed	**plít**	[pli:t]
weed (plant)	**plevel** (m)	[plɛvɛl]
watering can	**konev** (ž)	[konɛf]
to water (plants)	**zalévat**	[zalɛ:vat]
watering (act)	**zalévání** (s)	[zalɛ:va:ni:]
pitchfork	**vidle** (ž mn)	[vɪdlɛ]
rake	**hrábě** (ž mn)	[hra:be]
fertilizer	**hnojivo** (s)	[hnojɪvo]
to fertilize (vt)	**hnojit**	[hnojɪt]
manure (fertilizer)	**hnůj** (m)	[hnu:j]
field	**pole** (s)	[polɛ]

meadow	**louka** (ž)	[louka]
vegetable garden	**zelinářská zahrada** (ž)	[zɛlɪna:rʃska: zahrada]
orchard (e.g., apple ~)	**zahrada** (ž)	[zahrada]
to graze (vt)	**pást**	[pa:st]
herder (herdsman)	**pasák** (m)	[pasa:k]
pasture	**pastvina** (ž)	[pastvɪna]
cattle breeding	**živočišná výroba** (ž)	[ʒɪvoʧɪʃna: vi:roba]
sheep farming	**chov** (m) **ovcí**	[xov ovʦi:]
plantation	**plantáž** (ž)	[planta:ʃ]
row (garden bed ~s)	**záhonek** (m)	[za:honɛk]
hothouse	**skleník** (m)	[sklɛni:k]
drought (lack of rain)	**sucho** (s)	[suxo]
dry (~ summer)	**suchý**	[suxi:]
cereal crops	**obilniny** (ž mn)	[obɪlnɪnɪ]
to harvest, to gather	**sklízet**	[skli:zɛt]
miller (person)	**mlynář** (m)	[mlɪna:rʃ]
mill (e.g., gristmill)	**mlýn** (m)	[mli:n]
to grind (grain)	**mlít obilí**	[mli:t obɪli:]
flour	**mouka** (ž)	[mouka]
straw	**sláma** (ž)	[sla:ma]

121. Building. Building process

construction site	**staveniště** (s)	[stavɛnɪʃte]
to build (vt)	**stavět**	[stavet]
construction worker	**stavitel** (m)	[stavɪtɛl]
project	**projekt** (m)	[projɛkt]
architect	**architekt** (m)	[arxɪtɛkt]
worker	**dělník** (m)	[delni:k]
foundation (of a building)	**základ** (m)	[za:klat]
roof	**střecha** (ž)	[strʃɛxa]
foundation pile	**pilota** (ž)	[pɪlota]
wall	**zeď** (ž)	[zɛtʲ]
reinforcing bars	**armatura** (ž)	[armatura]
scaffolding	**lešení** (s)	[lɛʃɛni:]
concrete	**beton** (m)	[bɛton]
granite	**žula** (ž)	[ʒula]
stone	**kámen** (m)	[ka:mɛn]
brick	**cihla** (ž)	[ʦɪhla]
sand	**písek** (m)	[pi:sɛk]

cement	**cement** (m)	[ʦɛmɛnt]
plaster (for walls)	**omítka** (ž)	[omi:tka]
to plaster (vt)	**omítat**	[omi:tat]
paint	**barva** (ž)	[barva]
to paint (~ a wall)	**natírat**	[nati:rat]
barrel	**sud** (m)	[sut]
crane	**jeřáb** (m)	[jɛrʒa:p]
to lift, to hoist (vt)	**zvedat**	[zvɛdat]
to lower (vt)	**spouštět**	[spouʃtet]
bulldozer	**buldozer** (m)	[buldozɛr]
excavator	**rýpadlo** (s)	[ri:padlo]
scoop, bucket	**lžíce** (ž)	[lʒi:ʦɛ]
to dig (excavate)	**rýt**	[ri:t]
hard hat	**přilba** (ž)	[prʃɪlba]

122. Science. Research. Scientists

science	**věda** (ž)	[veda]
scientific (adj)	**vědecký**	[vedɛʦki:]
scientist	**vědec** (m)	[vedɛʦ]
theory	**teorie** (ž)	[tɛorɪe]
axiom	**axiom** (m)	[aksɪo:m]
analysis	**analýza** (ž)	[anali:za]
to analyze (vt)	**analyzovat**	[analɪzovat]
argument (strong ~)	**argument** (m)	[argumɛnt]
substance (matter)	**látka** (ž)	[la:tka]
hypothesis	**hypotéza** (ž)	[hɪpotɛ:za]
dilemma	**dilema** (s)	[dɪlɛma]
dissertation	**disertace** (ž)	[dɪsɛrtaʦɛ]
dogma	**dogma** (s)	[dogma]
doctrine	**doktrína** (ž)	[doktri:na]
research	**výzkum** (m)	[vi:skum]
to research (vt)	**zkoumat**	[skoumat]
tests (laboratory ~)	**kontrola** (ž)	[kontrola]
laboratory	**laboratoř** (ž)	[laboratorʃ]
method	**metoda** (ž)	[mɛtoda]
molecule	**molekula** (ž)	[molɛkula]
monitoring	**monitorování** (s)	[monɪtorova:ni:]
discovery (act, event)	**objev** (m)	[objɛf]
postulate	**postulát** (m)	[postula:t]
principle	**princip** (m)	[prɪnʦɪp]
forecast	**prognóza** (ž)	[progno:za]

to forecast (vt)	**předpovídat**	[prʒɛtpovi:dat]
synthesis	**syntéza** (ž)	[sintɛ:za]
trend (tendency)	**tendence** (ž)	[tɛndɛntsɛ]
theorem	**teorém** (s)	[tɛorɛ:m]
teachings	**nauka** (ž)	[nauka]
fact	**fakt** (m)	[fakt]
expedition	**výprava** (ž)	[vi:prava]
experiment	**experiment** (m)	[ɛkspɛrɪmɛnt]
academician	**akademik** (m)	[akadɛmɪk]
bachelor (e.g., ~ of Arts)	**bakalář** (m)	[bakala:rʃ]
doctor (PhD)	**doktor** (m)	[doktor]
Associate Professor	**docent** (m)	[dotsɛnt]
Master (e.g., ~ of Arts)	**magistr** (m)	[magɪstr]
professor	**profesor** (m)	[profɛsor]

Professions and occupations

123. Job search. Dismissal

job	**práce** (ž)	[pra:tsɛ]
staff (work force)	**stálí zaměstnanci** (m mn)	[sta:li: zamnestnantsɪ]
personnel	**personál** (m)	[pɛrsona:l]
career	**kariéra** (ž)	[karɪe:ra]
prospects (chances)	**vyhlídky** (ž mn)	[vɪhli:tkɪ]
skills (mastery)	**dovednost** (ž)	[dovɛdnost]
selection (screening)	**výběr** (m)	[vi:ber]
employment agency	**kádrová kancelář** (ž)	[ka:drova: kantsɛla:rʃ]
résumé	**resumé** (s)	[rɛzimɛ:]
job interview	**pohovor** (m)	[pohovor]
vacancy, opening	**neobsazené místo** (s)	[nɛopsazɛnɛ: mi:sto]
salary, pay	**plat** (m), **mzda** (ž)	[plat], [mzda]
fixed salary	**stálý plat** (m)	[sta:li: plat]
pay, compensation	**platba** (ž)	[platba]
position (job)	**funkce** (ž)	[fuŋktsɛ]
duty (of employee)	**povinnost** (ž)	[povɪnnost]
range of duties	**okruh** (m)	[okrux]
busy (I'm ~)	**zaměstnaný**	[zamnestnani:]
to fire (dismiss)	**propustit**	[propustɪt]
dismissal	**propuštění** (s)	[propuʃteni:]
unemployment	**nezaměstnanost** (ž)	[nɛzamnestnanost]
unemployed (n)	**nezaměstnaný** (m)	[nɛzamnestnani:]
retirement	**důchod** (m)	[du:xot]
to retire (from job)	**odejít do důchodu**	[odɛji:t do du:xodu]

124. Business people

director	**ředitel** (m)	[rʒɛdɪtɛl]
manager (director)	**správce** (m)	[spra:vtsɛ]
boss	**šéf** (m)	[ʃɛ:f]
superior	**vedoucí** (m)	[vɛdoutsɪ:]
superiors	**vedení** (s)	[vɛdɛni:]
president	**prezident** (m)	[prɛzɪdɛnt]

chairman	**předseda** (m)	[prʃɛtsɛda]
deputy (substitute)	**náměstek** (m)	[na:mnestɛk]
assistant	**pomocník** (m)	[pomotsni:k]
secretary	**sekretář** (m)	[sɛkrɛta:rʃ]
personal assistant	**osobní sekretář** (m)	[osobni: sɛkrɛta:rʃ]
businessman	**byznysmen** (m)	[bɪznɪsmen]
entrepreneur	**podnikatel** (m)	[podnɪkatɛl]
founder	**zakladatel** (m)	[zakladatɛl]
to found (vt)	**založit**	[zaloʒɪt]
incorporator	**zakladatel** (m)	[zakladatɛl]
partner	**partner** (m)	[partnɛr]
stockholder	**akcionář** (m)	[aktsɪona:rʃ]
millionaire	**milionář** (m)	[mɪlɪona:rʃ]
billionaire	**miliardář** (m)	[mɪlɪarda:rʃ]
owner, proprietor	**majitel** (m)	[majɪtɛl]
landowner	**vlastník** (m) **půdy**	[vlastni:k pu:dɪ]
client	**klient** (m)	[klɪent]
regular client	**stálý zákazník** (m)	[sta:li: za:kazni:k]
buyer (customer)	**zákazník** (m)	[za:kazni:k]
visitor	**návštěvník** (m)	[na:vʃtevni:k]
professional (n)	**profesionál** (m)	[profɛsɪona:l]
expert	**znalec** (m)	[znalɛts]
specialist	**odborník** (m)	[odborni:k]
banker	**bankéř** (m)	[baŋkɛ:rʃ]
broker	**broker** (m)	[brokɛr]
cashier, teller	**pokladník** (m)	[pokladni:k]
accountant	**účetní** (m, ž)	[u:tʃɛtni:]
security guard	**strážce** (m)	[stra:ʒtsɛ]
investor	**investor** (m)	[ɪnvɛstor]
debtor	**dlužník** (m)	[dluʒni:k]
creditor	**věřitel** (m)	[verʒɪtɛl]
borrower	**vypůjčovatel** (m)	[vɪpu:jtʃovatɛl]
importer	**dovozce** (m)	[dovoztsɛ]
exporter	**vývozce** (m)	[vi:voztsɛ]
manufacturer	**výrobce** (m)	[vi:robtsɛ]
distributor	**distributor** (m)	[dɪstrɪbutor]
middleman	**zprostředkovatel** (m)	[sprostrʃɛtkovatɛl]
consultant	**konzultant** (m)	[konzultant]
sales representative	**zástupce** (m)	[za:stuptsɛ]
agent	**agent** (m)	[agɛnt]
insurance agent	**pojišťovací agent** (m)	[pojɪʃtʲovatsi: agɛnt]

125. Service professions

cook	**kuchař** (m)	[kuxarʃ]
chef (kitchen chef)	**šéfkuchař** (m)	[ʃɛ:f kuxarʃ]
baker	**pekař** (m)	[pɛkarʃ]
bartender	**barman** (m)	[barman]
waiter	**číšník** (m)	[ʧi:ʃni:k]
waitress	**číšnice** (ž)	[ʧi:ʃnɪʦɛ]
lawyer, attorney	**advokát** (m)	[advoka:t]
lawyer (legal expert)	**právník** (m)	[pra:vni:k]
notary public	**notář** (m)	[nota:rʃ]
electrician	**elektromontér** (m)	[ɛlɛktromontɛ:r]
plumber	**instalatér** (m)	[ɪnstalatɛ:r]
carpenter	**tesař** (m)	[tɛsarʃ]
masseur	**masér** (m)	[masɛ:r]
masseuse	**masérka** (ž)	[masɛ:rka]
doctor	**lékař** (m)	[lɛ:karʃ]
taxi driver	**taxikář** (m)	[taksɪka:rʃ]
driver	**řidič** (m)	[rʒɪdɪʧ]
delivery man	**kurýr** (m)	[kuri:r]
chambermaid	**pokojská** (ž)	[pokojska:]
security guard	**strážce** (m)	[stra:ʒʦɛ]
flight attendant (fem.)	**letuška** (ž)	[lɛtuʃka]
schoolteacher	**učitel** (m)	[uʧɪtɛl]
librarian	**knihovník** (m)	[knɪhovni:k]
translator	**překladatel** (m)	[prʃɛkladatɛl]
interpreter	**tlumočník** (m)	[tlumoʧni:k]
guide	**průvodce** (m)	[pru:voʤɛ]
hairdresser	**holič** (m), **kadeřník** (m)	[holɪʧ], [kadɛrʒni:k]
mailman	**listonoš** (m)	[lɪstonoʃ]
salesman (store staff)	**prodavač** (m)	[prodavaʧ]
gardener	**zahradník** (m)	[zahradni:k]
domestic servant	**sluha** (m)	[sluha]
maid (female servant)	**služka** (ž)	[sluʃka]
cleaner (cleaning lady)	**uklízečka** (ž)	[ukli:zɛʧka]

126. Military professions and ranks

private	**vojín** (m)	[voji:n]
sergeant	**seržant** (m)	[sɛrʒant]

lieutenant	**poručík** (m)	[porutʃi:k]
captain	**kapitán** (m)	[kapɪta:n]
major	**major** (m)	[major]
colonel	**plukovník** (m)	[plukovni:k]
general	**generál** (m)	[gɛnɛra:l]
marshal	**maršál** (m)	[marʃa:l]
admiral	**admirál** (m)	[admɪra:l]
military (n)	**voják** (m)	[voja:k]
soldier	**voják** (m)	[voja:k]
officer	**důstojník** (m)	[du:stojni:k]
commander	**velitel** (m)	[vɛlɪtɛl]
border guard	**pohraničník** (m)	[pohranɪtʃni:k]
radio operator	**radista** (m)	[radɪsta]
scout (searcher)	**rozvědčík** (m)	[rozvedtʃi:k]
pioneer (sapper)	**ženista** (m)	[ʒenɪsta]
marksman	**střelec** (m)	[strʃɛlɛts]
navigator	**navigátor** (m)	[navɪga:tor]

127. Officials. Priests

king	**král** (m)	[kra:l]
queen	**královna** (ž)	[kra:lovna]
prince	**princ** (m)	[prɪnts]
princess	**princezna** (ž)	[prɪntsɛzna]
czar	**car** (m)	[tsar]
czarina	**carevna** (ž)	[tsarɛvna]
president	**prezident** (m)	[prɛzɪdɛnt]
Secretary (minister)	**ministr** (m)	[mɪnɪstr]
prime minister	**premiér** (m)	[prɛmje:r]
senator	**senátor** (m)	[sɛna:tor]
diplomat	**diplomat** (m)	[dɪplomat]
consul	**konzul** (m)	[konzul]
ambassador	**velvyslanec** (m)	[vɛlvɪslanɛts]
counselor (diplomatic officer)	**rada** (m)	[rada]
official, functionary (civil servant)	**úředník** (m)	[u:rʒɛdni:k]
prefect	**prefekt** (m)	[prɛfɛkt]
mayor	**primátor** (m)	[prɪma:tor]
judge	**soudce** (m)	[soudtsɛ]
prosecutor (e.g., district attorney)	**prokurátor** (m)	[prokura:tor]

missionary	**misionář** (m)	[mɪsɪona:rʃ]
monk	**mnich** (m)	[mnɪx]
abbot	**opat** (m)	[opat]
rabbi	**rabín** (m)	[rabi:n]
vizier	**vezír** (m)	[vɛzi:r]
shah	**šach** (m)	[ʃax]
sheikh	**šejk** (m)	[ʃɛjk]

128. Agricultural professions

beekeeper	**včelař** (m)	[vʧɛlarʃ]
herder, shepherd	**pasák** (m)	[pasa:k]
agronomist	**agronom** (m)	[agronom]
cattle breeder	**chovatel** (m)	[xovatɛl]
veterinarian	**zvěrolékař** (m)	[zverolɛ:karʃ]
farmer	**farmář** (m)	[farma:rʃ]
winemaker	**vinař** (m)	[vɪnarʃ]
zoologist	**zoolog** (m)	[zoolog]
cowboy	**kovboj** (m)	[kovboj]

129. Art professions

actor	**herec** (m)	[hɛrɛʦ]
actress	**herečka** (ž)	[hɛrɛʧka]
singer (masc.)	**zpěvák** (m)	[speva:k]
singer (fem.)	**zpěvačka** (ž)	[spevaʧka]
dancer (masc.)	**tanečník** (m)	[tanɛʧni:k]
dancer (fem.)	**tanečnice** (ž)	[tanɛʧnɪʦɛ]
performer (masc.)	**herec** (m)	[hɛrɛʦ]
performer (fem.)	**herečka** (ž)	[hɛrɛʧka]
musician	**hudebník** (m)	[hudɛbni:k]
pianist	**klavírista** (m)	[klavi:rɪsta]
guitar player	**kytarista** (m)	[kɪtarɪsta]
conductor (orchestra ~)	**dirigent** (m)	[dɪrɪgɛnt]
composer	**skladatel** (m)	[skladatɛl]
impresario	**impresário** (m)	[ɪmprɛsa:rɪo]
film director	**režisér** (m)	[rɛʒɪsɛ:r]
producer	**filmový producent** (m)	[fɪlmovi: produʦɛnt]
scriptwriter	**scenárista** (m)	[sʦɛna:rɪsta]
critic	**kritik** (m)	[krɪtɪk]

writer	**spisovatel** (m)	[spɪsovatɛl]
poet	**básník** (m)	[ba:sni:k]
sculptor	**sochař** (m)	[soxarʃ]
artist (painter)	**malíř** (m)	[mali:rʃ]
juggler	**žonglér** (m)	[ʒonglɛ:r]
clown	**klaun** (m)	[klaun]
acrobat	**akrobat** (m)	[akrobat]
magician	**kouzelník** (m)	[kouzɛlni:k]

130. Various professions

doctor	**lékař** (m)	[lɛ:karʃ]
nurse	**zdravotní sestra** (ž)	[zdravotni: sɛstra]
psychiatrist	**psychiatr** (m)	[psɪxɪatr]
dentist	**stomatolog** (m)	[stomatolog]
surgeon	**chirurg** (m)	[xɪrurg]
astronaut	**astronaut** (m)	[astronaut]
astronomer	**astronom** (m)	[astronom]
pilot	**pilot** (m)	[pɪlot]
driver (of taxi, etc.)	**řidič** (m)	[rʒɪdɪʧ]
engineer (train driver)	**strojvůdce** (m)	[strojvu:dʦɛ]
mechanic	**mechanik** (m)	[mɛxanɪk]
miner	**horník** (m)	[horni:k]
worker	**dělník** (m)	[delni:k]
locksmith	**zámečník** (m)	[za:mɛʧni:k]
joiner (carpenter)	**truhlář** (m)	[truhla:rʃ]
turner (lathe operator)	**soustružník** (m)	[soustruʒni:k]
construction worker	**stavitel** (m)	[stavɪtɛl]
welder	**svářeč** (m)	[sva:rʒɛʧ]
professor (title)	**profesor** (m)	[profɛsor]
architect	**architekt** (m)	[arxɪtɛkt]
historian	**historik** (m)	[hɪstorɪk]
scientist	**vědec** (m)	[vedɛʦ]
physicist	**fyzik** (m)	[fɪzɪk]
chemist (scientist)	**chemik** (m)	[xɛmɪk]
archeologist	**archeolog** (m)	[arxɛolog]
geologist	**geolog** (m)	[gɛolog]
researcher (scientist)	**výzkumník** (m)	[vi:skumni:k]
babysitter	**chůva** (ž)	[xu:va]
teacher, educator	**pedagog** (m)	[pɛdagog]
editor	**redaktor** (m)	[rɛdaktor]
editor-in-chief	**šéfredaktor** (m)	[ʃɛ:frɛdaktor]

correspondent	**zpravodaj** (m)	[spravodaj]
typist (fem.)	**písařka** (ž)	[pi:sarʃka]
designer	**návrhář** (m)	[na:vrha:rʃ]
computer expert	**odborník** (m) **na počítače**	[odborni:k na potʃi:tatʃɛ]
programmer	**programátor** (m)	[programa:tor]
engineer (designer)	**inženýr** (m)	[ɪnʒeni:r]
sailor	**námořník** (m)	[na:morʒni:k]
seaman	**námořník** (m)	[na:morʒni:k]
rescuer	**záchranář** (m)	[za:xrana:rʃ]
fireman	**hasič** (m)	[hasɪtʃ]
police officer	**policista** (m)	[polɪtsɪsta]
watchman	**hlídač** (m)	[hli:datʃ]
detective	**detektiv** (m)	[dɛtɛktɪf]
customs officer	**celník** (m)	[tsɛlni:k]
bodyguard	**osobní strážce** (m)	[osobni: stra:ʒtsɛ]
prison guard	**dozorce** (m)	[dozortsɛ]
inspector	**inspektor** (m)	[ɪnspɛktor]
sportsman	**sportovec** (m)	[sportovɛts]
trainer, coach	**trenér** (m)	[trɛnɛ:r]
butcher	**řezník** (m)	[rʒɛzni:k]
cobbler (shoe repairer)	**obuvník** (m)	[obuvni:k]
merchant	**obchodník** (m)	[obxodni:k]
loader (person)	**nakládač** (m)	[nakla:datʃ]
fashion designer	**modelář** (m)	[modɛla:rʃ]
model (fem.)	**modelka** (ž)	[modɛlka]

131. Occupations. Social status

schoolboy	**žák** (m)	[ʒa:k]
student (college ~)	**student** (m)	[studɛnt]
philosopher	**filozof** (m)	[fɪlozof]
economist	**ekonom** (m)	[ɛkonom]
inventor	**vynálezce** (m)	[vɪna:lɛztsɛ]
unemployed (n)	**nezaměstnaný** (m)	[nɛzamnestnani:]
retiree	**důchodce** (m)	[du:xodtsɛ]
spy, secret agent	**špión** (m)	[ʃpɪo:n]
prisoner	**vězeň** (m)	[vezɛnʲ]
striker	**stávkující** (m)	[sta:fkuji:tsi:]
bureaucrat	**byrokrat** (m)	[bɪrokrat]
traveler (globetrotter)	**cestovatel** (m)	[tsɛstovatɛl]
gay, homosexual (n)	**homosexuál** (m)	[homosɛksua:l]

hacker	**hacker** (m)	[hɛkr]
hippie	**hippie** (m)	[hɪppɪ]
bandit	**bandita** (m)	[bandɪta]
hit man, killer	**najatý vrah** (m)	[najati: vrax]
drug addict	**narkoman** (m)	[narkoman]
drug dealer	**drogový dealer** (m)	[drogovi: di:lɛr]
prostitute (fem.)	**prostitutka** (ž)	[prostɪtutka]
pimp	**kuplíř** (m)	[kupli:rʃ]
sorcerer	**čaroděj** (m)	[ʧarodej]
sorceress (evil ~)	**čarodějka** (ž)	[ʧarodejka]
pirate	**pirát** (m)	[pɪra:t]
slave	**otrok** (m)	[otrok]
samurai	**samuraj** (m)	[samuraj]
savage (primitive)	**divoch** (m)	[dɪvox]

Sports

132. Kinds of sports. Sportspersons

sportsman	**sportovec** (m)	[sportovɛts]
kind of sports	**sportovní disciplína** (ž)	[sportovni: dɪstsɪpli:na]
basketball	**basketbal** (m)	[baskɛtbal]
basketball player	**basketbalista** (m)	[baskɛtbalɪsta]
baseball	**baseball** (m)	[bɛjzbol]
baseball player	**hráč** (m) **baseballu**	[hra:ʧ bɛjzbolu]
soccer	**fotbal** (m)	[fotbal]
soccer player	**fotbalista** (m)	[fotbalɪsta]
goalkeeper	**brankář** (m)	[braŋka:rʃ]
hockey	**hokej** (m)	[hokɛj]
hockey player	**hokejista** (m)	[hokɛjɪsta]
volleyball	**volejbal** (m)	[volɛjbal]
volleyball player	**volejbalista** (m)	[volɛjbalɪsta]
boxing	**box** (m)	[boks]
boxer	**boxer** (m)	[boksɛr]
wrestling	**zápas** (m)	[za:pas]
wrestler	**zápasník** (m)	[za:pasni:k]
karate	**karate** (s)	[karatɛ]
karate fighter	**karatista** (m)	[karatɪsta]
judo	**džudo** (s)	[ʤudo]
judo athlete	**džudista** (m)	[ʤudɪsta]
tennis	**tenis** (m)	[tɛnɪs]
tennis player	**tenista** (m)	[tɛnɪsta]
swimming	**plavání** (s)	[plava:ni:]
swimmer	**plavec** (m)	[plavɛts]
fencing	**šerm** (m)	[ʃɛrm]
fencer	**šermíř** (m)	[ʃɛrmi:rʃ]
chess	**šachy** (m mn)	[ʃaxɪ]
chess player	**šachista** (m)	[ʃaxɪsta]

alpinism	**horolezectví** (s)	[horolɛzɛʦstvi:]
alpinist	**horolezec** (m)	[horolɛzɛʦ]
running	**běh** (m)	[bex]
runner	**běžec** (m)	[beʒeʦ]
athletics	**lehká atletika** (ž)	[lɛhka: atlɛtɪka]
athlete	**atlet** (m)	[atlɛt]
horseback riding	**jízda** (ž) **na koni**	[ji:zda na konɪ]
horse rider	**jezdec** (m)	[jɛzdɛʦ]
figure skating	**krasobruslení** (s)	[krasobruslɛni:]
figure skater (masc.)	**krasobruslař** (m)	[krasobruslarʃ]
figure skater (fem.)	**krasobruslařka** (ž)	[krasobruslarʃka]
powerlifting	**těžká atletika** (ž)	[teʃka: atlɛtɪka]
powerlifter	**vzpěrač** (m)	[vsperaʧ]
car racing	**automobilové závody** (m mn)	[automobɪlovɛ: za:vodɪ]
racer (driver)	**závodník** (m)	[za:vodni:k]
cycling	**cyklistika** (ž)	[ʦɪklɪstɪka]
cyclist	**cyklista** (m)	[ʦɪklɪsta]
broad jump	**daleké skoky** (m mn)	[dalekɛ: skokɪ]
pole vault	**skoky** (m mn) **o tyči**	[skokɪ o tɪʧɪ]
jumper	**skokan** (m)	[skokan]

133. Kinds of sports. Miscellaneous

football	**americký fotbal** (m)	[amerɪʦki: fotbal]
badminton	**badminton** (m)	[badmɪnton]
biathlon	**biatlon** (m)	[bɪatlon]
billiards	**kulečník** (m)	[kulɛʧni:k]
bobsled	**bobový sport** (m)	[bobovi: sport]
bodybuilding	**kulturistika** (ž)	[kulturɪstɪka]
water polo	**vodní pólo** (s)	[vodni: po:lo]
handball	**házená** (ž)	[ha:zɛna:]
golf	**golf** (m)	[golf]
rowing, crew	**veslování** (s)	[vɛslova:ni:]
scuba diving	**potápění** (s)	[pota:peni:]
cross-country skiing	**lyžařské závody** (m mn)	[lɪʒarʃskɛ: za:vodɪ]
table tennis (ping-pong)	**stolní tenis** (m)	[stolni: tɛnɪs]
sailing	**plachtění** (s)	[plaxteni:]
rally racing	**rallye** (s)	[rali:]

rugby	**ragby** (s)	[ragbɪ]
snowboarding	**snowboarding** (m)	[snoubordɪŋk]
archery	**lukostřelba** (ž)	[lukostrʃɛlba]

134. Gym

barbell	**vzpěračská činka** (ž)	[vsperaʧska: ʧɪŋka]
dumbbells	**činky** (ž mn)	[ʧɪŋkɪ]
training machine	**trenažér** (m)	[trɛnaʒe:r]
exercise bicycle	**kolový trenažér** (m)	[kolovi: trɛnaʒe:r]
treadmill	**běžecký pás** (m)	[beʒeʦki: pa:s]
horizontal bar	**hrazda** (ž)	[hrazda]
parallel bars	**bradla** (s mn)	[bradla]
vault (vaulting horse)	**kůň** (m)	[ku:nʲ]
mat (exercise ~)	**žíněnka** (ž)	[ʒi:neŋka]
jump rope	**švihadlo** (s)	[ʃvɪhadlo]
aerobics	**aerobik** (m)	[aɛrobɪk]
yoga	**jóga** (ž)	[jo:ga]

135. Hockey

hockey	**hokej** (m)	[hokɛj]
hockey player	**hokejista** (m)	[hokɛjɪsta]
to play hockey	**hrát hokej**	[hra:t hokɛj]
ice	**led** (m)	[lɛt]
puck	**puk** (m)	[puk]
hockey stick	**hokejka** (ž)	[hokejka]
ice skates	**brusle** (ž mn)	[bruslɛ]
board (ice hockey rink ~)	**hrazení** (s)	[hrazɛni:]
shot	**hod** (m)	[hot]
goaltender	**brankář** (m)	[braŋka:rʃ]
goal (score)	**gól** (m)	[go:l]
to score a goal	**vstřelit branku**	[vstrʃɛlɪt braŋku]
period	**třetina** (ž)	[trʃɛtɪna]
substitutes bench	**lavice** (ž) **náhradníků**	[lavɪʦɛ na:hradni:ku:]

136. Soccer

soccer	**fotbal** (m)	[fotbal]
soccer player	**fotbalista** (m)	[fotbalɪsta]

to play soccer	**hrát fotbal**	[hra:t fotbal]
major league	**nejvyšší liga** (ž)	[nɛjvɪʃi: lɪga]
soccer club	**fotbalový klub** (m)	[fotbalovi: klup]
coach	**trenér** (m)	[trɛnɛ:r]
owner, proprietor	**majitel** (m)	[majɪtɛl]
team	**mužstvo** (s)	[muʒstvo]
team captain	**kapitán** (m) **mužstva**	[kapɪta:n muʒstva]
player	**hráč** (m)	[hra:ʧ]
substitute	**náhradník** (m)	[na:hradni:k]
forward	**útočník** (m)	[u:toʧni:k]
center forward	**střední útočník** (m)	[strʃɛdni: u:toʧni:k]
scorer	**střelec** (m)	[strʃɛlɛʦ]
defender, back	**obránce** (m)	[obra:nʦɛ]
midfielder, halfback	**záložník** (m)	[za:loʒni:k]
match	**zápas** (ž)	[za:pas]
to meet (vi, vt)	**utkávat se**	[utka:vat sɛ]
final	**finále** (s)	[fɪna:lɛ]
semi-final	**semifinále** (s)	[sɛmɪfɪna:lɛ]
championship	**mistrovství** (s)	[mɪstrovstvi:]
period, half	**poločas** (m)	[poloʧas]
first period	**první poločas** (m)	[prvni: poloʧas]
half-time	**poločas** (m)	[poloʧas]
goal	**brána** (ž)	[bra:na]
goalkeeper	**brankář** (m)	[braŋka:rʃ]
goalpost	**tyč** (ž)	[tɪʧ]
crossbar	**břevno** (s)	[brʒɛvno]
net	**síť** (ž)	[si:tʲ]
to concede a goal	**pustit gól**	[pustɪt go:l]
ball	**míč** (m)	[mi:ʧ]
pass	**přihrávka** (ž)	[prʃɪhra:fka]
kick	**kop** (m)	[kop]
to kick (~ the ball)	**vystřelit**	[vɪstrʒɛlɪt]
free kick (direct ~)	**pokutový kop** (m)	[pokutovi: kop]
corner kick	**kop** (m) **z rohu**	[kop z rohu]
attack	**útok** (m)	[u:tok]
counterattack	**protiútok** (m)	[protɪu:tok]
combination	**kombinace** (ž)	[kombɪnaʦɛ]
referee	**rozhodčí** (m)	[rozhodʧi:]
to blow the whistle	**hvízdat**	[hvi:zdat]
whistle (sound)	**zahvízdnutí** (s)	[zahvi:zdnuti:]
foul, misconduct	**přestupek** (m)	[prʃɛstupɛk]
to commit a foul	**porušit**	[poruʃɪt]
to send off	**vyloučit**	[vɪlouʧɪt]
yellow card	**žlutá karta** (ž)	[ʒluta: karta]

red card	**červená karta** (ž)	[ʧɛrvɛna: karta]
disqualification	**diskvalifikace** (ž)	[dɪskvalɪfɪkaʦɛ]
to disqualify (vt)	**diskvalifikovat**	[dɪskvalɪfɪkovat]
penalty kick	**penalta** (ž)	[pɛnalta]
wall	**zeď** (ž)	[zɛtʲ]
to score (vi, vt)	**vstřelit**	[vstrʃɛlɪt]
goal (score)	**gól** (m)	[go:l]
to score a goal	**vstřelit branku**	[vstrʃɛlɪt braŋku]
substitution	**náhrada** (ž)	[na:hrada]
to replace (a player)	**vystřídat**	[vɪstrʃi:dat]
rules	**pravidla** (s mn)	[pravɪdla]
tactics	**taktika** (ž)	[taktɪka]
stadium	**stadión** (m)	[stadɪo:n]
stand (bleachers)	**tribuna** (ž)	[trɪbuna]
fan, supporter	**fanoušek** (m)	[fanouʃɛk]
to shout (vi)	**křičet**	[krʃɪʧɛt]
scoreboard	**tabló** (s)	[tablo:]
score	**skóre** (s)	[sko:rɛ]
defeat	**prohra** (ž)	[prohra]
to lose (not win)	**prohrát**	[prohra:t]
tie	**remíza** (ž)	[rɛmi:za]
to tie (vi)	**remizovat**	[rɛmɪzovat]
victory	**vítězství** (s)	[vi:tezstvi:]
to win (vi, vt)	**zvítězit**	[zvi:tezɪt]
champion	**mistr** (m)	[mɪstr]
best (adj)	**nejlepší**	[nɛjlɛpʃi:]
to congratulate (vt)	**blahopřát**	[blahoprʃa:t]
commentator	**komentátor** (m)	[komɛnta:tor]
to commentate (vt)	**komentovat**	[komɛntovat]
broadcast	**přenos** (m)	[prʃɛnos]

137. Alpine skiing

skis	**lyže** (ž mn)	[lɪʒe]
to ski (vi)	**lyžovat**	[lɪʒovat]
mountain-ski resort	**sjezdařské středisko** (s)	[sjɛzdarʃskɛ: strʃɛdɪsko]
ski lift	**vlek** (m)	[vlɛk]
ski poles	**hole** (ž mn)	[holɛ]
slope	**svah** (m)	[svax]
slalom	**slalom** (m)	[slalom]

138. Tennis. Golf

golf	**golf** (m)	[golf]
golf club	**golfový klub** (m)	[golfovi: klup]
golfer	**hráč** (m) **golfu**	[hra:tʃ golfu]
hole	**lůžko** (s)	[lu:ʃko]
club	**hůl** (ž)	[hu:l]
golf trolley	**golfový vozík** (m)	[golfovi: vozi:k]
tennis	**tenis** (m)	[tɛnɪs]
tennis court	**kurt** (m)	[kurt]
serve	**podání** (s)	[poda:ni:]
to serve (vt)	**servírovat**	[sɛrvi:rovat]
racket	**raketa** (ž)	[rakɛta]
net	**síť** (ž)	[si:tʲ]
ball	**míč** (m)	[mi:tʃ]

139. Chess

chess	**šachy** (m mn)	[ʃaxɪ]
chessmen	**šachy** (m mn)	[ʃaxɪ]
chess player	**šachista** (m)	[ʃaxɪsta]
chessboard	**šachovnice** (ž)	[ʃaxovnɪtsɛ]
chessman	**figura** (ž)	[fɪgura]
White (white pieces)	**bílé** (ž mn)	[bi:lɛ:]
Black (black pieces)	**černé** (ž mn)	[tʃɛrnɛ:]
pawn	**pěšec** (m)	[peʃɛts]
bishop	**střelec** (m)	[strʃɛlɛts]
knight	**kůň** (m)	[ku:nʲ]
rook	**věž** (ž)	[veʃ]
queen	**královna** (ž)	[kra:lovna]
king	**král** (m)	[kra:l]
move	**tah** (m)	[tax]
to move (vi, vt)	**táhnout**	[ta:hnout]
to sacrifice (vt)	**nechat sebrat**	[nɛxat sɛbrat]
castling	**rošáda** (ž)	[roʃa:da]
check	**šach** (m)	[ʃax]
checkmate	**mat** (m)	[mat]
chess tournament	**šachový turnaj** (m)	[ʃaxovi: turnaj]
Grand Master	**velmistr** (m)	[vɛlmɪstr]
combination	**kombinace** (ž)	[kombɪnatsɛ]
game (in chess)	**partie** (ž)	[partɪe]
checkers	**dáma** (ž)	[da:ma]

140. Boxing

boxing	**box** (m)	[boks]
fight (bout)	**boj** (m)	[boj]
boxing match	**souboj** (m)	[souboj]
round (in boxing)	**kolo** (s)	[kolo]
ring	**ring** (m)	[rɪng]
gong	**gong** (m)	[gong]
punch	**úder** (m)	[u:dɛr]
knockdown	**knock-down** (m)	[nok-daun]
knockout	**knokaut** (m)	[knokaut]
to knock out	**knokautovat**	[knokautovat]
boxing glove	**boxerská rukavice** (ž)	[boksɛrska: rukavɪʦɛ]
referee	**rozhodčí** (m)	[rozhodʧi:]
lightweight	**lehká váha** (ž)	[lɛhka: va:ha]
middleweight	**střední váha** (ž)	[strʃɛdni: va:ha]
heavyweight	**těžká váha** (ž)	[teʃka: va:ha]

141. Sports. Miscellaneous

Olympic Games	**Olympijské hry** (ž mn)	[olɪmpɪjskɛ: hrɪ]
winner	**vítěz** (m)	[vi:tez]
to be winning	**vítězit**	[vi:tezɪt]
to win (vi)	**vyhrát**	[vɪhra:t]
leader	**vůdce** (m)	[vu:dʦɛ]
to lead (vi)	**vést**	[vɛ:st]
first place	**první místo** (s)	[prvni: mi:sto]
second place	**druhé místo** (s)	[druhɛ: mi:sto]
third place	**třetí místo** (s)	[trʃɛti: mi:sto]
medal	**medaile** (ž)	[mɛdajlɛ]
trophy	**trofej** (ž)	[trofɛj]
prize cup (trophy)	**pohár** (m)	[poha:r]
prize (in game)	**cena** (ž)	[ʦɛna]
main prize	**hlavní cena** (ž)	[hlavni: ʦɛna]
record	**rekord** (m)	[rɛkort]
to set a record	**vytvořit rekord**	[vɪtvorʒɪt rɛkort]
final	**finále** (s)	[fɪna:lɛ]
final (adj)	**finální**	[fɪna:lni:]
champion	**mistr** (m)	[mɪstr]
championship	**mistrovství** (s)	[mɪstrovstvi:]

stadium	**stadión** (m)	[stadɪo:n]
stand (bleachers)	**tribuna** (ž)	[trɪbuna]
fan, supporter	**fanoušek** (m)	[fanouʃɛk]
opponent, rival	**soupeř** (m)	[soupɛrʃ]
start (start line)	**start** (m)	[start]
finish line	**cíl** (m)	[ʦi:l]
defeat	**prohra** (ž)	[prohra]
to lose (not win)	**prohrát**	[prohra:t]
referee	**rozhodčí** (m)	[rozhodʧi:]
jury (judges)	**porota, jury** (ž)	[porota], [ʒiri]
score	**skóre** (s)	[sko:rɛ]
tie	**remíza** (ž)	[rɛmi:za]
to tie (vi)	**remizovat**	[rɛmɪzovat]
point	**bod** (m)	[bot]
result (final score)	**výsledek** (m)	[vi:slɛdɛk]
period	**poločas** (m)	[poloʧas]
half-time	**poločas** (m)	[poloʧas]
doping	**doping** (m)	[dopɪŋk]
to penalize (vt)	**trestat**	[trɛstat]
to disqualify (vt)	**diskvalifikovat**	[dɪskvalɪfɪkovat]
apparatus	**nářadí** (s)	[na:rʒadi:]
javelin	**oštěp** (m)	[oʃtep]
shot (metal ball)	**koule** (ž)	[koulɛ]
ball (snooker, etc.)	**koule** (ž)	[koulɛ]
aim (target)	**cíl** (m)	[ʦi:l]
target	**terč** (m)	[tɛrʧ]
to shoot (vi)	**střílet**	[strʃi:lɛt]
accurate (~ shot)	**přesný**	[prʃɛsni:]
trainer, coach	**trenér** (m)	[trɛnɛ:r]
to train (sb)	**trénovat**	[trɛ:novat]
to train (vi)	**trénovat**	[trɛ:novat]
training	**trénink** (m)	[trɛ:nɪŋk]
gym	**tělocvična** (ž)	[teloʦvɪʧna]
exercise (physical)	**cvičení** (s)	[ʦvɪʧɛni:]
warm-up (athlete ~)	**rozcvička** (ž)	[rozʦvɪʧka]

Education

142. School

school	**škola** (ž)	[ʃkola]
principal (headmaster)	**ředitel** (m) **školy**	[rʒɛdɪtɛl ʃkolɪ]
pupil (boy)	**žák** (m)	[ʒa:k]
pupil (girl)	**žákyně** (ž)	[ʒa:kɪne]
schoolboy	**žák** (m)	[ʒa:k]
schoolgirl	**žákyně** (ž)	[ʒa:kɪne]
to teach (sb)	**učit**	[uʧɪt]
to learn (language, etc.)	**učit se**	[uʧɪt sɛ]
to learn by heart	**učit se nazpaměť**	[uʧɪt sɛ naspamnetʲ]
to learn (~ to count, etc.)	**učit se**	[uʧɪt sɛ]
to be in school	**chodí za školu**	[xodi: za ʃkolu]
to go to school	**jít do školy**	[ji:t do ʃkolɪ]
alphabet	**abeceda** (ž)	[abɛʦɛda]
subject (at school)	**předmět** (m)	[prʃɛdmnet]
classroom	**třída** (ž)	[trʃi:da]
lesson	**hodina** (ž)	[hodɪna]
recess	**přestávka** (ž)	[prʃɛsta:fka]
school bell	**zvonění** (s)	[zvoneni:]
school desk	**školní lavice** (ž)	[ʃkolni: lavɪʦɛ]
chalkboard	**tabule** (ž)	[tabulɛ]
grade	**známka** (ž)	[zna:mka]
good grade	**dobrá známka** (ž)	[dobra: zna:mka]
bad grade	**špatná známka** (ž)	[ʃpatna: zna:mka]
to give a grade	**dávat známku**	[da:vat zna:mku]
mistake, error	**chyba** (ž)	[xɪba]
to make mistakes	**dělat chyby**	[delat xɪbɪ]
to correct (an error)	**opravovat**	[opravovat]
cheat sheet	**tahák** (m)	[taha:k]
homework	**domácí úloha** (ž)	[doma:ʦi: u:loha]
exercise (in education)	**cvičení** (s)	[ʦvɪʧɛni:]
to be present	**být přítomen**	[bi:t prʃi:tomɛn]
to be absent	**chybět**	[xɪbet]
to miss school	**chybět ve škole**	[xɪbet ve ʃkolɛ]

to punish (vt)	**trestat**	[trɛstat]
punishment	**trest** (m)	[trɛst]
conduct (behavior)	**chování** (s)	[xova:ni:]
report card	**žákovská knížka** (ž)	[ʒa:kovska: kni:ʃka]
pencil	**tužka** (ž)	[tuʃka]
eraser	**guma** (ž)	[guma]
chalk	**křída** (ž)	[krʃi:da]
pencil case	**penál** (m)	[pɛna:l]
schoolbag	**brašna** (ž)	[braʃna]
pen	**pero** (s)	[pɛro]
school notebook	**sešit** (m)	[sɛʃɪt]
textbook	**učebnice** (ž)	[uʧɛbnɪʦɛ]
drafting compass	**kružidlo** (s)	[kruʒɪdlo]
to make technical drawings	**rýsovat**	[ri:sovat]
technical drawing	**výkres** (m)	[vi:krɛs]
poem	**báseň** (ž)	[ba:sɛnʲ]
by heart (adv)	**nazpaměť**	[naspamnetʲ]
to learn by heart	**učit se nazpaměť**	[uʧɪt sɛ naspamnetʲ]
school vacation	**prázdniny** (ž mn)	[pra:zdnɪnɪ]
to be on vacation	**mít prázdniny**	[mi:t pra:zdnɪnɪ]
to spend one's vacation	**strávit prázdniny**	[stra:vɪt pra:zdnɪnɪ]
test (written math ~)	**písemka** (ž)	[pi:sɛmka]
essay (composition)	**sloh** (m)	[slox]
dictation	**diktát** (m)	[dɪkta:t]
exam (examination)	**zkouška** (ž)	[skouʃka]
to take an exam	**dělat zkoušky**	[delat skouʃkɪ]
experiment (e.g., chemistry ~)	**pokus** (m)	[pokus]

143. College. University

academy	**akademie** (ž)	[akadɛmɪe]
university	**univerzita** (ž)	[unɪvɛrzɪta]
faculty (e.g., ~ of Medicine)	**fakulta** (ž)	[fakulta]
student (masc.)	**student** (m)	[studɛnt]
student (fem.)	**studentka** (ž)	[studɛntka]
lecturer (teacher)	**vyučující** (m)	[vɪuʧuji:ʦi:]
lecture hall, room	**posluchárna** (ž)	[posluxa:rna]
graduate	**absolvent** (m)	[apsolvɛnt]
diploma	**diplom** (m)	[dɪplom]

dissertation	**disertace** (ž)	[dɪsɛrtat͡sɛ]
study (report)	**bádání** (s)	[ba:da:ni:]
laboratory	**laboratoř** (ž)	[laboratorʃ]
lecture	**přednáška** (ž)	[prʃɛdna:ʃka]
coursemate	**spolužák** (m)	[spoluʒa:k]
scholarship	**stipendium** (s)	[stɪpɛndɪum]
academic degree	**akademická hodnost** (ž)	[akadɛmɪt͡ska: hodnost]

144. Sciences. Disciplines

mathematics	**matematika** (ž)	[matɛmatɪka]
algebra	**algebra** (ž)	[algɛbra]
geometry	**geometrie** (ž)	[gɛomɛtrɪe]
astronomy	**astronomie** (ž)	[astronomɪe]
biology	**biologie** (ž)	[bɪologɪe]
geography	**zeměpis** (m)	[zɛmnepɪs]
geology	**geologie** (ž)	[gɛologɪe]
history	**historie** (ž)	[hɪstorɪe]
medicine	**lékařství** (s)	[lɛ:karʃstvi:]
pedagogy	**pedagogika** (ž)	[pɛdagogɪka]
law	**právo** (s)	[pra:vo]
physics	**fyzika** (ž)	[fɪzɪka]
chemistry	**chemie** (ž)	[xɛmɪe]
philosophy	**filozofie** (ž)	[fɪlozofɪe]
psychology	**psychologie** (ž)	[psɪxologɪe]

145. Writing system. Orthography

grammar	**mluvnice** (ž)	[mluvnɪt͡sɛ]
vocabulary	**slovní zásoba** (ž)	[slovni: za:soba]
phonetics	**hláskosloví** (s)	[hla:skoslovi:]
noun	**podstatné jméno** (s)	[podsta:tnɛ: jmɛ:no]
adjective	**přídavné jméno** (s)	[prʃi:davnɛ: jmɛ:no]
verb	**sloveso** (s)	[slovɛso]
adverb	**příslovce** (s)	[prʃi:slovt͡sɛ]
pronoun	**zájmeno** (s)	[za:jmɛno]
interjection	**citoslovce** (s)	[t͡sɪtoslovt͡sɛ]
preposition	**předložka** (ž)	[prʃɛdloʃka]
root	**slovní základ** (m)	[slovni: za:klat]
ending	**koncovka** (ž)	[kont͡sofka]
prefix	**předpona** (ž)	[prʃɛtpona]

syllable	**slabika** (ž)	[slabɪka]
suffix	**přípona** (ž)	[prʃi:pona]
stress mark	**přízvuk** (m)	[prʃi:zvuk]
apostrophe	**odsuvník** (m)	[otsuvni:k]
period, dot	**tečka** (ž)	[tɛʧka]
comma	**čárka** (ž)	[ʧa:rka]
semicolon	**středník** (m)	[strʃɛdni:k]
colon	**dvojtečka** (ž)	[dvojtɛʧka]
ellipsis	**tři tečky** (ž mn)	[trʃɪ tɛʧkɪ]
question mark	**otazník** (m)	[otazni:k]
exclamation point	**vykřičník** (m)	[vɪkrʃɪʧni:k]
quotation marks	**uvozovky** (ž mn)	[uvozofkɪ]
in quotation marks	**v uvozovkách**	[f uvozofka:x]
parenthesis	**závorky** (ž mn)	[za:vorkɪ]
in parenthesis	**v závorkách**	[v za:vorkax]
hyphen	**spojovník** (m)	[spojovni:k]
dash	**pomlčka** (ž)	[pomlʧka]
space (between words)	**mezera** (ž)	[mɛzɛra]
letter	**písmeno** (s)	[pi:smɛno]
capital letter	**velké písmeno** (s)	[vɛlkɛ: pi:smɛno]
vowel (n)	**samohláska** (ž)	[samohla:ska]
consonant (n)	**souhláska** (ž)	[souhla:ska]
sentence	**věta** (ž)	[veta]
subject	**podmět** (m)	[podmnet]
predicate	**přísudek** (m)	[prʃi:sudɛk]
line	**řádek** (m)	[rʒa:dɛk]
on a new line	**z nového řádku**	[z novɛ:ho rʒa:tku]
paragraph	**odstavec** (m)	[otstavɛʦ]
word	**slovo** (s)	[slovo]
group of words	**slovní spojení** (s)	[slovni: spojɛni:]
expression	**výraz** (m)	[vi:raz]
synonym	**synonymum** (s)	[sɪnonɪmum]
antonym	**antonymum** (s)	[antonɪmum]
rule	**pravidlo** (s)	[pravɪdlo]
exception	**výjimka** (ž)	[vi:jɪmka]
correct (adj)	**správný**	[spra:vni:]
conjugation	**časování** (s)	[ʧasova:ni:]
declension	**skloňování** (s)	[sklonʲova:ni:]
nominal case	**pád** (m)	[pa:t]
question	**otázka** (ž)	[ota:ska]

to underline (vt)	**podtrhnout**	[podtrhnout]
dotted line	**tečkování** (s)	[tɛʧkova:ni:]

146. Foreign languages

language	**jazyk** (m)	[jazɪk]
foreign (adj)	**cizí**	[ʦɪzi:]
foreign language	**cizí jazyk** (m)	[ʦɪzi: jazɪk]
to study (vt)	**studovat**	[studovat]
to learn (language, etc.)	**učit se**	[uʧɪt sɛ]
to read (vi, vt)	**číst**	[ʧi:st]
to speak (vi, vt)	**mluvit**	[mluvɪt]
to understand (vt)	**rozumět**	[rozumnet]
to write (vt)	**psát**	[psa:t]
fast (adv)	**rychle**	[rɪxlɛ]
slowly (adv)	**pomalu**	[pomalu]
fluently (adv)	**plynně**	[plɪnne]
rules	**pravidla** (s mn)	[pravɪdla]
grammar	**mluvnice** (ž)	[mluvnɪʦɛ]
vocabulary	**slovní zásoba** (ž)	[slovni: za:soba]
phonetics	**hláskosloví** (s)	[hla:skoslovi:]
textbook	**učebnice** (ž)	[uʧɛbnɪʦɛ]
dictionary	**slovník** (m)	[slovni:k]
teach-yourself book	**učebnice** (ž) **pro samouky**	[uʧɛbnɪʦɛ pro samoukɪ]
phrasebook	**konverzace** (ž)	[konvɛrzaʦɛ]
cassette, tape	**kazeta** (ž)	[kazɛta]
videotape	**videokazeta** (ž)	[vɪdɛokazɛta]
CD, compact disc	**CD disk** (m)	[ʦɛ:dɛ: dɪsk]
DVD	**DVD** (s)	[dɛvɛdɛ]
alphabet	**abeceda** (ž)	[abɛʦɛda]
to spell (vt)	**hláskovat**	[hla:skovat]
pronunciation	**výslovnost** (ž)	[vi:slovnost]
accent	**cizí přízvuk** (m)	[ʦɪzi: prʃi:zvuk]
with an accent	**s cizím přízvukem**	[s ʦɪzi:m prʃi:zvukɛm]
without an accent	**bez cizího přízvuku**	[bɛz ʦɪzi:ho prʃi:zvuku]
word	**slovo** (s)	[slovo]
meaning	**smysl** (m)	[smɪsl]
course (e.g., a French ~)	**kurzy** (m mn)	[kurzɪ]
to sign up	**zapsat se**	[zapsat sɛ]
teacher	**vyučující** (m)	[vɪuʧuji:ʦi:]
translation (process)	**překlad** (m)	[prʃɛklat]

translation (text, etc.)	**překlad** (m)	[prʃɛklat]
translator	**překladatel** (m)	[prʃɛkladatɛl]
interpreter	**tlumočník** (m)	[tlumotʃni:k]
polyglot	**polyglot** (m)	[polɪglot]
memory	**paměť** (ž)	[pamnetʲ]

147. Fairy tale characters

Santa Claus	**svatý Mikuláš** (m)	[svati: mɪkula:ʃ]
Cinderella	**Popelka** (ž)	[popɛlka]
mermaid	**rusalka** (ž)	[rusalka]
Neptune	**Neptun** (m)	[nɛptun]
magician, wizard	**čaroděj** (m)	[tʃarodej]
fairy	**čarodějka** (ž)	[tʃarodejka]
magic (adj)	**čarodějný**	[tʃarodejni:]
magic wand	**čarovný proutek** (m)	[tʃarovni: proutɛk]
fairy tale	**pohádka** (ž)	[poha:tka]
miracle	**zázrak** (m)	[za:zrak]
dwarf	**gnóm** (m)	[gno:m]
to turn into ...	**proměnit se**	[promnenɪt sɛ]
ghost	**přízrak** (m)	[prʃi:zrak]
phantom	**přízrak** (m)	[prʃi:zrak]
monster	**příšera** (ž)	[prʃi:ʃɛra]
dragon	**drak** (m)	[drak]
giant	**obr** (m)	[obr]

148. Zodiac Signs

Aries	**Skopec** (m)	[skopɛʦ]
Taurus	**Býk** (m)	[bi:k]
Gemini	**Blíženci** (m mn)	[bli:ʒenʦɪ]
Cancer	**Rak** (m)	[rak]
Leo	**Lev** (m)	[lɛf]
Virgo	**Panna** (ž)	[panna]
Libra	**Váhy** (ž mn)	[va:hɪ]
Scorpio	**Štír** (m)	[ʃti:r]
Sagittarius	**Střelec** (m)	[strʃɛlɛʦ]
Capricorn	**Kozorožec** (m)	[kozoroʒeʦ]
Aquarius	**Vodnář** (m)	[vodna:rʃ]
Pisces	**Ryby** (ž mn)	[rɪbɪ]
character	**povaha** (ž)	[povaha]
character traits	**povahové vlastnosti** (ž mn)	[povahovɛ: vlastnostɪ]

behavior	**chování** (s)	[xova:ni:]
to tell fortunes	**hádat**	[ha:dat]
fortune-teller	**věštkyně** (ž)	[veʃtkɪne]
horoscope	**horoskop** (m)	[horoskop]

Arts

149. Theater

theater	**divadlo** (s)	[dɪvadlo]
opera	**opera** (ž)	[opɛra]
operetta	**opereta** (ž)	[opɛrɛta]
ballet	**balet** (m)	[balɛt]
theater poster	**plakát** (m)	[plaka:t]
troupe (theatrical company)	**soubor** (m)	[soubor]
tour	**pohostinská vystoupení** (s mn)	[pohostɪnska: vɪstoupɛni:]
to be on tour	**hostovat**	[hostovat]
to rehearse (vi, vt)	**zkoušet**	[skouʃɛt]
rehearsal	**zkouška** (ž)	[skouʃka]
repertoire	**repertoár** (m)	[rɛpɛrtoa:r]
performance	**představení** (s)	[prʃɛtstavɛni:]
theatrical show	**hra** (ž)	[hra]
play	**hra** (ž)	[hra]
ticket	**vstupenka** (ž)	[vstupɛŋka]
box office (ticket booth)	**pokladna** (ž)	[pokladna]
lobby, foyer	**vestibul** (m)	[vɛstɪbul]
coat check (cloakroom)	**šatna** (ž)	[ʃatna]
coat check tag	**lístek** (m) **s číslem**	[li:stɛk s ʧi:slem]
binoculars	**kukátko** (s)	[kuka:tko]
usher	**uvaděčka** (ž)	[uvadeʧka]
orchestra seats	**přízemí** (s)	[prʃi:zɛmi:]
balcony	**balkón** (m)	[balko:n]
dress circle	**první balkón** (m)	[prvni: balko:n]
box	**lóže** (ž)	[lo:ʒe]
row	**řada** (ž)	[rʒada]
seat	**místo** (s)	[mi:sto]
audience	**obecenstvo** (s)	[obɛʦɛnstvo]
spectator	**divák** (m)	[dɪva:k]
to clap (vi, vt)	**tleskat**	[tlɛskat]
applause	**potlesk** (m)	[potlɛsk]
ovation	**ovace** (ž)	[ovaʦɛ]
stage	**jeviště** (s)	[jɛvɪʃte]
curtain	**opona** (ž)	[opona]

scenery	**dekorace** (ž)	[dɛkoraʦɛ]
backstage	**kulisy** (ž mn)	[kulɪsɪ]
scene (e.g., the last ~)	**scéna** (ž)	[sʦɛ:na]
act	**jednání** (s)	[jɛdna:ni:]
intermission	**přestávka** (ž)	[prʃɛsta:fka]

150. Cinema

actor	**herec** (m)	[hɛrɛʦ]
actress	**herečka** (ž)	[hɛrɛʧka]
movies (industry)	**kinematografie** (ž)	[kɪnɛmatografɪɛ]
movie	**film** (m)	[fɪlm]
episode	**díl** (m)	[di:l]
detective movie	**detektivka** (ž)	[dɛtɛktɪfka]
action movie	**akční film** (m)	[akʧni: fɪlm]
adventure movie	**dobrodružný film** (m)	[dobrodruʒni: fɪlm]
sci-fi movie	**vědecko-fantastický film** (m)	[vɛdɛʦko-fantastɪʦki: fɪlm]
horror movie	**horor** (m)	[horor]
comedy movie	**filmová komedie** (ž)	[fɪlmova: komɛdɪɛ]
melodrama	**melodrama** (s)	[mɛlodrama]
drama	**drama** (s)	[drama]
fictional movie	**umělecký film** (m)	[umnelɛʦki: fɪlm]
documentary	**dokumentární film** (m)	[dokumɛnta:rni: fɪlm]
cartoon	**kreslený film** (m)	[krɛslɛni: fɪlm]
silent movies	**němý film** (m)	[nemi: fɪlm]
role (part)	**role** (ž)	[rolɛ]
leading role	**hlavní role** (ž)	[hlavni: rolɛ]
to play (vi, vt)	**hrát**	[hra:t]
movie star	**filmová hvězda** (ž)	[fɪlmova: hvezda]
well-known (adj)	**slavný**	[slavni:]
famous (adj)	**známý**	[zna:mi:]
popular (adj)	**oblíbený**	[obli:bɛni:]
script (screenplay)	**scénář** (m)	[sʦɛ:na:rʃ]
scriptwriter	**scenárista** (m)	[sʦɛna:rɪsta]
movie director	**režisér** (m)	[rɛʒɪsɛ:r]
producer	**filmový producent** (m)	[fɪlmovi: produʦɛnt]
assistant	**asistent** (m)	[asɪstɛnt]
cameraman	**kameraman** (m)	[kamɛraman]
stuntman	**kaskadér** (m)	[kaskadɛ:r]
double (stand-in)	**dvojník** (m)	[dvojni:k]
to shoot a movie	**natáčet film**	[nata:ʧɛt fɪlm]

audition, screen test	**zkušební natáčení** (s)	[skuʃɛbni: nata:ʧɛni:]
shooting	**natáčení** (s)	[nata:ʧɛni:]
movie crew	**filmová skupina** (ž)	[fɪlmova: skupɪna]
movie set	**natáčecí prostor** (m)	[nata:ʧɛʦi: prostor]
camera	**filmová kamera** (ž)	[fɪlmova: kamɛra]
movie theater	**biograf** (m)	[bɪograf]
screen (e.g., big ~)	**plátno** (s)	[pla:tno]
to show a movie	**promítat film**	[promi:tat fɪlm]
soundtrack	**zvuková stopa** (ž)	[zvukova: stopa]
special effects	**triky** (m mn)	[trɪkɪ]
subtitles	**titulky** (m mn)	[tɪtulkɪ]
credits	**titulky** (m mn)	[tɪtulkɪ]
translation	**překlad** (m)	[prʃɛklat]

151. Painting

art	**umění** (s)	[umneni:]
fine arts	**krásná umění** (s mn)	[kra:sna: umneni:]
art gallery	**galerie** (ž)	[galɛrɪe]
art exhibition	**výstava** (ž) **obrazů**	[vi:stava obrazu:]
painting (art)	**malířství** (s)	[mali:rʃstvi:]
graphic art	**grafika** (ž)	[grafɪka]
abstract art	**abstraktní umění** (s)	[apstraktni: umneni:]
impressionism	**impresionismus** (m)	[ɪmprɛsɪonɪzmus]
picture (painting)	**obraz** (m)	[obraz]
drawing	**kresba** (ž)	[krɛzba]
poster	**plakát** (m)	[plaka:t]
illustration (picture)	**ilustrace** (ž)	[ɪlustraʦɛ]
miniature	**miniatura** (ž)	[mɪnɪatura]
copy (of painting, etc.)	**kopie** (ž)	[kopɪe]
reproduction	**reprodukce** (ž)	[rɛprodukʦɛ]
mosaic	**mozaika** (ž)	[mozaɪka]
stained glass window	**skleněná mozaika** (ž)	[sklɛnena: mozaɪka]
fresco	**freska** (ž)	[frɛska]
engraving	**rytina** (ž)	[rɪtɪna]
bust (sculpture)	**bysta** (ž)	[bɪsta]
sculpture	**skulptura** (ž)	[skulptura]
statue	**socha** (ž)	[soxa]
plaster of Paris	**sádra** (ž)	[sa:dra]
plaster (as adj)	**sádrový**	[sa:drovi:]
portrait	**portrét** (m)	[portrɛ:t]
self-portrait	**autoportrét** (m)	[autoportrɛ:t]

landscape painting	**krajina** (ž)	[krajɪna]
still life	**zátiší** (s)	[za:tɪʃi:]
caricature	**karikatura** (ž)	[karɪkatura]
sketch	**náčrt** (m)	[na:ʧrt]
paint	**barva** (ž)	[barva]
watercolor paint	**vodová barva** (ž)	[vodova: barva]
oil (paint)	**olejová barva** (ž)	[olɛjova: barva]
pencil	**tužka** (ž)	[tuʃka]
India ink	**tuž** (ž)	[tuʃ]
charcoal	**uhel** (m)	[uhɛl]
to draw (vi, vt)	**kreslit**	[krɛslɪt]
to paint (vi, vt)	**malovat**	[malovat]
to pose (vi)	**být modelem**	[bi:t modɛlɛm]
artist's model (masc.)	**živý model** (m)	[ʒɪvi: modɛl]
artist's model (fem.)	**modelka** (ž)	[modɛlka]
artist (painter)	**malíř** (m)	[mali:rʃ]
work of art	**dílo** (s)	[di:lo]
masterpiece	**veledílo** (s)	[vɛlɛdi:lo]
studio (artist's workroom)	**dílna** (ž)	[di:lna]
canvas (cloth)	**plátno** (s)	[pla:tno]
easel	**malířský stojan** (m)	[malirʒski: stojan]
palette	**paleta** (ž)	[palɛta]
frame (picture ~, etc.)	**rám** (m)	[ra:m]
restoration	**restaurace** (ž)	[rɛstauraʦɛ]
to restore (vt)	**restaurovat**	[rɛstaurovat]

152. Literature & Poetry

literature	**literatura** (ž)	[lɪtɛratura]
author (writer)	**autor** (m)	[autor]
pseudonym	**pseudonym** (m)	[psɛudonɪm]
book	**kniha** (ž)	[knɪha]
volume	**díl** (m)	[di:l]
table of contents	**obsah** (m)	[opsax]
page	**stránka** (ž)	[stra:ŋka]
main character	**hlavní hrdina** (m)	[hlavni: hrdɪna]
autograph	**autogram** (m)	[autogram]
short story	**povídka** (ž)	[povi:tka]
story (novella)	**novela** (ž)	[novɛla]
novel	**román** (m)	[roma:n]
work (writing)	**spis** (m)	[spɪs]
fable	**bajka** (ž)	[bajka]

detective novel	**detektivka** (ž)	[dɛtɛktɪfka]
poem (verse)	**báseň** (ž)	[ba:sɛnʲ]
poetry	**poezie** (ž)	[poɛzɪe]
poem (epic, ballad)	**báseň** (ž)	[ba:sɛnʲ]
poet	**básník** (m)	[ba:sni:k]
fiction	**beletrie** (ž)	[bɛlɛtrɪe]
science fiction	**vědecko-fantastická literatura** (ž)	[vɛdɛʦko-fantastɪʦka lɪtɛratura]
adventures	**dobrodružství** (s)	[dobrodruʒstvi:]
educational literature	**školní literatura** (ž)	[ʃkolni: lɪtɛratura]
children's literature	**dětská literatura** (ž)	[detska: lɪtɛratura]

153. Circus

circus	**cirkus** (m)	[ʦɪrkus]
traveling circus	**cirkusový stan** (m)	[ʦɪrkusovi: stan]
program	**program** (m)	[program]
performance	**představení** (s)	[prʃɛtstavɛni:]
act (circus ~)	**výstup** (m)	[vi:stup]
circus ring	**aréna** (ž)	[arɛ:na]
pantomime (act)	**pantomima** (ž)	[pantomɪma]
clown	**klaun** (m)	[klaun]
acrobat	**akrobat** (m)	[akrobat]
acrobatics	**akrobatika** (ž)	[akrobatɪka]
gymnast	**gymnasta** (m)	[gɪmnasta]
acrobatic gymnastics	**gymnastika** (ž)	[gɪmnastɪka]
somersault	**salto** (s)	[salto]
athlete (strongman)	**atlet** (m)	[atlɛt]
tamer (e.g., lion ~)	**krotitel** (m)	[krotɪtɛl]
rider (circus horse ~)	**jezdec** (m)	[jɛzdɛʦ]
assistant	**asistent** (m)	[asɪstɛnt]
stunt	**trik** (m)	[trɪk]
magic trick	**kouzlo** (s)	[kouzlo]
conjurer, magician	**kouzelník** (m)	[kouzɛlni:k]
juggler	**žonglér** (m)	[ʒonglɛ:r]
to juggle (vi, vt)	**žonglovat**	[ʒonglovat]
animal trainer	**cvičitel** (m)	[ʦvɪʧɪtɛl]
animal training	**drezůra** (ž)	[drɛzu:ra]
to train (animals)	**cvičit**	[ʦvɪʧɪt]

154. Music. Pop music

music	**hudba** (ž)	[hudba]
musician	**hudebník** (m)	[hudɛbni:k]
musical instrument	**hudební nástroj** (m)	[hudɛbni: na:stroj]
to play ...	**hrát na ...**	[hra:t na]
guitar	**kytara** (ž)	[kɪtara]
violin	**housle** (ž mn)	[houslɛ]
cello	**violoncello** (s)	[vɪolonʧelo]
double bass	**basa** (ž)	[basa]
harp	**harfa** (ž)	[harfa]
piano	**pianino** (s)	[pɪanɪno]
grand piano	**klavír** (m)	[klavi:r]
organ	**varhany** (ž mn)	[varhanɪ]
wind instruments	**dechové nástroje** (m mn)	[dɛxovɛ: na:strojɛ]
oboe	**hoboj** (m)	[hoboj]
saxophone	**saxofon** (m)	[saksofon]
clarinet	**klarinet** (m)	[klarɪnɛt]
flute	**flétna** (ž)	[flɛ:tna]
trumpet	**trubka** (ž)	[trupka]
accordion	**akordeon** (m)	[akordɛon]
drum	**buben** (m)	[bubɛn]
duo	**duo** (s)	[duo]
trio	**trio** (s)	[trɪo]
quartet	**kvarteto** (s)	[kvartɛto]
choir	**sbor** (m)	[zbor]
orchestra	**orchestr** (m)	[orxɛstr]
pop music	**populární hudba** (ž)	[popula:rni: hudba]
rock music	**rocková hudba** (ž)	[rokova: hudba]
rock group	**roková kapela** (ž)	[rokova: kapɛla]
jazz	**jazz** (m)	[ʤɛs]
idol	**idol** (m)	[ɪdol]
admirer, fan	**ctitel** (m)	[ʦtɪtɛl]
concert	**koncert** (m)	[konʦɛrt]
symphony	**symfonie** (ž)	[sɪmfonɪe]
composition	**skladba** (ž)	[skladba]
to compose (write)	**složit**	[sloʒɪt]
singing (n)	**zpěv** (m)	[spef]
song	**píseň** (ž)	[pi:sɛnʲ]
tune (melody)	**melodie** (ž)	[mɛlodɪe]
rhythm	**rytmus** (m)	[rɪtmus]
blues	**blues** (s)	[blu:s]

sheet music	**noty** (ž mn)	[notɪ]
baton	**taktovka** (ž)	[taktofka]
bow	**smyčec** (m)	[smɪʧɛʦ]
string	**struna** (ž)	[struna]
case (e.g., guitar ~)	**pouzdro** (s)	[pouzdro]

Rest. Entertainment. Travel

155. Trip. Travel

tourism, travel	**turistika** (ž)	[turɪstɪka]
tourist	**turista** (m)	[turɪsta]
trip, voyage	**cestování** (s)	[ʦɛstova:ni:]
adventure	**příhoda** (ž)	[prʃi:hoda]
trip, journey	**cesta** (ž)	[ʦɛsta]
vacation	**dovolená** (ž)	[dovolɛna:]
to be on vacation	**mít dovolenou**	[mi:t dovolɛnou]
rest	**odpočinek** (m)	[otpoʧɪnɛk]
train	**vlak** (m)	[vlak]
by train	**vlakem**	[vlakɛm]
airplane	**letadlo** (s)	[lɛtadlo]
by airplane	**letadlem**	[lɛtadlɛm]
by car	**autem**	[autɛm]
by ship	**lodí**	[lodi:]
luggage	**zavazadla** (s mn)	[zavazadla]
suitcase	**kufr** (m)	[kufr]
luggage cart	**vozík** (m) **na zavazadla**	[vozi:k na zavazadla]
passport	**pas** (m)	[pas]
visa	**vízum** (s)	[vi:zum]
ticket	**jízdenka** (ž)	[ji:zdɛŋka]
air ticket	**letenka** (ž)	[lɛtɛŋka]
guidebook	**průvodce** (m)	[pru:vodʦɛ]
map (tourist ~)	**mapa** (ž)	[mapa]
area (rural ~)	**krajina** (ž)	[krajɪna]
place, site	**místo** (s)	[mi:sto]
exotica (n)	**exotika** (ž)	[ɛgzotɪka]
exotic (adj)	**exotický**	[ɛgzotɪʦki:]
amazing (adj)	**podivuhodný**	[podɪvuhodni:]
group	**skupina** (ž)	[skupɪna]
excursion, sightseeing tour	**výlet** (m)	[vi:lɛt]
guide (person)	**průvodce** (m)	[pru:vodʦɛ]

156. Hotel

hotel	**hotel** (m)	[hotɛl]
motel	**motel** (m)	[motɛl]
three-star (~ hotel)	**tři hvězdy**	[trʃɪ hvezdɪ]
five-star	**pět hvězd**	[pet hvezt]
to stay (in a hotel, etc.)	**ubytovat se**	[ubɪtovat sɛ]
room	**pokoj** (m)	[pokoj]
single room	**jednolůžkový pokoj** (m)	[jɛdnolu:ʃkovi: pokoj]
double room	**dvoulůžkový pokoj** (m)	[dvoulu:ʃkovi: pokoj]
to book a room	**rezervovat pokoj**	[rɛzɛrvovat pokoj]
half board	**polopenze** (ž)	[polopɛnzɛ]
full board	**plná penze** (ž)	[plna: pɛnzɛ]
with bath	**s koupelnou**	[s koupɛlnou]
with shower	**se sprchou**	[sɛ sprxou]
satellite television	**satelitní televize** (ž)	[satɛlɪtni: tɛlɛvɪzɛ]
air-conditioner	**klimatizátor** (m)	[klɪmatɪza:tor]
towel	**ručník** (m)	[rutʃni:k]
key	**klíč** (m)	[kli:tʃ]
administrator	**recepční** (m)	[rɛtsɛptʃni:]
chambermaid	**pokojská** (ž)	[pokojska:]
porter, bellboy	**nosič** (m)	[nosɪtʃ]
doorman	**vrátný** (m)	[vra:tni:]
restaurant	**restaurace** (ž)	[rɛstauratsɛ]
pub, bar	**bar** (m)	[bar]
breakfast	**snídaně** (ž)	[sni:dane]
dinner	**večeře** (ž)	[vɛtʃɛrʒɛ]
buffet	**obložený stůl** (m)	[oblozeni: stu:l]
lobby	**vstupní hala** (ž)	[vstupni: hala]
elevator	**výtah** (m)	[vi:tax]
DO NOT DISTURB	**NERUŠIT**	[nɛruʃɪt]
NO SMOKING	**ZÁKAZ KOUŘENÍ**	[za:kaz kourʒɛni:]

157. Books. Reading

book	**kniha** (ž)	[knɪha]
author	**autor** (m)	[autor]
writer	**spisovatel** (m)	[spɪsovatɛl]
to write (~ a book)	**napsat**	[napsat]
reader	**čtenář** (m)	[tʃtɛna:rʃ]
to read (vi, vt)	**číst**	[tʃi:st]

reading (activity)	**četba** (ž)	[ʧɛtba]
silently (to oneself)	**pro sebe**	[pro sɛbɛ]
aloud (adv)	**nahlas**	[nahlas]
to publish (vt)	**vydávat**	[vɪda:vat]
publishing (process)	**vydání** (s)	[vɪda:ni:]
publisher	**vydavatel** (m)	[vɪdavatɛl]
publishing house	**nakladatelství** (s)	[nakladatɛlstvi:]
to come out (be released)	**vyjít**	[vɪji:t]
release (of a book)	**vydání** (s)	[vɪda:ni:]
print run	**náklad** (m)	[na:klat]
bookstore	**knihkupectví** (s)	[knɪxkupɛʦtvi:]
library	**knihovna** (ž)	[knɪhovna]
story (novella)	**novela** (ž)	[novɛla]
short story	**povídka** (ž)	[povi:tka]
novel	**román** (m)	[roma:n]
detective novel	**detektivka** (ž)	[dɛtɛktɪfka]
memoirs	**paměti** (ž mn)	[pamnetɪ]
legend	**legenda** (ž)	[lɛgɛnda]
myth	**mýtus** (m)	[mi:tus]
poetry, poems	**básně** (ž mn)	[ba:sne]
autobiography	**vlastní životopis** (m)	[vlastni: ʒɪvotopɪs]
selected works	**výbor** (m) **z díla**	[vi:bor z di:la]
science fiction	**fantastika** (ž)	[fantastɪka]
title	**název** (m)	[na:zɛf]
introduction	**úvod** (m)	[u:vot]
title page	**titulní list** (m)	[tɪtulni: lɪst]
chapter	**kapitola** (ž)	[kapɪtola]
extract	**úryvek** (m)	[u:rɪvɛk]
episode	**epizoda** (ž)	[ɛpɪzoda]
plot (storyline)	**námět** (m)	[na:mnet]
contents	**obsah** (m)	[opsax]
table of contents	**obsah** (m)	[opsax]
main character	**hlavní hrdina** (m)	[hlavni: hrdɪna]
volume	**svazek** (m)	[svazɛk]
cover	**obálka** (ž)	[oba:lka]
binding	**vazba** (ž)	[vazba]
bookmark	**záložka** (ž)	[za:loʃka]
page	**stránka** (ž)	[stra:ŋka]
to page through	**listovat**	[lɪstovat]
margins	**okraj** (m)	[okraj]
annotation (marginal note, etc.)	**poznámka** (ž) **na okraj**	[pozna:mka na okraj]

footnote	**poznámka** (ž)	[pozna:mka]
text	**text** (m)	[tɛkst]
type, font	**písmo** (s)	[pi:smo]
misprint, typo	**chyba** (ž) **tisku**	[xɪba tɪsku]
translation	**překlad** (m)	[prʃɛklat]
to translate (vt)	**překládat**	[prʃɛkla:dat]
original (n)	**originál** (m)	[orɪgɪna:l]
famous (adj)	**slavný**	[slavni:]
unknown (not famous)	**neznámý**	[nɛzna:mi:]
interesting (adj)	**zajímavý**	[zaji:mavi:]
bestseller	**bestseller** (m)	[bɛstsɛlɛr]
dictionary	**slovník** (m)	[slovni:k]
textbook	**učebnice** (ž)	[uʧɛbnɪʦɛ]
encyclopedia	**encyklopedie** (ž)	[ɛnʦɪklopɛdɪe]

158. Hunting. Fishing

hunting	**lov** (m)	[lof]
to hunt (vi, vt)	**lovit**	[lovɪt]
hunter	**lovec** (m)	[lovɛʦ]
to shoot (vi)	**střílet**	[strʃi:lɛt]
rifle	**puška** (ž)	[puʃka]
bullet (shell)	**náboj** (m)	[na:boj]
shot (lead balls)	**broky** (m mn)	[brokɪ]
steel trap	**past** (ž)	[past]
snare (for birds, etc.)	**léčka** (ž)	[lɛ:ʧka]
to lay a steel trap	**líčit past**	[li:ʧɪt past]
poacher	**pytlák** (m)	[pɪtla:k]
game (in hunting)	**zvěřina** (ž)	[zverʒɪna]
hound dog	**lovecký pes** (m)	[lovɛʦki: pɛs]
safari	**safari** (s)	[safarɪ]
mounted animal	**vycpané zvíře** (s)	[vɪʦpanɛ: zvi:rʒɛ]
fisherman, angler	**rybář** (m)	[rɪba:rʃ]
fishing (angling)	**rybaření** (s)	[rɪbarʒɛni:]
to fish (vi)	**lovit ryby**	[lovɪt rɪbɪ]
fishing rod	**udice** (ž)	[udɪʦɛ]
fishing line	**vlas** (m)	[vlas]
hook	**háček** (m)	[ha:ʧɛk]
float, bobber	**splávek** (m)	[spla:vɛk]
bait	**návnada** (ž)	[na:vnada]
to cast a line	**hodit udici**	[hodɪt udɪʦɪ]
to bite (ab. fish)	**brát**	[bra:t]

catch (of fish)	**úlovek** (m)	[u:lovɛk]
ice-hole	**otvor** (m) **v ledu**	[otvor v lɛdu]
fishing net	**síť** (ž)	[si:tʲ]
boat	**loďka** (ž)	[lotʲka]
to net (to fish with a net)	**lovit sítí**	[lovɪt si:ti:]
to cast[throw] the net	**házet síť**	[ha:zɛt si:tʲ]
to haul the net in	**vytahovat síť**	[vɪtahovat si:tʲ]
whaler (person)	**velrybář** (m)	[vɛlrɪba:rʃ]
whaleboat	**velrybářská loď** (ž)	[vɛlrɪba:rʃska: lotʲ]
harpoon	**harpuna** (ž)	[harpuna]

159. Games. Billiards

billiards	**kulečník** (m)	[kulɛtʃni:k]
billiard room, hall	**kulečníková herna** (ž)	[kulɛtʃni:kova: hɛrna]
ball (snooker, etc.)	**kulečníková koule** (ž)	[kulɛtʃni:kova: koulɛ]
to pocket a ball	**strefit se koulí**	[strɛfɪt sɛ kouli:]
cue	**tágo** (s)	[ta:go]
pocket	**otvor** (m) **v kulečníku**	[otvor v kulɛtʃni:ku]

160. Games. Playing cards

diamonds	**kára** (s mn)	[ka:ra]
spades	**piky** (m mn)	[pɪkɪ]
hearts	**srdce** (s mn)	[srdtsɛ]
clubs	**kříže** (m mn)	[krʃi:ʒe]
ace	**eso** (s)	[ɛso]
king	**král** (m)	[kra:l]
queen	**dáma** (ž)	[da:ma]
jack, knave	**kluk** (m)	[kluk]
playing card	**karta** (ž)	[karta]
cards	**karty** (ž mn)	[kartɪ]
trump	**trumf** (m)	[trumf]
deck of cards	**karty** (ž mn)	[kartɪ]
point	**bod** (m)	[bot]
to deal (vi, vt)	**rozdávat**	[rozda:vat]
to shuffle (cards)	**míchat**	[mi:xat]
lead, turn (n)	**vynášení** (s)	[vɪna:ʃɛni:]
cardsharp	**falešný hráč** (m)	[falɛʃni: hra:tʃ]

161. Casino. Roulette

casino	**kasino** (s)	[kasi:no]
roulette (game)	**ruleta** (ž)	[rulɛta]
bet	**sázka** (ž)	[sa:ska]
to place bets	**sázet**	[sa:zɛt]
red	**červené** (s)	[ʧɛrvɛnɛ:]
black	**černé** (s)	[ʧɛrnɛ:]
to bet on red	**sázet na červené**	[sa:zɛt na ʧɛrvɛnɛ:]
to bet on black	**sázet na černé**	[sa:zɛt na ʧɛrnɛ:]
croupier (dealer)	**krupiér** (m)	[krupjɛ:r]
to spin the wheel	**otáčet buben**	[ota:ʧɛt bubɛn]
rules (of game)	**pravidla** (s mn) **hry**	[pravɪdla hrɪ]
chip	**žeton** (m)	[ʒeton]
to win (vi, vt)	**vyhrát**	[vɪhra:t]
win (winnings)	**výhra** (ž)	[vi:hra]
to lose (~ 100 dollars)	**prohrát**	[prohra:t]
loss (losses)	**prohra** (ž)	[prohra]
player	**hráč** (m)	[hra:ʧ]
blackjack (card game)	**hra** (ž) **jednadvacet**	[hra jɛdnadvaʦɛt]
craps (dice game)	**hra** (ž) **v kostky**	[hra v kostkɪ]
dice (a pair of ~)	**kostky** (ž mn)	[kostkɪ]
slot machine	**hrací automat** (m)	[hraʦi: automat]

162. Rest. Games. Miscellaneous

to stroll (vi, vt)	**procházet se**	[proxa:zɛt sɛ]
stroll (leisurely walk)	**procházka** (ž)	[proxa:ska]
car ride	**vyjížďka** (ž)	[vɪji:ʒtʲka]
adventure	**příhoda** (ž)	[prʃi:hoda]
picnic	**piknik** (m)	[pɪknɪk]
game (chess, etc.)	**hra** (ž)	[hra]
player	**hráč** (m)	[hra:ʧ]
game (one ~ of chess)	**partie** (ž)	[partɪe]
collector (e.g., philatelist)	**sběratel** (m)	[zberatɛl]
to collect (stamps, etc.)	**sbírat**	[zbi:rat]
collection	**sbírka** (ž)	[zbi:rka]
crossword puzzle	**křížovka** (ž)	[krʃi:ʒofka]
racetrack (horse racing venue)	**hipodrom** (m)	[hɪpodrom]
disco (discotheque)	**diskotéka** (ž)	[dɪskotɛ:ka]

sauna	**sauna** (ž)	[sauna]
lottery	**loterie** (ž)	[lotɛrɪe]
camping trip	**túra** (ž)	[tu:ra]
camp	**tábor** (m)	[ta:bor]
tent (for camping)	**stan** (m)	[stan]
compass	**kompas** (m)	[kompas]
camper	**turista** (m)	[turɪsta]
to watch (movie, etc.)	**dívat se na ...**	[di:vat sɛ na]
viewer	**televizní divák** (m)	[tɛlɛvɪzni: dɪva:k]
TV show (TV program)	**televizní pořad** (m)	[tɛlevɪzni: porʒat]

163. Photography

camera (photo)	**fotoaparát** (m)	[fotoapara:t]
photo, picture	**fotografie** (ž)	[fotografɪe]
photographer	**fotograf** (m)	[fotograf]
photo studio	**fotografický salón** (m)	[fotografɪʦki: salo:n]
photo album	**fotoalbum** (s)	[fotoalbum]
camera lens	**objektiv** (m)	[objɛktɪf]
telephoto lens	**teleobjektiv** (m)	[tɛlɛobjɛktɪf]
filter	**filtr** (m)	[fɪltr]
lens	**čočka** (ž)	[ʧoʧka]
optics (high-quality ~)	**optika** (ž)	[optɪka]
diaphragm (aperture)	**clona** (ž)	[ʦlona]
exposure time (shutter speed)	**expozice** (ž)	[ɛkspozɪʦɛ]
viewfinder	**hledáček** (m)	[hlɛda:ʧɛk]
digital camera	**digitální kamera** (ž)	[dɪgɪta:lni: kamɛra]
tripod	**stativ** (m)	[statɪf]
flash	**blesk** (m)	[blɛsk]
to photograph (vt)	**fotografovat**	[fotografovat]
to take pictures	**fotografovat**	[fotografovat]
to have one's picture taken	**fotografovat se**	[fotografovat sɛ]
focus	**ostrost** (ž)	[ostrost]
to focus	**zaostřovat**	[zaostrʃovat]
sharp, in focus (adj)	**ostrý**	[ostri:]
sharpness	**ostrost** (ž)	[ostrost]
contrast	**kontrast** (m)	[kontrast]
contrast (as adj)	**kontrastní**	[kontrastni:]
picture (photo)	**snímek** (m)	[sni:mɛk]
negative (n)	**negativ** (m)	[nɛgatɪf]

film (a roll of ~)	**film** (m)	[fɪlm]
frame (still)	**záběr** (m)	[za:ber]
to print (photos)	**tisknout**	[tɪsknout]

164. Beach. Swimming

beach	**pláž** (ž)	[pla:ʃ]
sand	**písek** (m)	[pi:sɛk]
deserted (beach)	**pustý**	[pusti:]
suntan	**opálení** (s)	[opa:lɛni:]
to get a tan	**opalovat se**	[opalovat sɛ]
tan (adj)	**opálený**	[opa:lɛni:]
sunscreen	**krém** (m) **na opalování**	[krɛ:m na opalova:ni:]
bikini	**bikiny** (mn)	[bɪkɪnɪ]
bathing suit	**dámské plavky** (ž mn)	[damske plafkɪ]
swim trunks	**plavky** (ž mn)	[plafkɪ]
swimming pool	**bazén** (m)	[bazɛ:n]
to swim (vi)	**plavat**	[plavat]
shower	**sprcha** (ž)	[sprxa]
to change (one's clothes)	**převlékat se**	[prʃɛvlɛ:kat sɛ]
towel	**ručník** (m)	[rutʃni:k]
boat	**loďka** (ž)	[lotʲka]
motorboat	**motorový člun** (m)	[motorovi: tʃlun]
water ski	**vodní lyže** (ž mn)	[vodni: lɪʒe]
paddle boat	**vodní bicykl** (m)	[vodni: bɪtsɪkl]
surfing	**surfování** (s)	[surfova:ni:]
surfer	**surfař** (m)	[surfarʃ]
scuba set	**potápěčský dýchací přístroj** (m)	[pota:petʃski: di:xatsi: prʃi:stroj]
flippers (swim fins)	**ploutve** (ž mn)	[ploutvɛ]
mask (diving ~)	**maska** (ž)	[maska]
diver	**potápěč** (m)	[pota:petʃ]
to dive (vi)	**potápět se**	[pota:pet sɛ]
underwater (adv)	**pod vodou**	[pod vodou]
beach umbrella	**slunečník** (m)	[slunɛtʃni:k]
sunbed (lounger)	**rozkládací lehátko** (s)	[roskla:datsi: lɛha:tko]
sunglasses	**sluneční brýle** (mn)	[slunɛtʃni: bri:lɛ]
air mattress	**nafukovací matrace** (ž)	[nafukovatsi: matratsɛ]
to play (amuse oneself)	**hrát**	[hra:t]
to go for a swim	**koupat se**	[koupat sɛ]
beach ball	**míč** (m)	[mi:tʃ]
to inflate (vt)	**nafukovat**	[nafukovat]

inflatable, air (adj)	**nafukovací**	[nafukovaʦi:]
wave	**vlna** (ž)	[vlna]
buoy (line of ~s)	**bóje** (ž)	[bo:jɛ]
to drown (ab. person)	**topit se**	[topɪt sɛ]
to save, to rescue	**zachraňovat**	[zaxranʲovat]
life vest	**záchranná vesta** (ž)	[za:xranna: vɛsta]
to observe, to watch	**pozorovat**	[pozorovat]
lifeguard	**záchranář** (m)	[za:xrana:rʃ]

TECHNICAL EQUIPMENT. TRANSPORTATION

Technical equipment

165. Computer

computer	**počítač** (m)	[potʃi:tatʃ]
notebook, laptop	**notebook** (m)	[noutbu:k]
to turn on	**zapnout**	[zapnout]
to turn off	**vypnout**	[vɪpnout]
keyboard	**klávesnice** (ž)	[kla:vɛsnɪtsɛ]
key	**klávesa** (ž)	[kla:vɛsa]
mouse	**myš** (ž)	[mɪʃ]
mouse pad	**podložka** (ž) **pro myš**	[podloʃka pro mɪʃ]
button	**tlačítko** (s)	[tlatʃi:tko]
cursor	**kurzor** (m)	[kurzor]
monitor	**monitor** (m)	[monɪtor]
screen	**obrazovka** (ž)	[obrazofka]
hard disk	**pevný disk** (m)	[pɛvni: dɪsk]
hard disk capacity	**rozměr** (m) **disku**	[rozmner dɪsku]
memory	**paměť** (ž)	[pamnetʲ]
random access memory	**operační paměť** (ž)	[opɛratʃni: pamnetʲ]
file	**soubor** (m)	[soubor]
folder	**složka** (ž)	[sloʃka]
to open (vt)	**otevřít**	[otɛvrʒi:t]
to close (vt)	**zavřít**	[zavrʒi:t]
to save (vt)	**uložit**	[uloʒɪt]
to delete (vt)	**vymazat**	[vɪmazat]
to copy (vt)	**zkopírovat**	[skopi:rovat]
to sort (vt)	**uspořádat**	[usporʒa:dat]
to transfer (copy)	**zkopírovat**	[skopi:rovat]
program	**program** (m)	[program]
software	**programové vybavení** (s)	[programovɛ: vɪbavɛni:]
programmer	**programátor** (m)	[programa:tor]
to program (vt)	**programovat**	[programovat]
hacker	**hacker** (m)	[hɛkr]
password	**heslo** (s)	[hɛslo]

virus	**virus** (m)	[vɪrus]
to find, to detect	**zjistit**	[zjɪstɪt]
byte	**byte** (m)	[bajt]
megabyte	**megabyte** (m)	[mɛgabajt]
data	**data** (s mn)	[data]
database	**databáze** (ž)	[databa:zɛ]
cable (USB, etc.)	**kabel** (m)	[kabɛl]
to disconnect (vt)	**odpojit**	[otpojɪt]
to connect (sth to sth)	**připojit**	[prʃɪpojɪt]

166. Internet. E-mail

Internet	**internet** (m)	[ɪntɛrnɛt]
browser	**prohlížeč** (m)	[prohli:ʒetʃ]
search engine	**vyhledávací zdroj** (m)	[vɪhlɛda:vatsi: zdroj]
provider	**dodavatel** (m)	[dodavatɛl]
webmaster	**web-master** (m)	[vɛb-mastɛr]
website	**webové stránky** (ž mn)	[vɛbovɛ: stra:ŋkɪ]
webpage	**webová stránka** (ž)	[vɛbova: stra:ŋka]
address (e-mail ~)	**adresa** (ž)	[adrɛsa]
address book	**adresář** (m)	[adrɛsa:rʃ]
mailbox	**e-mailová schránka** (ž)	[i:mɛjlova: sxra:ŋka]
mail	**pošta** (ž)	[poʃta]
full (adj)	**přeplněný**	[prʃɛplneni:]
message	**zpráva** (ž)	[spra:va]
incoming messages	**příchozí zprávy** (ž mn)	[pʃi:xozi: spra:vɪ]
outgoing messages	**odchozí zprávy** (ž mn)	[otxozi: spra:vɪ]
sender	**odesílatel** (m)	[odɛsi:latɛl]
to send (vt)	**odeslat**	[odɛslat]
sending (of mail)	**odeslání** (s)	[odɛsla:ni:]
receiver	**příjemce** (m)	[prʃi:jɛmtsɛ]
to receive (vt)	**dostat**	[dostat]
correspondence	**korespondence** (ž)	[korɛspondɛntsɛ]
to correspond (vi)	**korespondovat**	[korɛspondovat]
file	**soubor** (m)	[soubor]
to download (vt)	**stáhnout**	[sta:hnout]
to create (vt)	**vytvořit**	[vɪtvorʒɪt]
to delete (vt)	**vymazat**	[vɪmazat]
deleted (adj)	**vymazaný**	[vɪmazani:]
connection (ADSL, etc.)	**spojení** (s)	[spojɛni:]

speed	**rychlost** (ž)	[rɪxlost]
modem	**modem** (m)	[modɛm]
access	**přístup** (m)	[prʃi:stup]
port (e.g., input ~)	**port** (m)	[port]
connection (make a ~)	**připojení** (s)	[prʃɪpojɛni:]
to connect to ... (vi)	**připojit se**	[prʃɪpojɪt sɛ]
to select (vt)	**vybrat**	[vɪbrat]
to search (for ...)	**hledat**	[hlɛdat]

167. Electricity

electricity	**elektřina** (ž)	[ɛlɛktrʃɪna]
electric, electrical (adj)	**elektrický**	[ɛlɛktrɪʦki:]
electric power plant	**elektrárna** (ž)	[ɛlɛktra:rna]
energy	**energie** (ž)	[ɛnɛrgɪe]
electric power	**elektrická energie** (ž)	[ɛlɛktrɪʦka: ɛnɛrgɪe]
light bulb	**žárovka** (ž)	[ʒa:rofka]
flashlight	**baterka** (ž)	[batɛrka]
street light	**pouliční lampa** (ž)	[poulɪʧni: lampa]
light	**světlo** (s)	[svetlo]
to turn on	**zapínat**	[zapi:nat]
to turn off	**vypínat**	[vɪpi:nat]
to turn off the light	**zhasnout světlo**	[zhasnout svetlo]
to burn out (vi)	**přepálit se**	[prʃɛpa:lɪt sɛ]
short circuit	**krátké spojení** (s)	[kra:tkɛ: spojɛni:]
broken wire	**přetržení** (s)	[prʃɛtrʒeni:]
contact (electrical ~)	**kontakt** (m)	[kontakt]
light switch	**vypínač** (m)	[vɪpi:naʧ]
wall socket	**zásuvka** (ž)	[za:sufka]
plug	**zástrčka** (ž)	[za:strʧka]
extension cord	**prodlužovák** (m)	[prodluʒova:k]
fuse	**pojistka** (ž)	[pojɪstka]
cable, wire	**vodič** (m)	[vodɪʧ]
wiring	**vedení** (s)	[vɛdɛni:]
ampere	**ampér** (m)	[ampɛ:r]
amperage	**intenzita** (ž) **proudu**	[ɪntɛnzɪta proudu]
volt	**volt** (m)	[volt]
voltage	**napětí** (s)	[napeti:]
electrical device	**elektrický přístroj** (m)	[ɛlɛktrɪʦki: prʃi:stroj]
indicator	**indikátor** (m)	[ɪndɪka:tor]
electrician	**elektrotechnik** (m)	[ɛlɛktrotɛxnɪk]

to solder (vt)	**letovat**	[lɛtovat]
soldering iron	**letovačka** (ž)	[lɛtovatʃka]
electric current	**proud** (m)	[prout]

168. Tools

tool, instrument	**nářadí** (s)	[na:rʒadi:]
tools	**nástroje** (m mn)	[nastrojɛ]
equipment (factory ~)	**zařízení** (s)	[zarʒi:zɛni:]
hammer	**kladivo** (s)	[kladɪvo]
screwdriver	**šroubovák** (m)	[ʃroubova:k]
ax	**sekera** (ž)	[sɛkɛra]
saw	**pila** (ž)	[pɪla]
to saw (vt)	**řezat**	[rʒɛzat]
plane (tool)	**hoblík** (m)	[hobli:k]
to plane (vt)	**hoblovat**	[hoblovat]
soldering iron	**letovačka** (ž)	[lɛtovatʃka]
to solder (vt)	**letovat**	[lɛtovat]
file (tool)	**pilník** (m)	[pɪlni:k]
carpenter pincers	**kleště** (ž mn)	[klɛʃte]
lineman's pliers	**ploché kleště** (ž mn)	[ploxɛ: klɛʃte]
chisel	**dláto** (s)	[dla:to]
drill bit	**vrták** (m)	[vrta:k]
electric drill	**svidřík** (m)	[svɪdrʒi:k]
to drill (vi, vt)	**vrtat**	[vrtat]
knife	**nůž** (m)	[nu:ʃ]
pocket knife	**kapesní nůž** (m)	[kapɛsni: nu:ʃ]
blade	**čepel** (ž)	[tʃɛpɛl]
sharp (blade, etc.)	**ostrý**	[ostri:]
dull, blunt (adj)	**tupý**	[tupi:]
to get blunt (dull)	**ztupit se**	[stupɪt sɛ]
to sharpen (vt)	**ostřit**	[ostrʃɪt]
bolt	**šroub** (m)	[ʃroup]
nut	**matice** (ž)	[matɪtsɛ]
thread (of a screw)	**závit** (m)	[za:vɪt]
wood screw	**vrut** (m)	[vrut]
nail	**hřebík** (m)	[hrʒɛbi:k]
nailhead	**hlavička** (ž)	[hlavɪtʃka]
ruler (for measuring)	**pravítko** (s)	[pravi:tko]
tape measure	**měřicí pásmo** (s)	[mnerʒɪtsi: pa:smo]
spirit level	**libela** (ž)	[lɪbɛla]

magnifying glass	**lupa** (ž)	[lupa]
measuring instrument	**měřicí přístroj** (m)	[mnerʒɪtsi: prʃi:stroj]
to measure (vt)	**měřit**	[mnerʒɪt]
scale (of thermometer, etc.)	**stupnice** (ž)	[stupnɪtsɛ]
readings	**údaje** (m mn)	[u:dajɛ]
compressor	**kompresor** (m)	[komprɛsor]
microscope	**mikroskop** (m)	[mɪkroskop]
pump (e.g., water ~)	**pumpa** (ž)	[pumpa]
robot	**robot** (m)	[robot]
laser	**laser** (m)	[lɛjzr]
wrench	**maticový klíč** (m)	[matɪtsovi: kli:tʃ]
adhesive tape	**lepicí páska** (ž)	[lɛpɪtsi: pa:ska]
glue	**lepidlo** (s)	[lɛpɪdlo]
sandpaper	**smirkový papír** (m)	[smɪrkovi: papi:r]
spring	**pružina** (ž)	[pruʒɪna]
magnet	**magnet** (m)	[magnɛt]
gloves	**rukavice** (ž mn)	[rukavɪtsɛ]
rope	**provaz** (m)	[provaz]
cord	**šňůra** (ž)	[ʃnu:ra]
wire (e.g., telephone ~)	**vodič** (m)	[vodɪtʃ]
cable	**kabel** (m)	[kabɛl]
sledgehammer	**palice** (ž)	[palɪtsɛ]
prybar	**sochor** (m)	[soxor]
ladder	**žebřík** (m)	[ʒebrʒi:k]
stepladder	**dvojitý žebřík** (m)	[dvojɪti: ʒebrʒi:k]
to screw (tighten)	**zakroutit**	[zakroutɪt]
to unscrew (lid, filter, etc.)	**odšroubovávat**	[otʃroubova:vat]
to tighten (e.g., with a clamp)	**svírat**	[svi:rat]
to glue, to stick	**přilepit**	[prʃɪlɛpɪt]
to cut (vt)	**řezat**	[rʒɛzat]
malfunction (fault)	**porucha** (ž)	[poruxa]
repair (mending)	**oprava** (ž)	[oprava]
to repair, to fix (vt)	**opravovat**	[opravovat]
to adjust (machine, etc.)	**seřizovat**	[sɛrʒɪzovat]
to check (to examine)	**zkoušet**	[skouʃɛt]
checking	**kontrola** (ž)	[kontrola]
readings	**údaj** (m)	[u:daj]
reliable, solid (machine)	**spolehlivý**	[spolɛhlɪvi:]
complex (adj)	**složitý**	[sloʒɪti:]
to rust (get rusted)	**rezavět**	[rɛzavet]

rusty, rusted (adj)	**rezavý**	[rɛzavi:]
rust	**rez** (ž)	[rɛz]

Transportation

169. Airplane

airplane	**letadlo** (s)	[lɛtadlo]
air ticket	**letenka** (ž)	[lɛtɛŋka]
airline	**letecká společnost** (ž)	[lɛtɛt͡ska: spolɛt͡ʃnost]
airport	**letiště** (s)	[lɛtɪʃte]
supersonic (adj)	**nadzvukový**	[nadzvukovi:]
captain	**velitel** (m) **posádky**	[vɛlɪtɛl posa:tkɪ]
crew	**posádka** (ž)	[posa:tka]
pilot	**pilot** (m)	[pɪlot]
flight attendant (fem.)	**letuška** (ž)	[lɛtuʃka]
navigator	**navigátor** (m)	[navɪga:tor]
wings	**křídla** (s mn)	[krʃi:dla]
tail	**ocas** (m)	[ot͡sas]
cockpit	**kabina** (ž)	[kabɪna]
engine	**motor** (m)	[motor]
undercarriage (landing gear)	**podvozek** (m)	[podvozɛk]
turbine	**turbína** (ž)	[turbi:na]
propeller	**vrtule** (ž)	[vrtulɛ]
black box	**černá skříňka** (ž)	[t͡ʃɛrna: skrʃi:nʲka]
yoke (control column)	**řídicí páka** (ž)	[rʒi:dɪt͡si: pa:ka]
fuel	**palivo** (s)	[palɪvo]
safety card	**předpis** (m)	[prʃɛtpɪs]
oxygen mask	**kyslíková maska** (ž)	[kɪsli:kova: maska]
uniform	**uniforma** (ž)	[unɪforma]
life vest	**záchranná vesta** (ž)	[za:xranna: vɛsta]
parachute	**padák** (m)	[pada:k]
takeoff	**start** (m) **letadla**	[start lɛtadla]
to take off (vi)	**vzlétat**	[vzlɛ:tat]
runway	**rozjezdová dráha** (ž)	[rozjɛzdova: dra:ha]
visibility	**viditelnost** (ž)	[vɪdɪtɛlnost]
flight (act of flying)	**let** (m)	[lɛt]
altitude	**výška** (ž)	[vi:ʃka]
air pocket	**vzdušná jáma** (ž)	[vzduʃna: jama]
seat	**místo** (s)	[mi:sto]
headphones	**sluchátka** (s mn)	[sluxa:tka]

folding tray (tray table)	**odklápěcí stolek** (m)	[otkla:petsi: stolɛk]
airplane window	**okénko** (s)	[okɛ:ŋko]
aisle	**chodba** (ž)	[xodba]

170. Train

train	**vlak** (m)	[vlak]
commuter train	**elektrický vlak** (m)	[ɛlɛktrɪtski: vlak]
express train	**rychlík** (m)	[rɪxli:k]
diesel locomotive	**motorová lokomotiva** (ž)	[motorova: lokomotɪva]
steam locomotive	**parní lokomotiva** (ž)	[parni: lokomotɪva]
passenger car	**vůz** (m)	[vu:z]
dining car	**jídelní vůz** (m)	[ji:dɛlni: vu:z]
rails	**koleje** (ž mn)	[kolɛjɛ]
railroad	**železnice** (ž mn)	[ʒelɛznɪtsɛ]
railway tie	**pražec** (m)	[praʒets]
platform (railway ~)	**nástupiště** (s)	[na:stupɪʃte]
track (~ 1, 2, etc.)	**kolej** (ž)	[kolɛj]
semaphore	**návěstidlo** (s)	[na:vestɪdlo]
station	**stanice** (ž)	[stanɪtsɛ]
engineer (train driver)	**strojvůdce** (m)	[strojvu:dtsɛ]
porter (of luggage)	**nosič** (m)	[nosɪtʃ]
car attendant	**průvodčí** (m)	[pru:vodtʃi:]
passenger	**cestující** (m)	[tsɛstuji:tsi:]
conductor (ticket inspector)	**revizor** (m)	[rɛvɪzor]
corridor (in train)	**chodba** (ž)	[xodba]
emergency brake	**záchranná brzda** (ž)	[za:xranna: brzda]
compartment	**oddělení** (s)	[oddelɛni:]
berth	**lůžko** (s)	[lu:ʃko]
upper berth	**horní lůžko** (s)	[horni: lu:ʃko]
lower berth	**dolní lůžko** (s)	[dolni: lu:ʃko]
bed linen, bedding	**lůžkoviny** (ž mn)	[lu:ʃkovɪnɪ]
ticket	**jízdenka** (ž)	[ji:zdɛŋka]
schedule	**jízdní řád** (m)	[ji:zdni: rʒa:t]
information display	**tabule** (ž)	[tabulɛ]
to leave, to depart	**odjíždět**	[odji:ʒdet]
departure (of train)	**odjezd** (m)	[odjɛst]
to arrive (ab. train)	**přijíždět**	[prʃɪji:ʒdet]
arrival	**příjezd** (m)	[prʃi:jɛst]
to arrive by train	**přijet vlakem**	[prʃɪɛt vlakɛm]
to get on the train	**nastoupit do vlaku**	[nastoupɪt do vlaku]

to get off the train	**vystoupit z vlaku**	[vɪstoupɪt z vlaku]
train wreck	**železniční neštěstí** (s)	[ʒelɛznɪʧni: nɛʃtesti:]
to derail (vi)	**vykolejit**	[vɪkolɛjɪt]
steam locomotive	**parní lokomotiva** (ž)	[parni: lokomotɪva]
stoker, fireman	**topič** (m)	[topɪʧ]
firebox	**topeniště** (s)	[topɛnɪʃte]
coal	**uhlí** (s)	[uhli:]

171. Ship

ship	**loď** (ž)	[lotʲ]
vessel	**loď** (ž)	[lotʲ]
steamship	**parník** (m)	[parni:k]
riverboat	**říční loď** (ž)	[riʧni lotʲ]
cruise ship	**linková loď** (ž)	[lɪŋkova: lotʲ]
cruiser	**křižník** (m)	[krʒɪʒni:k]
yacht	**jachta** (ž)	[jaxta]
tugboat	**vlek** (m)	[vlɛk]
barge	**vlečná nákladní loď** (ž)	[vlɛʧna: na:kladni: lotʲ]
ferry	**prám** (m)	[pra:m]
sailing ship	**plachetnice** (ž)	[plaxɛtnɪʦɛ]
brigantine	**brigantina** (ž)	[brɪganti:na]
ice breaker	**ledoborec** (m)	[lɛdoborɛʦ]
submarine	**ponorka** (ž)	[ponorka]
boat (flat-bottomed ~)	**loďka** (ž)	[lotʲka]
dinghy	**člun** (m)	[ʧlun]
lifeboat	**záchranný člun** (m)	[za:xranni: ʧlun]
motorboat	**motorový člun** (m)	[motorovi: ʧlun]
captain	**kapitán** (m)	[kapɪta:n]
seaman	**námořník** (m)	[na:morʒni:k]
sailor	**námořník** (m)	[na:morʒni:k]
crew	**posádka** (ž)	[posa:tka]
boatswain	**loďmistr** (m)	[lodʲmɪstr]
ship's boy	**plavčík** (m)	[plavʧi:k]
cook	**lodní kuchař** (m)	[lodni: kuxarʃ]
ship's doctor	**lodní lékař** (m)	[lodni: lɛ:karʃ]
deck	**paluba** (ž)	[paluba]
mast	**stěžeň** (m)	[steʒenʲ]
sail	**plachta** (ž)	[plaxta]
hold	**podpalubí** (s)	[potpalubi:]
bow (prow)	**příď** (ž)	[prʃi:tʲ]

stern	**záď** (ž)	[za:tʲ]
oar	**veslo** (s)	[vɛslo]
screw propeller	**lodní šroub** (m)	[lodni: ʃroup]
cabin	**kajuta** (ž)	[kajuta]
wardroom	**společenská místnost** (ž)	[spolɛʧɛnska: mi:stnost]
engine room	**strojovna** (ž)	[strojovna]
bridge	**kapitánský můstek** (m)	[kapɪta:nski: mu:stɛk]
radio room	**rádiová kabina** (ž)	[ra:dɪova: kabɪna]
wave (radio)	**vlna** (ž)	[vlna]
logbook	**lodní deník** (m)	[lodni: dɛni:k]
spyglass	**dalekohled** (m)	[dalɛkohlet]
bell	**zvon** (m)	[zvon]
flag	**vlajka** (ž)	[vlajka]
hawser (mooring ~)	**lano** (s)	[lano]
knot (bowline, etc.)	**uzel** (m)	[uzɛl]
deckrails	**zábradlí** (s)	[za:bradli:]
gangway	**schůdky** (m mn)	[sxu:tkɪ]
anchor	**kotva** (ž)	[kotva]
to weigh anchor	**zvednout kotvy**	[zvɛdnout kotvɪ]
to drop anchor	**spustit kotvy**	[spustɪt kotvɪ]
anchor chain	**kotevní řetěz** (m)	[kotɛvni: rʒɛtez]
port (harbor)	**přístav** (m)	[prʃi:staf]
quay, wharf	**přístaviště** (s)	[prʃi:stavɪʃte]
to berth (moor)	**přistávat**	[prʃɪsta:vat]
to cast off	**vyplouvat**	[vɪplouvat]
trip, voyage	**cestování** (s)	[ʦɛstova:ni:]
cruise (sea trip)	**výletní plavba** (ž)	[vi:lɛtni: plavba]
course (route)	**kurz** (m)	[kurs]
route (itinerary)	**trasa** (ž)	[trasa]
fairway (safe water channel)	**plavební dráha** (ž)	[plavɛbni: dra:ha]
shallows	**mělčina** (ž)	[mnelʧɪna]
to run aground	**najet na mělčinu**	[najɛt na mnelʧɪnu]
storm	**bouřka** (ž)	[bourʃka]
signal	**signál** (m)	[sɪgna:l]
to sink (vi)	**potápět se**	[pota:pet sɛ]
Man overboard!	**Muž přes palubu!**	[muʒ prʃɛs palubu]
SOS (distress signal)	**SOS**	[ɛs o: ɛs]
ring buoy	**záchranný kruh** (m)	[za:xranni: krux]

172. Airport

airport	**letiště** (s)	[lɛtɪʃte]
airplane	**letadlo** (s)	[lɛtadlo]
airline	**letecká společnost** (ž)	[lɛtɛʦka: spolɛʧnost]
air traffic controller	**dispečer** (m)	[dɪspɛʧɛr]
departure	**odlet** (m)	[odlɛt]
arrival	**přílet** (m)	[prʃi:lɛt]
to arrive (by plane)	**přiletět**	[prʃɪlɛtet]
departure time	**čas** (m) **odletu**	[ʧas odlɛtu]
arrival time	**čas** (m) **příletu**	[ʧas prʃilɛtu]
to be delayed	**mít zpoždění**	[mi:t spoʒdɛni:]
flight delay	**zpoždění** (s) **odletu**	[spoʒdeni: odlɛtu]
information board	**informační tabule** (ž)	[ɪnformaʧni: tabulɛ]
information	**informace** (ž)	[ɪnformaʦɛ]
to announce (vt)	**hlásit**	[hla:sɪt]
flight (e.g., next ~)	**let** (m)	[lɛt]
customs	**celnice** (ž)	[ʦɛlnɪʦɛ]
customs officer	**celník** (m)	[ʦɛlni:k]
customs declaration	**prohlášení** (s)	[prohla:ʃɛni:]
to fill out (vt)	**vyplnit**	[vɪplnɪt]
to fill out the declaration	**vyplnit prohlášení**	[vɪplnɪt prohla:ʃɛni:]
passport control	**pasová kontrola** (ž)	[pasova: kontrola]
luggage	**zavazadla** (s mn)	[zavazadla]
hand luggage	**příruční zavazadlo** (s)	[prʃi:ruʧni: zavazadlo]
luggage cart	**vozík** (m) **na zavazadla**	[vozi:k na zavazadla]
landing	**přistání** (s)	[prʃɪsta:ni:]
landing strip	**přistávací dráha** (ž)	[prʃɪsta:vaʦi: dra:ha]
to land (vi)	**přistávat**	[prʃɪsta:vat]
airstair (passenger stair)	**pojízdné schůdky** (m mn)	[poji:zdnɛ: sxu:tkɪ]
check-in	**registrace** (ž)	[rɛgɪstraʦɛ]
check-in counter	**přepážka** (ž) **registrace**	[prʃɛpa:ʃka rɛgɪstraʦɛ]
to check-in (vi)	**zaregistrovat se**	[zarɛgɪstrovat sɛ]
boarding pass	**palubní lístek** (m)	[palubni: li:stɛk]
departure gate	**příchod** (m) **k nástupu**	[prʃi:xot k na:stupu]
transit	**tranzit** (m)	[tranzɪt]
to wait (vt)	**čekat**	[ʧɛkat]
departure lounge	**čekárna** (ž)	[ʧɛka:rna]
to see off	**doprovázet**	[doprova:zɛt]
to say goodbye	**loučit se**	[louʧɪt sɛ]

173. Bicycle. Motorcycle

bicycle	**kolo** (s)	[kolo]
scooter	**skútr** (m)	[sku:tr]
motorcycle, bike	**motocykl** (m)	[mototsɪkl]
to go by bicycle	**jet na kole**	[jɛt na kolɛ]
handlebars	**řídítka** (s mn)	[rʒi:di:tka]
pedal	**pedál** (m)	[pɛda:l]
brakes	**brzdy** (ž mn)	[brzdɪ]
bicycle seat (saddle)	**sedlo** (s)	[sɛdlo]
pump	**pumpa** (ž)	[pumpa]
luggage rack	**nosič** (m)	[nosɪtʃ]
front lamp	**světlo** (s)	[svetlo]
helmet	**helma** (ž)	[hɛlma]
wheel	**kolo** (s)	[kolo]
fender	**blatník** (m)	[blatni:k]
rim	**věnec** (m)	[venɛts]
spoke	**paprsek** (m)	[paprsɛk]

Cars

174. Types of cars

automobile, car	**auto** (s)	[auto]
sports car	**sportovní auto** (s)	[sportovni: auto]
limousine	**limuzína** (ž)	[lɪmuzi:na]
off-road vehicle	**terénní vozidlo** (s)	[tɛrɛ:nni: vozɪdlo]
convertible (n)	**kabriolet** (m)	[kabrɪolɛt]
minibus	**mikrobus** (m)	[mɪkrobus]
ambulance	**sanitka** (ž)	[sanɪtka]
snowplow	**sněžný pluh** (m)	[sneʒni: plux]
truck	**náklaďák** (m)	[na:klad[j]a:k]
tanker truck	**cisterna** (ž)	[ʦɪstɛrna]
van (small truck)	**dodávka** (ž)	[doda:fka]
road tractor (trailer truck)	**tahač** (m)	[tahaʧ]
trailer	**přívěs** (m)	[prʃi:ves]
comfortable (adj)	**komfortní**	[komfortni:]
used (adj)	**ojetý**	[oeti:]

175. Cars. Bodywork

hood	**kapota** (ž)	[kapota]
fender	**blatník** (m)	[blatni:k]
roof	**střecha** (ž)	[strʃɛxa]
windshield	**ochranné sklo** (s)	[oxrannɛ: sklo]
rear-view mirror	**zpětné zrcátko** (s)	[spetnɛ: zrʦa:tko]
windshield washer	**ostřikovač** (m)	[ostrʃɪkovaʧ]
windshield wipers	**stírače** (m mn)	[sti:raʧɛ]
side window	**boční sklo** (s)	[boʧni: sklo]
window lift (power window)	**stahování okna** (s)	[stahova:ni: okna]
antenna	**anténa** (ž)	[antɛ:na]
sunroof	**střešní okno** (s)	[strʃɛʃni: okno]
bumper	**nárazník** (m)	[na:razni:k]
trunk	**kufr** (m)	[kufr]
roof luggage rack	**nosič** (m)	[nosɪʧ]
door	**dveře** (ž mn)	[dvɛrʒɛ]

door handle	**klika** (ž)	[klɪka]
door lock	**zámek** (m)	[za:mɛk]
license plate	**statní poznávací značka** (ž)	[statni: pozna:vaʦi: znaʧka]
muffler	**tlumič** (m)	[tlumɪʧ]
gas tank	**nádržka** (ž) **na benzín**	[na:drʃka na bɛnzi:n]
tailpipe	**výfuková trubka** (ž)	[vi:fukova: trupka]
gas, accelerator	**plyn** (m)	[plɪn]
pedal	**pedál** (m)	[pɛda:l]
gas pedal	**plynový pedál** (m)	[plɪnovi: pɛda:l]
brake	**brzda** (ž)	[brzda]
brake pedal	**brzdový pedál** (m)	[brzdovi: pɛda:l]
to brake (use the brake)	**brzdit**	[brzdɪt]
parking brake	**parkovací brzda** (ž)	[parkovaʦi: brzda]
clutch	**spojka** (ž)	[spojka]
clutch pedal	**spojkový pedál** (m)	[spojkovi: pɛda:l]
clutch disc	**spojkový kotouč** (m)	[spojkovi: kotouʧ]
shock absorber	**tlumič** (m)	[tlumɪʧ]
wheel	**kolo** (s)	[kolo]
spare tire	**náhradní kolo** (s)	[na:hradni: kolo]
tire	**pneumatika** (ž), **plášť** (m)	[pneumatɪka], [plaʃtʲ]
hubcap	**poklice** (ž)	[poklɪʦɛ]
driving wheels	**hnací kola** (s mn)	[hnaʦi: kola]
front-wheel drive (as adj)	**s pohonem předních kol**	[s pohonɛm prʃɛdni:x kol]
rear-wheel drive (as adj)	**s pohonem zadních kol**	[s pohonɛm zadni:x kol]
all-wheel drive (as adj)	**s pohonem všech kol**	[s pohonɛm vʃɛx kol]
gearbox	**převodová skříň** (ž)	[prʃɛvodova: skrʃi:nʲ]
automatic (adj)	**samočinný**	[samoʧɪnni:]
mechanical (adj)	**mechanický**	[mɛxanɪʦki:]
gear shift	**převodová páka** (ž)	[prʃɛvodova: pa:ka]
headlight	**světlo** (s)	[svetlo]
headlights	**světla** (s mn)	[svetla]
low beam	**potkávací světla** (s mn)	[potka:vaʦi: svetla]
high beam	**dálková světla** (s mn)	[da:lkova: svetla]
brake light	**brzdová světla** (s mn)	[brzdova: svetla]
parking lights	**obrysová světla** (s mn)	[obrɪsova: svetla]
hazard lights	**havarijní světla** (s mn)	[havarɪjni: svetla]
fog lights	**mlhovky** (ž mn)	[mlhofkɪ]
turn signal	**směrové světlo** (s)	[smnerovɛ: svetlo]
back-up light	**zpětné světlo** (s)	[spetnɛ svetlo]

176. Cars. Passenger compartment

car inside (interior)	**interiér** (m)	[ɪntɛrjɛ:r]
leather (as adj)	**kožený**	[koʒeni:]
velour (as adj)	**velurový**	[vɛlurovi:]
upholstery	**potah** (m)	[potax]
instrument (gage)	**přístroj** (m)	[prʃi:stroj]
dashboard	**přístrojová deska** (ž)	[prʃi:strojova: dɛska]
speedometer	**rychloměr** (m)	[rɪxlomner]
needle (pointer)	**ručička** (ž)	[rutʃɪtʃka]
odometer	**počítač** (m) **kilometrů**	[potʃi:tatʃ kɪlomɛtru:]
indicator (sensor)	**snímač** (m)	[sni:matʃ]
level	**hladina** (ž)	[hladɪna]
warning light	**lampička** (ž)	[lampɪtʃka]
steering wheel	**volant** (m)	[volant]
horn	**houkačka** (ž)	[houkatʃka]
button	**tlačítko** (s)	[tlatʃi:tko]
switch	**přepínač** (m)	[prʃɛpi:natʃ]
seat	**sedadlo** (s)	[sɛdadlo]
backrest	**opěradlo** (m)	[operadlo]
headrest	**podhlavník** (m)	[pothlavni:k]
seat belt	**bezpečnostní pás** (m)	[bɛzpɛtʃnostni: pa:s]
to fasten the belt	**připásat se**	[prʃɪpa:sat sɛ]
adjustment (of seats)	**regulování** (s)	[rɛgulova:ni:]
airbag	**nafukovací vak** (m)	[nafukovatsi: vak]
air-conditioner	**klimatizátor** (m)	[klɪmatɪza:tor]
radio	**rádio** (s)	[ra:dɪo]
CD player	**CD přehrávač** (m)	[tsɛ:dɛ: prʃɛhra:vatʃ]
to turn on	**zapnout**	[zapnout]
antenna	**anténa** (ž)	[antɛ:na]
glove box	**přihrádka** (ž)	[prʃɪhra:tka]
ashtray	**popelník** (m)	[popɛlni:k]

177. Cars. Engine

engine, motor	**motor** (m)	[motor]
diesel (as adj)	**dieselový**	[dɪzɪlovi:]
gasoline (as adj)	**benzínový**	[bɛnzi:novi:]
engine volume	**obsah** (m) **motoru**	[opsax motoru]
power	**výkon** (m)	[vi:kon]
horsepower	**koňská síla** (ž)	[konʲska: si:la]
piston	**píst** (m)	[pi:st]

cylinder	**cylindr** (m)	[ʦɪlɪndr]
valve	**ventil** (m)	[vɛntɪl]
injector	**injektor** (m)	[ɪnjɛktor]
generator (alternator)	**generátor** (m)	[genera:tor]
carburetor	**karburátor** (m)	[karbura:tor]
motor oil	**motorový olej** (m)	[motorovi: olɛj]
radiator	**chladič** (m)	[xladɪʧ]
coolant	**chladicí kapalina** (ž)	[xladɪʦi: kapalɪna]
cooling fan	**ventilátor** (m)	[vɛntɪla:tor]
battery (accumulator)	**akumulátor** (m)	[akumula:tor]
starter	**startér** (m)	[startɛ:r]
ignition	**zapalování** (s)	[zapalova:ni:]
spark plug	**zapalovací svíčka** (ž)	[zapalovaʦi: svi:ʧka]
terminal (of battery)	**svorka** (ž)	[svorka]
positive terminal	**plus** (m)	[plus]
negative terminal	**minus** (m)	[mi:nus]
fuse	**pojistka** (ž)	[pojɪstka]
air filter	**vzduchový filtr** (m)	[vzduxovi: fɪltr]
oil filter	**olejový filtr** (m)	[olɛjovi: fɪltr]
fuel filter	**palivový filtr** (m)	[palɪvovi: fɪltr]

178. Cars. Crash. Repair

car crash	**havárie** (ž)	[hava:rɪe]
traffic accident	**dopravní nehoda** (ž)	[dopravni: nɛhoda]
to crash (into the wall, etc.)	**narazit**	[narazɪt]
to get smashed up	**rozbít se**	[rozbi:t sɛ]
damage	**poškození** (s)	[poʃkozɛni:]
intact (unscathed)	**celý**	[ʦɛli:]
breakdown	**porucha** (ž)	[poruxa]
to break down (vi)	**porouchat se**	[porouxat sɛ]
towrope	**vlečné lano** (s)	[vlɛʧnɛ: lano]
puncture	**píchnutí** (s)	[pi:xnuti:]
to be flat	**splasknout**	[splasknout]
to pump up	**nafukovat**	[nafukovat]
pressure	**tlak** (m)	[tlak]
to check (to examine)	**prověřit**	[proverʒɪt]
repair	**oprava** (ž)	[oprava]
auto repair shop	**opravna** (ž)	[opravna]
spare part	**náhradní díl** (m)	[na:hradni: di:l]
part	**díl** (m)	[di:l]

bolt (with nut)	**šroub** (m)	[ʃroup]
screw (fastener)	**šroub** (m)	[ʃroup]
nut	**matice** (ž)	[matɪʦɛ]
washer	**podložka** (ž)	[podloʃka]
bearing (e.g., ball ~)	**ložisko** (s)	[loʒɪsko]
tube	**trubka** (ž)	[trupka]
gasket (head ~)	**vložka** (ž)	[vloʃka]
cable, wire	**vodič** (m)	[vodɪʧ]
jack	**zvedák** (m)	[zvɛda:k]
wrench	**francouzský klíč** (m)	[franʦouski: kli:ʧ]
hammer	**kladivo** (s)	[kladɪvo]
pump	**pumpa** (ž)	[pumpa]
screwdriver	**šroubovák** (m)	[ʃroubova:k]
fire extinguisher	**hasicí přístroj** (m)	[hasɪʦi: prʃi:stroj]
warning triangle	**výstražný trojúhelník** (ž)	[vi:straʒni: troju:hɛlnik]
to stall (vi)	**zhasínat**	[zhasi:nat]
stall (n)	**zastavení** (s)	[zastavɛni:]
to be broken	**být porouchaný**	[bi:t porouxani:]
to overheat (vi)	**přehřát se**	[prʃɛhrʒa:t sɛ]
to be clogged up	**ucpat se, být ucpaný**	[uʦpat se], [bi:t uʦpani:]
to freeze up (pipes, etc.)	**zamrznout**	[zamrznout]
to burst (vi, ab. tube)	**puknout**	[puknout]
pressure	**tlak** (m)	[tlak]
level	**hladina** (ž)	[hladɪna]
slack (~ belt)	**slabý**	[slabi:]
dent	**promáčknutí** (s)	[proma:ʧknuti:]
knocking noise (engine)	**klapot** (m)	[klapot]
crack	**prasklina** (ž)	[prasklɪna]
scratch	**rýha** (ž)	[ri:ha]

179. Cars. Road

road	**cesta** (ž)	[ʦɛsta]
highway	**dálnice** (ž)	[da:lnɪʦɛ]
freeway	**silnice** (ž)	[sɪlnɪʦɛ]
direction (way)	**směr** (m)	[smner]
distance	**vzdálenost** (ž)	[vzda:lɛnost]
bridge	**most** (m)	[most]
parking lot	**parkoviště** (s)	[parkovɪʃte]
square	**náměstí** (s)	[na:mnesti:]
interchange	**nadjezd** (m)	[nadjɛzt]
tunnel	**podjezd** (m)	[podjɛzt]

gas station	**benzínová stanice** (ž)	[bɛnzi:nova: stanɪʦɛ]
parking lot	**parkoviště** (s)	[parkovɪʃte]
gas pump (fuel dispenser)	**benzínová pumpa** (ž)	[bɛnzi:nova: pumpa]
auto repair shop	**autoopravna** (ž)	[autoopravna]
to get gas (to fill up)	**natankovat**	[nataŋkovat]
fuel	**palivo** (s)	[palɪvo]
jerrycan	**kanystr** (m)	[kanɪstr]
asphalt	**asfalt** (m)	[asfalt]
road markings	**označení** (s)	[oznaʧɛni:]
curb	**obrubník** (m)	[obrubni:k]
guardrail	**ochranné zábradlí** (s)	[oxrannɛ: za:bradli:]
ditch	**příkop** (m)	[prʃi:kop]
roadside (shoulder)	**krajnice** (ž)	[krajnɪʦɛ]
lamppost	**sloup** (m)	[sloup]
to drive (a car)	**řídit**	[rʒi:dɪt]
to turn (e.g., ~ left)	**zatáčet**	[zata:ʧɛt]
to make a U-turn	**otáčet se**	[ota:ʧɛt sɛ]
reverse (~ gear)	**zpáteční rychlost** (ž)	[spa:tɛʧni: rɪxlost]
to honk (vi)	**houkat**	[houkat]
honk (sound)	**houkání** (s)	[houka:ni:]
to get stuck (in the mud, etc.)	**uváznout**	[uva:znout]
to spin the wheels	**prokluzovat**	[prokluzovat]
to cut, to turn off (vt)	**zastavovat**	[zastavovat]
speed	**rychlost** (ž)	[rɪxlost]
to exceed the speed limit	**překročit dovolenou rychlost**	[prʃɛkroʧɪt dovolɛnou rɪxlost]
to give a ticket	**pokutovat**	[pokutovat]
traffic lights	**semafor** (m)	[sɛmafor]
driver's license	**řidičský průkaz** (m)	[rʒɪdɪʧski: pru:kaz]
grade crossing	**přejezd** (m)	[prʃɛjɛzt]
intersection	**křižovatka** (ž)	[krʃɪʒovatka]
crosswalk	**přechod** (m) **pro chodce**	[prʃɛxot pro xoʦɛ]
bend, curve	**zatáčka** (ž)	[zata:ʧka]
pedestrian zone	**pěší zóna** (ž)	[peʃi: zo:na]

180. Traffic signs

rules of the road	**dopravní předpisy** (m mn)	[dopravni: prʃɛtpɪsɪ]
road sign (traffic sign)	**značka** (ž)	[znaʧka]
passing (overtaking)	**předjíždění** (s)	[prʃɛdji:ʒdeni:]
curve	**zatáčka** (ž)	[zata:ʧka]
U-turn	**otáčení** (s)	[ota:ʧɛni:]
traffic circle	**kruhový objezd** (m)	[kruhovi: objɛzt]
No entry	**zákaz vjezdu**	[za:kaz vjɛzdu]

No vehicles allowed	**zákaz provozu**	[za:kaz provozu]
No passing	**zákaz předjíždění**	[za:kaz prʃɛdji:ʒdeni:]
No parking	**zákaz stání**	[za:kaz sta:ni:]
No stopping	**zákaz zastavení**	[za:kaz zastavɛni:]
dangerous bend	**ostrá zatáčka** (ž)	[ostra: zata:ʧka]
steep descent	**nebezpečné klesání** (s)	[nebɛspɛʧnɛ: klesa:ni:]
one-way traffic	**jednosměrný provoz** (m)	[jɛdnosmnerni: provoz]
crosswalk	**přechod** (m) **pro chodce**	[prʃɛxot pro xodʦɛ]
slippery road	**nebezpečí smyku** (ž)	[nɛbɛspɛʧi: smɪku]
YIELD	**dej přednost v jízdě**	[dɛj prʃɛdnost v ji:zde]

PEOPLE. LIFE EVENTS

Life events

181. Holidays. Event

celebration, holiday	**svátek** (m)	[sva:tɛk]
national day	**národní svátek** (m)	[na:rodni: sva:tɛk]
public holiday	**sváteční den** (m)	[sva:tɛtʃni: dɛn]
to commemorate (vt)	**oslavovat**	[oslavovat]
event (happening)	**událost** (ž)	[uda:lost]
event (organized activity)	**akce** (ž)	[aktsɛ]
banquet (party)	**banket** (m)	[baŋkɛt]
reception (formal party)	**recepce** (ž)	[rɛtsɛptsɛ]
feast	**hostina** (ž)	[hostɪna]
anniversary	**výročí** (s)	[vi:rotʃi:]
jubilee	**jubileum** (s)	[jubɪlɛjum]
to celebrate (vt)	**oslavit**	[oslavɪt]
New Year	**Nový rok** (m)	[novi: rok]
Happy New Year!	**Šťastný nový rok!**	[ʃtʲastni: novi: rok]
Santa Claus	**svatý Mikuláš** (m)	[svati: mɪkula:ʃ]
Christmas	**Vánoce** (ž mn)	[va:notsɛ]
Merry Christmas!	**Veselé Vánoce!**	[vɛsɛlɛ: va:notsɛ]
Christmas tree	**vánoční stromek** (m)	[va:notʃni: stromɛk]
fireworks (fireworks show)	**ohňostroj** (m)	[ohnʲostroj]
wedding	**svatba** (ž)	[svatba]
groom	**ženich** (m)	[ʒenɪx]
bride	**nevěsta** (ž)	[nɛvesta]
to invite (vt)	**zvát**	[zva:t]
invitation card	**pozvánka** (ž)	[pozva:ŋka]
guest	**host** (m)	[host]
to visit (~ your parents, etc.)	**jít na návštěvu**	[ji:t na na:vʃtevu]
to meet the guests	**vítat hosty**	[vitat hostɪ]
gift, present	**dárek** (m)	[da:rɛk]
to give (sth as present)	**darovat**	[darovat]
to receive gifts	**dostávat dárky**	[dosta:vat da:rkɪ]

bouquet (of flowers)	**kytice** (ž)	[kɪtɪʦɛ]
congratulations	**blahopřání** (s)	[blahoprʃa:ni:]
to congratulate (vt)	**blahopřát**	[blahoprʃa:t]
greeting card	**blahopřejný lístek** (m)	[blahoprʃɛjni: li:stɛk]
to send a postcard	**poslat lístek**	[poslat li:stɛk]
to get a postcard	**dostat lístek**	[dostat li:stɛk]
toast	**přípitek** (m)	[prʃi:pɪtɛk]
to offer (a drink, etc.)	**častovat**	[ʧastovat]
champagne	**šampaňské** (s)	[ʃampanʲskɛ:]
to enjoy oneself	**bavit se**	[bavɪt sɛ]
merriment (gaiety)	**zábava** (ž)	[za:bava]
joy (emotion)	**radost** (ž)	[radost]
dance	**tanec** (m)	[tanɛʦ]
to dance (vi, vt)	**tančit**	[tanʧɪt]
waltz	**valčík** (m)	[valʧi:k]
tango	**tango** (s)	[tango]

182. Funerals. Burial

cemetery	**hřbitov** (m)	[hrʒbɪtof]
grave, tomb	**hrob** (m)	[hrop]
cross	**kříž** (m)	[krʃi:ʃ]
gravestone	**náhrobek** (m)	[na:hrobɛk]
fence	**ohrádka** (ž)	[ohra:tka]
chapel	**kaple** (ž)	[kaplɛ]
death	**úmrtí** (s)	[u:mrti:]
to die (vi)	**umřít**	[umrʒi:t]
the deceased	**zemřelý** (m)	[zɛmrʒɛli:]
mourning	**smutek** (m)	[smutɛk]
to bury (vt)	**pohřbívat**	[pohrʒbi:vat]
funeral home	**pohřební ústav** (m)	[pohrʒɛbni: u:staf]
funeral	**pohřeb** (m)	[pohrʒɛp]
wreath	**věnec** (m)	[venɛʦ]
casket, coffin	**rakev** (ž)	[rakɛf]
hearse	**katafalk** (m)	[katafalk]
shroud	**pohřební roucho** (m)	[pohrʒɛbni: rouxo]
funeral procession	**pohřební průvod** (m)	[pohrʒɛbni: pru:vot]
funerary urn	**popelnice** (ž)	[popɛlnɪʦɛ]
crematory	**krematorium** (s)	[krɛmatorɪum]
obituary	**nekrolog** (m)	[nɛkrolog]
to cry (weep)	**plakat**	[plakat]
to sob (vi)	**vzlykat**	[vzlɪkat]

183. War. Soldiers

platoon	**četa** (ž)	[tʃɛta]
company	**rota** (ž)	[rota]
regiment	**pluk** (m)	[pluk]
army	**armáda** (ž)	[arma:da]
division	**divize** (ž)	[dɪvɪzɛ]
section, squad	**oddíl** (m)	[oddi:l]
host (army)	**vojsko** (s)	[vojsko]
soldier	**voják** (m)	[voja:k]
officer	**důstojník** (m)	[du:stojni:k]
private	**vojín** (m)	[voji:n]
sergeant	**seržant** (m)	[sɛrʒant]
lieutenant	**poručík** (m)	[porutʃi:k]
captain	**kapitán** (m)	[kapɪta:n]
major	**major** (m)	[major]
colonel	**plukovník** (m)	[plukovni:k]
general	**generál** (m)	[gɛnɛra:l]
sailor	**námořník** (m)	[na:morʒni:k]
captain	**kapitán** (m)	[kapɪta:n]
boatswain	**loďmistr** (m)	[lodʲmɪstr]
artilleryman	**dělostřelec** (m)	[delostrʃɛlɛts]
paratrooper	**výsadkář** (m)	[vi:satka:rʃ]
pilot	**letec** (m)	[lɛtɛts]
navigator	**navigátor** (m)	[navɪga:tor]
mechanic	**mechanik** (m)	[mɛxanɪk]
pioneer (sapper)	**ženista** (m)	[ʒenɪsta]
parachutist	**parašutista** (m)	[paraʃutɪsta]
reconnaissance scout	**rozvědčík** (m)	[rozvedtʃi:k]
sniper	**odstřelovač** (m)	[otstrʃɛlovatʃ]
patrol (group)	**hlídka** (ž)	[hli:tka]
to patrol (vt)	**hlídkovat**	[hli:tkovat]
sentry, guard	**strážný** (m)	[stra:ʒni:]
warrior	**vojín** (m)	[voji:n]
patriot	**vlastenec** (m)	[vlastɛnɛts]
hero	**hrdina** (m)	[hrdɪna]
heroine	**hrdinka** (ž)	[hrdɪŋka]
traitor	**zrádce** (m)	[zra:dtsɛ]
to betray (vt)	**zradit**	[zradɪt]
deserter	**zběh** (m)	[zbex]
to desert (vi)	**dezertovat**	[dɛzɛrtovat]
mercenary	**žoldnéř** (m)	[ʒoldnɛ:rʃ]

recruit	**branec** (m)	[branɛʦ]
volunteer	**dobrovolník** (m)	[dobrovolni:k]
dead (n)	**zabitý** (m)	[zabɪti:]
wounded (n)	**raněný** (m)	[raneni:]
prisoner of war	**zajatec** (m)	[zajatɛʦ]

184. War. Military actions. Part 1

war	**válka** (ž)	[va:lka]
to be at war	**bojovat**	[bojovat]
civil war	**občanská válka** (ž)	[obʧanska: va:lka]
treacherously (adv)	**věrolomně**	[verolomne]
declaration of war	**vyhlášení** (s)	[vɪhla:ʃɛni:]
to declare (~ war)	**vyhlásit**	[vɪhla:sɪt]
aggression	**agrese** (ž)	[agrɛsɛ]
to attack (invade)	**přepadat**	[prʃɛpadat]
to invade (vt)	**uchvacovat**	[uxvaʦovat]
invader	**uchvatitel** (m)	[uxvatɪtɛl]
conqueror	**dobyvatel** (m)	[dobɪvatɛl]
defense	**obrana** (ž)	[obrana]
to defend (a country, etc.)	**bránit**	[bra:nɪt]
to defend (against ...)	**bránit se**	[bra:nɪt sɛ]
enemy, hostile	**nepřítel** (m)	[nɛprʃi:tɛl]
enemy (as adj)	**nepřátelský**	[nɛprʃa:tɛlski:]
strategy	**strategie** (ž)	[stratɛgɪe]
tactics	**taktika** (ž)	[taktɪka]
order	**rozkaz** (m)	[roskas]
command (order)	**povel** (m)	[povɛl]
to order (vt)	**rozkazovat**	[roskazovat]
mission	**úkol** (m)	[u:kol]
secret (adj)	**tajný**	[tajni:]
battle	**bitva** (ž)	[bɪtva]
combat	**boj** (m)	[boj]
attack	**útok** (m)	[u:tok]
charge (assault)	**útok** (m)	[u:tok]
to storm (vt)	**dobývat útokem**	[dobi:vat u:tokɛm]
siege (to be under ~)	**obležení** (s)	[oblɛʒeni:]
offensive (n)	**ofenzíva** (ž)	[ofɛnzi:va]
to go on the offensive	**zahájit ofenzivu**	[zaha:jɪt ofɛnzivu]
retreat	**ústup** (m)	[u:stup]

to retreat (vi)	**ustupovat**	[ustupovat]
encirclement	**obklíčení** (s)	[opkli:ʧɛni:]
to encircle (vt)	**obkličovat**	[opklɪʧovat]
bombing (by aircraft)	**bombardování** (s)	[bombardova:ni:]
to drop a bomb	**shodit pumu**	[sxodɪt pumu]
to bomb (vt)	**bombardovat**	[bombardovat]
explosion	**výbuch** (m)	[vi:bux]
shot	**výstřel** (m)	[vi:strʃɛl]
to fire (~ a shot)	**vystřelit**	[vɪstrʒɛlɪt]
firing (burst of ~)	**střelba** (ž)	[strʃɛlba]
to aim (to point a weapon)	**mířit**	[mi:rʒɪt]
to point (a gun)	**zamířit**	[zami:rʒɪt]
to hit (the target)	**zasáhnout**	[zasa:hnout]
to sink (~ a ship)	**potopit**	[potopɪt]
hole (in a ship)	**trhlina** (ž)	[trhlɪna]
to founder, to sink (vi)	**topit se**	[topɪt sɛ]
front (war ~)	**fronta** (ž)	[fronta]
evacuation	**evakuace** (ž)	[ɛvakuaʦɛ]
to evacuate (vt)	**evakuovat**	[ɛvakuovat]
trench	**zákop** (m)	[za:kop]
barbwire	**ostnatý drát** (m)	[ostnati: dra:t]
barrier (anti tank ~)	**zátaras** (m)	[za:taras]
watchtower	**věž** (ž)	[veʃ]
military hospital	**vojenská nemocnice** (ž)	[vojɛnska: nɛmoʦnɪʦɛ]
to wound (vt)	**zranit**	[zranɪt]
wound	**rána** (ž)	[ra:na]
wounded (n)	**raněný** (m)	[raneni:]
to be wounded	**utrpět zranění**	[utrpet zraneni:]
serious (wound)	**těžký**	[teʃki:]

185. War. Military actions. Part 2

captivity	**zajetí** (s)	[zajɛti:]
to take captive	**zajmout**	[zajmout]
to be held captive	**být v zajetí**	[bi:t v zajɛti:]
to be taken captive	**dostat se do zajetí**	[dostat sɛ do zajɛti:]
concentration camp	**koncentrační tábor** (m)	[konʦɛntraʧni: ta:bor]
prisoner of war	**zajatec** (m)	[zajatɛʦ]
to escape (vi)	**utéci**	[utɛ:ʦɪ]
to betray (vt)	**zradit**	[zradɪt]
betrayer	**zrádce** (m)	[zra:dʦɛ]

betrayal	**zrada** (ž)	[zrada]
to execute (by firing squad)	**zastřelit**	[zastrʃɛlɪt]
execution (by firing squad)	**smrt** (ž) **zastřelením**	[smrt zastrʃɛlɛni:m]
equipment (military gear)	**výstroj** (ž)	[vi:stroj]
shoulder board	**nárameník** (m)	[na:ramɛni:k]
gas mask	**plynová maska** (ž)	[plɪnova: maska]
field radio	**vysílačka** (ž)	[vɪsi:latʃka]
cipher, code	**šifra** (ž)	[ʃɪfra]
secrecy	**konspirace** (ž)	[konspɪratsɛ]
password	**heslo** (s)	[hɛslo]
land mine	**mina** (ž)	[mɪna]
to mine (road, etc.)	**zaminovat**	[zamɪnovat]
minefield	**minové pole** (s)	[mɪnovɛ: polɛ]
air-raid warning	**letecký poplach** (m)	[lɛtɛtski: poplax]
alarm (alert signal)	**poplach** (m)	[poplax]
signal	**signál** (m)	[sɪgna:l]
signal flare	**světlice** (ž)	[svetlɪtsɛ]
headquarters	**štáb** (m)	[ʃta:p]
reconnaissance	**rozvědka** (ž)	[rozvetka]
situation	**situace** (ž)	[sɪtuatsɛ]
report	**hlášení** (s)	[hla:ʃɛni:]
ambush	**záloha** (ž)	[za:loha]
reinforcement (of army)	**posila** (ž)	[posɪla]
target	**terč** (m)	[tɛrtʃ]
proving ground	**střelnice** (ž)	[strʃɛlnɪtsɛ]
military exercise	**manévry** (m mn)	[manɛ:vrɪ]
panic	**panika** (ž)	[panɪka]
devastation	**rozvrat** (m)	[rozvrat]
destruction, ruins	**zpustošení** (s)	[spustoʃɛni:]
to destroy (vt)	**zpustošit**	[spustoʃɪt]
to survive (vi, vt)	**přežít**	[prʃɛʒi:t]
to disarm (vt)	**odzbrojit**	[odzbrojɪt]
to handle (~ a gun)	**zacházet**	[zaxa:zɛt]
Attention!	**Pozor!**	[pozor]
At ease!	**Pohov!**	[pohof]
feat, act of courage	**hrdinský čin** (m)	[hrdɪnski: tʃɪn]
oath (vow)	**přísaha** (ž)	[prʃi:saha]
to swear (an oath)	**přísahat**	[prʃi:sahat]
decoration (medal, etc.)	**vyznamenání** (s)	[vɪznamɛna:ni:]
to award (give medal to)	**vyznamenávat**	[vɪznamɛna:vat]

medal	**medaile** (ž)	[mɛdajlɛ]
order (e.g., ~ of Merit)	**řád** (m)	[rʒa:t]
victory	**vítězství** (s)	[vi:tezstvi:]
defeat	**porážka** (ž)	[pora:ʃka]
armistice	**příměří** (s)	[prʃi:mnerʒi:]
standard (battle flag)	**prapor** (m)	[prapor]
glory (honor, fame)	**sláva** (ž)	[sla:va]
parade	**vojenská přehlídka** (ž)	[vojɛnska: prʃɛhli:tka]
to march (on parade)	**pochodovat**	[poxodovat]

186. Weapons

weapons	**zbraň** (ž)	[zbranʲ]
firearms	**střelná zbraň** (ž)	[strʃɛlna: zbranʲ]
cold weapons (knives, etc.)	**bodná a sečná zbraň** (ž)	[bodna: a sɛʧna: zbranʲ]
chemical weapons	**chemická zbraň** (ž)	[xɛmɪʦka: zbranʲ]
nuclear (adj)	**jaderný**	[jadɛrni:]
nuclear weapons	**jaderná zbraň** (ž)	[jadɛrna: zbranʲ]
bomb	**puma** (ž)	[puma]
atomic bomb	**atomová puma** (ž)	[atomova: puma]
pistol (gun)	**pistole** (ž)	[pɪstolɛ]
rifle	**puška** (ž)	[puʃka]
submachine gun	**samopal** (m)	[samopal]
machine gun	**kulomet** (m)	[kulomɛt]
muzzle	**ústí** (s) **hlavně**	[u:sti: hlavne]
barrel	**hlaveň** (ž)	[hlavɛnʲ]
caliber	**ráž** (ž)	[ra:ʃ]
trigger	**kohoutek** (m)	[kohoutɛk]
sight (aiming device)	**hledí** (s)	[hlɛdi:]
magazine	**zásobník** (m)	[za:sobni:k]
butt (shoulder stock)	**pažba** (ž)	[paʒba]
hand grenade	**granát** (m)	[grana:t]
explosive	**výbušnina** (ž)	[vi:buʃnɪna]
bullet	**kulka** (ž)	[kulka]
cartridge	**náboj** (m)	[na:boj]
charge	**nálož** (ž)	[na:loʃ]
ammunition	**střelivo** (s)	[strʃɛlɪvo]
bomber (aircraft)	**bombardér** (m)	[bombardɛ:r]
fighter	**stíhačka** (ž)	[sti:haʧka]

helicopter	**vrtulník** (m)	[vrtulni:k]
anti-aircraft gun	**protiletadlové dělo** (s)	[protɪlɛtadlovɛ: delo]
tank	**tank** (m)	[taŋk]
tank gun	**tankové dělo** (s)	[taŋkovɛ: delo]
artillery	**dělostřelectvo** (s)	[delostrʃɛlɛtstvo]
gun (cannon, howitzer)	**dělo** (s)	[delo]
to lay (a gun)	**zamířit**	[zami:rʒɪt]
shell (projectile)	**střela** (ž)	[strʃɛla]
mortar bomb	**mina** (ž)	[mɪna]
mortar	**minomet** (m)	[mɪnomɛt]
splinter (shell fragment)	**střepina** (ž)	[strʃɛpɪna]
submarine	**ponorka** (ž)	[ponorka]
torpedo	**torpédo** (s)	[torpɛ:do]
missile	**raketa** (ž)	[rakɛta]
to load (gun)	**nabíjet**	[nabi:jɛt]
to shoot (vi)	**střílet**	[strʃi:lɛt]
to point at (the cannon)	**mířit**	[mi:rʒɪt]
bayonet	**bodák** (m)	[boda:k]
rapier	**kord** (m)	[kort]
saber (e.g., cavalry ~)	**šavle** (ž)	[ʃavlɛ]
spear (weapon)	**kopí** (s)	[kopi:]
bow	**luk** (m)	[luk]
arrow	**šíp** (m)	[ʃi:p]
musket	**mušketa** (ž)	[muʃkɛta]
crossbow	**samostříl** (m)	[samostrʃi:l]

187. Ancient people

primitive (prehistoric)	**prvobytný**	[prvobɪtni:]
prehistoric (adj)	**prehistorický**	[prɛhɪstorɪtski:]
ancient (~ civilization)	**starobylý**	[starobɪli:]
Stone Age	**Doba** (ž) **kamenná**	[doba kamɛnna:]
Bronze Age	**Doba** (ž) **bronzová**	[doba bronzova:]
Ice Age	**Doba** (ž) **ledová**	[doba lɛdova:]
tribe	**kmen** (m)	[kmɛn]
cannibal	**lidojed** (m)	[lɪdojɛt]
hunter	**lovec** (m)	[lovɛts]
to hunt (vi, vt)	**lovit**	[lovɪt]
mammoth	**mamut** (m)	[mamut]
cave	**jeskyně** (ž)	[jɛskɪne]
fire	**oheň** (m)	[ohɛnʲ]
campfire	**táborák** (m)	[taborak]

cave painting	**jeskynní malba** (ž)	[jɛskɪnni: malba]
tool (e.g., stone ax)	**pracovní nástroje** (m mn)	[pratsovni: na:strojɛ]
spear	**oštěp** (m)	[oʃtep]
stone ax	**kamenná sekera** (ž)	[kamɛnna: sɛkɛra]
to be at war	**bojovat**	[bojovat]
to domesticate (vt)	**ochočovat**	[oxotʃovat]
idol	**modla** (ž)	[modla]
to worship (vt)	**klanět se**	[klanet sɛ]
superstition	**pověra** (ž)	[povera]
rite	**obřad** (m)	[oprʃat]
evolution	**evoluce** (ž)	[ɛvolutsɛ]
development	**rozvoj** (m)	[rozvoj]
disappearance (extinction)	**vymizení** (s)	[vɪmɪzɛni:]
to adapt oneself	**přizpůsobovat se**	[prʃɪspu:sobovat sɛ]
archeology	**archeologie** (ž)	[arxɛologɪɛ]
archeologist	**archeolog** (m)	[arxɛolog]
archeological (adj)	**archeologický**	[arxɛologɪtski:]
excavation site	**vykopávky** (ž mn)	[vɪkopa:fkɪ]
excavations	**vykopávky** (ž mn)	[vɪkopa:fkɪ]
find (object)	**objev** (m)	[objɛf]
fragment	**část** (ž)	[tʃa:st]

188. Middle Ages

people (ethnic group)	**lid, národ** (m)	[lɪt], [na:rot]
peoples	**národy** (m mn)	[na:rodɪ]
tribe	**kmen** (m)	[kmɛn]
tribes	**kmeny** (m mn)	[kmɛnɪ]
barbarians	**barbaři** (m mn)	[barbarʒɪ]
Gauls	**Galové** (m mn)	[galovɛ:]
Goths	**Gótové** (m mn)	[go:tovɛ:]
Slavs	**Slované** (m mn)	[slovanɛ:]
Vikings	**Vikingové** (m mn)	[vɪkɪngovɛ:]
Romans	**Římané** (m mn)	[rʒi:manɛ:]
Roman (adj)	**římský**	[rʒi:mski:]
Byzantines	**obyvatelé Byzantské říše** (m mn)	[obɪvatɛlɛ: bɪzantskɛ: rʃi:ʃɛ]
Byzantium	**Byzantská říše** (ž)	[bɪzantska: rʃi:ʃɛ]
Byzantine (adj)	**byzantský**	[bɪzantski:]
emperor	**císař** (m)	[tsi:sarʃ]
leader, chief (tribal ~)	**vůdce** (m)	[vu:dtsɛ]
powerful (~ king)	**mocný**	[motsni:]

king	**král** (m)	[kra:l]
ruler (sovereign)	**vladař** (m)	[vladarʃ]
knight	**rytíř** (m)	[rɪti:rʃ]
feudal lord	**feudál** (m)	[fɛuda:l]
feudal (adj)	**feudální**	[fɛuda:lni:]
vassal	**vasal** (m)	[vasal]
duke	**vévoda** (m)	[vɛ:voda]
earl	**hrabě** (m)	[hrabe]
baron	**barel** (m)	[barɛl]
bishop	**biskup** (m)	[bɪskup]
armor	**brnění** (s)	[brneni:]
shield	**štít** (m)	[ʃti:t]
sword	**meč** (m)	[mɛʧ]
visor	**hledí** (s)	[hlɛdi:]
chainmail	**kroužková košile** (ž)	[krouʃkova: koʃɪlɛ]
Crusade	**křižácká výprava** (ž)	[krʃɪʒa:ʦka: vi:prava]
crusader	**křižák** (m)	[krʃɪʒa:k]
territory	**území** (s)	[u:zɛmi:]
to attack (invade)	**přepadat**	[prʃɛpadat]
to conquer (vt)	**dobýt**	[dobi:t]
to occupy (invade)	**zmocnit se**	[zmoʦnɪt sɛ]
siege (to be under ~)	**obležení** (s)	[oblɛʒeni:]
besieged (adj)	**obklíčený**	[opkli:ʧɛni:]
to besiege (vt)	**obkličovat**	[opklɪʧovat]
inquisition	**inkvizice** (ž)	[ɪŋkvɪzɪʦɛ]
inquisitor	**inkvizitor** (m)	[ɪŋkvɪzɪtor]
torture	**mučení** (s)	[muʧɛni:]
cruel (adj)	**krutý**	[kruti:]
heretic	**kacíř** (m)	[kaʦi:rʃ]
heresy	**bludařství** (s)	[bludarʃstvi:]
seafaring	**mořeplavba** (ž)	[morʒɛplavba]
pirate	**pirát** (m)	[pɪra:t]
piracy	**pirátství** (s)	[pɪra:tstvi:]
boarding (attack)	**abordáž** (ž)	[aborda:ʃ]
loot, booty	**kořist** (ž)	[korʒɪst]
treasures	**bohatství** (s)	[bohatstvi:]
discovery	**objevení** (s)	[objɛvɛni:]
to discover (new land, etc.)	**objevit**	[objɛvɪt]
expedition	**výprava** (ž)	[vi:prava]
musketeer	**mušketýr** (m)	[muʃkɛti:r]
cardinal	**kardinál** (m)	[kardɪna:l]
heraldry	**heraldika** (ž)	[hɛraldɪka]
heraldic (adj)	**heraldický**	[hɛraldɪʦki:]

189. Leader. Chief. Authorities

king	**král** (m)	[kra:l]
queen	**královna** (ž)	[kra:lovna]
royal (adj)	**královský**	[kra:lovski:]
kingdom	**království** (s)	[kra:lovstvi:]
prince	**princ** (m)	[prɪnʦ]
princess	**princezna** (ž)	[prɪnʦɛzna]
president	**prezident** (m)	[prɛzɪdɛnt]
vice-president	**viceprezident** (m)	[vɪʦɛprɛzɪdɛnt]
senator	**senátor** (m)	[sɛna:tor]
monarch	**monarcha** (m)	[monarxa]
ruler (sovereign)	**vladař** (m)	[vladarʃ]
dictator	**diktátor** (m)	[dɪkta:tor]
tyrant	**tyran** (m)	[tɪran]
magnate	**magnát** (m)	[magna:t]
director	**ředitel** (m)	[rʒɛdɪtɛl]
chief	**šéf** (m)	[ʃɛ:f]
manager (director)	**správce** (m)	[spra:vʦɛ]
boss	**bos** (m)	[bos]
owner	**majitel** (m)	[majɪtɛl]
leader	**vůdce** (m)	[vu:dʦɛ]
head (~ of delegation)	**hlava** (m)	[hlava]
authorities	**úřady** (m mn)	[u:rʒadɪ]
superiors	**vedení** (s)	[vɛdɛni:]
governor	**gubernátor** (m)	[gubɛrna:tor]
consul	**konzul** (m)	[konzul]
diplomat	**diplomat** (m)	[dɪplomat]
mayor	**primátor** (m)	[prɪma:tor]
sheriff	**šerif** (m)	[ʃɛrɪf]
emperor	**císař** (m)	[ʦi:sarʃ]
tsar, czar	**car** (m)	[ʦar]
pharaoh	**faraón** (m)	[farao:n]
khan	**chán** (m)	[xa:n]

190. Road. Way. Directions

road	**cesta** (ž)	[ʦɛsta]
way (direction)	**cesta** (ž)	[ʦɛsta]
freeway	**silnice** (ž)	[sɪlnɪʦɛ]
highway	**dálnice** (ž)	[da:lnɪʦɛ]

interstate	**národní trasa** (ž)	[na:rodni: trasa]
main road	**hlavní silnice** (ž)	[hlavni: sɪlnɪʦɛ]
dirt road	**polní cesta** (ž)	[polni: ʦɛsta]
pathway	**stezka** (ž)	[stɛska]
footpath (troddenpath)	**stezka** (ž)	[stɛska]
Where?	**Kde?**	[gdɛ]
Where (to)?	**Kam?**	[kam]
From where?	**Odkud?**	[otkut]
direction (way)	**směr** (m)	[smner]
to point (~ the way)	**ukázat**	[uka:zat]
to the left	**vlevo**	[vlɛvo]
to the right	**vpravo**	[vpravo]
straight ahead (adv)	**rovně**	[rovne]
back (e.g., to turn ~)	**zpátky**	[spa:tkɪ]
bend, curve	**zatáčka** (ž)	[zata:ʧka]
to turn (e.g., ~ left)	**zatáčet**	[zata:ʧɛt]
to make a U-turn	**otáčet se**	[ota:ʧɛt sɛ]
to be visible (mountains, castle, etc.)	**být vidět**	[bi:t vɪdet]
to appear (come into view)	**ukázat se**	[uka:zat sɛ]
stop, halt (e.g., during a trip)	**zastávka** (ž)	[zasta:fka]
to rest, to pause (vi)	**odpočinout**	[otpoʧɪnout]
rest (pause)	**odpočinek** (m)	[otpoʧɪnɛk]
to lose one's way	**zabloudit**	[zabloudɪt]
to lead to ... (ab. road)	**vést k ...**	[vɛ:st k]
to come out (e.g., on the highway)	**dostat se k ...**	[dostat sɛ k]
stretch (of road)	**úsek** (m)	[u:sɛk]
asphalt	**asfalt** (m)	[asfalt]
curb	**obrubník** (m)	[obrubni:k]
ditch	**příkop** (m)	[prʃi:kop]
manhole	**poklop** (m)	[poklop]
roadside (shoulder)	**krajnice** (ž)	[krajnɪʦɛ]
pit, pothole	**jáma** (ž)	[ja:ma]
to go (on foot)	**jít**	[ji:t]
to pass (overtake)	**předejít**	[prʃɛdɛji:t]
step (footstep)	**krok** (m)	[krok]
on foot (adv)	**pěšky**	[peʃkɪ]
to block (road)	**zatarasit**	[zatarasɪt]
boom gate	**závory** (ž mn)	[za:vorɪ]
dead end	**slepá ulice** (ž)	[slɛpa: ulɪʦɛ]

191. Breaking the law. Criminals. Part 1

bandit	**bandita** (m)	[bandɪta]
crime	**zločin** (m)	[zloʧɪn]
criminal (person)	**zločinec** (m)	[zloʧɪnɛʦ]
thief	**zloděj** (m)	[zlodej]
to steal (vi, vt)	**krást**	[kra:st]
stealing (larceny)	**loupež** (ž)	[loupɛʃ]
theft	**krádež** (ž)	[kra:dɛʃ]
to kidnap (vt)	**unést**	[unɛ:st]
kidnapping	**únos** (m)	[u:nos]
kidnapper	**únosce** (m)	[u:nosʦɛ]
ransom	**výkupné** (s)	[vi:kupnɛ:]
to demand ransom	**žádat výkupné**	[ʒa:dat vi:kupnɛ:]
to rob (vt)	**loupit**	[loupɪt]
robbery	**loupež** (ž)	[loupɛʃ]
robber	**lupič** (m)	[lupɪʧ]
to extort (vt)	**vydírat**	[vɪdi:rat]
extortionist	**vyděrač** (m)	[vɪderaʧ]
extortion	**vyděračství** (s)	[vɪderaʧstvi:]
to murder, to kill	**zabít**	[zabi:t]
murder	**vražda** (ž)	[vraʒda]
murderer	**vrah** (m)	[vrax]
gunshot	**výstřel** (m)	[vi:strʃɛl]
to fire (~ a shot)	**vystřelit**	[vɪstrʒɛlɪt]
to shoot to death	**zastřelit**	[zastrʃɛlɪt]
to shoot (vi)	**střílet**	[strʃi:lɛt]
shooting	**střelba** (ž)	[strʃɛlba]
incident (fight, etc.)	**nehoda** (ž)	[nɛhoda]
fight, brawl	**rvačka** (ž)	[rvaʧka]
Help!	**Pomoc!**	[pomoʦ]
victim	**oběť** (ž)	[obetʲ]
to damage (vt)	**poškodit**	[poʃkodɪt]
damage	**škoda** (ž)	[ʃkoda]
dead body, corpse	**mrtvola** (ž)	[mrtvola]
grave (~ crime)	**těžký**	[teʃki:]
to attack (vt)	**napadnout**	[napadnout]
to beat (to hit)	**bít**	[bi:t]
to beat up	**zbít**	[zbi:t]
to take (rob of sth)	**odebrat**	[odɛbrat]
to stab to death	**zabít**	[zabi:t]

to maim (vt)	**zmrzačit**	[zmrzatʃɪt]
to wound (vt)	**zranit**	[zranɪt]
blackmail	**vyděračství** (s)	[vɪderatʃstvi:]
to blackmail (vt)	**vydírat**	[vɪdi:rat]
blackmailer	**vyděrač** (m)	[vɪderatʃ]
protection racket	**vyděračství** (s)	[vɪderatʃstvi:]
racketeer	**vyděrač** (m)	[vɪderatʃ]
gangster	**gangster** (m)	[gangstɛr]
mafia, Mob	**mafie** (ž)	[mafɪe]
pickpocket	**kapsář** (m)	[kapsa:rʃ]
burglar	**kasař** (m)	[kasarʃ]
smuggling	**pašování** (s)	[paʃova:ni:]
smuggler	**pašerák** (m)	[paʃɛra:k]
forgery	**padělání** (s)	[padela:ni:]
to forge (counterfeit)	**padělat**	[padelat]
fake (forged)	**padělaný**	[padelani:]

192. Breaking the law. Criminals. Part 2

rape	**znásilnění** (s)	[zna:sɪlneni:]
to rape (vt)	**znásilnit**	[zna:sɪlnɪt]
rapist	**násilník** (m)	[na:sɪlni:k]
maniac	**maniak** (m)	[manɪak]
prostitute (fem.)	**prostitutka** (ž)	[prostɪtutka]
prostitution	**prostituce** (ž)	[prostɪtutsɛ]
pimp	**kuplíř** (m)	[kupli:rʃ]
drug addict	**narkoman** (m)	[narkoman]
drug dealer	**drogový dealer** (m)	[drogovi: di:lɛr]
to blow up (bomb)	**vyhodit do povětří**	[vɪhodɪt do povetrʃi:]
explosion	**výbuch** (m)	[vi:bux]
to set fire	**zapálit**	[zapa:lɪt]
arsonist	**žhář** (m)	[ʒha:rʃ]
terrorism	**terorismus** (m)	[tɛrorɪzmus]
terrorist	**terorista** (m)	[tɛrorɪsta]
hostage	**rukojmí** (m)	[rukojmi:]
to swindle (deceive)	**oklamat**	[oklamat]
swindle, deception	**podvod** (m)	[podvot]
swindler	**podvodník** (m)	[podvodni:k]
to bribe (vt)	**podplatit**	[potplatɪt]
bribery	**podplácení** (s)	[potpla:tsɛni:]

bribe	**úplatek** (m)	[u:platɛk]
poison	**jed** (m)	[jɛt]
to poison (vt)	**otrávit**	[otra:vɪt]
to poison oneself	**otrávit se**	[otra:vɪt sɛ]
suicide (act)	**sebevražda** (ž)	[sɛbɛvraʒda]
suicide (person)	**sebevrah** (m)	[sɛbɛvrax]
to threaten (vt)	**vyhrožovat**	[vɪhroʒovat]
threat	**vyhrůžka** (ž)	[vɪhru:ʃka]
to make an attempt	**páchat atentát**	[pa:xat atenta:t]
attempt (attack)	**atentát** (m)	[atɛnta:t]
to steal (a car)	**unést**	[unɛ:st]
to hijack (a plane)	**unést**	[unɛ:st]
revenge	**pomsta** (ž)	[pomsta]
to avenge (get revenge)	**mstít se**	[msti:t sɛ]
to torture (vt)	**mučit**	[muʧɪt]
torture	**mučení** (s)	[muʧɛni:]
to torment (vt)	**trápit**	[tra:pɪt]
pirate	**pirát** (m)	[pɪra:t]
hooligan	**chuligán** (m)	[xulɪga:n]
armed (adj)	**ozbrojený**	[ozbrojɛni:]
violence	**násilí** (s)	[na:sɪli:]
illegal (unlawful)	**nelegální**	[nɛlɛga:lni:]
spying (espionage)	**špionáž** (ž)	[ʃpɪona:ʃ]
to spy (vi)	**špehovat**	[ʃpɛhovat]

193. Police. Law. Part 1

justice	**justice** (ž)	[justiʦɛ]
court (see you in ~)	**soud** (m)	[sout]
judge	**soudce** (m)	[soudʦɛ]
jurors	**porotci** (m mn)	[porotʦɪ]
jury trial	**porota** (ž)	[porota]
to judge, to try (vt)	**soudit**	[soudɪt]
lawyer, attorney	**advokát** (m)	[advoka:t]
defendant	**obžalovaný** (m)	[obʒalovani:]
dock	**lavice** (ž) **obžalovaných**	[lavɪʦɛ obʒalovani:x]
charge	**žaloba** (ž)	[ʒaloba]
accused	**obžalovaný** (m)	[obʒalovani:]
sentence	**rozsudek** (m)	[rozsudɛk]
to sentence (vt)	**odsoudit**	[otsoudɪt]

guilty (culprit)	**viník** (m)	[vɪni:k]
to punish (vt)	**potrestat**	[potrɛstat]
punishment	**trest** (m)	[trɛst]
fine (penalty)	**pokuta** (ž)	[pokuta]
life imprisonment	**doživotní vězení** (s)	[doʒɪvotni: vezɛni:]
death penalty	**trest** (m) **smrti**	[trɛst smrtɪ]
electric chair	**elektrické křeslo** (s)	[ɛlɛktrɪtskɛ: krʃɛslo]
gallows	**šibenice** (ž)	[ʃɪbɛnɪtsɛ]
to execute (vt)	**popravit**	[popravɪt]
execution	**poprava** (ž)	[poprava]
prison, jail	**vězení** (s)	[vezɛni:]
cell	**cela** (ž)	[tsɛla]
escort (convoy)	**ozbrojený doprovod** (m)	[ozbrojɛni: doprovot]
prison guard	**dozorce** (m)	[dozortsɛ]
prisoner	**vězeň** (m)	[vezɛnʲ]
handcuffs	**pouta** (s mn)	[pouta]
to handcuff (vt)	**nasadit pouta**	[nasadɪt pouta]
prison break	**útěk** (m)	[u:tek]
to break out (vi)	**uprchnout**	[uprxnout]
to disappear (vi)	**zmizet**	[zmɪzɛt]
to release (from prison)	**propustit**	[propustɪt]
amnesty	**amnestie** (ž)	[amnɛstɪe]
police	**policie** (ž)	[polɪtsɪe]
police officer	**policista** (m)	[polɪtsɪsta]
police station	**policejní stanice** (ž)	[polɪtsɛjni: stanɪtsɛ]
billy club	**gumový obušek** (m)	[gumovi: obuʃɛk]
bullhorn	**hlásná trouba** (ž)	[hla:sna: trouba]
patrol car	**policejní vůz** (m)	[polɪtsɛjni: vu:z]
siren	**houkačka** (ž)	[houkatʃka]
to turn on the siren	**zapnout houkačku**	[zapnout houkatʃku]
siren call	**houkání** (s)	[houka:ni:]
crime scene	**místo** (s) **činu**	[mi:sto tʃɪnu]
witness	**svědek** (m)	[svedɛk]
freedom	**svoboda** (ž)	[svoboda]
accomplice	**spolupachatel** (m)	[spolupaxatɛl]
to flee (vi)	**zmizet**	[zmɪzɛt]
trace (to leave a ~)	**stopa** (ž)	[stopa]

194. Police. Law. Part 2

search (investigation)	**pátrání** (s)	[pa:tra:ni:]
to look for ...	**pátrat**	[pa:trat]

suspicion	**podezření** (s)	[podɛzrʒɛni:]
suspicious (e.g., ~ vehicle)	**podezřelý**	[podɛzrʒɛli:]
to stop (cause to halt)	**zastavit**	[zastavɪt]
to detain (keep in custody)	**zadržet**	[zadrʒet]
case (lawsuit)	**případ** (m)	[prʃi:pat]
investigation	**vyšetřování** (s)	[vɪʃɛtrʃova:ni:]
detective	**detektiv** (m)	[dɛtɛktɪf]
investigator	**vyšetřovatel** (m)	[vɪʃɛtrʃovatɛl]
hypothesis	**verze** (ž)	[vɛrzɛ]
motive	**motiv** (m)	[motɪf]
interrogation	**výslech** (m)	[vi:slɛx]
to interrogate (vt)	**vyslýchat**	[vɪsli:xat]
to question (~ neighbors, etc.)	**vyslýchat**	[vɪsli:xat]
check (identity ~)	**kontrola** (ž)	[kontrola]
round-up (raid)	**zátah** (m)	[za:tax]
search (~ warrant)	**prohlídka** (ž)	[prohli:tka]
chase (pursuit)	**stíhání** (s)	[sti:ha:ni:]
to pursue, to chase	**pronásledovat**	[prona:slɛdovat]
to track (a criminal)	**sledovat**	[slɛdovat]
arrest	**zatčení** (s)	[zatʧɛni:]
to arrest (sb)	**zatknout**	[zatknout]
to catch (thief, etc.)	**chytit**	[xɪtɪt]
capture	**chycení** (s)	[xɪʦɛni:]
document	**dokument** (m)	[dokumɛnt]
proof (evidence)	**důkaz** (m)	[du:kaz]
to prove (vt)	**dokazovat**	[dokazovat]
footprint	**stopa** (ž)	[stopa]
fingerprints	**otisky** (m mn) **prstů**	[otɪskɪ prstu:]
piece of evidence	**důkaz** (m)	[du:kaz]
alibi	**alibi** (s)	[alɪbɪ]
innocent (not guilty)	**nevinný**	[nɛvɪnni:]
injustice	**nespravedlivost** (ž)	[nɛspravɛdlɪvost]
unjust, unfair (adj)	**nespravedlivý**	[nɛspra:vɛdlɪvi:]
criminal (adj)	**kriminální**	[krɪmɪna:lni:]
to confiscate (vt)	**konfiskovat**	[konfɪskovat]
drug (illegal substance)	**droga** (ž)	[droga]
weapon, gun	**zbraň** (ž)	[zbranʲ]
to disarm (vt)	**odzbrojit**	[odzbrojɪt]
to order (command)	**rozkazovat**	[roskazovat]
to disappear (vi)	**zmizet**	[zmɪzɛt]
law	**zákon** (m)	[za:kon]
legal, lawful (adj)	**zákonný**	[za:konni:]
illegal, illicit (adj)	**nezákonný**	[nɛza:konni:]

responsibility (blame)	**odpovědnost** (ž)	[otpovednost]
responsible (adj)	**odpovědný**	[otpovedni:]

NATURE

The Earth. Part 1

195. Outer space

space	**kosmos** (m)	[kosmos]
space (as adj)	**kosmický**	[kosmɪʦki:]
outer space	**kosmický prostor** (m)	[kosmɪʦki: prostor]
world, universe	**vesmír** (m)	[vɛsmi:r]
world	**svět** (m)	[svet]
galaxy	**galaxie** (ž)	[galaksɪe]
star	**hvězda** (ž)	[hvezda]
constellation	**souhvězdí** (s)	[souhvezdi:]
planet	**planeta** (ž)	[planɛta]
satellite	**družice** (ž)	[druʒɪʦɛ]
meteorite	**meteorit** (m)	[mɛtɛorɪt]
comet	**kometa** (ž)	[komɛta]
asteroid	**asteroid** (m)	[astɛroɪt]
orbit	**oběžná dráha** (ž)	[obeʒna: dra:ha]
to revolve (~ around the Earth)	**otáčet se**	[ota:ʧɛt sɛ]
atmosphere	**atmosféra** (ž)	[atmosfɛ:ra]
the Sun	**Slunce** (s)	[sluntsɛ]
solar system	**sluneční soustava** (ž)	[slunɛʧni: soustava]
solar eclipse	**sluneční zatmění** (s)	[slunɛʧni: zatmneni:]
the Earth	**Země** (ž)	[zɛmnɛ]
the Moon	**Měsíc** (m)	[mnesi:ʦ]
Mars	**Mars** (m)	[mars]
Venus	**Venuše** (ž)	[vɛnuʃɛ]
Jupiter	**Jupiter** (m)	[jupɪtɛr]
Saturn	**Saturn** (m)	[saturn]
Mercury	**Merkur** (m)	[mɛrkur]
Uranus	**Uran** (m)	[uran]
Neptune	**Neptun** (m)	[nɛptun]
Pluto	**Pluto** (s)	[pluto]
Milky Way	**Mléčná dráha** (ž)	[mlɛ:ʧna: dra:ha]

Great Bear (Ursa Major)	**Velká medvědice** (ž)	[vɛlka: mɛdvedɪʦɛ]
North Star	**Polárka** (ž)	[pola:rka]
Martian	**Marťan** (m)	[martʲan]
extraterrestrial (n)	**mimozemšťan** (m)	[mɪmozɛmʃtʲan]
alien	**vetřelec** (m)	[vɛtrʃɛlɛʦ]
flying saucer	**létající talíř** (m)	[lɛ:taji:ʦi: tali:rʃ]
spaceship	**kosmická loď** (ž)	[kosmɪʦka: lotʲ]
space station	**orbitální stanice** (ž)	[orbɪta:lni: stanɪʦɛ]
blast-off	**start** (m)	[start]
engine	**motor** (m)	[motor]
nozzle	**tryska** (ž)	[trɪska]
fuel	**palivo** (s)	[palɪvo]
cockpit, flight deck	**kabina** (ž)	[kabɪna]
antenna	**anténa** (ž)	[antɛ:na]
porthole	**okénko** (s)	[okɛ:ŋko]
solar panel	**sluneční baterie** (ž)	[slunɛʧni: batɛrɪe]
spacesuit	**skafandr** (m)	[skafandr]
weightlessness	**beztížný stav** (m)	[bɛzti:ʒni: staf]
oxygen	**kyslík** (m)	[kɪsli:k]
docking (in space)	**spojení** (s)	[spojɛni:]
to dock (vi, vt)	**spojovat se**	[spojovat sɛ]
observatory	**observatoř** (ž)	[opsɛrvatorʃ]
telescope	**teleskop** (m)	[tɛlɛskop]
to observe (vt)	**pozorovat**	[pozorovat]
to explore (vt)	**zkoumat**	[skoumat]

196. The Earth

the Earth	**Země** (ž)	[zɛmnɛ]
the globe (the Earth)	**zeměkoule** (ž)	[zɛmnekoulɛ]
planet	**planeta** (ž)	[planɛta]
atmosphere	**atmosféra** (ž)	[atmosfɛ:ra]
geography	**zeměpis** (m)	[zɛmnepɪs]
nature	**příroda** (ž)	[prʃi:roda]
globe (table ~)	**glóbus** (m)	[glo:bus]
map	**mapa** (ž)	[mapa]
atlas	**atlas** (m)	[atlas]
Europe	**Evropa** (ž)	[ɛvropa]
Asia	**Asie** (ž)	[azɪe]
Africa	**Afrika** (ž)	[afrɪka]

Australia	**Austrálie** (ž)	[austra:lɪe]
America	**Amerika** (ž)	[amɛrɪka]
North America	**Severní Amerika** (ž)	[sɛvɛrni: amɛrɪka]
South America	**Jižní Amerika** (ž)	[jɪʒni: amɛrɪka]
Antarctica	**Antarktida** (ž)	[antarkti:da]
the Arctic	**Arktida** (ž)	[arktɪda]

197. Cardinal directions

north	**sever** (m)	[sɛvɛr]
to the north	**na sever**	[na sɛvɛr]
in the north	**na severu**	[na sɛvɛru]
northern (adj)	**severní**	[sɛvɛrni:]
south	**jih** (m)	[jɪx]
to the south	**na jih**	[na jɪx]
in the south	**na jihu**	[na jɪhu]
southern (adj)	**jižní**	[jɪʒni:]
west	**západ** (m)	[za:pat]
to the west	**na západ**	[na za:pat]
in the west	**na západě**	[na za:pade]
western (adj)	**západní**	[za:padni:]
east	**východ** (m)	[vi:xot]
to the east	**na východ**	[na vi:xot]
in the east	**na východě**	[na vi:xode]
eastern (adj)	**východní**	[vi:xodni:]

198. Sea. Ocean

sea	**moře** (s)	[morʒɛ]
ocean	**oceán** (m)	[ot͡sɛa:n]
gulf (bay)	**záliv** (m)	[za:lɪf]
straits	**průliv** (m)	[pru:lɪf]
land (solid ground)	**země** (ž)	[zɛmnɛ]
continent (mainland)	**pevnina** (ž)	[pɛvnɪna]
island	**ostrov** (m)	[ostrof]
peninsula	**poloostrov** (m)	[poloostrof]
archipelago	**souostroví** (s)	[souostrovi:]
bay, cove	**zátoka** (ž)	[za:toka]
harbor	**přístav** (m)	[prʃi:staf]
lagoon	**laguna** (ž)	[lagu:na]
cape	**mys** (m)	[mɪs]
atoll	**atol** (m)	[atol]

reef	**útes** (m)	[u:tɛs]
coral	**korál** (m)	[kora:l]
coral reef	**korálový útes** (m)	[kora:lovi: u:tɛs]
deep (adj)	**hluboký**	[hluboki:]
depth (deep water)	**hloubka** (ž)	[hloupka]
abyss	**hlubina** (ž)	[hlubɪna]
trench (e.g., Mariana ~)	**prohlubeň** (ž)	[prohlubɛnʲ]
current (Ocean ~)	**proud** (m)	[prout]
to surround (bathe)	**omývat**	[omi:vat]
shore	**břeh** (m)	[brʒɛx]
coast	**pobřeží** (s)	[pobrʒɛʒi:]
flow (flood tide)	**příliv** (m)	[prʃi:lɪf]
ebb (ebb tide)	**odliv** (m)	[odlɪf]
shoal	**mělčina** (ž)	[mnelʧɪna]
bottom (~ of the sea)	**dno** (s)	[dno]
wave	**vlna** (ž)	[vlna]
crest (~ of a wave)	**hřbet** (m) **vlny**	[hrʒbɛt vlnɪ]
spume (sea foam)	**pěna** (ž)	[pena]
storm (sea storm)	**bouřka** (ž)	[bourʃka]
hurricane	**hurikán** (m)	[hurɪka:n]
tsunami	**tsunami** (s)	[tsunamɪ]
calm (dead ~)	**bezvětří** (s)	[bɛzvetrʃi:]
quiet, calm (adj)	**klidný**	[klɪdni:]
pole	**pól** (m)	[po:l]
polar (adj)	**polární**	[pola:rni:]
latitude	**šířka** (ž)	[ʃi:rʃka]
longitude	**délka** (ž)	[dɛ:lka]
parallel	**rovnoběžka** (ž)	[rovnobeʃka]
equator	**rovník** (m)	[rovni:k]
sky	**obloha** (ž)	[obloha]
horizon	**horizont** (m)	[horɪzont]
air	**vzduch** (m)	[vzdux]
lighthouse	**maják** (m)	[maja:k]
to dive (vi)	**potápět se**	[pota:pet sɛ]
to sink (ab. boat)	**potopit se**	[potopɪt sɛ]
treasures	**bohatství** (s)	[bohatstvi:]

199. Seas' and Oceans' names

Atlantic Ocean	**Atlantický oceán** (m)	[atlantɪtski: otsɛa:n]
Indian Ocean	**Indický oceán** (m)	[ɪndɪtski: otsɛa:n]

Pacific Ocean	**Tichý oceán** (m)	[tɪxi: otsɛa:n]
Arctic Ocean	**Severní ledový oceán** (m)	[sɛvɛrni: lɛdovi: otsɛa:n]
Black Sea	**Černé moře** (s)	[ʧɛrnɛ: morʒɛ]
Red Sea	**Rudé moře** (s)	[rudɛ: morʒɛ]
Yellow Sea	**Žluté moře** (s)	[ʒlutɛ: morʒɛ]
White Sea	**Bílé moře** (s)	[bi:lɛ: morʒɛ]
Caspian Sea	**Kaspické moře** (s)	[kaspɪtskɛ: morʒɛ]
Dead Sea	**Mrtvé moře** (s)	[mrtvɛ: morʒɛ]
Mediterranean Sea	**Středozemní moře** (s)	[strʃɛdozɛmni: morʒɛ]
Aegean Sea	**Egejské moře** (s)	[ɛgɛjskɛ: morʒɛ]
Adriatic Sea	**Jaderské moře** (s)	[jadɛrskɛ: morʒɛ]
Arabian Sea	**Arabské moře** (s)	[arapskɛ: morʒɛ]
Sea of Japan	**Japonské moře** (s)	[japonskɛ: morʒɛ]
Bering Sea	**Beringovo moře** (s)	[bɛrɪngovo morʒɛ]
South China Sea	**Jihočínské moře** (s)	[jɪhoʧi:nskɛ: morʒɛ]
Coral Sea	**Korálové moře** (s)	[kora:lovɛ: morʒɛ]
Tasman Sea	**Tasmanovo moře** (s)	[tasmanovo morʒɛ]
Caribbean Sea	**Karibské moře** (s)	[karɪpskɛ: morʒɛ]
Barents Sea	**Barentsovo moře** (s)	[barɛntsovo morʒɛ]
Kara Sea	**Karské moře** (s)	[karskɛ: morʒɛ]
North Sea	**Severní moře** (s)	[sɛvɛrni: morʒɛ]
Baltic Sea	**Baltské moře** (s)	[baltskɛ: morʒɛ]
Norwegian Sea	**Norské moře** (s)	[norskɛ: morʒɛ]

200. Mountains

mountain	**hora** (ž)	[hora]
mountain range	**horské pásmo** (s)	[horskɛ: pa:smo]
mountain ridge	**horský hřbet** (m)	[horski: hrʒbɛt]
summit, top	**vrchol** (m)	[vrxol]
peak	**štít** (m)	[ʃti:t]
foot (~ of the mountain)	**úpatí** (s)	[u:pati:]
slope (mountainside)	**svah** (m)	[svax]
volcano	**sopka** (ž)	[sopka]
active volcano	**činná sopka** (ž)	[ʧɪnna: sopka]
dormant volcano	**vyhaslá sopka** (ž)	[vɪhasla: sopka]
eruption	**výbuch** (m)	[vi:bux]
crater	**kráter** (m)	[kra:tɛr]
magma	**magma** (ž)	[magma]
lava	**láva** (ž)	[la:va]

molten (~ lava)	**rozžhavený**	[rozʒhavɛni:]
canyon	**kaňon** (m)	[kan^jon]
gorge	**soutěska** (ž)	[souteska]
crevice	**rozsedlina** (ž)	[rozsɛdlɪna]
abyss (chasm)	**propast** (ž)	[propast]
pass, col	**průsmyk** (m)	[pru:smɪk]
plateau	**plató** (s)	[plato:]
cliff	**skála** (ž)	[ska:la]
hill	**kopec** (m)	[kopɛʦ]
glacier	**ledovec** (m)	[lɛdovɛʦ]
waterfall	**vodopád** (m)	[vodopa:t]
geyser	**vřídlo** (s)	[vrʒi:dlo]
lake	**jezero** (s)	[jɛzɛro]
plain	**rovina** (ž)	[rovɪna]
landscape	**krajina** (ž)	[krajɪna]
echo	**ozvěna** (ž)	[ozvena]
alpinist	**horolezec** (m)	[horolɛzɛʦ]
rock climber	**horolezec** (m)	[horolɛzɛʦ]
to conquer (in climbing)	**dobývat**	[dobi:vat]
climb (an easy ~)	**výstup** (m)	[vi:stup]

201. Mountains names

The Alps	**Alpy** (mn)	[alpɪ]
Mont Blanc	**Mont Blanc** (m)	[monblaŋ]
The Pyrenees	**Pyreneje** (mn)	[pɪrɛnɛjɛ]
The Carpathians	**Karpaty** (mn)	[karpatɪ]
The Ural Mountains	**Ural** (m)	[ural]
The Caucasus Mountains	**Kavkaz** (m)	[kafkaz]
Mount Elbrus	**Elbrus** (m)	[ɛlbrus]
The Altai Mountains	**Altaj** (m)	[altaj]
The Tian Shan	**Ťan-šan** (ž)	[t^jan-ʃan]
The Pamir Mountains	**Pamír** (m)	[pami:r]
The Himalayas	**Himaláje** (mn)	[hɪmala:jɛ]
Mount Everest	**Mount Everest** (m)	[mount ɛvɛrɛst]
The Andes	**Andy** (mn)	[andɪ]
Mount Kilimanjaro	**Kilimandžáro** (s)	[kɪlɪmanʤa:ro]

202. Rivers

river	**řeka** (ž)	[rʒɛka]
spring (natural source)	**pramen** (m)	[pramɛn]

riverbed (river channel)	**koryto** (s)	[korɪto]
basin (river valley)	**povodí** (s)	[povodi:]
to flow into ...	**vlévat se**	[vlɛ:vat sɛ]
tributary	**přítok** (m)	[prʃi:tok]
bank (of river)	**břeh** (m)	[brʒɛx]
current (stream)	**proud** (m)	[prout]
downstream (adv)	**po proudu**	[po proudu]
upstream (adv)	**proti proudu**	[protɪ proudu]
inundation	**povodeň** (ž)	[povodɛnʲ]
flooding	**záplava** (ž)	[za:plava]
to overflow (vi)	**rozlévat se**	[rozlɛ:vat sɛ]
to flood (vt)	**zaplavovat**	[zaplavovat]
shallow (shoal)	**mělčina** (ž)	[mnelʧɪna]
rapids	**peřej** (ž)	[pɛrʒɛj]
dam	**přehrada** (ž)	[prʃɛhrada]
canal	**průplav** (m)	[pru:plaf]
reservoir (artificial lake)	**vodní nádrž** (ž)	[vodni: na:drʃ]
sluice, lock	**zdymadlo** (s)	[zdɪmadlo]
water body (pond, etc.)	**vodojem** (m)	[vodojɛm]
swamp (marshland)	**bažina** (ž)	[baʒɪna]
bog, marsh	**slať** (ž)	[slatʲ]
whirlpool	**vír** (m)	[vi:r]
stream (brook)	**potok** (m)	[potok]
drinking (ab. water)	**pitný**	[pɪtni:]
fresh (~ water)	**sladký**	[slatki:]
ice	**led** (m)	[lɛt]
to freeze over (ab. river, etc.)	**zamrznout**	[zamrznout]

203. Rivers' names

Seine	**Seina** (ž)	[se:na]
Loire	**Loira** (ž)	[loa:ra]
Thames	**Temže** (ž)	[tɛmʒe]
Rhine	**Rýn** (m)	[ri:n]
Danube	**Dunaj** (m)	[dunaj]
Volga	**Volha** (ž)	[volha]
Don	**Don** (m)	[don]
Lena	**Lena** (ž)	[lɛna]
Yellow River	**Chuang-chež** (ž)	[xuan-xɛ]

Yangtze	**Jang-c'-ťiang** (ž)	[jang-ʦɛ-tʲang]
Mekong	**Mekong** (m)	[mɛkong]
Ganges	**Ganga** (ž)	[ganga]
Nile River	**Nil** (m)	[nɪl]
Congo River	**Kongo** (s)	[kongo]
Okavango River	**Okavango** (s)	[okavango]
Zambezi River	**Zambezi** (ž)	[zambɛzɪ]
Limpopo River	**Limpopo** (s)	[lɪmpopo]
Mississippi River	**Mississippi** (ž)	[mɪsɪsɪpɪ]

204. Forest

forest, wood	**les** (m)	[lɛs]
forest (as adj)	**lesní**	[lɛsni:]
thick forest	**houština** (ž)	[houʃtɪna]
grove	**háj** (m)	[ha:j]
forest clearing	**mýtina** (ž)	[mi:tɪna]
thicket	**houští** (s)	[houʃti:]
scrubland	**křoví** (s)	[krʃovi:]
footpath (troddenpath)	**stezka** (ž)	[stɛska]
gully	**rokle** (ž)	[roklɛ]
tree	**strom** (m)	[strom]
leaf	**list** (m)	[lɪst]
leaves (foliage)	**listí** (s)	[lɪsti:]
fall of leaves	**padání** (s) **listí**	[pada:ni: lɪsti:]
to fall (ab. leaves)	**opadávat**	[opada:vat]
top (of the tree)	**vrchol** (m)	[vrxol]
branch	**větev** (ž)	[vetɛf]
bough	**suk** (m)	[suk]
bud (on shrub, tree)	**pupen** (m)	[pupɛn]
needle (of pine tree)	**jehla** (ž)	[jɛhla]
pine cone	**šiška** (ž)	[ʃɪʃka]
tree hollow	**dutina** (ž)	[dutɪna]
nest	**hnízdo** (s)	[hni:zdo]
burrow (animal hole)	**doupě** (s)	[doupe]
trunk	**kmen** (m)	[kmɛn]
root	**kořen** (m)	[korʒɛn]
bark	**kůra** (ž)	[ku:ra]
moss	**mech** (m)	[mɛx]
to uproot (remove trees or tree stumps)	**klučit**	[kluʧɪt]

to chop down	**kácet**	[ka:ʦɛt]
to deforest (vt)	**odlesnit**	[odlesnɪt]
tree stump	**pařez** (m)	[parʒɛz]
campfire	**oheň** (m)	[ohɛnʲ]
forest fire	**požár** (m)	[poʒa:r]
to extinguish (vt)	**hasit**	[hasɪt]
forest ranger	**hajný** (m)	[hajni:]
protection	**ochrana** (ž)	[oxrana]
to protect (~ nature)	**chránit**	[xra:nɪt]
poacher	**pytlák** (m)	[pɪtla:k]
steel trap	**past** (ž)	[past]
to gather, to pick (vt)	**sbírat**	[zbi:rat]
to lose one's way	**zabloudit**	[zabloudɪt]

205. Natural resources

natural resources	**přírodní zdroje** (m mn)	[prʃi:rodni: zdrojɛ]
minerals	**užitkové nerosty** (m mn)	[uʒɪtkovɛ: nɛrostɪ]
deposits	**ložisko** (s)	[loʒɪsko]
field (e.g., oilfield)	**naleziště** (s)	[nalezɪʃte]
to mine (extract)	**dobývat**	[dobi:vat]
mining (extraction)	**těžba** (ž)	[teʒba]
ore	**ruda** (ž)	[ruda]
mine (e.g., for coal)	**důl** (m)	[du:l]
shaft (mine ~)	**šachta** (ž)	[ʃaxta]
miner	**horník** (m)	[horni:k]
gas (natural ~)	**plyn** (m)	[plɪn]
gas pipeline	**plynovod** (m)	[plɪnovot]
oil (petroleum)	**ropa** (ž)	[ropa]
oil pipeline	**ropovod** (m)	[ropovot]
oil well	**ropová věž** (ž)	[ropova: veʃ]
derrick (tower)	**vrtná věž** (ž)	[vrtna: veʃ]
tanker	**tanková loď** (ž)	[taŋkova: lotʲ]
sand	**písek** (m)	[pi:sɛk]
limestone	**vápenec** (m)	[va:pɛnɛʦ]
gravel	**štěrk** (m)	[ʃterk]
peat	**rašelina** (ž)	[raʃɛlɪna]
clay	**hlína** (ž)	[hli:na]
coal	**uhlí** (s)	[uhli:]
iron (ore)	**železo** (s)	[ʒelɛzo]
gold	**zlato** (s)	[zlato]
silver	**stříbro** (s)	[strʃi:bro]

nickel	**nikl** (m)	[nɪkl]
copper	**měď** (ž)	[mnetʲ]
zinc	**zinek** (m)	[zɪnɛk]
manganese	**mangan** (m)	[mangan]
mercury	**rtuť** (ž)	[rtutʲ]
lead	**olovo** (s)	[olovo]
mineral	**minerál** (m)	[mɪnɛra:l]
crystal	**krystal** (m)	[krɪstal]
marble	**mramor** (m)	[mramor]
uranium	**uran** (m)	[uran]

The Earth. Part 2

206. Weather

weather	**počasí** (s)	[potʃasi:]
weather forecast	**předpověď** (ž) **počasí**	[prʃɛtpovetʲ potʃasi:]
temperature	**teplota** (ž)	[tɛplota]
thermometer	**teploměr** (m)	[tɛplomner]
barometer	**barometr** (m)	[baromɛtr]
humid (adj)	**vlhký**	[vlxki:]
humidity	**vlhkost** (ž)	[vlxkost]
heat (extreme ~)	**horko** (s)	[horko]
hot (torrid)	**horký**	[horki:]
it's hot	**horko**	[horko]
it's warm	**teplo**	[tɛplo]
warm (moderately hot)	**teplý**	[tɛpli:]
it's cold	**je zima**	[jɛ zɪma]
cold (adj)	**studený**	[studɛni:]
sun	**slunce** (s)	[sluntsɛ]
to shine (vi)	**svítit**	[svi:tɪt]
sunny (day)	**slunečný**	[slunɛtʃni:]
to come up (vi)	**vzejít**	[vzɛji:t]
to set (vi)	**zapadnout**	[zapadnout]
cloud	**mrak** (m)	[mrak]
cloudy (adj)	**oblačný**	[oblatʃni:]
rain cloud	**mračno** (s)	[mratʃno]
somber (gloomy)	**pochmurný**	[poxmurni:]
rain	**déšť** (m)	[dɛ:ʃtʲ]
it's raining	**prší**	[prʃɪ:]
rainy (~ day, weather)	**deštivý**	[dɛʃtɪvi:]
to drizzle (vi)	**mrholit**	[mrholɪt]
pouring rain	**liják** (m)	[lɪja:k]
downpour	**liják** (m)	[lɪja:k]
heavy (e.g., ~ rain)	**silný**	[sɪlni:]
puddle	**kaluž** (ž)	[kaluʃ]
to get wet (in rain)	**moknout**	[moknout]
fog (mist)	**mlha** (ž)	[mlha]
foggy	**mlhavý**	[mlhavi:]

snow	**sníh** (m)	[sni:x]
it's snowing	**sněží**	[sneʒi:]

207. Severe weather. Natural disasters

thunderstorm	**bouřka** (ž)	[bourʃka]
lightning (~ strike)	**blesk** (m)	[blɛsk]
to flash (vi)	**blýskat se**	[bli:skat sɛ]
thunder	**hřmění** (s)	[hrʒmneni:]
to thunder (vi)	**hřmít**	[hrʒmi:t]
it's thundering	**hřmí**	[hrʒmi:]
hail	**kroupy** (ž mn)	[kroupɪ]
it's hailing	**padají kroupy**	[padaji: kroupɪ]
to flood (vt)	**zaplavit**	[zaplavɪt]
flood, inundation	**povodeň** (ž)	[povodɛnʲ]
earthquake	**zemětřesení** (s)	[zɛmnetrʃɛsɛni:]
tremor, shoke	**otřes** (m)	[otrʃɛs]
epicenter	**epicentrum** (s)	[ɛpɪʦɛntrum]
eruption	**výbuch** (m)	[vi:bux]
lava	**láva** (ž)	[la:va]
twister	**smršť** (ž)	[smrʃtʲ]
tornado	**tornádo** (s)	[torna:do]
typhoon	**tajfun** (m)	[tajfun]
hurricane	**hurikán** (m)	[hurɪka:n]
storm	**bouřka** (ž)	[bourʃka]
tsunami	**tsunami** (s)	[tsunamɪ]
cyclone	**cyklón** (m)	[ʦiklo:n]
bad weather	**nečas** (m)	[nɛʧas]
fire (accident)	**požár** (m)	[poʒa:r]
disaster	**katastrofa** (ž)	[katastrofa]
meteorite	**meteorit** (m)	[mɛtɛorɪt]
avalanche	**lavina** (ž)	[lavɪna]
snowslide	**lavina** (ž)	[lavɪna]
blizzard	**metelice** (ž)	[mɛtɛlɪʦɛ]
snowstorm	**vánice** (ž)	[va:nɪʦɛ]

208. Noises. Sounds

silence (quiet)	**ticho** (s)	[tɪxo]
sound	**zvuk** (m)	[zvuk]

noise	**hluk** (m)	[hluk]
to make noise	**hlučet**	[hluʧɛt]
noisy (adj)	**hlučný**	[hluʧni:]
loudly (to speak, etc.)	**hlasitě**	[hlasɪte]
loud (voice, etc.)	**hlasitý**	[hlasɪti:]
constant (e.g., ~ noise)	**neustálý**	[nɛusta:li:]
cry, shout (n)	**křik** (m)	[krʃɪk]
to cry, to shout (vi)	**křičet**	[krʃɪʧɛt]
whisper	**šepot** (m)	[ʃɛpot]
to whisper (vi, vt)	**šeptat**	[ʃɛptat]
barking (dog's ~)	**štěkot** (m)	[ʃtekot]
to bark (vi)	**štěkat**	[ʃtekat]
groan (of pain, etc.)	**sténání** (s)	[stɛ:na:ni:]
to groan (vi)	**sténat**	[stɛ:nat]
cough	**kašel** (m)	[kaʃɛl]
to cough (vi)	**kašlat**	[kaʃlat]
whistle	**hvízdání** (s)	[hvi:zda:ni:]
to whistle (vi)	**hvízdat**	[hvi:zdat]
knock (at the door)	**klepání** (s)	[klɛpa:ni:]
to knock (on the door)	**klepat**	[klɛpat]
to crack (vi)	**cvrčet**	[ʦvrʧɛt]
crack (cracking sound)	**třesk** (m)	[trʃɛsk]
siren	**houkačka** (ž)	[houkaʧka]
whistle (factory ~, etc.)	**houkání** (s)	[houka:ni:]
to whistle (ab. train)	**hučet**	[huʧɛt]
honk (car horn sound)	**houkačka** (ž)	[houkaʧka]
to honk (vi)	**houkat**	[houkat]

209. Winter

winter (n)	**zima** (ž)	[zɪma]
winter (as adj)	**zimní**	[zɪmni:]
in winter	**v zimě**	[v zɪmne]
snow	**sníh** (m)	[sni:x]
it's snowing	**sněží**	[sneʒi:]
snowfall	**sněžení** (s)	[sneʒeni:]
snowdrift	**závěj** (ž)	[za:vej]
snowflake	**sněhová vločka** (ž)	[snehova: vloʧka]
snowball	**sněhová koule** (ž)	[snehova: koulɛ]
snowman	**sněhulák** (m)	[snehula:k]
icicle	**rampouch** (m)	[rampoux]

December	**prosinec** (m)	[prosɪnɛʦ]
January	**leden** (m)	[lɛdɛn]
February	**únor** (m)	[u:nor]
frost (severe ~, freezing cold)	**mráz** (m)	[mra:z]
frosty (weather, air)	**mrazivý**	[mrazɪvi:]
below zero (adv)	**pod nulou**	[pod nulou]
first frost	**mrazíky** (m mn)	[mrazi:kɪ]
hoarfrost	**jinovatka** (ž)	[jɪnovatka]
cold (cold weather)	**chlad** (m)	[xlat]
it's cold	**chladno**	[xladno]
fur coat	**kožich** (m)	[koʒɪx]
mittens	**palčáky** (m mn)	[palʧa:kɪ]
to get sick	**onemocnět**	[onɛmoʦnet]
cold (illness)	**nachlazení** (s)	[naxlazɛni:]
to catch a cold	**nachladit se**	[naxladɪt sɛ]
ice	**led** (m)	[lɛt]
black ice	**náledí** (s)	[na:lɛdi:]
to freeze over (ab. river, etc.)	**zamrznout**	[zamrznout]
ice floe	**kra** (ž)	[kra]
skis	**lyže** (ž mn)	[lɪʒe]
skier	**lyžař** (m)	[lɪʒarʃ]
to ski (vi)	**lyžovat**	[lɪʒovat]
to skate (vi)	**bruslit**	[bruslɪt]

Fauna

210. Mammals. Predators

predator	**šelma** (ž)	[ʃɛlma]
tiger	**tygr** (m)	[tɪgr]
lion	**lev** (m)	[lɛf]
wolf	**vlk** (m)	[vlk]
fox	**liška** (ž)	[lɪʃka]
jaguar	**jaguár** (m)	[jagua:r]
leopard	**levhart** (m)	[lɛvhart]
cheetah	**gepard** (m)	[gɛpart]
black panther	**panter** (m)	[pantɛr]
puma	**puma** (ž)	[puma]
snow leopard	**pardál** (m)	[parda:l]
lynx	**rys** (m)	[rɪs]
coyote	**kojot** (m)	[kojot]
jackal	**šakal** (m)	[ʃakal]
hyena	**hyena** (ž)	[hɪena]

211. Wild animals

animal	**zvíře** (s)	[zvi:rʒɛ]
beast (animal)	**zvíře** (s)	[zvi:rʒɛ]
squirrel	**veverka** (ž)	[vɛvɛrka]
hedgehog	**ježek** (m)	[jɛʒek]
hare	**zajíc** (m)	[zaji:ʦ]
rabbit	**králík** (m)	[kra:li:k]
badger	**jezevec** (m)	[jɛzɛvɛʦ]
raccoon	**mýval** (m)	[mi:val]
hamster	**křeček** (m)	[krʃɛʧɛk]
marmot	**svišť** (m)	[svɪʃtʲ]
mole	**krtek** (m)	[krtɛk]
mouse	**myš** (ž)	[mɪʃ]
rat	**krysa** (ž)	[krɪsa]
bat	**netopýr** (m)	[nɛtopi:r]
ermine	**hranostaj** (m)	[hranostaj]
sable	**sobol** (m)	[sobol]

marten	**kuna** (ž)	[kuna]
weasel	**lasice** (ž)	[lasɪʦɛ]
mink	**norek** (m)	[norɛk]
beaver	**bobr** (m)	[bobr]
otter	**vydra** (ž)	[vɪdra]
horse	**kůň** (m)	[ku:nʲ]
moose	**los** (m)	[los]
deer	**jelen** (m)	[jɛlɛn]
camel	**velbloud** (m)	[vɛlblout]
bison	**bizon** (m)	[bɪzon]
wisent	**zubr** (m)	[zubr]
buffalo	**buvol** (m)	[buvol]
zebra	**zebra** (ž)	[zɛbra]
antelope	**antilopa** (ž)	[antɪlopa]
roe deer	**srnka** (ž)	[srŋka]
fallow deer	**daněk** (m)	[danek]
chamois	**kamzík** (m)	[kamzi:k]
wild boar	**vepř** (m)	[vɛprʃ]
whale	**velryba** (ž)	[vɛlrɪba]
seal	**tuleň** (m)	[tulɛnʲ]
walrus	**mrož** (m)	[mroʃ]
fur seal	**lachtan** (m)	[laxtan]
dolphin	**delfín** (m)	[dɛlfi:n]
bear	**medvěd** (m)	[mɛdvet]
polar bear	**bílý medvěd** (m)	[bi:li: mɛdvet]
panda	**panda** (ž)	[panda]
monkey	**opice** (ž)	[opɪʦɛ]
chimpanzee	**šimpanz** (m)	[ʃɪmpanz]
orangutan	**orangutan** (m)	[orangutan]
gorilla	**gorila** (ž)	[gorɪla]
macaque	**makak** (m)	[makak]
gibbon	**gibon** (m)	[gɪbon]
elephant	**slon** (m)	[slon]
rhinoceros	**nosorožec** (m)	[nosoroʒeʦ]
giraffe	**žirafa** (ž)	[ʒɪrafa]
hippopotamus	**hroch** (m)	[hrox]
kangaroo	**klokan** (m)	[klokan]
koala (bear)	**koala** (ž)	[koala]
mongoose	**promyka** (ž) **indická**	[promɪka ɪndɪʦka:]
chinchilla	**činčila** (ž)	[ʧɪnʧɪla]
skunk	**skunk** (m)	[skuŋk]
porcupine	**dikobraz** (m)	[dɪkobras]

212. Domestic animals

cat	**kočka** (ž)	[kotʃka]
tomcat	**kocour** (m)	[kotsour]
dog	**pes** (m)	[pɛs]
horse	**kůň** (m)	[ku:nʲ]
stallion (male horse)	**hřebec** (m)	[hrʒɛbɛts]
mare	**kobyla** (ž)	[kobɪla]
cow	**kráva** (ž)	[kra:va]
bull	**býk** (m)	[bi:k]
ox	**vůl** (m)	[vu:l]
sheep (ewe)	**ovce** (ž)	[ovtsɛ]
ram	**beran** (m)	[bɛran]
goat	**koza** (ž)	[koza]
billy goat, he-goat	**kozel** (m)	[kozɛl]
donkey	**osel** (m)	[osɛl]
mule	**mul** (m)	[mul]
pig, hog	**prase** (s)	[prasɛ]
piglet	**prasátko** (s)	[prasa:tko]
rabbit	**králík** (m)	[kra:li:k]
hen (chicken)	**slepice** (ž)	[slɛpɪtsɛ]
rooster	**kohout** (m)	[kohout]
duck	**kachna** (ž)	[kaxna]
drake	**kačer** (m)	[katʃɛr]
goose	**husa** (ž)	[husa]
tom turkey, gobbler	**krocan** (m)	[krotsan]
turkey (hen)	**krůta** (ž)	[kru:ta]
domestic animals	**domácí zvířata** (s mn)	[doma:tsi: zvi:rʒata]
tame (e.g., ~ hamster)	**ochočený**	[oxotʃɛni:]
to tame (vt)	**ochočovat**	[oxotʃovat]
to breed (vt)	**chovat**	[xovat]
farm	**farma** (ž)	[farma]
poultry	**drůbež** (ž)	[dru:bɛʃ]
cattle	**dobytek** (m)	[dobɪtɛk]
herd (cattle)	**stádo** (s)	[sta:do]
stable	**stáj** (ž)	[sta:j]
pigpen	**vepřín** (m)	[vɛprʃi:n]
cowshed	**kravín** (m)	[kravi:n]
rabbit hutch	**králíkárna** (ž)	[kra:li:ka:rna]
hen house	**kurník** (m)	[kurni:k]

213. Dogs. Dog breeds

dog	**pes** (m)	[pɛs]
sheepdog	**vlčák** (m)	[vlʧa:k]
German shepherd	**německý ovčák** (m)	[nemɛʦki: ofʧa:k]
poodle	**pudl** (m)	[pudl]
dachshund	**jezevčík** (m)	[ezɛvʧi:k]
bulldog	**buldok** (m)	[buldok]
boxer	**boxer** (m)	[boksɛr]
mastiff	**mastif** (m)	[mastɪf]
Rottweiler	**rotvajler** (m)	[rotvajlɛr]
Doberman	**dobrman** (m)	[dobrman]
basset	**basset** (m)	[basɛt]
bobtail	**bobtail** (m)	[bobtɛjl]
Dalmatian	**dalmatin** (m)	[dalmatɪn]
cocker spaniel	**kokršpaněl** (m)	[kokrʃpanel]
Newfoundland	**novofoundlandský pes** (m)	[novofaundlɛndski: pɛs]
Saint Bernard	**bernardýn** (m)	[bɛrnardi:n]
husky	**husky** (m)	[haskɪ]
Chow Chow	**Čau-čau** (m)	[ʧau-ʧau]
spitz	**špic** (m)	[ʃpɪʦ]
pug	**mopsl** (m)	[mopsl]

214. Sounds made by animals

barking (n)	**štěkot** (m)	[ʃtekot]
to bark (vi)	**štěkat**	[ʃtekat]
to meow (vi)	**mňoukat**	[mnʲoukat]
to purr (vi)	**mručet**	[mruʧɛt]
to moo (vi)	**bučet**	[buʧɛt]
to bellow (bull)	**řvát**	[rʒva:t]
to growl (vi)	**vrčet**	[vrʧɛt]
howl (n)	**vytí** (s)	[vɪti:]
to howl (vi)	**výt**	[vi:t]
to whine (vi)	**skučet**	[skuʧɛt]
to bleat (sheep)	**blekotat**	[blɛkotat]
to oink, to grunt (pig)	**chrochtat**	[xroxtat]
to squeal (vi)	**vřískat**	[vrʒi:skat]
to croak (vi)	**kuňkat**	[kunʲkat]
to buzz (insect)	**bzučet**	[bzuʧɛt]

to chirp (crickets, grasshopper)	**cvrčet**	[ʦvrʧɛt]

215. Young animals

cub	**mládě** (s)	[mla:de]
kitten	**kotě** (s)	[kote]
baby mouse	**myší mládě** (s)	[mɪʃi: mla:de]
puppy	**štěně** (s)	[ʃtene]
leveret	**zajíček** (m)	[zai:ʧɛk]
baby rabbit	**králíček** (m)	[kra:li:ʧɛk]
wolf cub	**vlče** (s)	[vlʧɛ]
fox cub	**liščí mládě** (s)	[lɪʃʧi: mla:de]
bear cub	**medvídě** (s)	[mɛdvi:de]
lion cub	**lvíče** (s)	[lvi:ʧɛ]
tiger cub	**tygří mládě** (s)	[tɪgrʒi: mla:de]
elephant calf	**slůně** (s)	[slu:ne]
piglet	**prasátko** (s)	[prasa:tko]
calf (young cow, bull)	**tele** (s)	[tɛlɛ]
kid (young goat)	**kůzle** (s)	[ku:zlɛ]
lamb	**jehně** (s)	[jɛhne]
fawn (young deer)	**jelení mládě** (s)	[jɛlɛni: mla:de]
young camel	**velbloudí mládě** (s)	[vɛlbloudi: mla:de]
snakelet (baby snake)	**hádě** (s)	[ha:de]
froglet (baby frog)	**žabička** (ž)	[ʒabɪʧka]
baby bird	**ptáče** (s)	[pta:ʧɛ]
chick (of chicken)	**kuře** (s)	[kurʒɛ]
duckling	**kačátko** (s)	[kaʧa:tko]

216. Birds

bird	**pták** (m)	[pta:k]
pigeon	**holub** (m)	[holup]
sparrow	**vrabec** (m)	[vrabɛʦ]
tit (great tit)	**sýkora** (ž)	[si:kora]
magpie	**straka** (ž)	[straka]
raven	**havran** (m)	[havran]
crow	**vrána** (ž)	[vra:na]
jackdaw	**kavka** (ž)	[kafka]
rook	**polní havran** (m)	[polni: havran]
duck	**kachna** (ž)	[kaxna]
goose	**husa** (ž)	[husa]

pheasant **bažant** (m) [baʒant]
eagle **orel** (m) [orɛl]
hawk **jestřáb** (m) [jɛstrʃa:p]
falcon **sokol** (m) [sokol]

vulture **sup** (m) [sup]
condor (Andean ~) **kondor** (m) [kondor]

swan **labuť** (ž) [labutʲ]
crane **jeřáb** (m) [jɛrʒa:p]
stork **čáp** (m) [ʧa:p]

parrot **papoušek** (m) [papouʃɛk]
hummingbird **kolibřík** (m) [kolɪbrʒi:k]
peacock **páv** (m) [pa:f]

ostrich **pštros** (m) [pʃtros]
heron **volavka** (ž) [volafka]

flamingo **plameňák** (m) [plamɛnʲa:k]
pelican **pelikán** (m) [pɛlɪka:n]

nightingale **slavík** (m) [slavi:k]
swallow **vlaštovka** (ž) [vlaʃtofka]

thrush **drozd** (m) [drozt]
song thrush **zpěvný drozd** (m) [spevni: drozt]
blackbird **kos** (m) [kos]

swift **rorejs** (m) [rorɛjs]
lark **skřivan** (m) [skrʃɪvan]
quail **křepel** (m) [krʃɛpɛl]

woodpecker **datel** (m) [datɛl]
cuckoo **kukačka** (ž) [kukaʧka]
owl **sova** (ž) [sova]
eagle owl **výr** (m) [vi:r]
wood grouse **tetřev** (m) **hlušec** [tɛtrʃɛv hluʃɛʦ]

black grouse **tetřev** (m) [tɛtrʃɛf]
partridge **koroptev** (ž) [koroptɛf]

starling **špaček** (m) [ʃpaʧɛk]
canary **kanár** (m) [kana:r]
hazel grouse **jeřábek** (m) [jɛrʒa:bɛk]

chaffinch **pěnkava** (ž) [peŋkava]
bullfinch **hejl** (m) [hɛjl]

seagull **racek** (m) [raʦɛk]
albatross **albatros** (m) [albatros]
penguin **tučňák** (m) [tuʧnʲa:k]

217. Birds. Singing and sounds

to sing (vi)	**zpívat**	[spi:vat]
to call (animal, bird)	**křičet**	[krʃɪʧɛt]
to crow (rooster)	**kokrhat**	[kokrhat]
cock-a-doodle-doo	**kykyryký**	[kɪkɪrɪki:]
to cluck (hen)	**kdákat**	[gda:kat]
to caw (crow call)	**krákat**	[kra:kat]
to quack (duck call)	**káchat**	[ka:xat]
to cheep (vi)	**kvičet**	[kvɪʧɛt]
to chirp, to twitter	**cvrlikat**	[ʦvrlɪkat]

218. Fish. Marine animals

bream	**cejn** (m)	[ʦɛjn]
carp	**kapr** (m)	[kapr]
perch	**okoun** (m)	[okoun]
catfish	**sumec** (m)	[sumɛʦ]
pike	**štika** (ž)	[ʃtɪka]
salmon	**losos** (m)	[losos]
sturgeon	**jeseter** (m)	[jɛsɛtɛr]
herring	**sleď** (ž)	[slɛtʲ]
Atlantic salmon	**losos** (m)	[losos]
mackerel	**makrela** (ž)	[makrɛla]
flatfish	**platýs** (m)	[plati:s]
zander, pike perch	**candát** (m)	[ʦanda:t]
cod	**treska** (ž)	[trɛska]
tuna	**tuňák** (m)	[tunʲa:k]
trout	**pstruh** (m)	[pstrux]
eel	**úhoř** (m)	[u:horʃ]
electric ray	**rejnok** (m) **elektrický**	[rɛjnok ɛlɛktrɪʦki:]
moray eel	**muréna** (ž)	[murɛ:na]
piranha	**piraňa** (ž)	[pɪranʲja]
shark	**žralok** (m)	[ʒralok]
dolphin	**delfín** (m)	[dɛlfi:n]
whale	**velryba** (ž)	[vɛlrɪba]
crab	**krab** (m)	[krap]
jellyfish	**medúza** (ž)	[mɛdu:za]
octopus	**chobotnice** (ž)	[xobotnɪʦɛ]
starfish	**hvězdice** (ž)	[hvezdɪʦɛ]
sea urchin	**ježovka** (ž)	[jɛʒofka]

seahorse	**mořský koníček** (m)	[morʃski: koni:ʧɛk]
oyster	**ústřice** (ž)	[u:strʃɪʦɛ]
shrimp	**kreveta** (ž)	[krɛvɛta]
lobster	**humr** (m)	[humr]
spiny lobster	**langusta** (ž)	[langusta]

219. Amphibians. Reptiles

snake	**had** (m)	[hat]
venomous (snake)	**jedovatý**	[jɛdovati:]
viper	**zmije** (ž)	[zmɪjɛ]
cobra	**kobra** (ž)	[kobra]
python	**krajta** (ž)	[krajta]
boa	**hroznýš** (m)	[hrozni:ʃ]
grass snake	**užovka** (ž)	[uʒofka]
rattle snake	**chřestýš** (m)	[xrʃɛsti:ʃ]
anaconda	**anakonda** (ž)	[anakonda]
lizard	**ještěrka** (ž)	[jɛʃterka]
iguana	**leguán** (m)	[lɛgua:n]
monitor lizard	**varan** (m)	[varan]
salamander	**mlok** (m)	[mlok]
chameleon	**chameleón** (m)	[xamɛlɛo:n]
scorpion	**štír** (m)	[ʃti:r]
turtle	**želva** (ž)	[ʒelva]
frog	**žába** (ž)	[ʒa:ba]
toad	**ropucha** (ž)	[ropuxa]
crocodile	**krokodýl** (m)	[krokodi:l]

220. Insects

insect, bug	**hmyz** (m)	[hmɪz]
butterfly	**motýl** (m)	[moti:l]
ant	**mravenec** (m)	[mravɛnɛʦ]
fly	**moucha** (ž)	[mouxa]
mosquito	**komár** (m)	[koma:r]
beetle	**brouk** (m)	[brouk]
wasp	**vosa** (ž)	[vosa]
bee	**včela** (ž)	[vʧɛla]
bumblebee	**čmelák** (m)	[ʧmɛla:k]
gadfly (botfly)	**střeček** (m)	[strʃɛʧɛk]
spider	**pavouk** (m)	[pavouk]
spiderweb	**pavučina** (ž)	[pavuʧɪna]

dragonfly	**vážka** (ž)	[va:ʃka]
grasshopper	**kobylka** (ž)	[kobɪlka]
moth (night butterfly)	**motýl** (m)	[moti:l]
cockroach	**šváb** (m)	[ʃva:p]
tick	**klíště** (s)	[kli:ʃte]
flea	**blecha** (ž)	[blɛxa]
midge	**muška** (ž)	[muʃka]
locust	**saranče** (ž)	[sarantʃɛ]
snail	**hlemýžď** (m)	[hlɛmi:ʒtʲ]
cricket	**cvrček** (m)	[tsvrtʃɛk]
lightning bug	**svatojánská muška** (ž)	[svatoja:nska: muʃka]
ladybug	**slunéčko** (s) **sedmitečné**	[slunɛ:tʃko sɛdmɪtɛtʃnɛ:]
cockchafer	**chroust** (m)	[xroust]
leech	**piavice** (ž)	[pɪavɪtsɛ]
caterpillar	**housenka** (ž)	[housɛŋka]
earthworm	**červ** (m)	[tʃɛrf]
larva	**larva** (ž)	[larva]

221. Animals. Body parts

beak	**zobák** (m)	[zoba:k]
wings	**křídla** (s mn)	[krʃi:dla]
foot (of bird)	**běhák** (m)	[beha:k]
feathers (plumage)	**opeření** (s)	[opɛrʒɛni:]
feather	**pero** (s)	[pɛro]
crest	**chochol** (m)	[xoxol]
gills	**žábry** (ž mn)	[ʒa:brɪ]
spawn	**jikry** (ž mn)	[jɪkrɪ]
larva	**larva** (ž)	[larva]
fin	**ploutev** (ž)	[ploutɛf]
scales (of fish, reptile)	**šupiny** (ž mn)	[ʃupɪnɪ]
fang (canine)	**kel** (m)	[kɛl]
paw (e.g., cat's ~)	**tlapa** (ž)	[tlapa]
muzzle (snout)	**čumák** (m)	[tʃuma:k]
maw (mouth)	**tlama** (ž)	[tlama]
tail	**ocas** (m)	[otsas]
whiskers	**vousy** (m mn)	[vousɪ]
hoof	**kopyto** (s)	[kopɪto]
horn	**roh** (m)	[rox]
carapace	**krunýř** (m)	[kruni:rʃ]
shell (of mollusk)	**škeble** (ž)	[ʃkɛblɛ]
eggshell	**skořápka** (ž)	[skorʒa:pka]
animal's hair (pelage)	**srst** (ž)	[srst]
pelt (hide)	**kůže** (ž)	[ku:ʒe]

222. Actions of animals

to fly (vi)	**létat**	[lɛ:tat]
to fly in circles	**kroužit**	[krouʒɪt]
to fly away	**odletět**	[odlɛtet]
to flap (~ the wings)	**mávat**	[ma:vat]
to peck (vi)	**zobat**	[zobat]
to sit on eggs	**sedět na vejcích**	[sɛdet na vɛjʦi:x]
to hatch out (vi)	**vyklubávat se**	[vɪkluba:vat sɛ]
to build a nest	**hnízdit**	[hni:zdɪt]
to slither, to crawl	**plazit se**	[plazɪt sɛ]
to sting, to bite (insect)	**štípat**	[ʃti:pat]
to bite (ab. animal)	**kousat**	[kousat]
to sniff (vt)	**čenichat**	[ʧɛnɪxat]
to bark (vi)	**štěkat**	[ʃtekat]
to hiss (snake)	**syčet**	[sɪʧɛt]
to scare (vt)	**strašit**	[straʃɪt]
to attack (vt)	**útočit**	[u:toʧɪt]
to gnaw (bone, etc.)	**hryzat**	[hrɪzat]
to scratch (with claws)	**škrábat**	[ʃkra:bat]
to hide (vi)	**schovávat se**	[sxova:vat sɛ]
to play (kittens, etc.)	**hrát si**	[hra:t sɪ]
to hunt (vi, vt)	**lovit**	[lovɪt]
to hibernate (vi)	**být v spánku**	[bi:t v spa:ŋku]
to go extinct	**vymřít**	[vɪmrʒi:t]

223. Animals. Habitats

habitat	**životní prostředí** (s)	[ʒɪvotni: prostrʃɛdi:]
migration	**stěhování** (s)	[stehova:ni:]
mountain	**hora** (ž)	[hora]
reef	**útes** (m)	[u:tɛs]
cliff	**skála** (ž)	[ska:la]
forest	**les** (m)	[lɛs]
jungle	**džungle** (ž)	[ʤunglɛ]
savanna	**savana** (ž)	[savana]
tundra	**tundra** (ž)	[tundra]
steppe	**step** (ž)	[stɛp]
desert	**poušť** (ž)	[pouʃtʲ]
oasis	**oáza** (ž)	[oa:za]
sea	**moře** (s)	[morʒɛ]

lake	**jezero** (s)	[jɛzɛro]
ocean	**oceán** (m)	[otsɛa:n]
swamp (marshland)	**bažina** (ž)	[baʒɪna]
freshwater (adj)	**sladkovodní**	[slatkovodni:]
pond	**rybník** (m)	[rɪbni:k]
river	**řeka** (ž)	[rʒɛka]
den (bear's ~)	**brloh** (m)	[brlox]
nest	**hnízdo** (s)	[hni:zdo]
tree hollow	**dutina** (ž)	[dutɪna]
burrow (animal hole)	**doupě** (s)	[doupe]
anthill	**mraveniště** (s)	[mravɛnɪʃte]

224. Animal care

zoo	**zoologická zahrada** (ž)	[zoologɪtska: zahrada]
nature preserve	**přírodní rezervace** (ž)	[prʃi:rodni: rɛzɛrvatsɛ]
breeder (cattery, kennel, etc.)	**obora** (ž)	[obora]
open-air cage	**voliéra** (ž)	[volɪe:ra]
cage	**klec** (ž)	[klɛts]
doghouse (kennel)	**bouda** (ž)	[bouda]
dovecot	**holubník** (m)	[holubni:k]
aquarium (fish tank)	**akvárium** (s)	[akva:rɪum]
dolphinarium	**delfinárium** (s)	[dɛlfɪna:rum]
to breed (animals)	**chovat**	[xovat]
brood, litter	**potomstvo** (s)	[potomstvo]
to tame (vt)	**ochočovat**	[oxotʃovat]
to train (animals)	**cvičit**	[tsvɪtʃɪt]
feed (fodder, etc.)	**krmivo** (s)	[krmɪvo]
to feed (vt)	**krmit**	[krmɪt]
pet store	**obchod** (m) **se zvířaty**	[obxot sɛ zvi:rʒatɪ]
muzzle (for dog)	**košík** (m)	[koʃi:k]
collar (e.g., dog ~)	**obojek** (m)	[obojɛk]
name (of animal)	**jméno** (s)	[jmɛ:no]
pedigree (of dog)	**rodokmen** (m)	[rodokmɛn]

225. Animals. Miscellaneous

pack (wolves)	**smečka** (ž)	[smɛtʃka]
flock (birds)	**hejno** (s)	[hɛjno]
shoal, school (fish)	**hejno** (s)	[hɛjno]
herd (horses)	**stádo** (s)	[sta:do]

male (n)	**samec** (m)	[samɛʦ]
female (n)	**samice** (ž)	[samɪʦɛ]
hungry (adj)	**hladový**	[hladovi:]
wild (adj)	**divoký**	[dɪvoki:]
dangerous (adj)	**nebezpečný**	[nɛbɛzpɛʧni:]

226. Horses

horse	**kůň** (m)	[ku:nʲ]
breed (race)	**plemeno** (s)	[plɛmɛno]
foal	**hříbě** (s)	[hrʒi:be]
mare	**kobyla** (ž)	[kobɪla]
mustang	**mustang** (m)	[mustaŋg]
pony	**pony** (m)	[ponɪ]
draft horse	**tahoun** (m)	[tahoun]
mane	**hříva** (ž)	[hrʒi:va]
tail	**ocas** (m)	[oʦas]
hoof	**kopyto** (s)	[kopɪto]
horseshoe	**podkova** (ž)	[potkova]
to shoe (vt)	**okovat**	[okovat]
blacksmith	**kovář** (m)	[kova:rʃ]
saddle	**sedlo** (s)	[sɛdlo]
stirrup	**třmen** (m)	[trʃmɛn]
bridle	**uzda** (ž)	[uzda]
reins	**opratě** (ž mn)	[oprate]
whip (for riding)	**bičík** (m)	[bɪʧi:k]
rider	**jezdec** (m)	[jɛzdɛʦ]
to saddle up (vt)	**osedlat**	[osɛdlat]
to mount a horse	**vsednout**	[vsɛdnout]
gallop	**cval** (m)	[ʦval]
to gallop (vi)	**jet cvalem**	[jɛt ʦvalɛm]
trot (n)	**klus** (m)	[klus]
at a trot (adv)	**klusem**	[klusɛm]
to go at a trot	**jet klusem**	[jɛt klusɛm]
racehorse	**dostihový kůň** (m)	[dostɪhovi: ku:nʲ]
horse racing	**dostihy** (m mn)	[dostɪhɪ]
stable	**stáj** (ž)	[sta:j]
to feed (vt)	**krmit**	[krmɪt]
hay	**seno** (s)	[sɛno]
to water (animals)	**napájet**	[napa:jɛt]

to wash (horse)	**hřebelcovat**	[hrʒɛbɛlʦovat]
horse-drawn cart	**povoz** (m)	[povos]
to graze (vi)	**pást se**	[pa:st sɛ]
to neigh (vi)	**řehtat**	[rʒɛxtat]
to kick (to buck)	**kopnout**	[kopnout]

Flora

227. Trees

tree	**strom** (m)	[strom]
deciduous (adj)	**listnatý**	[lɪstnati:]
coniferous (adj)	**jehličnatý**	[jɛhlɪʧnati:]
evergreen (adj)	**stálezelená**	[sta:lɛzɛlɛna:]
apple tree	**jabloň** (ž)	[jablonʲ]
pear tree	**hruška** (ž)	[hruʃka]
sweet cherry tree	**třešně** (ž)	[trʃɛʃne]
sour cherry tree	**višně** (ž)	[vɪʃne]
plum tree	**švestka** (ž)	[ʃvɛstka]
birch	**bříza** (ž)	[brʒi:za]
oak	**dub** (m)	[dup]
linden tree	**lípa** (ž)	[li:pa]
aspen	**osika** (ž)	[osɪka]
maple	**javor** (m)	[javor]
spruce	**smrk** (m)	[smrk]
pine	**borovice** (ž)	[borovɪʦɛ]
larch	**modřín** (m)	[modrʒi:n]
fir tree	**jedle** (ž)	[jɛdlɛ]
cedar	**cedr** (m)	[ʦɛdr]
poplar	**topol** (m)	[topol]
rowan	**jeřáb** (m)	[jɛrʒa:p]
willow	**jíva** (ž)	[ji:va]
alder	**olše** (ž)	[olʃɛ]
beech	**buk** (m)	[buk]
elm	**jilm** (m)	[jɪlm]
ash (tree)	**jasan** (m)	[jasan]
chestnut	**kaštan** (m)	[kaʃtan]
magnolia	**magnólie** (ž)	[magno:lɪe]
palm tree	**palma** (ž)	[palma]
cypress	**cypřiš** (m)	[ʦɪprʃɪʃ]
mangrove	**mangróvie** (ž)	[mangro:vɪe]
baobab	**baobab** (m)	[baobap]
eucalyptus	**eukalypt** (m)	[ɛukalɪpt]
sequoia	**sekvoje** (ž)	[sɛkvojɛ]

228. Shrubs

bush	**keř** (m)	[kɛrʃ]
shrub	**křoví** (s)	[krʃoviː]
grapevine	**vinná réva** (s)	[vɪnnaː reːva]
vineyard	**vinice** (ž)	[vɪnɪʦɛ]
raspberry bush	**maliny** (ž mn)	[malɪnɪ]
blackcurrant bush	**černý rybíz** (m)	[ʧɛrniː rɪbiːz]
redcurrant bush	**červený rybíz** (m)	[ʧɛrvɛniː rɪbiːz]
gooseberry bush	**angrešt** (m)	[angrɛʃt]
acacia	**akácie** (ž)	[akaːʦɪe]
barberry	**dřišťál** (m)	[drʒɪʃtʲaːl]
jasmine	**jasmín** (m)	[jasmiːn]
juniper	**jalovec** (m)	[jalovɛʦ]
rosebush	**růžový keř** (m)	[ruːʒoviː kɛrʃ]
dog rose	**šípek** (m)	[ʃiːpɛk]

229. Mushrooms

mushroom	**houba** (ž)	[houba]
edible mushroom	**jedlá houba** (ž)	[jɛdlaː houba]
poisonous mushroom	**jedovatá houba** (ž)	[jɛdovataː houba]
cap (of mushroom)	**klobouk** (m)	[klobouk]
stipe (of mushroom)	**nožička** (ž)	[noʒɪʧka]
cep (Boletus edulis)	**hřib** (m)	[hrʒɪp]
orange-cap boletus	**křemenáč** (m)	[krʃɛmɛnaːʧ]
birch bolete	**kozák** (m)	[kozaːk]
chanterelle	**liška** (ž)	[lɪʃka]
russula	**holubinka** (ž)	[holubɪŋka]
morel	**smrž** (m)	[smrʃ]
fly agaric	**muchomůrka** (ž) **červená**	[muxomuːrka ʧɛrvɛnaː]
death cap	**prašivka** (ž)	[praʃɪfka]

230. Fruits. Berries

fruit	**ovoce** (s), **plod** (m)	[ovoʦɛ], [plot]
fruits	**ovoce** (s mn)	[ovoʦɛ]
apple	**jablko** (s)	[jablko]
pear	**hruška** (ž)	[hruʃka]
plum	**švestka** (ž)	[ʃvɛstka]
strawberry (garden ~)	**zahradní jahody** (ž mn)	[zahradniː jahodɪ]

sour cherry	**višně** (ž)	[vɪʃne]
sweet cherry	**třešně** (ž mn)	[trʃɛʃne]
grape	**hroznové víno** (s)	[hroznovɛ: vi:no]
raspberry	**maliny** (ž mn)	[malɪnɪ]
blackcurrant	**černý rybíz** (m)	[ʧɛrni: rɪbi:z]
redcurrant	**červený rybíz** (m)	[ʧɛrvɛni: rɪbi:z]
gooseberry	**angrešt** (m)	[angrɛʃt]
cranberry	**klikva** (ž)	[klɪkva]
orange	**pomeranč** (m)	[pomɛranʧ]
mandarin	**mandarinka** (ž)	[mandarɪŋka]
pineapple	**ananas** (m)	[ananas]
banana	**banán** (m)	[bana:n]
date	**datle** (ž)	[datlɛ]
lemon	**citrón** (m)	[ʦɪtro:n]
apricot	**meruňka** (ž)	[mɛrunʲka]
peach	**broskev** (ž)	[broskɛf]
kiwi	**kiwi** (s)	[kɪvɪ]
grapefruit	**grapefruit** (m)	[grɛjpfru:t]
berry	**bobule** (ž)	[bobulɛ]
berries	**bobule** (ž mn)	[bobulɛ]
cowberry	**brusinky** (ž mn)	[brusɪŋkɪ]
wild strawberry	**jahody** (ž mn)	[jahodɪ]
bilberry	**borůvky** (ž mn)	[boru:fkɪ]

231. Flowers. Plants

flower	**květina** (ž)	[kvetɪna]
bouquet (of flowers)	**kytice** (ž)	[kɪtɪʦɛ]
rose (flower)	**růže** (ž)	[ru:ʒe]
tulip	**tulipán** (m)	[tulɪpa:n]
carnation	**karafiát** (m)	[karafɪa:t]
gladiolus	**mečík** (m)	[mɛʧi:k]
cornflower	**chrpa** (ž)	[xrpa]
harebell	**zvoneček** (m)	[zvonɛʧɛk]
dandelion	**pampeliška** (ž)	[pampɛlɪʃka]
camomile	**heřmánek** (m)	[hɛrʒma:nɛk]
aloe	**aloe** (s)	[aloɛ]
cactus	**kaktus** (m)	[kaktus]
rubber plant, ficus	**fíkus** (m)	[fi:kus]
lily	**lilie** (ž)	[lɪlɪe]
geranium	**geránie** (ž)	[gera:nɪe]
hyacinth	**hyacint** (m)	[hɪaʦɪnt]

mimosa	**citlivka** (ž)	[ʦɪtlɪfka]
narcissus	**narcis** (m)	[narʦɪs]
nasturtium	**potočnice** (ž)	[potoʧnɪʦɛ]
orchid	**orchidej** (ž)	[orxɪdɛj]
peony	**pivoňka** (ž)	[pɪvonʲka]
violet	**fialka** (ž)	[fɪalka]
pansy	**maceška** (ž)	[maʦɛʃka]
forget-me-not	**pomněnka** (ž)	[pomneŋka]
daisy	**sedmikráska** (ž)	[sɛdmɪkra:ska]
poppy	**mák** (m)	[ma:k]
hemp	**konopě** (ž)	[konope]
mint	**máta** (ž)	[ma:ta]
lily of the valley	**konvalinka** (ž)	[konvalɪŋka]
snowdrop	**sněženka** (ž)	[sneʒeŋka]
nettle	**kopřiva** (ž)	[koprʃɪva]
sorrel	**šťovík** (m)	[ʃtʲovi:k]
water lily	**leknín** (m)	[lɛkni:n]
fern	**kapradí** (s)	[kapradi:]
lichen	**lišejník** (m)	[lɪʃɛjni:k]
conservatory (greenhouse)	**oranžérie** (ž)	[oranʒe:rɪe]
lawn	**trávník** (m)	[tra:vni:k]
flowerbed	**květinový záhonek** (m)	[kvetɪnovi: za:honɛk]
plant	**rostlina** (ž)	[rostlɪna]
grass	**tráva** (ž)	[tra:va]
blade of grass	**stéblo** (s) **trávy**	[stɛ:blo tra:vɪ]
leaf	**list** (m)	[lɪst]
petal	**okvětní lístek** (m)	[okvetni: li:stɛk]
stem	**stéblo** (s)	[stɛ:blo]
tuber	**hlíza** (ž)	[hli:za]
young plant (shoot)	**výhonek** (m)	[vi:honɛk]
thorn	**osten** (m)	[ostɛn]
to blossom (vi)	**kvést**	[kvɛ:st]
to fade, to wither	**vadnout**	[vadnout]
smell (odor)	**vůně** (ž)	[vu:ne]
to cut (flowers)	**uříznout**	[urʒi:znout]
to pick (a flower)	**utrhnout**	[utrhnout]

232. Cereals, grains

grain	**obilí** (s)	[obɪli:]
cereal crops	**obilniny** (ž mn)	[obɪlnɪnɪ]

ear (of barley, etc.)	**klas** (m)	[klas]
wheat	**pšenice** (ž)	[pʃɛnɪʦɛ]
rye	**žito** (s)	[ʒɪto]
oats	**oves** (m)	[ovɛs]
millet	**jáhly** (ž mn)	[ja:hlɪ]
barley	**ječmen** (m)	[jɛʧmɛn]
corn	**kukuřice** (ž)	[kukurʒɪʦɛ]
rice	**rýže** (ž)	[ri:ʒe]
buckwheat	**pohanka** (ž)	[pohaŋka]
pea plant	**hrách** (m)	[hra:x]
kidney bean	**fazole** (ž)	[fazolɛ]
soy	**sója** (ž)	[so:ja]
lentil	**čočka** (ž)	[ʧoʧka]
beans (pulse crops)	**boby** (m mn)	[bobɪ]

233. Vegetables. Greens

vegetables	**zelenina** (ž)	[zɛlɛnɪna]
greens	**zelenina** (ž)	[zɛlɛnɪna]
tomato	**rajské jablíčko** (s)	[rajskɛ: jabli:ʧko]
cucumber	**okurka** (ž)	[okurka]
carrot	**mrkev** (ž)	[mrkɛf]
potato	**brambory** (ž mn)	[bramborɪ]
onion	**cibule** (ž)	[ʦɪbulɛ]
garlic	**česnek** (m)	[ʧɛsnɛk]
cabbage	**zelí** (s)	[zɛli:]
cauliflower	**květák** (m)	[kveta:k]
Brussels sprouts	**růžičková kapusta** (ž)	[ru:ʒɪʧkova: kapusta]
broccoli	**brokolice** (ž)	[brokolɪʦɛ]
beet	**červená řepa** (ž)	[ʧɛrvena: rʒɛpa]
eggplant	**lilek** (m)	[lɪlɛk]
zucchini	**cukina, cuketa** (ž)	[ʦukɪna], [ʦuketa]
pumpkin	**tykev** (ž)	[tɪkɛf]
turnip	**vodní řepa** (ž)	[vodni: rʒɛpa]
parsley	**petržel** (ž)	[pɛtrʒel]
dill	**kopr** (m)	[kopr]
lettuce	**salát** (m)	[sala:t]
celery	**celer** (m)	[ʦɛlɛr]
asparagus	**chřest** (m)	[xrʃɛst]
spinach	**špenát** (m)	[ʃpɛna:t]
pea	**hrách** (m)	[hra:x]
beans	**boby** (m mn)	[bobɪ]
corn (maize)	**kukuřice** (ž)	[kukurʒɪʦɛ]

kidney bean	**fazole** (ž)	[fazolɛ]
pepper	**pepř** (m)	[pɛprʃ]
radish	**ředkvička** (ž)	[rʒɛtkvɪtʃka]
artichoke	**artyčok** (m)	[artɪtʃok]

REGIONAL GEOGRAPHY

Countries. Nationalities

234. Western Europe

Europe	**Evropa** (ž)	[ɛvropa]
European Union	**Evropská unie** (ž)	[ɛuropska: unɪe]
European (n)	**Evropan** (m)	[ɛvropan]
European (adj)	**evropský**	[ɛvropski:]
Austria	**Rakousko** (s)	[rakousko]
Austrian (masc.)	**Rakušan** (m)	[rakuʃan]
Austrian (fem.)	**Rakušanka** (ž)	[rakuʃaŋka]
Austrian (adj)	**rakouský**	[rakouski:]
Great Britain	**Velká Británie** (ž)	[vɛlka: brɪta:nɪe]
England	**Anglie** (ž)	[anglɪe]
British (masc.)	**Angličan** (m)	[anglɪʧan]
British (fem.)	**Angličanka** (ž)	[anglɪʧanka]
English, British (adj)	**anglický**	[anglɪʦki:]
Belgium	**Belgie** (ž)	[bɛlgɪe]
Belgian (masc.)	**Belgičan** (m)	[bɛlgɪʧan]
Belgian (fem.)	**Belgičanka** (ž)	[bɛlgɪʧaŋka]
Belgian (adj)	**belgický**	[bɛlgɪʦki:]
Germany	**Německo** (s)	[nemɛʦko]
German (masc.)	**Němec** (m)	[nemɛʦ]
German (fem.)	**Němka** (ž)	[nemka]
German (adj)	**německý**	[nemɛʦki:]
Netherlands	**Nizozemí** (s)	[nɪzozɛmi:]
Holland	**Holandsko** (s)	[holandsko]
Dutch (masc.)	**Holanďan** (m)	[holandʲan]
Dutch (fem.)	**Holanďanka** (ž)	[holandʲaŋka]
Dutch (adj)	**holandský**	[holandski:]
Greece	**Řecko** (s)	[rʒɛʦko]
Greek (masc.)	**Řek** (m)	[rʒɛk]
Greek (fem.)	**Řekyně** (ž)	[rʒɛkɪne]
Greek (adj)	**řecký**	[rʒɛʦki:]
Denmark	**Dánsko** (s)	[da:nsko]
Dane (masc.)	**Dán** (m)	[da:n]

Dane (fem.)	**Dánka** (ž)	[da:ŋka]
Danish (adj)	**dánský**	[da:nski:]
Ireland	**Irsko** (s)	[ɪrsko]
Irish (masc.)	**Ir** (m)	[ɪr]
Irish (fem.)	**Irka** (ž)	[ɪrka]
Irish (adj)	**irský**	[ɪrski:]
Iceland	**Island** (m)	[ɪslant]
Icelander (masc.)	**Islanďan** (m)	[ɪslandʲan]
Icelander (fem.)	**Islanďanka** (ž)	[ɪslandʲaŋka]
Icelandic (adj)	**islandský**	[ɪslantski:]
Spain	**Španělsko** (s)	[ʃpanelsko]
Spaniard (masc.)	**Španěl** (m)	[ʃpanel]
Spaniard (fem.)	**Španělka** (ž)	[ʃpanelka]
Spanish (adj)	**španělský**	[ʃpanelski:]
Italy	**Itálie** (ž)	[ɪta:lɪe]
Italian (masc.)	**Ital** (m)	[ɪtal]
Italian (fem.)	**Italka** (ž)	[ɪtalka]
Italian (adj)	**italský**	[ɪtalski:]
Cyprus	**Kypr** (m)	[kɪpr]
Cypriot (masc.)	**Kypřan** (m)	[kɪprʃan]
Cypriot (fem.)	**Kypřanka** (ž)	[kɪprʃaŋka]
Cypriot (adj)	**kyperský**	[kɪpɛrski:]
Malta	**Malta** (ž)	[malta]
Maltese (masc.)	**Malťan** (m)	[maltʲan]
Maltese (fem.)	**Malťanka** (ž)	[maltʲaŋka]
Maltese (adj)	**maltský**	[maltski:]
Norway	**Norsko** (s)	[norsko]
Norwegian (masc.)	**Nor** (m)	[nor]
Norwegian (fem.)	**Norka** (ž)	[norka]
Norwegian (adj)	**norský**	[norski:]
Portugal	**Portugalsko** (s)	[portugalsko]
Portuguese (masc.)	**Portugalec** (m)	[portugalɛts]
Portuguese (fem.)	**Portugalka** (ž)	[portugalka]
Portuguese (adj)	**portugalský**	[portugalski:]
Finland	**Finsko** (s)	[fɪnsko]
Finn (masc.)	**Fin** (m)	[fɪn]
Finn (fem.)	**Finka** (ž)	[fɪŋka]
Finnish (adj)	**finský**	[fɪnski:]
France	**Francie** (ž)	[frantsɪe]
French (masc.)	**Francouz** (m)	[frantsous]
French (fem.)	**Francouzka** (ž)	[frantsouska]
French (adj)	**francouzský**	[frantsouski:]

Sweden	**Švédsko** (s)	[ʃvɛ:tsko]
Swede (masc.)	**Švéd** (m)	[ʃvɛ:t]
Swede (fem.)	**Švédka** (ž)	[ʃvɛ:tka]
Swedish (adj)	**švédský**	[ʃvɛ:dski:]
Switzerland	**Švýcarsko** (s)	[ʃvi:ʦarsko]
Swiss (masc.)	**Švýcar** (m)	[ʃvi:ʦar]
Swiss (fem.)	**Švýcarka** (ž)	[ʃvi:ʦarka]
Swiss (adj)	**švýcarský**	[ʃvi:ʦarski:]
Scotland	**Skotsko** (s)	[skotsko]
Scottish (masc.)	**Skot** (m)	[skot]
Scottish (fem.)	**Skotka** (ž)	[skotka]
Scottish (adj)	**skotský**	[skotski:]
Vatican	**Vatikán** (m)	[vatɪka:n]
Liechtenstein	**Lichtenštejnsko** (s)	[lɪxtɛnʃtɛjnsko]
Luxembourg	**Lucembursko** (s)	[luʦɛmbursko]
Monaco	**Monako** (s)	[monako]

235. Central and Eastern Europe

Albania	**Albánie** (ž)	[alba:nɪe]
Albanian (masc.)	**Albánec** (m)	[alba:nɛʦ]
Albanian (fem.)	**Albánka** (ž)	[alba:ŋka]
Albanian (adj)	**albánský**	[alba:nski:]
Bulgaria	**Bulharsko** (s)	[bulharsko]
Bulgarian (masc.)	**Bulhar** (m)	[bulhar]
Bulgarian (fem.)	**Bulharka** (ž)	[bulharka]
Bulgarian (adj)	**bulharský**	[bulharski:]
Hungary	**Maďarsko** (s)	[madʲarsko]
Hungarian (masc.)	**Maďar** (m)	[madʲar]
Hungarian (fem.)	**Maďarka** (ž)	[madʲarka]
Hungarian (adj)	**maďarský**	[madʲarski:]
Latvia	**Lotyšsko** (s)	[lotɪʃsko]
Latvian (masc.)	**Lotyš** (m)	[lotɪʃ]
Latvian (fem.)	**Lotyška** (ž)	[lotɪʃka]
Latvian (adj)	**lotyšský**	[lotɪʃski:]
Lithuania	**Litva** (ž)	[lɪtva]
Lithuanian (masc.)	**Litevec** (m)	[lɪtɛvɛʦ]
Lithuanian (fem.)	**Litevka** (ž)	[lɪtɛfka]
Lithuanian (adj)	**litevský**	[lɪtɛvski:]
Poland	**Polsko** (s)	[polsko]
Pole (masc.)	**Polák** (m)	[pola:k]
Pole (fem.)	**Polka** (ž)	[polka]

Polish (adj)	**polský**	[polski:]
Romania	**Rumunsko** (s)	[rumunsko]
Romanian (masc.)	**Rumun** (m)	[rumun]
Romanian (fem.)	**Rumunka** (ž)	[rumuŋka]
Romanian (adj)	**rumunský**	[rumunski:]
Serbia	**Srbsko** (s)	[srpsko]
Serbian (masc.)	**Srb** (m)	[srp]
Serbian (fem.)	**Srbka** (ž)	[srpka]
Serbian (adj)	**srbský**	[srpski:]
Slovakia	**Slovensko** (s)	[slovɛnsko]
Slovak (masc.)	**Slovák** (m)	[slova:k]
Slovak (fem.)	**Slovenka** (ž)	[slovɛŋka]
Slovak (adj)	**slovenský**	[slovɛnski:]
Croatia	**Chorvatsko** (s)	[xorvatsko]
Croatian (masc.)	**Chorvat** (m)	[xorvat]
Croatian (fem.)	**Chorvatka** (ž)	[xorvatka]
Croatian (adj)	**chorvatský**	[xorvatski:]
Czech Republic	**Česko** (s)	[ʧɛsko]
Czech (masc.)	**Čech** (m)	[ʧɛx]
Czech (fem.)	**Češka** (ž)	[ʧɛʃka]
Czech (adj)	**český**	[ʧɛski:]
Estonia	**Estonsko** (s)	[ɛstonsko]
Estonian (masc.)	**Estonec** (m)	[ɛstonɛʦ]
Estonian (fem.)	**Estonka** (ž)	[ɛstoŋka]
Estonian (adj)	**estonský**	[ɛstonski:]
Bosnia and Herzegovina	**Bosna a Hercegovina** (ž)	[bosna a hɛrʦɛgovɪna]
Macedonia (Republic of ~)	**Makedonie** (ž)	[makɛdonɪe]
Slovenia	**Slovinsko** (s)	[slovɪnsko]
Montenegro	**Černá Hora** (ž)	[ʧɛrna: hora]

236. Former USSR countries

Azerbaijan	**Ázerbájdžán** (m)	[a:zɛrba:jʤa:n]
Azerbaijani (masc.)	**Ázerbájdžánec** (m)	[a:zɛrba:jʤa:nɛʦ]
Azerbaijani (fem.)	**Ázerbájdžánka** (ž)	[a:zɛrba:jʤa:ŋka]
Azerbaijani, Azeri (adj)	**ázerbájdžánský**	[a:zɛrba:jʤa:nski:]
Armenia	**Arménie** (ž)	[armɛ:nɪe]
Armenian (masc.)	**Armén** (m)	[armɛ:n]
Armenian (fem.)	**Arménka** (ž)	[armɛ:ŋka]
Armenian (adj)	**arménský**	[armɛ:nski:]
Belarus	**Bělorusko** (s)	[belorusko]
Belarusian (masc.)	**Bělorus** (m)	[belorus]

Belarusian (fem.)	**Běloruska** (ž)	[beloruska]
Belarusian (adj)	**běloruský**	[beloruski:]
Georgia	**Gruzie** (ž)	[gruzɪe]
Georgian (masc.)	**Gruzín** (m)	[gruzi:n]
Georgian (fem.)	**Gruzínka** (ž)	[gruzi:ŋka]
Georgian (adj)	**gruzínský**	[gruzi:nski:]
Kazakhstan	**Kazachstán** (m)	[kazaxsta:n]
Kazakh (masc.)	**Kazach** (m)	[kazax]
Kazakh (fem.)	**Kazaška** (ž)	[kazaʃka]
Kazakh (adj)	**kazašský**	[kazaʃski:]
Kirghizia	**Kyrgyzstán** (m)	[kɪrgɪsta:n]
Kirghiz (masc.)	**Kyrgyz** (m)	[kɪrgɪs]
Kirghiz (fem.)	**Kyrgyzka** (ž)	[kɪrgɪska]
Kirghiz (adj)	**kyrgyzský**	[kɪrgɪski:]
Moldova, Moldavia	**Moldavsko** (s)	[moldavsko]
Moldavian (masc.)	**Moldavan** (m)	[moldavan]
Moldavian (fem.)	**Moldavanka** (ž)	[moldavaŋka]
Moldavian (adj)	**moldavský**	[moldavski:]
Russia	**Rusko** (s)	[rusko]
Russian (masc.)	**Rus** (m)	[rus]
Russian (fem.)	**Ruska** (ž)	[ruska]
Russian (adj)	**ruský**	[ruski:]
Tajikistan	**Tádžikistán** (m)	[ta:ʤɪkɪsta:n]
Tajik (masc.)	**Tádžik** (m)	[ta:ʤɪk]
Tajik (fem.)	**Tádžička** (ž)	[ta:ʤɪʧka]
Tajik (adj)	**tádžický**	[ta:ʤɪʦki:]
Turkmenistan	**Turkmenistán** (m)	[turkmɛnɪsta:n]
Turkmen (masc.)	**Turkmen** (m)	[turkmɛn]
Turkmen (fem.)	**Turkmenka** (ž)	[turkmɛŋka]
Turkmenian (adj)	**turkmenský**	[turkmɛnski:]
Uzbekistan	**Uzbekistán** (m)	[uzbɛkɪsta:n]
Uzbek (masc.)	**Uzbek** (m)	[uzbɛk]
Uzbek (fem.)	**Uzbečka** (ž)	[uzbɛʧka]
Uzbek (adj)	**uzbecký**	[uzbɛʦki:]
Ukraine	**Ukrajina** (ž)	[ukrajɪna]
Ukrainian (masc.)	**Ukrajinec** (m)	[ukrajɪnɛʦ]
Ukrainian (fem.)	**Ukrajinka** (ž)	[ukrajɪŋka]
Ukrainian (adj)	**ukrajinský**	[ukrajɪnski:]

237. Asia

Asia	**Asie** (ž)	[azɪe]
Asian (adj)	**asijský**	[azɪjski:]

Vietnam	**Vietnam** (m)	[vjɛtnam]
Vietnamese (masc.)	**Vietnamec** (m)	[vjɛtnamɛʦ]
Vietnamese (fem.)	**Vietnamka** (ž)	[vjɛtnamka]
Vietnamese (adj)	**vietnamský**	[vjɛtnamski:]
India	**Indie** (ž)	[ɪndɪe]
Indian (masc.)	**Ind** (m)	[ɪnd]
Indian (fem.)	**Indka** (ž)	[ɪntka]
Indian (adj)	**indický**	[ɪndɪʦki:]
Israel	**Izrael** (m)	[ɪzraɛl]
Israeli (masc.)	**Izraelec** (m)	[ɪzraɛlɛʦ]
Israeli (fem.)	**Izraelka** (ž)	[ɪzraɛlka]
Israeli (adj)	**izraelský**	[ɪzraɛlski:]
Jew (n)	**Žid** (m)	[ʒɪt]
Jewess (n)	**Židovka** (ž)	[ʒɪdofka]
Jewish (adj)	**židovský**	[ʒɪdovski:]
China	**Čína** (ž)	[ʧi:na]
Chinese (masc.)	**Číňan** (m)	[ʧi:nʲan]
Chinese (fem.)	**Číňanka** (ž)	[ʧi:nʲaŋka]
Chinese (adj)	**čínský**	[ʧi:nski:]
Korean (masc.)	**Korejec** (m)	[korɛjɛʦ]
Korean (fem.)	**Korejka** (ž)	[korɛjka]
Korean (adj)	**korejský**	[korɛjski:]
Lebanon	**Libanon** (m)	[lɪbanon]
Lebanese (masc.)	**Libanonec** (m)	[lɪbanonɛʦ]
Lebanese (fem.)	**Libanonka** (ž)	[lɪbanoŋka]
Lebanese (adj)	**libanonský**	[lɪbanonski:]
Mongolia	**Mongolsko** (s)	[mongolsko]
Mongolian (masc.)	**Mongol** (m)	[mongol]
Mongolian (fem.)	**Mongolka** (ž)	[mongolka]
Mongolian (adj)	**mongolský**	[mongolski:]
Malaysia	**Malajsie** (ž)	[malajzɪe]
Malaysian (masc.)	**Malajec** (m)	[malajɛʦ]
Malaysian (fem.)	**Malajka** (ž)	[malajka]
Malaysian (adj)	**malajský**	[malajski:]
Pakistan	**Pákistán** (m)	[pa:kɪsta:n]
Pakistani (masc.)	**Pákistánec** (m)	[pa:kɪsta:nɛʦ]
Pakistani (fem.)	**Pákistánka** (ž)	[pa:kɪsta:ŋka]
Pakistani (adj)	**pákistánský**	[pa:kɪsta:nski:]
Saudi Arabia	**Saúdská Arábie** (ž)	[sau:dska: ara:bɪe]
Arab (masc.)	**Arab** (m)	[arap]
Arab (fem.)	**Arabka** (ž)	[arapka]
Arab, Arabic (adj)	**arabský**	[arapski:]

Thailand	**Thajsko** (s)	[tajsko]
Thai (masc.)	**Thajec** (m)	[tajɛʦ]
Thai (fem.)	**Thajka** (ž)	[tajka]
Thai (adj)	**thajský**	[tajski:]
Taiwan	**Tchaj-wan** (m)	[tajvan]
Taiwanese (masc.)	**Tchajwanec** (m)	[tajvanɛʦ]
Taiwanese (fem.)	**Tchajwanka** (ž)	[tajvaŋka]
Taiwanese (adj)	**tchajwanský**	[tajvanski:]
Turkey	**Turecko** (s)	[turɛʦko]
Turk (masc.)	**Turek** (m)	[turɛk]
Turk (fem.)	**Turkyně** (ž)	[turkɪne]
Turkish (adj)	**turecký**	[turɛʦki:]
Japan	**Japonsko** (s)	[japonsko]
Japanese (masc.)	**Japonec** (m)	[japonɛʦ]
Japanese (fem.)	**Japonka** (ž)	[japoŋka]
Japanese (adj)	**japonský**	[japonski:]
Afghanistan	**Afghánistán** (m)	[afga:nɪsta:n]
Bangladesh	**Bangladéš** (m)	[bangladɛ:ʃ]
Indonesia	**Indonésie** (ž)	[ɪndonɛ:zɪe]
Jordan	**Jordánsko** (s)	[jorda:nsko]
Iraq	**Irák** (m)	[ɪra:k]
Iran	**Írán** (m)	[i:ra:n]
Cambodia	**Kambodža** (ž)	[kambodʒa]
Kuwait	**Kuvajt** (m)	[kuvajt]
Laos	**Laos** (m)	[laos]
Myanmar	**Barma** (ž)	[barma]
Nepal	**Nepál** (m)	[nɛpa:l]
United Arab Emirates	**Spojené arabské emiráty** (m mn)	[spojɛnɛ: arapskɛ: ɛmɪra:tɪ]
Syria	**Sýrie** (ž)	[si:rɪe]
Palestine	**Palestinská autonomie** (ž)	[palɛstɪnska: autonomɪe]
South Korea	**Jižní Korea** (ž)	[jɪʒni: korɛa]
North Korea	**Severní Korea** (ž)	[sevɛrni: korɛa]

238. North America

United States of America	**Spojené státy americké** (m mn)	[spojɛnɛ: sta:tɪ amɛrɪʦkɛ:]
American (masc.)	**Američan** (m)	[amɛrɪʧan]
American (fem.)	**Američanka** (ž)	[amɛrɪʧaŋka]
American (adj)	**americký**	[amɛrɪʦki:]
Canada	**Kanada** (ž)	[kanada]
Canadian (masc.)	**Kanaďan** (m)	[kanadʲan]

Canadian (fem.)	**Kanaďanka** (ž)	[kanadʲaŋka]
Canadian (adj)	**kanadský**	[kanadski:]
Mexico	**Mexiko** (s)	[mɛksɪko]
Mexican (masc.)	**Mexičan** (m)	[mɛksɪʧan]
Mexican (fem.)	**Mexičanka** (ž)	[mɛksɪʧaŋka]
Mexican (adj)	**mexický**	[mɛksɪʦski:]

239. Central and South America

Argentina	**Argentina** (ž)	[argɛntɪna]
Argentinian (masc.)	**Argentinec** (m)	[argɛntɪnɛʦ]
Argentinian (fem.)	**Argentinka** (ž)	[argɛntɪŋka]
Argentinian (adj)	**argentinský**	[argɛntɪnski:]
Brazil	**Brazílie** (ž)	[brazi:lɪe]
Brazilian (masc.)	**Brazilec** (m)	[brazɪlɛʦ]
Brazilian (fem.)	**Brazilka** (ž)	[brazɪlka]
Brazilian (adj)	**brazilský**	[brazɪlski:]
Colombia	**Kolumbie** (ž)	[kolumbɪe]
Colombian (masc.)	**Kolumbijec** (m)	[kolumbɪjɛʦ]
Colombian (fem.)	**Kolumbijka** (ž)	[kolumbɪjka]
Colombian (adj)	**kolumbijský**	[kolumbɪjski:]
Cuba	**Kuba** (ž)	[kuba]
Cuban (masc.)	**Kubánec** (m)	[kuba:nɛʦ]
Cuban (fem.)	**Kubánka** (ž)	[kuba:ŋka]
Cuban (adj)	**kubánský**	[kuba:nski:]
Chile	**Chile** (s)	[ʧɪlɛ]
Chilean (masc.)	**Chilan** (m)	[ʧɪlan]
Chilean (fem.)	**Chilanka** (ž)	[ʧɪlaŋka]
Chilean (adj)	**chilský**	[ʧɪlski:]
Bolivia	**Bolívie** (ž)	[boli:vɪe]
Venezuela	**Venezuela** (ž)	[vɛnɛzuɛla]
Paraguay	**Paraguay** (ž)	[paragvaj]
Peru	**Peru** (s)	[pɛru]
Suriname	**Surinam** (m)	[surɪnam]
Uruguay	**Uruguay** (ž)	[urugvaj]
Ecuador	**Ekvádor** (m)	[ɛkva:dor]
The Bahamas	**Bahamy** (ž mn)	[bahamɪ]
Haiti	**Haiti** (s)	[haɪtɪ]
Dominican Republic	**Dominikánská republika** (ž)	[domɪnɪka:nska: rɛpublɪka]
Panama	**Panama** (ž)	[panama]
Jamaica	**Jamajka** (ž)	[jamajka]

240. Africa

Egypt	**Egypt** (m)	[ɛgɪpt]
Egyptian (masc.)	**Egypťan** (m)	[ɛgɪptʲan]
Egyptian (fem.)	**Egypťanka** (ž)	[ɛgɪptʲaŋka]
Egyptian (adj)	**egyptský**	[ɛgɪptski:]
Morocco	**Maroko** (s)	[maroko]
Moroccan (masc.)	**Maročan** (m)	[marotʃan]
Moroccan (fem.)	**Maročanka** (ž)	[marotʃaŋka]
Moroccan (adj)	**marocký**	[marotski:]
Tunisia	**Tunisko** (s)	[tunɪsko]
Tunisian (masc.)	**Tunisan** (m)	[tunɪsan]
Tunisian (fem.)	**Tunisanka** (ž)	[tunɪsaŋka]
Tunisian (adj)	**tuniský**	[tunɪski:]
Ghana	**Ghana** (ž)	[gana]
Zanzibar	**Zanzibar** (m)	[zanzɪbar]
Kenya	**Keňa** (ž)	[kɛnʲa]
Libya	**Libye** (ž)	[lɪbɪe]
Madagascar	**Madagaskar** (m)	[madagaskar]
Namibia	**Namibie** (ž)	[namɪbɪe]
Senegal	**Senegal** (m)	[sɛnɛgal]
Tanzania	**Tanzanie** (ž)	[tanzanɪe]
South Africa	**Jihoafrická republika** (ž)	[jɪhoafrɪtska: rɛpublɪka]
African (masc.)	**Afričan** (m)	[afrɪtʃan]
African (fem.)	**Afričanka** (ž)	[afrɪtʃaŋka]
African (adj)	**africký**	[afrɪtski:]

241. Australia. Oceania

Australia	**Austrálie** (ž)	[austra:lɪe]
Australian (masc.)	**Australan** (m)	[australan]
Australian (fem.)	**Australanka** (ž)	[australaŋka]
Australian (adj)	**australský**	[australski:]
New Zealand	**Nový Zéland** (m)	[novi: zɛ:lant]
New Zealander (masc.)	**Novozélanďan** (m)	[novozɛ:landʲan]
New Zealander (fem.)	**Novozélanďanka** (ž)	[novozɛ:landʲaŋka]
New Zealand (as adj)	**novozélandský**	[novozɛ:landski:]
Tasmania	**Tasmánie** (ž)	[tasma:nɪe]
French Polynesia	**Francouzská Polynésie** (ž)	[frantsouska: polɪnɛ:zɪe]

242. Cities

Amsterdam	**Amsterodam** (m)	[amstɛrodam]
Ankara	**Ankara** (ž)	[aŋkara]
Athens	**Atény** (ž mn)	[atɛ:nɪ]
Baghdad	**Bagdád** (m)	[bagda:t]
Bangkok	**Bangkok** (m)	[bangkok]
Barcelona	**Barcelona** (ž)	[barsɛlona]
Beijing	**Peking** (m)	[pɛkɪŋk]
Beirut	**Bejrút** (m)	[bɛjru:t]
Berlin	**Berlín** (m)	[bɛrli:n]
Mumbai (Bombay)	**Bombaj** (ž)	[bombaj]
Bonn	**Bonn** (m)	[bonn]
Bordeaux	**Bordeaux** (s)	[bordo:]
Bratislava	**Bratislava** (ž)	[bratɪslava]
Brussels	**Brusel** (m)	[brusɛl]
Bucharest	**Bukurešť** (ž)	[bukurɛʃtʲ]
Budapest	**Budapešť** (ž)	[budapɛʃtʲ]
Cairo	**Káhira** (ž)	[ka:hɪra]
Kolkata (Calcutta)	**Kalkata** (ž)	[kalkata]
Chicago	**Chicago** (s)	[ʧɪka:go]
Copenhagen	**Kodaň** (ž)	[kodanʲ]
Dar-es-Salaam	**Dar es Salaam** (m)	[dar ɛs sala:m]
Delhi	**Dillí** (s)	[dɪli:]
Dubai	**Dubaj** (m)	[dubaj]
Dublin	**Dublin** (m)	[dublɪn]
Düsseldorf	**Düsseldorf** (m)	[disldorf]
Florence	**Florencie** (ž)	[florɛntsɪe]
Frankfurt	**Frankfurt** (m)	[fraŋkfurt]
Geneva	**Ženeva** (ž)	[ʒenɛva]
The Hague	**Haag** (m)	[ha:g]
Hamburg	**Hamburk** (m)	[hamburk]
Hanoi	**Hanoj** (m)	[hanoj]
Havana	**Havana** (ž)	[havana]
Helsinki	**Helsinky** (ž mn)	[hɛlsɪŋkɪ]
Hiroshima	**Hirošima** (ž)	[hɪroʃɪma]
Hong Kong	**Hongkong** (m)	[hoŋkong]
Istanbul	**Istanbul** (m)	[ɪstanbul]
Jerusalem	**Jeruzalém** (m)	[jɛruzalɛ:m]
Kyiv	**Kyjev** (m)	[kɪef]
Kuala Lumpur	**Kuala Lumpur** (m)	[kuala lumpur]
Lisbon	**Lisabon** (m)	[lɪsabon]
London	**Londýn** (m)	[londi:n]
Los Angeles	**Los Angeles** (s)	[los ɛnʒɛlis]

Lyons	**Lyon** (m)	[ɪon]
Madrid	**Madrid** (m)	[madrɪt]
Marseille	**Marseille** (ž)	[marsɛj]
Mexico City	**Mexiko** (s)	[mɛksɪko]
Miami	**Miami** (s)	[majamɪ]
Montreal	**Montreal** (m)	[monrɛal]
Moscow	**Moskva** (ž)	[moskva]
Munich	**Mnichov** (m)	[mnɪxof]
Nairobi	**Nairobi** (s)	[najrobɪ]
Naples	**Neapol** (m)	[nɛapol]
New York	**New York** (m)	[nju: jork]
Nice	**Nizza** (ž)	[nɪʦa]
Oslo	**Oslo** (s)	[oslo]
Ottawa	**Otava** (ž)	[otava]
Paris	**Paříž** (ž)	[parʒi:ʃ]
Prague	**Praha** (ž)	[praha]
Rio de Janeiro	**Rio de Janeiro** (s)	[rɪodɛʒanɛ:ro]
Rome	**Řím** (m)	[rʒi:m]
Saint Petersburg	**Sankt-Petěrburg** (m)	[saŋkt-pɛterburg]
Seoul	**Soul** (m)	[soul]
Shanghai	**Šanghaj** (ž)	[ʃangxaj]
Singapore	**Singapur** (m)	[sɪngapur]
Stockholm	**Stockholm** (m)	[stokholm]
Sydney	**Sydney** (s)	[sɪdnɛj]
Taipei	**Tchaj-pej** (s)	[taj-pɛj]
Tokyo	**Tokio** (s)	[tokɪo]
Toronto	**Toronto** (s)	[toronto]
Venice	**Benátky** (ž mn)	[bɛna:tkɪ]
Vienna	**Vídeň** (ž)	[vi:dɛnʲ]
Warsaw	**Varšava** (ž)	[varʃava]
Washington	**Washington** (m)	[voʃɪnkton]

243. Politics. Government. Part 1

politics	**politika** (ž)	[polɪtɪka]
political (adj)	**politický**	[polɪtɪʦki:]
politician	**politik** (m)	[polɪtɪk]
state (country)	**stát** (m)	[sta:t]
citizen	**občan** (m)	[obʧan]
citizenship	**státní příslušnost** (ž)	[sta:tni: prʃi:sluʃnost]
national emblem	**státní znak** (m)	[sta:tni: znak]
national anthem	**státní hymna** (ž)	[sta:tni: hɪmna]
government	**vláda** (ž)	[vla:da]

head of state	**hlava** (m) **státu**	[hlava sta:tu]
parliament	**parlament** (m)	[parlamɛnt]
party	**strana** (ž)	[strana]
capitalism	**kapitalismus** (m)	[kapɪtalɪzmus]
capitalist (adj)	**kapitalistický**	[kapɪtalɪstɪʦki:]
socialism	**socialismus** (m)	[soʦɪalɪzmus]
socialist (adj)	**socialistický**	[soʦɪalɪstɪʦki:]
communism	**komunismus** (m)	[komunɪzmus]
communist (adj)	**komunistický**	[komunɪstɪʦki:]
communist (n)	**komunista** (m)	[komunɪsta]
democracy	**demokracie** (ž)	[dɛmokraʦɪe]
democrat	**demokrat** (m)	[dɛmokrat]
democratic (adj)	**demokratický**	[dɛmokratɪʦki:]
Democratic party	**demokratická strana** (ž)	[dɛmokratɪʦka: strana]
liberal (n)	**liberál** (m)	[lɪbɛra:l]
liberal (adj)	**liberální**	[lɪbɛra:lni:]
conservative (n)	**konzervativec** (m)	[konzɛrvatɪvɛʦ]
conservative (adj)	**konzervativní**	[konzɛrvatɪvni:]
republic (n)	**republika** (ž)	[rɛpublɪka]
republican (n)	**republikán** (m)	[rɛpublɪka:n]
Republican party	**republikánská strana** (ž)	[rɛpublɪka:nska: strana]
elections	**volby** (ž mn)	[volbɪ]
to elect (vt)	**volit**	[volɪt]
elector, voter	**volič** (m)	[volɪʧ]
election campaign	**volební kampaň** (ž)	[volɛbni: kampanʲ]
voting (n)	**hlasování** (s)	[hlasova:ni:]
to vote (vi)	**hlasovat**	[hlasovat]
suffrage, right to vote	**hlasovací právo** (s)	[hlasovaʦi: pra:vo]
candidate	**kandidát** (m)	[kandɪda:t]
to be a candidate	**kandidovat**	[kandɪdovat]
campaign	**kampaň** (ž)	[kampanʲ]
opposition (as adj)	**opoziční**	[opozɪʧni:]
opposition (n)	**opozice** (ž)	[opozɪʦɛ]
visit	**návštěva** (ž)	[na:vʃteva]
official visit	**oficiální návštěva** (ž)	[ofɪʦɪa:lni: na:fʃteva]
international (adj)	**mezinárodní**	[mɛzɪna:rodni:]
negotiations	**jednání** (s)	[jɛdna:ni:]
to negotiate (vi)	**jednat**	[jɛdnat]

244. Politics. Government. Part 2

society	**společnost** (ž)	[spolɛʧnost]
constitution	**ústava** (ž)	[u:stava]
power (political control)	**moc** (ž)	[moʦ]
corruption	**korupce** (ž)	[koruptsɛ]
law (justice)	**zákon** (m)	[za:kon]
legal (legitimate)	**zákonný**	[za:konni:]
justice (fairness)	**spravedlivost** (ž)	[spravɛdlɪvost]
just (fair)	**spravedlivý**	[spravɛdlɪvi:]
committee	**výbor** (m)	[vi:bor]
bill (draft law)	**návrh** (m) **zákona**	[na:vrx za:kona]
budget	**rozpočet** (m)	[rozpoʧɛt]
policy	**politika** (ž)	[polɪtɪka]
reform	**reforma** (ž)	[rɛforma]
radical (adj)	**radikální**	[radɪka:lni:]
power (strength, force)	**síla** (ž)	[si:la]
powerful (adj)	**silný**	[sɪlni:]
supporter	**stoupenec** (m)	[stoupɛnɛʦ]
influence	**vliv** (m)	[vlɪf]
regime (e.g., military ~)	**režim** (m)	[rɛʒɪm]
conflict	**konflikt** (m)	[konflɪkt]
conspiracy (plot)	**spiknutí** (s)	[spɪknuti:]
provocation	**provokace** (ž)	[provokaʦɛ]
to overthrow (regime, etc.)	**svrhnout**	[svrhnout]
overthrow (of government)	**svržení** (s)	[svrʒeni:]
revolution	**revoluce** (ž)	[rɛvoluʦɛ]
coup d'état	**převrat** (m)	[prʃɛvrat]
military coup	**vojenský převrat** (m)	[vojɛnski: prʃɛvrat]
crisis	**krize** (ž)	[krɪzɛ]
economic recession	**hospodářský pokles** (m)	[hospoda:rʃski: poklɛs]
demonstrator (protester)	**demonstrant** (m)	[dɛmonstrant]
demonstration	**demonstrace** (ž)	[dɛmonstraʦɛ]
martial law	**válečný stav** (m)	[va:lɛʧni: staf]
military base	**základna** (ž)	[za:kladna]
stability	**stabilita** (ž)	[stabɪlɪta]
stable (adj)	**stabilní**	[stabɪlni:]
exploitation	**vykořisťování** (s)	[vɪkorʒɪstʲova:ni:]
to exploit (workers)	**vykořisťovat**	[vɪkorʒɪstʲovat]
racism	**rasismus** (m)	[rasɪzmus]
racist	**rasista** (m)	[rasɪsta]

fascism	**fašismus** (m)	[faʃɪzmus]
fascist	**fašista** (m)	[faʃɪsta]

245. Countries. Miscellaneous

foreigner	**cizinec** (m)	[ʦɪzɪnɛʦ]
foreign (adj)	**cizí**	[ʦɪzi:]
abroad (in a foreign country)	**v zahraničí**	[v zahranɪʧi:]
emigrant	**emigrant** (m)	[ɛmɪgrant]
emigration	**emigrace** (ž)	[ɛmɪgraʦɛ]
to emigrate (vi)	**emigrovat**	[ɛmɪgrovat]
the West	**Západ** (m)	[za:pat]
the East	**Východ** (m)	[vi:xot]
the Far East	**Dálný východ** (m)	[da:lni: vi:xot]
civilization	**civilizace** (ž)	[ʦɪvɪlɪzaʦɛ]
humanity (mankind)	**lidstvo** (s)	[lɪdstvo]
the world (earth)	**svět** (m)	[svet]
peace	**mír** (m)	[mi:r]
worldwide (adj)	**světový**	[svetovi:]
homeland	**vlast** (ž)	[vlast]
people (population)	**lid** (m)	[lɪt]
population	**obyvatelstvo** (s)	[obɪvatɛlstvo]
people (a lot of ~)	**lidé** (m mn)	[lɪdɛ:]
nation (people)	**národ** (m)	[na:rot]
generation	**generace** (ž)	[gɛnɛraʦɛ]
territory (area)	**území** (s)	[u:zɛmi:]
region	**region** (m)	[rɛgɪon]
state (part of a country)	**stát** (m)	[sta:t]
tradition	**tradice** (ž)	[tradɪʦɛ]
custom (tradition)	**zvyk** (m)	[zvɪk]
ecology	**ekologie** (ž)	[ɛkologɪe]
Indian (Native American)	**Indián** (m)	[ɪndɪa:n]
Gypsy (masc.)	**Rom** (m)	[rom]
Gypsy (fem.)	**Romka** (ž)	[romka]
Gypsy (adj)	**romský**	[romski:]
empire	**říše** (ž)	[rʒi:ʃɛ]
colony	**kolonie** (ž)	[kolonɪe]
slavery	**otroctví** (s)	[otroʦtvi:]
invasion	**vpád** (m)	[vpa:t]
famine	**hlad** (m)	[hlat]

246. Major religious groups. Confessions

religion	**náboženství** (s)	[na:boʒenstvi:]
religious (adj)	**náboženský**	[na:boʒenski:]
faith, belief	**víra** (ž)	[vi:ra]
to believe (in God)	**věřit**	[verʒɪt]
believer	**věřící** (m)	[verʒi:ʦi:]
atheism	**ateizmus** (m)	[atɛɪzmus]
atheist	**ateista** (m)	[atɛɪsta]
Christianity	**křesťanství** (s)	[krʃɛstʲanstvi:]
Christian (n)	**křesťan** (m)	[krʃɛstʲan]
Christian (adj)	**křesťanský**	[krʃɛstʲanski:]
Catholicism	**katolicismus** (m)	[katolɪʦɪzmus]
Catholic (n)	**katolík** (m)	[katoli:k]
Catholic (adj)	**katolický**	[katolɪʦki:]
Protestantism	**protestantismus** (m)	[protɛstantɪzmus]
Protestant Church	**protestantská církev** (ž)	[protɛstanʦka: ʦi:rkɛf]
Protestant (n)	**protestant** (m)	[protɛstant]
Orthodoxy	**pravoslaví** (s)	[pravoslavi:]
Orthodox Church	**pravoslavná církev** (ž)	[pravoslavna: ʦi:rkɛf]
Orthodox (n)	**pravoslavný** (m)	[pravoslavni:]
Presbyterianism	**presbyteriánství** (s)	[prɛzbɪtɛrɪa:nstvi:]
Presbyterian Church	**presbyteriánská církev** (ž)	[prɛzbɪtɛrɪa:nska: ʦi:rkɛf]
Presbyterian (n)	**presbyterián** (m)	[prɛzbɪtɛrɪa:n]
Lutheranism	**luteránská církev** (ž)	[lutɛra:nska: ʦi:rkɛf]
Lutheran (n)	**luterán** (m)	[lutɛra:n]
Baptist Church	**baptismus** (m)	[baptɪzmus]
Baptist (n)	**baptista** (m)	[baptɪsta]
Anglican Church	**anglikánská církev** (ž)	[anglɪka:nska: ʦi:rkɛf]
Anglican (n)	**anglikán** (m)	[anglɪka:n]
Mormonism	**Mormonism** (m)	[mormonɪzm]
Mormon (n)	**mormon** (m)	[mormon]
Judaism	**judaismus** (m)	[judaɪzmus]
Jew (n)	**žid** (m)	[ʒɪt]
Buddhism	**buddhismus** (m)	[budhɪzmus]
Buddhist (n)	**buddhista** (m)	[budhɪsta]
Hinduism	**hinduismus** (m)	[hɪndujɪzmus]
Hindu (n)	**Hinduista** (m)	[hɪnduɪsta]

Islam	**islám** (m)	[ɪsla:m]
Muslim (n)	**muslim** (m)	[muslɪm]
Muslim (adj)	**muslimský**	[muslɪmski:]
Shiah Islam	**šíitský islám** (m)	[ʃi:ɪtski: ɪsla:m]
Shiite (n)	**šíita** (ž)	[ʃi:ɪta]
Sunni Islam	**Sunnitský islám** (m)	[sunnɪtski: ɪsla:m]
Sunnite (n)	**Sunnita** (m)	[sunnɪta]

247. Religions. Priests

priest	**kněz** (m)	[knez]
the Pope	**Papež** (m)	[papɛʃ]
monk, friar	**mnich** (m)	[mnɪx]
nun	**jeptiška** (ž)	[jɛptɪʃka]
pastor	**pastor** (m)	[pastor]
abbot	**opat** (m)	[opat]
vicar (parish priest)	**vikář** (m)	[vɪka:rʃ]
bishop	**biskup** (m)	[bɪskup]
cardinal	**kardinál** (m)	[kardɪna:l]
preacher	**kazatel** (m)	[kazatɛl]
preaching	**kázání** (s)	[ka:za:ni:]
parishioners	**farnost** (ž)	[farnost]
believer	**věřící** (m)	[verʒi:ʦi:]
atheist	**ateista** (m)	[atɛɪsta]

248. Faith. Christianity. Islam

Adam	**Adam** (m)	[adam]
Eve	**Eva** (ž)	[ɛva]
God	**Bůh** (m)	[bu:x]
the Lord	**Pán** (m)	[pa:n]
the Almighty	**Všemohoucí** (m)	[vʃɛmohouʦi:]
sin	**hřích** (m)	[hrʒi:x]
to sin (vi)	**hřešit**	[hrʒɛʃɪt]
sinner (masc.)	**hříšník** (m)	[hrʒiʃni:k]
sinner (fem.)	**hříšnice** (ž)	[hrʒɪʃnɪʦɛ]
hell	**peklo** (s)	[pɛklo]
paradise	**ráj** (m)	[ra:j]
Jesus	**Ježíš** (m)	[jɛʒi:ʃ]

Jesus Christ	**Ježíš Kristus** (m)	[jɛʒi:ʃ krɪstus]
the Holy Spirit	**Duch** (m) **Svatý**	[dux svati:]
the Savior	**Spasitel** (m)	[spasɪtɛl]
the Virgin Mary	**Bohorodička** (ž)	[bohorodɪʧka]
the Devil	**ďábel** (m)	[dʲa:bɛl]
devil's (adj)	**ďábelský**	[dʲa:bɛlski:]
Satan	**satan** (m)	[satan]
satanic (adj)	**satanský**	[satanski:]
angel	**anděl** (m)	[andel]
guardian angel	**anděl** (m) **strážný**	[andel stra:ʒni:]
angelic (adj)	**andělský**	[andelski:]
apostle	**apoštol** (m)	[apoʃtol]
archangel	**archanděl** (m)	[arxandel]
the Antichrist	**antikrist** (m)	[antɪkrɪst]
Church	**Církev** (ž)	[ʦi:rkɛf]
Bible	**Bible** (ž)	[bɪblɛ]
biblical (adj)	**biblický**	[bɪblɪʦki:]
Old Testament	**Starý zákon** (m)	[stari: za:kon]
New Testament	**Nový zákon** (m)	[novi: za:kon]
Gospel	**Evangelium** (s)	[ɛvangɛlɪum]
Holy Scripture	**Písmo** (s) **svaté**	[pi:smo svatɛ:]
Heaven	**nebeské království** (s)	[nɛbɛskɛ: kra:lovstvi:]
Commandment	**přikázání** (s)	[prʃɪka:za:ni:]
prophet	**prorok** (m)	[prorok]
prophecy	**proroctví** (s)	[proroʦtvi:]
Allah	**Alláh** (m)	[ala:x]
Mohammed	**Mohamed** (m)	[mohamɛt]
the Koran	**Korán** (m)	[kora:n]
mosque	**mešita** (ž)	[mɛʃɪta]
mullah	**Mullah** (m)	[mulla]
prayer	**modlitba** (ž)	[modlɪtba]
to pray (vi, vt)	**modlit se**	[modlɪt sɛ]
pilgrimage	**pouť** (ž)	[poutʲ]
pilgrim	**poutník** (m)	[poutni:k]
Mecca	**Mekka** (ž)	[mɛka]
church	**kostel** (m)	[kostɛl]
temple	**chrám** (m)	[xra:m]
cathedral	**katedrála** (ž)	[katɛdra:la]
Gothic (adj)	**gotický**	[gotɪʦki:]
synagogue	**synagóga** (ž)	[sinago:ga]
mosque	**mešita** (ž)	[mɛʃɪta]
chapel	**kaple** (ž)	[kaplɛ]

abbey	**opatství** (s)	[opatstvi:]
convent	**klášter** (m)	[kla:ʃtɛr]
monastery	**klášter** (m)	[kla:ʃtɛr]
bell (church ~s)	**zvon** (m)	[zvon]
bell tower	**zvonice** (ž)	[zvonɪʦɛ]
to ring (ab. bells)	**zvonit**	[zvonɪt]
cross	**kříž** (m)	[krʃi:ʃ]
cupola (roof)	**kopule** (ž)	[kopulɛ]
icon	**ikona** (ž)	[ɪkona]
soul	**duše** (ž)	[duʃɛ]
fate (destiny)	**osud** (m)	[osut]
evil (n)	**zlo** (s)	[zlo]
good (n)	**dobro** (s)	[dobro]
vampire	**upír** (m)	[upi:r]
witch (evil ~)	**čarodějnice** (ž)	[ʧarodejnɪʦɛ]
demon	**démon** (m)	[dɛ:mon]
spirit	**duch** (m)	[dux]
redemption (giving us ~)	**vykoupení** (s)	[vɪkoupɛni:]
to redeem (vt)	**vykoupit**	[vɪkoupɪt]
church service, mass	**bohoslužba** (ž)	[bohosluʒba]
to say mass	**sloužit**	[slouʒɪt]
confession	**zpověď** (ž)	[spovetʲ]
to confess (vi)	**zpovídat se**	[spovi:dat sɛ]
saint (n)	**světec** (m)	[svetɛʦ]
sacred (holy)	**posvátný**	[posva:tni:]
holy water	**svěcená voda** (ž)	[svetsɛna: voda]
ritual (n)	**ritus** (m)	[rɪtus]
ritual (adj)	**rituální**	[rɪtua:lni:]
sacrifice	**oběť** (ž)	[obetʲ]
superstition	**pověra** (ž)	[povera]
superstitious (adj)	**pověrčivý**	[poverʧɪvi:]
afterlife	**posmrtný život** (m)	[posmrtni: ʒɪvot]
eternal life	**věčný život** (m)	[vetʃni: ʒɪvot]

MISCELLANEOUS

249. Various useful words

background (green ~)	**pozadí** (s)	[pozadi:]
balance (of situation)	**rovnováha** (ž)	[rovnova:ha]
barrier (obstacle)	**zábrana** (ž)	[za:brana]
base (basis)	**základna** (ž)	[za:kladna]
beginning	**začátek** (m)	[zatʃa:tɛk]
category	**kategorie** (ž)	[katɛgorɪe]
cause (reason)	**důvod** (m)	[du:vot]
choice	**volba** (ž)	[volba]
coincidence	**shoda** (ž)	[sxoda]
comfortable (~ chair)	**pohodlný**	[pohodlni:]
comparison	**srovnání** (s)	[srovna:ni:]
compensation	**kompenzace** (ž)	[kompɛnzatsɛ]
degree (extent, amount)	**stupeň** (m)	[stupɛnʲ]
development	**rozvoj** (m)	[rozvoj]
difference	**rozdíl** (m)	[rozdi:l]
effect (e.g., of drugs)	**efekt** (m)	[ɛfɛkt]
effort (exertion)	**úsilí** (s)	[u:sɪli:]
element	**prvek** (m)	[prvɛk]
end (finish)	**skončení** (s)	[skontʃɛni:]
example (illustration)	**příklad** (m)	[prʃi:klat]
fact	**fakt** (m)	[fakt]
frequent (adj)	**častý**	[tʃasti:]
growth (development)	**růst** (m)	[ru:st]
help	**pomoc** (ž)	[pomots]
ideal	**ideál** (m)	[ɪdɛa:l]
kind (sort, type)	**druh** (m)	[drux]
labyrinth	**labyrint** (m)	[labɪrɪnt]
mistake, error	**chyba** (ž)	[xɪba]
moment	**moment** (m)	[momɛnt]
object (thing)	**předmět** (m)	[prʃɛdmnet]
obstacle	**překážka** (ž)	[prʃɛka:ʃka]
original (original copy)	**originál** (m)	[orɪgɪna:l]
part (~ of sth)	**část** (ž)	[tʃa:st]
particle, small part	**částice** (ž)	[tʃa:stɪtsɛ]
pause (break)	**pauza** (ž)	[pauza]

position	**pozice** (ž)	[pozɪtsɛ]
principle	**princip** (m)	[prɪntsɪp]
problem	**problém** (m)	[problɛ:m]
process	**proces** (m)	[protsɛs]
progress	**pokrok** (m)	[pokrok]
property (quality)	**vlastnost** (ž)	[vlastnost]
reaction	**reakce** (ž)	[rɛaktsɛ]
risk	**riziko** (s)	[rɪzɪko]
secret	**tajemství** (s)	[tajɛmstvi:]
series	**řada** (ž)	[rʒada]
shape (outer form)	**tvar** (m)	[tvar]
situation	**situace** (ž)	[sɪtuatsɛ]
solution	**řešení** (s)	[rʒɛʃɛni:]
standard (adj)	**standardní**	[standardni:]
standard (level of quality)	**standard** (m)	[standart]
stop (pause)	**přestávka** (ž)	[prʃɛsta:fka]
style	**sloh** (m)	[slox]
system	**systém** (m)	[sɪstɛ:m]
table (chart)	**tabulka** (ž)	[tabulka]
tempo, rate	**tempo** (s)	[tɛmpo]
term (word, expression)	**termín** (m)	[tɛrmi:n]
thing (object, item)	**věc** (ž)	[vets]
truth (e.g., moment of ~)	**pravda** (ž)	[pravda]
turn (please wait your ~)	**pořadí** (s)	[porʒadi:]
type (sort, kind)	**typ** (m)	[tɪp]
urgent (adj)	**neodkladný**	[nɛotkladni:]
urgently (adv)	**neodkladně**	[nɛotkladne]
utility (usefulness)	**užitek** (m)	[uʒɪtɛk]
variant (alternative)	**varianta** (ž)	[varɪanta]
way (means, method)	**způsob** (m)	[spu:sop]
zone	**pásmo** (s)	[pa:smo]

250. Modifiers. Adjectives. Part 1

additional (adj)	**dodatečný**	[dodatɛtʃni:]
ancient (~ civilization)	**starobylý**	[starobɪli:]
artificial (adj)	**umělý**	[umneli:]
back, rear (adj)	**zadní**	[zadni:]
bad (adj)	**špatný**	[ʃpatni:]
beautiful (~ palace)	**překrásný**	[prʃɛkra:sni:]
beautiful (person)	**pěkný**	[pekni:]
big (in size)	**velký**	[vɛlki:]

bitter (taste)	**hořký**	[horʃki:]
blind (sightless)	**slepý**	[slɛpi:]
calm, quiet (adj)	**klidný**	[klɪdni:]
careless (negligent)	**nedbalý**	[nɛdbali:]
caring (~ father)	**starostlivý**	[starostlɪvi:]
central (adj)	**ústřední**	[u:strʃɛdni:]
cheap (low-priced)	**levný**	[lɛvni:]
cheerful (adj)	**veselý**	[vɛsɛli:]
children's (adj)	**dětský**	[detski:]
civil (~ law)	**občanský**	[obʧanski:]
clandestine (secret)	**podzemní**	[podzɛmni:]
clean (free from dirt)	**čistý**	[ʧɪsti:]
clear (explanation, etc.)	**srozumitelný**	[srozumɪtɛlni:]
clever (smart)	**moudrý**	[moudri:]
close (near in space)	**blízký**	[bli:ski:]
closed (adj)	**zavřený**	[zavrʒɛni:]
cloudless (sky)	**bezmračný**	[bɛzmraʧni:]
cold (drink, weather)	**studený**	[studɛni:]
compatible (adj)	**slučitelný**	[sluʧɪtɛlni:]
contented (satisfied)	**spokojený**	[spokojɛni:]
continuous (uninterrupted)	**nepřetržitý**	[nɛprʃɛtrʒɪti:]
cool (weather)	**chladný**	[xladni:]
dangerous (adj)	**nebezpečný**	[nɛbɛzpɛʧni:]
dark (room)	**temný**	[tɛmni:]
dead (not alive)	**mrtvý**	[mrtvi:]
dense (fog, smoke)	**hustý**	[husti:]
destitute (extremely poor)	**chudobný**	[xudobni:]
different (not the same)	**různý**	[ru:zni:]
difficult (decision)	**těžký**	[teʃki:]
difficult (problem, task)	**složitý**	[sloʒɪti:]
dim, faint (light)	**mdlý**	[mdli:]
dirty (not clean)	**špinavý**	[ʃpɪnavi:]
distant (in space)	**daleký**	[dalɛki:]
dry (clothes, etc.)	**suchý**	[suxi:]
easy (not difficult)	**snadný**	[snadni:]
empty (glass, room)	**prázdný**	[pra:zdni:]
even (e.g., ~ surface)	**rovný**	[rovni:]
exact (amount)	**přesný**	[prʃɛsni:]
excellent (adj)	**výborný**	[vi:borni:]
excessive (adj)	**nadměrný**	[nadmnerni:]
expensive (adj)	**drahý**	[drahi:]
exterior (adj)	**vnější**	[vnejʃi:]
far (the ~ East)	**vzdálený**	[vzda:lɛni:]

fast (quick)	**rychlý**	[rɪxli:]
fatty (food)	**tučný**	[tuʧni:]
fertile (land, soil)	**úrodný**	[u:rodni:]
flat (~ panel display)	**plochý**	[ploxi:]
foreign (adj)	**cizí**	[ʦɪzi:]
fragile (china, glass)	**křehký**	[krʃɛxki:]
free (at no cost)	**bezplatný**	[bɛzplatni:]
free (unrestricted)	**volný**	[volni:]
fresh (~ water)	**sladký**	[slatki:]
fresh (e.g., ~ bread)	**čerstvý**	[ʧɛrstvi:]
frozen (food)	**zmražený**	[zmraʒeni:]
full (completely filled)	**plný**	[plni:]
gloomy (house, forecast)	**pochmurný**	[poxmurni:]
good (book, etc.)	**dobrý**	[dobri:]
good, kind (kindhearted)	**dobrý**	[dobri:]
grateful (adj)	**vděčný**	[vdeʧni:]
happy (adj)	**šťastný**	[ʃtʲastni:]
hard (not soft)	**tvrdý**	[tvrdi:]
heavy (in weight)	**těžký**	[teʃki:]
hostile (adj)	**nepřátelský**	[nɛprʃa:tɛlski:]
hot (adj)	**teplý**	[tɛpli:]
huge (adj)	**obrovský**	[obrovski:]
humid (adj)	**vlhký**	[vlxki:]
hungry (adj)	**hladový**	[hladovi:]
ill (sick, unwell)	**nemocný**	[nɛmoʦni:]
immobile (adj)	**nehybný**	[nɛhɪbni:]
important (adj)	**důležitý**	[du:lɛʒɪti:]
impossible (adj)	**nemožný**	[nɛmoʒni:]
incomprehensible	**nesrozumitelný**	[nɛsrozumɪtɛlni:]
indispensable (adj)	**nutný**	[nutni:]
inexperienced (adj)	**nezkušený**	[nɛskuʃɛni:]
insignificant (adj)	**bezvýznamný**	[bɛzvi:znamni:]
interior (adj)	**vnitřní**	[vnɪtrʃni:]
joint (~ decision)	**společný**	[spolɛʧni:]
last (e.g., ~ week)	**minulý**	[mɪnuli:]
last (final)	**poslední**	[poslɛdni:]
left (e.g., ~ side)	**levý**	[lɛvi:]
legal (legitimate)	**zákonný**	[za:konni:]
light (in weight)	**lehký**	[lɛhki:]
light (pale color)	**světlý**	[svetli:]
limited (adj)	**omezený**	[omɛzɛni:]
liquid (fluid)	**tekutý**	[tɛkuti:]
long (e.g., ~ hair)	**dlouhý**	[dlouhi:]

loud (voice, etc.)	**hlasitý**	[hlasɪti:]
low (voice)	**tichý**	[tɪxi:]

251. Modifiers. Adjectives. Part 2

main (principal)	**hlavní**	[hlavni:]
matt, matte	**matový**	[matovi:]
meticulous (job)	**pečlivý**	[pɛʧlɪvi:]
mysterious (adj)	**záhadný**	[za:hadni:]
narrow (street, etc.)	**úzký**	[u:ski:]
native (~ country)	**rodný**	[rodni:]
nearby (adj)	**blízký**	[bli:ski:]
nearsighted (adj)	**krátkozraký**	[kra:tkozraki:]
needed (necessary)	**potřebný**	[potrʃɛbni:]
negative (~ response)	**záporný**	[za:porni:]
neighboring (adj)	**sousední**	[sousɛdni:]
nervous (adj)	**nervózní**	[nɛrvo:zni:]
new (adj)	**nový**	[novi:]
next (e.g., ~ week)	**příští**	[prʃi:ʃti:]
nice (agreeable)	**milý**	[mɪli:]
pleasant (voice)	**příjemný**	[prʃi:jɛmni:]
normal (adj)	**normální**	[norma:lni:]
not big (adj)	**nevelký**	[nɛvɛlki:]
not difficult (adj)	**snadný**	[snadni:]
obligatory (adj)	**povinný**	[povɪnni:]
old (house)	**starý**	[stari:]
open (adj)	**otevřený**	[otɛvrʒɛni:]
opposite (adj)	**protilehlý**	[protɪlɛhli:]
ordinary (usual)	**obvyklý**	[obvɪkli:]
original (unusual)	**originální**	[orɪgɪna:lni:]
past (recent)	**minulý**	[mɪnuli:]
permanent (adj)	**trvalý**	[trvali:]
personal (adj)	**osobní**	[osobni:]
polite (adj)	**zdvořilý**	[zdvorʒɪli:]
poor (not rich)	**chudý**	[xudi:]
possible (adj)	**možný**	[moʒni:]
present (current)	**přítomný**	[prʃi:tomni:]
previous (adj)	**předešlý**	[prʃɛdɛʃli:]
principal (main)	**základní**	[za:kladni:]
private (~ jet)	**soukromý**	[soukromi:]
probable (adj)	**pravděpodobný**	[pravdepodobni:]
prolonged (e.g., ~ applause)	**dlouhý**	[dlouhi:]

public (open to all)	**veřejný**	[vɛrʒɛjni:]
punctual (person)	**přesný**	[prʃɛsni:]
quiet (tranquil)	**tichý**	[tɪxi:]
rare (adj)	**vzácný**	[vza:ʦni:]
raw (uncooked)	**syrový**	[sɪrovi:]
right (not left)	**pravý**	[pravi:]
right, correct (adj)	**správný**	[spra:vni:]
ripe (fruit)	**zralý**	[zrali:]
risky (adj)	**nebezpečný**	[nɛbɛzpɛʧni:]
sad (~ look)	**smutný**	[smutni:]
sad (depressing)	**smutný**	[smutni:]
safe (not dangerous)	**bezpečný**	[bɛzpɛʧni:]
salty (food)	**slaný**	[slani:]
satisfied (customer)	**spokojený**	[spokojɛni:]
second hand (adj)	**použitý**	[pouʒɪti:]
shallow (water)	**mělký**	[mnelki:]
sharp (blade, etc.)	**ostrý**	[ostri:]
short (in length)	**krátký**	[kra:tki:]
short, short-lived (adj)	**krátkodobý**	[kra:tkodobi:]
significant (notable)	**významný**	[vi:znamni:]
similar (adj)	**podobný**	[podobni:]
simple (easy)	**jednoduchý**	[jɛdnoduxi:]
skinny	**vychrtlý**	[vɪxrtli:]
small (in size)	**malý**	[mali:]
smooth (surface)	**hladký**	[hlatki:]
soft (~ toys)	**měkký**	[mneki:]
solid (~ wall)	**pevný**	[pɛvni:]
sour (flavor, taste)	**kyselý**	[kɪsɛli:]
spacious (house, etc.)	**prostorný**	[prostorni:]
special (adj)	**speciální**	[spɛʦɪa:lni:]
straight (line, road)	**přímý**	[prʃi:mi:]
strong (person)	**silný**	[sɪlni:]
stupid (foolish)	**hloupý**	[hloupi:]
suitable (e.g., ~ for drinking)	**vhodný**	[vhodni:]
sunny (day)	**sluneční**	[slunɛʧni:]
superb, perfect (adj)	**vynikající**	[vɪnɪkaji:ʦi:]
swarthy (adj)	**snědý**	[snedi:]
sweet (sugary)	**sladký**	[slatki:]
tan (adj)	**opálený**	[opa:lɛni:]
tasty (delicious)	**chutný**	[xutni:]
tender (affectionate)	**něžný**	[neʒni:]
the highest (adj)	**nejvyšší**	[nɛjvɪʃi:]
the most important	**nejdůležitější**	[nɛjdu:lɛʒɪtejʃi:]

the nearest	**nejbližší**	[nɛjblɪʒʃi:]
the same, equal (adj)	**stejný**	[stɛjni:]
thick (e.g., ~ fog)	**hustý**	[husti:]
thick (wall, slice)	**tlustý**	[tlusti:]
thin (person)	**hubený**	[hubɛni:]
tight (~ shoes)	**těsný**	[tesni:]
tired (exhausted)	**unavený**	[unavɛni:]
tiring (adj)	**únavný**	[u:navni:]
transparent (adj)	**průhledný**	[pru:hlɛdni:]
unclear (adj)	**nejasný**	[nɛjasni:]
unique (exceptional)	**jedinečný**	[jɛdɪnɛʧni:]
various (adj)	**nejrůznější**	[nɛjru:znejʃi:]
warm (moderately hot)	**teplý**	[tɛpli:]
wet (e.g., ~ clothes)	**mokrý**	[mokri:]
whole (entire, complete)	**celý**	[ʦɛli:]
wide (e.g., ~ road)	**široký**	[ʃɪroki:]
young (adj)	**mladý**	[mladi:]

MAIN 500 VERBS

252. Verbs A-C

to accompany (vt)	**doprovázet**	[doprova:zɛt]
to accuse (vt)	**obviňovat**	[obvɪnʲovat]
to acknowledge (admit)	**přiznávat**	[prʃɪzna:vat]
to act (take action)	**jednat**	[jɛdnat]
to add (supplement)	**dodávat**	[doda:vat]
to address (speak to)	**obracet se**	[obratsɛt sɛ]
to admire (vi)	**obdivovat**	[obdɪvovat]
to advertise (vt)	**dělat reklamu**	[delat rɛklamu]
to advise (vt)	**radit**	[radɪt]
to affirm (assert)	**tvrdit**	[tvrdɪt]
to agree (say yes)	**souhlasit**	[souhlasɪt]
to aim (to point a weapon)	**mířit**	[mi:rʒɪt]
to allow (sb to do sth)	**dovolovat**	[dovolovat]
to amputate (vt)	**amputovat**	[amputovat]
to answer (vi, vt)	**odpovídat**	[otpovi:dat]
to apologize (vi)	**omlouvat se**	[omlouvat sɛ]
to appear (come into view)	**objevovat se**	[objɛvovat sɛ]
to applaud (vi, vt)	**tleskat**	[tlɛskat]
to appoint (assign)	**jmenovat**	[jmɛnovat]
to approach (come closer)	**přistupovat**	[prʃɪstupovat]
to arrive (ab. train)	**přijíždět**	[prʃɪji:ʒdet]
to ask (~ sb to do sth)	**prosit**	[prosɪt]
to aspire to ...	**toužit**	[touʒɪt]
to assist (help)	**asistovat**	[asɪstovat]
to attack (mil.)	**útočit**	[u:totʃɪt]
to attain (objectives)	**dosahovat**	[dosahovat]
to avenge (get revenge)	**mstít se**	[msti:t sɛ]
to avoid (danger, task)	**stranit se**	[stranɪt sɛ]
to award (give medal to)	**vyznamenat**	[vɪznamɛnat]
to battle (vi)	**zápasit**	[za:pasɪt]
to be (vi)	**být**	[bi:t]
to be a cause of ...	**způsobovat**	[spu:sobovat]
to be afraid	**bát se**	[ba:t sɛ]
to be angry (with ...)	**zlobit se**	[zlobɪt sɛ]

to be at war	**válčit**	[va:ltʃɪt]
to be based (on ...)	**zakládat se**	[zakla:dat sɛ]
to be bored	**nudit se**	[nudɪt sɛ]
to be convinced	**přesvědčovat se**	[prʃɛsvedtʃovat sɛ]
to be enough	**stačit**	[statʃɪt]
to be envious	**závidět**	[za:vɪdet]
to be indignant	**rozhořčovat se**	[rozhorʃtʃovat sɛ]
to be interested in ...	**zajímat se**	[zaji:mat sɛ]
to be lost in thought	**zamyslit se**	[zamɪslɪt sɛ]
to be lying (~ on the table)	**ležet**	[lɛʒet]
to be needed	**být potřebný**	[bi:t potrʃɛbni:]
to be perplexed (puzzled)	**být v rozpacích**	[bi:t v rozpatsi:x]
to be preserved	**zachovat se**	[zaxovat sɛ]
to be required	**být potřebný**	[bi:t potrʃɛbni:]
to be surprised	**divit se**	[dɪvɪt sɛ]
to be worried	**znepokojovat se**	[znɛpokojovat sɛ]
to beat (to hit)	**bít**	[bi:t]
to become (e.g., ~ old)	**stávat se**	[sta:vat sɛ]
to behave (vi)	**chovat se**	[xovat sɛ]
to believe (think)	**věřit**	[verʒɪt]
to belong to ...	**patřit**	[patrʃɪt]
to berth (moor)	**přistávat**	[prʃɪsta:vat]
to blind (other drivers)	**oslepovat**	[oslɛpovat]
to blow (wind)	**foukat**	[foukat]
to blush (vi)	**červenat se**	[tʃɛrvɛnat sɛ]
to boast (vi)	**vychloubat se**	[vɪxloubat sɛ]
to borrow (money)	**půjčovat si**	[pu:jtʃovat sɪ]
to break (branch, toy, etc.)	**lámat**	[la:mat]
to breathe (vi)	**dýchat**	[di:xat]
to bring (sth)	**přivážet**	[prʃɪva:ʒet]
to burn (paper, logs)	**pálit**	[pa:lɪt]
to buy (purchase)	**kupovat**	[kupovat]
to call (~ for help)	**volat**	[volat]
to call (yell for sb)	**zavolat**	[zavolat]
to calm down (vt)	**uklidňovat**	[uklɪdnʲovat]
can (v aux)	**moci**	[motsɪ]
to cancel (call off)	**zrušit**	[zruʃɪt]
to cast off (of a boat or ship)	**vyplouvat**	[vɪplouvat]
to catch (e.g., ~ a ball)	**chytat**	[xɪtat]
to change (~ one's opinion)	**změnit**	[zmnenɪt]
to change (exchange)	**měnit**	[mnenɪt]
to charm (vt)	**okouzlovat**	[okouzlovat]
to choose (select)	**vybírat**	[vɪbi:rat]

to chop off (with an ax)	**useknout**	[usɛknout]
to clean (e.g., kettle from scale)	**očišťovat**	[otʃɪʃtʲovat]
to clean (shoes, etc.)	**čistit**	[tʃɪstɪt]
to clean up (tidy)	**uklízet**	[ukli:zɛt]
to close (vt)	**zavírat**	[zavi:rat]
to comb one's hair	**česat se**	[tʃɛsat sɛ]
to come down (the stairs)	**jít dolů**	[ji:t dolu:]
to come out (book)	**vyjít**	[vɪji:t]
to compare (vt)	**porovnávat**	[porovna:vat]
to compensate (vt)	**hradit**	[hradɪt]
to compete (vi)	**konkurovat**	[koŋkurovat]
to compile (~ a list)	**sestavovat**	[sɛstavovat]
to complain (vi, vt)	**stěžovat si**	[steʒovat sɪ]
to complicate (vt)	**zkomplikovat**	[skomplɪkovat]
to compose (music, etc.)	**složit**	[sloʒɪt]
to compromise (reputation)	**kompromitovat se**	[kompromɪtovat sɛ]
to concentrate (vi)	**soustřeďovat se**	[soustrʃɛdʲovat sɛ]
to confess (criminal)	**přiznávat se**	[prʃɪzna:vat sɛ]
to confuse (mix up)	**plést**	[plɛ:st]
to congratulate (vt)	**blahopřát**	[blahoprʃa:t]
to consult (doctor, expert)	**konzultovat s ...**	[konzultovat s]
to continue (~ to do sth)	**pokračovat**	[pokratʃovat]
to control (vt)	**kontrolovat**	[kontrolovat]
to convince (vt)	**přesvědčovat**	[prʃɛsvedtʃovat]
to cooperate (vi)	**spolupracovat**	[spolupratsovat]
to coordinate (vt)	**koordinovat**	[koordɪnovat]
to correct (an error)	**opravovat**	[opravovat]
to cost (vt)	**stát**	[sta:t]
to count (money, etc.)	**počítat**	[potʃi:tat]
to count on ...	**spoléhat na ...**	[spolɛ:hat na]
to crack (ceiling, wall)	**praskat**	[praskat]
to create (vt)	**vytvořit**	[vɪtvorʒɪt]
to crush, to squash (~ a bug)	**rozšlápnout**	[rozʃla:pnout]
to cry (weep)	**plakat**	[plakat]
to cut off (with a knife)	**odřezat**	[odrʒɛzat]

253. Verbs D-G

to dare (~ to do sth)	**troufat si**	[troufat sɪ]
to date from ...	**datovat se**	[datovat sɛ]

to deceive (vi, vt)	**podvádět**	[podva:det]
to decide (~ to do sth)	**řešit**	[rʒɛʃɪt]
to decorate (tree, street)	**zdobit**	[zdobɪt]
to dedicate (book, etc.)	**věnovat**	[venovat]
to defend (a country, etc.)	**bránit**	[bra:nɪt]
to defend oneself	**bránit se**	[bra:nɪt sɛ]
to demand (request firmly)	**žádat**	[ʒa:dat]
to denounce (vt)	**donášet**	[dona:ʃɛt]
to deny (vt)	**popírat**	[popi:rat]
to depend on ...	**záviset**	[za:vɪsɛt]
to deprive (vt)	**zbavovat**	[zbavovat]
to deserve (vt)	**zasluhovat**	[zasluhovat]
to design (machine, etc.)	**projektovat**	[projɛktovat]
to desire (want, wish)	**přát**	[prʃa:t]
to despise (vt)	**pohrdat**	[pohrdat]
to destroy (documents, etc.)	**ničit**	[nɪʧɪt]
to differ (from sth)	**lišit se**	[lɪʃɪt sɛ]
to dig (tunnel, etc.)	**rýt**	[ri:t]
to direct (point the way)	**zaměřovat**	[zamnerʒovat]
to disappear (vi)	**zmizet**	[zmɪzɛt]
to discover (new land, etc.)	**objevovat**	[objɛvovat]
to discuss (vt)	**projednávat**	[projɛdna:vat]
to distribute (leaflets, etc.)	**šířit**	[ʃi:rʒɪt]
to disturb (vt)	**rušit**	[ruʃɪt]
to dive (vi)	**potápět se**	[pota:pet sɛ]
to divide (math)	**dělit**	[delɪt]
to do (vt)	**dělat**	[delat]
to do the laundry	**prát**	[pra:t]
to double (increase)	**zdvojnásobovat**	[zdvojna:sobovat]
to doubt (have doubts)	**pochybovat**	[poxɪbovat]
to draw a conclusion	**dělat závěr**	[delat za:ver]
to dream (daydream)	**snít**	[sni:t]
to dream (in sleep)	**snít**	[sni:t]
to drink (vi, vt)	**pít**	[pi:t]
to drive a car	**řídit**	[rʒi:dɪt]
to drive away (scare away)	**vyhnat**	[vɪhnat]
to drop (let fall)	**pouštět**	[pouʃtet]
to drown (ab. person)	**topit se**	[topɪt sɛ]
to dry (clothes, hair)	**sušit**	[suʃɪt]
to eat (vi, vt)	**jíst**	[ji:st]
to eavesdrop (vi)	**doslechnout se**	[doslɛxnout sɛ]

to emit (diffuse - odor, etc.)	**šířit**	[ʃi:rʒɪt]
to enjoy oneself	**bavit se**	[bavɪt sɛ]
to enter (on the list)	**vpisovat**	[vpɪsovat]
to enter (room, house, etc.)	**vstoupit**	[vstoupɪt]
to entertain (amuse)	**bavit**	[bavɪt]
to equip (fit out)	**zařizovat**	[zarʒɪzovat]
to examine (proposal)	**projednat**	[projɛdnat]
to exchange (sth)	**vyměňovat si**	[vɪmnenʲovat sɪ]
to excuse (forgive)	**omlouvat**	[omlouvat]
to exist (vi)	**existovat**	[ɛgzɪstovat]
to expect (anticipate)	**očekávat**	[otʃɛka:vat]
to expect (foresee)	**předvídat**	[prʃɛdvi:dat]
to expel (from school, etc.)	**vylučovat**	[vɪlutʃovat]
to explain (vt)	**vysvětlovat**	[vɪsvetlovat]
to express (vt)	**vyslovit**	[vɪslovɪt]
to extinguish (a fire)	**hasit**	[hasɪt]
to fall in love (with ...)	**zamilovat se**	[zamɪlovat sɛ]
to feed (provide food)	**krmit**	[krmɪt]
to fight (against the enemy)	**bojovat**	[bojovat]
to fight (vi)	**prát se**	[pra:t sɛ]
to fill (glass, bottle)	**plnit**	[plnɪt]
to find (~ lost items)	**nacházet**	[naxa:zɛt]
to finish (vt)	**končit**	[kontʃɪt]
to fish (angle)	**lovit ryby**	[lovɪt rɪbɪ]
to fit (ab. dress, etc.)	**hodit se**	[hodɪt sɛ]
to flatter (vt)	**lichotit**	[lɪxotɪt]
to fly (bird, plane)	**létat**	[lɛ:tat]
to follow ... (come after)	**následovat**	[na:slɛdovat]
to forbid (vt)	**zakazovat**	[zakazovat]
to force (compel)	**nutit**	[nutɪt]
to forget (vi, vt)	**zapomínat**	[zapomi:nat]
to forgive (pardon)	**odpouštět**	[otpouʃtet]
to form (constitute)	**tvořit**	[tvorʒɪt]
to get dirty (vi)	**ušpinit se**	[uʃpɪnɪt sɛ]
to get infected (with ...)	**nakazit se**	[nakazɪt sɛ]
to get irritated	**rozčilovat se**	[roztʃɪlovat sɛ]
to get married	**ženit se**	[ʒenɪt sɛ]
to get rid of ...	**zbavovat se**	[zbavovat sɛ]
to get tired	**unavovat se**	[unavovat sɛ]
to get up (arise from bed)	**vstávat**	[vsta:vat]

to give (vt)	**dávat**	[da:vat]
to give a bath (to bath)	**koupat**	[koupat]
to give a hug, to hug (vt)	**objímat**	[obji:mat]
to give in (yield to)	**ustupovat**	[ustupovat]
to glimpse (vt)	**uvidět**	[uvɪdet]
to go (by car, etc.)	**jet**	[jɛt]
to go (on foot)	**jít**	[ji:t]
to go for a swim	**koupat se**	[koupat sɛ]
to go out (for dinner, etc.)	**vyjít**	[vɪji:t]
to go to bed (go to sleep)	**jít spát**	[ji:t spa:t]
to greet (vt)	**zdravit**	[zdravɪt]
to grow (plants)	**pěstovat**	[pestovat]
to guarantee (vt)	**zaručovat**	[zarutʃovat]
to guess (the answer)	**rozluštit**	[rozluʃtɪt]

254. Verbs H-M

to hand out (distribute)	**rozdat**	[rozdat]
to hang (curtains, etc.)	**věšet**	[veʃɛt]
to have (vt)	**mít**	[mi:t]
to have a try	**pokusit se**	[pokusɪt sɛ]
to have breakfast	**snídat**	[sni:dat]
to have dinner	**večeřet**	[vɛtʃɛrʒɛt]
to have lunch	**obědvat**	[obedvat]
to head (group, etc.)	**řídit**	[rʒi:dɪt]
to hear (vt)	**slyšet**	[slɪʃɛt]
to heat (vt)	**zahřívat**	[zahrʒi:vat]
to help (vt)	**pomáhat**	[poma:hat]
to hide (vt)	**schovávat**	[sxova:vat]
to hire (e.g., ~ a boat)	**najímat**	[naji:mat]
to hire (staff)	**zaměstnávat**	[zamnestna:vat]
to hope (vi, vt)	**doufat**	[doufat]
to hunt (for food, sport)	**lovit**	[lovɪt]
to hurry (vi)	**spěchat**	[spexat]
to imagine (to picture)	**představovat si**	[prʃɛtstavovat sɪ]
to imitate (vt)	**napodobovat**	[napodobovat]
to implore (vt)	**snažně prosit**	[snaʒne prosɪt]
to import (vt)	**dovážet**	[dova:ʒet]
to increase (vi)	**zvětšovat se**	[zvetʃovat sɛ]
to increase (vt)	**zvětšovat**	[zvetʃovat]
to infect (vt)	**infikovat**	[ɪnfɪkovat]
to influence (vt)	**působit**	[pu:sobɪt]
to inform (e.g., ~ the police about)	**sdělovat**	[zdelovat]

to inform (vt)	**informovat**	[ɪnformovat]
to inherit (vt)	**dědit**	[dedɪt]
to inquire (about ...)	**informovat se**	[ɪnformovat sɛ]
to insert (put in)	**zasazovat**	[zasazovat]
to insinuate (imply)	**narážet**	[nara:ʒet]
to insist (vi, vt)	**trvat**	[trvat]
to inspire (vt)	**podněcovat**	[podnet͡sovat]
to instruct (teach)	**instruovat**	[ɪnstruovat]
to insult (offend)	**urážet**	[ura:ʒet]
to interest (vt)	**zajímat**	[zaji:mat]
to intervene (vi)	**vměšovat se**	[vmneʃovat sɛ]
to introduce (sb to sb)	**seznamovat**	[sɛznamovat]
to invent (machine, etc.)	**vynalézat**	[vɪnalɛ:zat]
to invite (vt)	**zvát**	[zva:t]
to iron (clothes)	**žehlit**	[ʒehlɪt]
to irritate (annoy)	**rozčilovat**	[rozt͡ʃɪlovat]
to isolate (vt)	**izolovat**	[ɪzolovat]
to join (political party, etc.)	**připojovat se**	[prʃɪpojovat sɛ]
to joke (be kidding)	**žertovat**	[ʒertovat]
to keep (old letters, etc.)	**uchovávat**	[uxova:vat]
to keep silent, to hush	**mlčet**	[mlt͡ʃɛt]
to kill (vt)	**zabíjet**	[zabi:jɛt]
to knock (on the door)	**klepat**	[klɛpat]
to know (sb)	**znát**	[zna:t]
to know (sth)	**vědět**	[vedet]
to laugh (vi)	**smát se**	[sma:t sɛ]
to launch (start up)	**spouštět**	[spouʃtet]
to leave (~ for Mexico)	**odjíždět**	[odji:ʒdet]
to leave (forget sth)	**zapomínat**	[zapomi:nat]
to leave (spouse)	**opouštět**	[opouʃtet]
to liberate (city, etc.)	**osvobozovat**	[osvobozovat]
to lie (~ on the floor)	**ležet**	[lɛʒet]
to lie (tell untruth)	**lhát**	[lha:t]
to light (campfire, etc.)	**zapálit**	[zapa:lɪt]
to light up (illuminate)	**osvětlovat**	[osvetlovat]
to like (I like ...)	**líbit se**	[li:bɪt sɛ]
to limit (vt)	**omezovat**	[omɛzovat]
to listen (vi)	**poslouchat**	[poslouxat]
to live (~ in France)	**bydlet**	[bɪdlɛt]
to live (exist)	**žít**	[ʒi:t]
to load (gun)	**nabíjet**	[nabi:jɛt]
to load (vehicle, etc.)	**nakládat**	[nakla:dat]
to look (I'm just ~ing)	**dívat se**	[di:vat sɛ]
to look for ... (search)	**hledat**	[hlɛdat]

to look like (resemble)	**být podobný**	[bi:t podobni:]
to lose (umbrella, etc.)	**ztrácet**	[stra:ʦɛt]
to love (e.g., ~ dancing)	**mít rád**	[mi:t ra:t]
to love (sb)	**milovat**	[mɪlovat]
to lower (blind, head)	**spouštět**	[spouʃtet]
to make (~ dinner)	**vařit**	[varʒɪt]
to make a mistake	**mýlit se**	[mi:lɪt sɛ]
to make angry	**zlobit**	[zlobɪt]
to make easier	**usnadnit**	[usnadnɪt]
to make multiple copies	**rozmnožit**	[rozmnoʒɪt]
to make the acquaintance	**seznamovat se**	[sɛznamovat sɛ]
to make use (of ...)	**používat**	[pouʒi:vat]
to manage, to run	**řídit**	[rʒi:dɪt]
to mark (make a mark)	**označit**	[oznaʧɪt]
to mean (signify)	**znamenat**	[znamɛnat]
to memorize (vt)	**zapamatovat si**	[zapamatovat sɪ]
to mention (talk about)	**zmiňovat se**	[zmɪnʲovat sɛ]
to miss (school, etc.)	**zameškávat**	[zameʃka:vat]
to mix (combine, blend)	**směšovat**	[smneʃovat]
to mock (make fun of)	**vysmívat se**	[vɪsmi:vat sɛ]
to move (to shift)	**přemisťovat**	[prʃɛmɪstʲovat]
to multiply (math)	**násobit**	[na:sobɪt]
must (v aux)	**musit**	[musɪt]

255. Verbs N-R

to name, to call (vt)	**nazývat**	[nazi:vat]
to negotiate (vi)	**jednat**	[jɛdnat]
to note (write down)	**poznamenat si**	[poznamenat sɪ]
to notice (see)	**všímat si**	[vʃi:mat sɪ]
to obey (vi, vt)	**podřizovat se**	[podrʒɪzovat sɛ]
to object (vi, vt)	**namítat**	[nami:tat]
to observe (see)	**pozorovat**	[pozorovat]
to offend (vt)	**urážet**	[ura:ʒet]
to omit (word, phrase)	**vynechávat**	[vɪnɛxa:vat]
to open (vt)	**otvírat**	[otvi:rat]
to order (in restaurant)	**objednávat**	[objɛdna:vat]
to order (mil.)	**rozkazovat**	[roskazovat]
to organize (concert, party)	**pořádat**	[porʒa:dat]
to overestimate (vt)	**přeceňovat**	[prʃɛʦɛnʲovat]
to own (possess)	**vlastnit**	[vlastnɪt]
to participate (vi)	**zúčastnit se**	[zu:ʧastnɪt sɛ]
to pass through (by car, etc.)	**míjet**	[mi:jɛt]

to pay (vi, vt)	**platit**	[platɪt]
to peep, spy on	**nahlížet**	[nahli:ʒet]
to penetrate (vt)	**pronikat**	[pronɪkat]
to permit (vt)	**dovolovat**	[dovolovat]
to pick (flowers)	**trhat**	[trhat]
to place (put, set)	**rozmisťovat**	[rozmɪstʲovat]
to plan (~ to do sth)	**plánovat**	[pla:novat]
to play (actor)	**hrát**	[hra:t]
to play (children)	**hrát**	[hra:t]
to point (~ the way)	**ukázat**	[uka:zat]
to pour (liquid)	**nalévat**	[nalɛ:vat]
to pray (vi, vt)	**modlit se**	[modlɪt sɛ]
to prefer (vt)	**dávat přednost**	[da:vat prʃɛdnost]
to prepare (~ a plan)	**připravit**	[prʃɪpravɪt]
to present (sb to sb)	**představovat**	[prʃɛtstavovat]
to preserve (peace, life)	**zachovávat**	[zaxova:vat]
to prevail (vt)	**převládat**	[prʃɛvla:dat]
to progress (move forward)	**postupovat**	[postupovat]
to promise (vt)	**slibovat**	[slɪbovat]
to pronounce (vt)	**vyslovovat**	[vɪslovovat]
to propose (vt)	**nabízet**	[nabi:zɛt]
to protect (e.g., ~ nature)	**chránit**	[xra:nɪt]
to protest (vi)	**protestovat**	[protɛstovat]
to prove (vt)	**dokazovat**	[dokazovat]
to provoke (vt)	**provokovat**	[provokovat]
to pull (~ the rope)	**táhnout**	[ta:hnout]
to punish (vt)	**trestat**	[trɛstat]
to push (~ the door)	**strkat**	[strkat]
to put away (vt)	**skladovat**	[skladovat]
to put in order	**dávat do pořádku**	[da:vat do porʒa:tku]
to put, to place	**klást**	[kla:st]
to quote (cite)	**citovat**	[ʦɪtovat]
to reach (arrive at)	**dosahovat**	[dosahovat]
to read (vi, vt)	**číst**	[ʧi:st]
to realize (a dream)	**uskutečňovat**	[uskutɛʧnʲovat]
to recognize (identify sb)	**poznávat**	[pozna:vat]
to recommend (vt)	**doporučovat**	[doporuʧovat]
to recover (~ from flu)	**uzdravovat se**	[uzdravovat sɛ]
to redo (do again)	**předělávat**	[prʃɛdela:vat]
to reduce (speed, etc.)	**zmenšovat**	[zmɛnʃovat]
to refuse (~ sb)	**odmítat**	[odmi:tat]
to regret (be sorry)	**litovat**	[lɪtovat]

to reinforce (vt)	**upevňovat**	[upɛvnʲovat]
to remember (Do you ~ me?)	**pamatovat**	[pamatovat]
to remember (I can't ~ her name)	**vzpomínat**	[vspomi:nat]
to remind of ...	**připomínat**	[prʃɪpomi:nat]
to remove (~ a stain)	**odstraňovat**	[otstranʲovat]
to remove (~ an obstacle)	**odstraňovat**	[otstranʲovat]
to rent (sth from sb)	**pronajímat si**	[pronaji:mat sɪ]
to repair (mend)	**opravovat**	[opravovat]
to repeat (say again)	**opakovat**	[opakovat]
to report (make a report)	**podávat zprávu**	[poda:vat spra:vu]
to reproach (vt)	**vyčítat**	[vɪʧi:tat]
to reserve, to book	**rezervovat**	[rɛzɛrvovat]
to restrain (hold back)	**zabraňovat**	[zabranʲovat]
to return (come back)	**vracet se**	[vraʦɛʦɛ]
to risk, to take a risk	**riskovat**	[rɪskovat]
to rub out (erase)	**setřít**	[sɛtrʃi:t]
to run (move fast)	**běžet**	[beʒet]
to rush (hurry sb)	**popohánět**	[popoha:net]

256. Verbs S-W

to satisfy (please)	**uspokojovat**	[uspokojovat]
to save (rescue)	**zachraňovat**	[zaxranʲovat]
to say (~ thank you)	**říci**	[rʒi:ʦɪ]
to scold (vt)	**nadávat**	[nada:vat]
to scratch (with claws)	**škrábat**	[ʃkra:bat]
to select (to pick)	**vyhledat si**	[vɪhlɛdat sɪ]
to sell (goods)	**prodávat**	[proda:vat]
to send (a letter)	**odesílat**	[odɛsi:lat]
to send back (vt)	**odeslat zpět**	[odɛslat spet]
to sense (~ danger)	**cítit**	[ʦi:tɪt]
to sentence (vt)	**odsuzovat**	[otsuzovat]
to serve (in restaurant)	**obsluhovat**	[opsluhovat]
to settle (a conflict)	**urovnávat**	[urovna:vat]
to shake (vt)	**třást**	[trʃa:st]
to shave (vi)	**holit se**	[holɪt sɛ]
to shine (gleam)	**zářit**	[za:rʒɪt]
to shiver (with cold)	**chvět se**	[xvet sɛ]
to shoot (vi)	**střílet**	[strʃi:lɛt]
to shout (vi)	**křičet**	[krʃɪʧɛt]

to show (to display)	**ukazovat**	[ukazovat]
to shudder (vi)	**zachvívat se**	[zaxvi:vat sɛ]
to sigh (vi)	**vzdechnout**	[vzdɛxnout]
to sign (document)	**podepisovat**	[podɛpɪsovat]
to signify (mean)	**znamenat**	[znamɛnat]
to simplify (vt)	**zjednodušovat**	[zjɛdnoduʃovat]
to sin (vi)	**hřešit**	[hrʒɛʃɪt]
to sit (be sitting)	**sedět**	[sɛdet]
to sit down (vi)	**sednout si**	[sɛdnout sɪ]
to smell (emit an odor)	**vonět**	[vonet]
to smell (inhale the odor)	**čichat**	[ʧɪxat]
to smile (vi)	**usmívat se**	[usmi:vat sɛ]
to snap (vi, ab. rope)	**roztrhat se**	[roztrhat sɛ]
to solve (problem)	**vyřešit**	[vɪrʒɛʃɪt]
to sow (seed, crop)	**sít**	[si:t]
to spill (liquid)	**rozlévat**	[rozlɛ:vat]
to spit (vi)	**plivat**	[plɪvat]
to stand (toothache, cold)	**trpět**	[trpet]
to start (begin)	**začínat**	[zaʧi:nat]
to steal (money, etc.)	**krást**	[kra:st]
to stop (for pause, etc.)	**zastavovat se**	[zastavovat sɛ]
to stop (please ~ calling me)	**zastavovat**	[zastavovat]
to stop talking	**zmlknout**	[zmlknout]
to stroke (caress)	**hladit**	[hladɪt]
to study (vt)	**studovat**	[studovat]
to suffer (feel pain)	**trápit se**	[tra:pɪt sɛ]
to support (cause, idea)	**podpořit**	[potporʒɪt]
to suppose (assume)	**předpokládat**	[prʃɛtpokla:dat]
to surface (ab. submarine)	**vyplouvat**	[vɪplouvat]
to surprise (amaze)	**udivovat**	[udɪvovat]
to suspect (vt)	**podezírat**	[podɛzi:rat]
to swim (vi)	**plavat**	[plavat]
to take (get hold of)	**brát**	[bra:t]
to take a bath	**mýt se**	[mi:t sɛ]
to take a rest	**odpočívat**	[otpoʧi:vat]
to take away (e.g., about waiter)	**odnášet**	[odna:ʃɛt]
to take off (airplane)	**vzlétat**	[vzlɛ:tat]
to take off (painting, curtains, etc.)	**sundávat**	[sunda:vat]
to take pictures	**fotografovat**	[fotografovat]
to talk to ...	**mluvit s ...**	[mluvɪt s]

to teach (give lessons)	**vyučovat**	[vɪuʧovat]
to tear off, to rip off (vt)	**odtrhnout**	[odtrhnout]
to tell (story, joke)	**povídat**	[povi:dat]
to thank (vt)	**děkovat**	[dekovat]
to think (believe)	**mít za to**	[mi:t za to]
to think (vi, vt)	**myslit**	[mɪslɪt]
to threaten (vt)	**vyhrožovat**	[vɪhroʒovat]
to throw (stone, etc.)	**házet**	[ha:zɛt]
to tie to ...	**uvazovat**	[uvazovat]
to tie up (prisoner)	**svazovat**	[svazovat]
to tire (make tired)	**unavovat**	[unavovat]
to touch (one's arm, etc.)	**dotýkat se**	[doti:kat sɛ]
to tower (over ...)	**vypínat se**	[vɪpi:nat sɛ]
to train (animals)	**cvičit**	[ʦvɪʧɪt]
to train (sb)	**trénovat**	[trɛ:novat]
to train (vi)	**trénovat**	[trɛ:novat]
to transform (vt)	**transformovat**	[transformovat]
to translate (vt)	**překládat**	[prʃɛkla:dat]
to treat (illness)	**léčit**	[lɛ:ʧɪt]
to trust (vt)	**důvěřovat**	[du:verʒovat]
to try (attempt)	**pokoušet se**	[pokouʃɛt sɛ]
to turn (e.g., ~ left)	**zatáčet**	[zata:ʧɛt]
to turn away (vi)	**odvracet se**	[odvraʦɛt sɛ]
to turn off (the light)	**zhasínat**	[zhasi:nat]
to turn on (computer, etc.)	**zapínat**	[zapi:nat]
to turn over (stone, etc.)	**převrátit**	[prʃɛvra:tɪt]
to underestimate (vt)	**podceňovat**	[podʦɛnʲovat]
to underline (vt)	**podtrhnout**	[podtrhnout]
to understand (vt)	**rozumět**	[rozumnet]
to undertake (vt)	**podnikat**	[podnɪkat]
to unite (vt)	**sjednocovat**	[sjɛdnoʦovat]
to untie (vt)	**odvazovat**	[odvazovat]
to use (phrase, word)	**použít**	[pouʒi:t]
to vaccinate (vt)	**dělat očkování**	[delat oʧkova:ni:]
to vote (vi)	**hlasovat**	[hlasovat]
to wait (vt)	**čekat**	[ʧɛkat]
to wake (sb)	**budit**	[budɪt]
to want (wish, desire)	**chtít**	[xti:t]
to warn (of the danger)	**upozorňovat**	[upozornʲovat]
to wash (clean)	**mýt**	[mi:t]
to water (plants)	**zalévat**	[zalɛ:vat]
to wave (the hand)	**mávat**	[ma:vat]
to weigh (have weight)	**vážit**	[va:ʒɪt]

to work (vi)	**pracovat**	[pratsovat]
to worry (make anxious)	**znepokojovat**	[znɛpokojovat]
to worry (vi)	**znepokojovat se**	[znɛpokojovat sɛ]
to wrap (parcel, etc.)	**zabalovat**	[zabalovat]
to wrestle (sport)	**zápasit**	[za:pasɪt]
to write (vt)	**psát**	[psa:t]
to write down	**zapisovat si**	[zapɪsovat sɪ]

Made in the USA
Lexington, KY
15 August 2018